# THE INVESTOR'S COOKBOOK
## A GUIDE TO WEALTH CREATION

by

Dr. John J. Baxevanis

DORRANCE
PUBLISHING CO
EST. 1920
PITTSBURGH, PENNSYLVANIA 15222

The contents of this work, including, but not limited to, the accuracy of events, people, and places depicted; opinions expressed; permission to use previously published materials included; and any advice given or actions advocated are solely the responsibility of the author, who assumes all liability for said work and indemnifies the publisher against any claims stemming from publication of the work.

Dorrance Publishing Co
701 Smithfield Street
Pittsburgh, PA 15222
Visit our website at *www.dorrancebookstore.com*

ISBN: 978-1-4809-1073-7
eISBN: 978-1-4809-1395-0

# Table of Contents

# Acknowledgments

To James and Dean: The future belongs to them, but only if they remain knowledgeable, diligent, and patient.

To their cousins: Haig, Tia, and Seth.

To the finest geographer ever: Dr. John D. Eyre of Chapel Hill.

# Introduction

There are many moments when we see but not observe. Mediterranean settlements have narrow streets, whitewashed exteriors, huddled buildings, tall ceilings, terrazzo flooring, stonewalls, and louvered/shuttered windows. The look to the untrained eye is as far removed from a Scandinavian scenograph as anything imagined. The strange, unfamiliar, and non-automobile accommodating settlements appear chaotic, but once you live there, you realize that this seemingly haphazard agglomeration of stone and red tiled roof is a natural, air-conditioned *bourg* of the first order, meant to keep man and beast cool during the seven-month, hot summer. Such is the world of investing: at first chaotic, confusing, perplexing, complicated, and wrought with danger. The sooner you understand the investing landscape, the better. Teach yourself the power of observation and learn to become a better and more successful investor. Acquire the basics of economic history, monetary policy, and the machinations of the oldest streets in Manhattan. A formal university education is not required; just spare moments from mindless sport and reality programming. Read the classics, visit the library and, above all, ask questions. The sooner you train your mind to acquire and process new information, the more successful you will become in the world of investing. Successful investing is never a product of luck, but the residue of diligent, patient, and resolute planning. This tome is organized in six chapters, all of which are intended to introduce the neophyte, the character of investing, from womb to the great beyond.

Chapter 1 frames the investment world in terms of geography, factors that produce economic growth, the concentration of wealth, and investment opportunities. Chapter 2 offers the asset allocations of cash, bonds, and equities. Chapter 3 attempts to offer sensible behavioral guidelines. Chapter 4 offers a discussion on the cyclical and secular nature of economic activity and their importance in investing. Chapter 5 offers a smorgasbord of investment recipes from birth to retirement. Chapter 6 presents resource material. In the final analysis, you, the investor, must learn to be relatively agnostic to markets and become a money manager. A Ph.D. is not necessary to invest successfully. In the investing kitchen, you will assemble only the ingredients that you will need to successful investing: knowledge, prudence, confidence, asset diversification, risk management, patience, and discipline. The investment strategies enunciated in the following pages are suggestions. Choose ingredients wisely and follow the recipes to "critical mass," or the stage that one can stop working and enjoy a lifestyle consistent with your comfort zone. Never be arrogant. Remember, "Slow and steady wins the race." You will thank yourself profusely once you inculcate these simple principles.

This book is unusual in that it is not written by a corporate executive, muckraker, stockbroker, or financial analyst. I am an outsider to the professional world of investing and a retired university professor who has made every possible mistake that a mortal can think of; hence, the tome is intended to help investors avoid potential mistakes and, in the process, maximize financial returns. The money that I have made was not the result of professional associations, but personal investment experience. In terms of disclosures, I am not a registered stockbroker, advisor, banker, or a person affiliated with any aspect of commercial markets. My family and I have accounts with the Vanguard Group, Schwab and Co., Fidelity Investments, Dodge and Cox, and Meridian Funds. For brevity and simplicity, the Vanguard Group is used as the "default" investment vehicle for illustrative purposes. Under no circumstances do I endorse or seek to solicit and gain any financial advantage or reward from any institution mentioned. I have tried to be as objective and factually accurate as possible. For those errors encountered, I apologize profusely, and under no circumstances should anyone follow my suggestions blindly. Do your due diligence often; be skeptical and develop an adversarial attitude toward the subject of investing. My comments are an articulation of beliefs and judgments for educational purposes and should not be construed as recommendations to buy and sell anything. When in doubt, seek professional advice. A note of caution is in order. Although not every subject can be dealt with in minute detail, illustrative material kept to a minimum to conserve space. And since legislation governing a number of specific issues is constantly changing, details are left out as to minimize confusion.

Gastronomy is quite similar to investing; hence, the title of this book and the nature of its structure. Before you begin cooking: procure a recipe; acquire and assemble ingredients; cut, peel, trim, chop, simmer, boil, bake, roast, etc. for a variable period; and enjoy. The investor must look at investing in a similar fashion. You need a strategy/plan, and you need to acquire investment knowledge, select the best investments, and dissect them in detail in terms of characteristics. Finally, a good word from the Austrian economists who maintain: "It's not what you don't know that will hurt you; it's what you think you know that can destroy your wealth." I do hope that the information contained herein will supply sufficient information for the average person to invest wisely. Since we live in the "Information Age," the prudent investor needs to read as much as possible in order to remain current and informed.

# CHAPTER 1

# THE KITCHEN

*If it doesn't add value, it is waste.* - Henry Ford

*"The $US is geared to accommodate absolutely unlimited credit for two purposes–consumption and financial speculation…the borrowing pulls future spending into the present…at the expense of such spending in the future."* - Kurt Richebacher

# The Unequal Distribution of Wealth

## Measuring Wealth

Economic development is a process by which an economy's real national income increases over a protracted period. "Process" refers to the operation of certain forces that operate over time and represent significance when they lead to the discovery of additional resources, institutional and organizational modifications, capital accumulation, better techniques of production, and changes in demographic structure. Economic growth, in the Aristotelian sense, is neither inevitable nor mechanical, but the result of human will. In this connection, there are a number of self-evident axioms. No nation is permanently fixed into a developed, emergent, or developing category, as these terms are relative to each other and in constant flux. All nations contain ingredients of progressive and historic backwater elements. All nations develop economically in stages that exhibit "stop and go" features. No nation "progresses" on a straight path forever in any direction. Economic growth in one area produces less growth in others.

1. Gross Domestic Product (GDP) measures the total output of all goods and services. The primary driver of GDP growth is capital investment in the production of goods and services (minus inflation), but because its definition varies by country, comparisons are misleading. What is not reported is the considerable underground economy that amounts to 45%-plus of global GDP, and in this connection, the disparity between developed and underdeveloped nations is enormous. Except for the recent rise of Emerging Markets (EMs), the pattern of global wealth distribution has been relatively constant for 125 years. Statistics, for the year 1888, from the *Mulhall's Dictionary of Statistics* indicate that world factory output was but $22.4 billion, of which the top 12 countries accounted for more than 99% of total: US $7.2 billion; UK $4.1; Germany $2.9; France $2.4; Russia $1.8; Austria-Hungary $1.2; Italy $.6; Belgium $.5; Spain $.4; Sweden $.2; Netherlands $.1; Switzerland $.1; and the rest of world $.5. It is evident that the US and UK, with 50% of secondary output, dominated the secondary sector. By 1913, secondary output rose to $89 billion of which the following 13 nations represented 86% of global production: US (34.4%), UK (10.4%), Germany (10.3%), Russia (9.5%), France

(5%), Japan (4%), Italy (2.5%), Canada (2.2%), Poland (1.7%), Austria-Hungary (1.5%), Belgium (1.4%), Sweden (1.1%), India (1.1%). By 1947 the world generated $153 billion of secondary goods, of which the US produced $86.9, or more than 55%; W. Germany and the USSR $18 each; UK $15.6; France $6.7; Canada $5.6; Italy $3.6; Poland $2.8; Japan $2.5; Sweden $2.1; Austria $2; Belgium $1.9; India $1.7; Czechoslovakia .4. Secondary output increased sevenfold by 1964 with the US and Canada (38% each), Europe including Russia (40%), and the rest of the world 22%. In 1990 Western industrial countries and Japan had about 55% of global secondary share, Russia and Eastern Europe 11%, China 6%, India 2%, and the rest of the world 26%. As of 2011, the richest nations in terms of GDP were US, China, Japan, Germany, UK, India, and France, collectively 55% of global GDP. It is estimated that the aggregate value of all global financial assets amounted to $230 trillion. Gold accounts for less than $1.4 trillion, or 0.5% of global assets.

The key economic metric derived from GDP figures is per capita income. The world's developed markets (DMs) containing 15% of the world's population, are responsible for 56% of global GDP, and are characterized as being "modern" in the sense that science and technology have been applied to solve age-old problems and create secular societies. Third World markets and EMs contain 85% of the world's population, but only 44% of GDP. TWs are mainly confined to Africa, south of the Sahara, with the exception of South Africa, most of Latin America, and portions of Asia. They have 25% of world population, but 9% of GDP. The top global quintile receives about 62% of all income, the second largest 23%, and the other three combined receive 15%. The richest 1% own about 41% of global assets for the year 2010, and the bottom 50% owned less than 2%. Per capita income in the richest 20 countries is $33,000, and for the 50 poorest nations less than $1,500.

The Institute for Policy Studies reported in 2000 that the top 200 corporations' combined sales are bigger than the combined economies of all countries minus the biggest 10. In terms of GDP comparisons in 1999, General Motors was bigger than Denmark, DaimlerChrysler bigger than Poland, Royal Dutch/Shell bigger than Venezuela, IBM bigger than Singapore, and Sony was bigger than Pakistan. In 1999 sales of General Motors, Wal-Mart, Exxon Mobil, Ford Motor, and DaimlerChrysler were bigger than the GDPs of 152 countries. For the year 2008, the distribution of the 100 largest corporations was: US 31, Germany 13, France 10, UK, 9, Japan 8, Italy and Korea 4 each, China, Spain, and Switzerland 3 each, Russia and the Netherlands 2 each, and 1 each for Netherlands, Belgium, Luxembourg, Mexico, Norway, Brazil, Finland, and Malaysia. It is interesting to note that Europe contained 51, the US 31, and the rest of the world more than doubled their number since 2000. A slightly broader picture emerges when the geography of the world's 500 largest corporations for 2012 are analyzed. Asia had 188, Europe 162, US 132, and Latin America 13. Note also that of the 100 largest economies in the world, 59 were corporations and only 41 were countries based on a comparison of corporate sales and country GDP. Sales from the top 200 corporations are growing at a faster rate than global GDP. They have many venues: headquarters in one country, production of various products in many countries, financing from several other nations, design, marketing and accounting offices located in still others, and products and services sold globally. Many have lost their national identity, and more important, their national loyalty.

2. Purchasing Power Parity (PPP) seeks to measure the anomalies that have arisen between global domestic prices and exchange rates. As such, historical global GDP comparisons are no longer considered accurate. The effective PPP figures for EMs present a very different picture, as the metrics are based on local purchasing power and not on international currency disparities and, hence, are more realistic. When peripheral areas like New Zealand and Australia, are included, Asia represents the world's largest economy. The geography of economic performance, dominated by North Atlantic nations has been broken, and now diffused to Asia and Latin American nations. Over the course of the past 30 years, East Asia has increased income sevenfold, South Asia fourfold, Latin America doubled, but Sub-Saharan Africa declined 2%. DMs continue to increase income levels but at much slower rates than Asia. The five BRICS nations (Brazil, Russia, India, China and South Africa), by 2030, will collectively exceed the combined GDP of the US, Japan, Germany, UK, France, and Italy.

3. Although the geography of wealth has always exhibited pockets of extreme concentration, the spacial distribution patterns of the new millennium are quite remarkable. The richest 2% live in Anglo-America (35%), Western and Southern Europe (42%), and the Middle East, China, India, Singapore, Taiwan, Korea, Australia, and Japan (23%); 97% of the richest 1% lives in the Northern Hemisphere. More remarkable is the fact that wealth and the most lucrative economic professions are not only concentrated in the richest countries, but also clustered in the largest metropolises. In the US, more than 85% of the nation's wealth is concentrated in the 55 largest metropolitan areas. Furthermore, company headquarters of the 500 largest corporations, ranked, by state, for 2008 according to Fortune Magazine were: Texas (58), New York (55), California (52), Illinois 33), Ohio (28), Pennsylvania (25), New Jersey (23), Michigan (22), Minnesota (19), Virginia (19), Florida (14), North Carolina (14), Georgia, Massachusetts and Connecticut 12 each, and 10 each in Colorado, Washington, and Wisconsin. In terms of urban concentration, New York had 43, Houston 25, Chicago 12, Dallas 12, and Atlanta 10, collectively about 21% of the national total. If one includes corporate headquarters located in suburban fringes, the percentage would rise to 68%. Fifty percent of US GDP emanates from just five states: California, Texas, New York, Florida, and Illinois, and 75% of that are from just eight metropolitan areas. The concentration of income is even more remarkable when one compares the income generated in one square mile in mid-Manhattan is more than several million times that of Montana. Forty-five thousand Americans are worth more than \$50 million. According to magazine reports, the geography of global millionaires in 2011 exceeded 15 million with the US ranking number one followed by China

and Russia. In terms of percentage relative to population: Singapore ranks number one followed by Switzerland, Qatar, Hong Kong, Kuwait, United Arab Emirates, US, Taiwan, Israel, and Belgium. The distribution of global billionaires exhibits a similar pattern. In 2013, 1,453 billionaires were worth $6 trillion. The US leads the list with 480, followed by China, Russia, UK, Germany, and India. The top 1% control 47% of global assets.

4. Human Development Index is a UN metric for life expectancy, literacy, education, GDP, and standard of living per capita. According to the index, European countries rank as the best places to live; Norway ranks first followed by Sweden, Australia, Canada, Netherlands, Belgium, US, UK, France, and Germany. Tokyo is the world's most expensive city, followed by Paris, Oslo, Zurich, London, Hong Kong, Sydney, Stockholm, Frankfurt, and Singapore. A related index, Legatum Prosperity, seeks to define global prosperity by measuring economy, education, entrepreneurship & opportunity, governance, health, personal freedom, safety and security, and social capital. The 20 leading countries are Norway, Denmark, Sweden, Australia, New Zealand, Canada, Finland, Netherlands, Switzerland, Ireland, Luxembourg, US, UK, Germany, Iceland, Austria, Belgium, Hong Kong, Singapore, and Taiwan.

5. Capital markets consist of money and foreign exchange markets, security markets, and commercial property. Capital concentration and current movements are mainly in areas with high saving rates, high R&D budgets, a legal system that protects private property, maintains lower taxes, a progressive government, etc. There are about 80 nations with active stock exchanges, but the spacial variations of number of transactions, total volume in dollars, and economic significance to the local and global economy vary enormously. The US has about 41% of the global equity market, and Europe and EMs 29% each. Although the US remains the largest equity market, over the course of the past 55 years the US portion of the global equity market declined from 90% in 1950, to 66% in 1980, and 55% in 1990. EMs rose from less than 3% in 1980 to 29% in 2012. NYSE is the largest stock exchange in the world by a factor of four, but 50 years ago, it was larger by a factor of 20. The global equity market capitalization at the end of 2012 was $40 trillion, the bond market was $90 trillion, the derivative market exceeded $700 trillion, and the global currency market is a $2.2 trillion dollar a day market. The 50 largest banks exhibit the following spacial features for 2009: Germany (8), US (7), France and China (5 each), UK and Japan (4 each), Netherlands (3), Switzerland, Spain and Belgium (2 each), and Italy, Sweden, Denmark, Canada, Australia, India, Hong Kong, and Singapore (1 each). Aggregate financial assets and income of the world's largest 50 banks and the 25 leading securities firms confirms the dominance of New York, Tokyo, London, Paris, Shanghai, Hong Kong, Singapore, Mumbai, St. Petersburg, and Frankfurt. They are also the main centers of venture capital concentration.

6. Aggregate consumption is another important wealth concentration metric. The list of variables that one may include to separate the super-rich from the poorest include the following: the number of cars per 1,000 people, square feet of livable space, electrical use per capita, percent of population in tertiary activities, the percent of population urbanized, water use, highway connectivity, foreign trade per capita, capitalization of agricultural land per acre, etc. Among the countless metrics are the following exhibiting considerable interest: the generation of electricity. The relationship between electrical production and GDP growth is direct and significant. Over the past two decades electrical generation has grown by 2.5% annually; hence, any deviation from the average becomes an inflection point. Globally, electric power, as consumption per capita reveals that DMs consume 10 times is more than TWs, and that the most rapid growth occurs in EMs (5%). This rapid growth, for more than 40% of the world's population, places an enormous demand on copper and other raw materials, which means that the commodity boom will last a long time, as $10 trillion in electrical infrastructure will be spent by 2025.

7. The dramatic growth in world trade exhibits a similar relationship. International trade has increased from $5 trillion in 1960 to more than $29 trillion in 2012, of which fuel and related items are the most important followed by secondary products. Before the Age of Discovery, the world was a compilation of local and regional markets, but slowly during the early 16th century, colonialism connected global suppliers and producers. These commercial ties increased in intensity as the Industrial Revolution gained strength in the 19th century, and rose sharply after 1980. Global trade was controlled by North Atlantic nations until Japan entered this elite group in 1960. EMs are now the leading producers of goods. In 1952, the US, UK, Canada, W. Germany, and France accounted for nearly 50% of world trade. In 1962, the percentage increased to 62%. The following countries are responsible for more than 85% of global trade by value: China, Germany, Japan, US, India, Korea, UK, Brazil, Netherlands, Italy, Canada, Belgium, Hong Kong, Russia, Mexico, Australia, Saudi Arabia, Iran, Turkey, Brazil, and Taiwan. Concentrating on high value-added consumer commodities, pharmaceuticals, and quality precision industrial products, Western Europe enjoys a positive trade balance with the rest of the world. The magnitude of international trade reveals a number of interesting elements: (a) exports from EMs are larger than those from DMs; (b) exports from DMs are branded names, discretionary consumer products, financials, high tech goods, and military weaponry; (c) export of commercial services is increasing faster than secondary goods from EMs; and (d) trade is increasing 6% annually as it is a function of rapid innovation and discovery in secondary and tertiary output, and the reduction and elimination of economic dislocations. Scandinavia, China, Japan, Taiwan, Singapore, Switzerland, UK, Australia, Israel, and Canada dominate global economic competitiveness. After centuries of isolation, EMs and TWs are now reinserting themselves, and account for 59% all exports.

# Developed Market Characteristics

1. The population is highly urbanized, tertiary in employment with information and high-tech industries dominating. 2. DMs contain a higher number of scientists and skilled individuals as percent of total, nearly all concentrated in the largest metropolitan areas. 3. Since the Industrial Revolution, every generation has been punctuated by new technologies and higher standards and levels of living. 4. They have been the largest recipients of the "brain drain," dominate R&D, engineering, and global financial management. Japan ranks first in R&D as percent of GDP with 3.3%, the US and China spend 2.4% each, and the EU 2.2%. In terms of percentage of R&D funding growth, China, with 10%-plus, ranks first. 5. Nearly all DMs have slower than historic GDP growth rates, high unemployment, high taxation, large and rising debts, and high entitlement costs. GDP growth rates in DMs have been declining for the past generation and are now less than 2%. Since 2000, most DMs have lost market share to EMs. 6. In an attempt to counterbalance the current, destabilizing, economic forces between developed and emerging economies, DMs have pursued policies of reflation keeping interest rates at generational low levels. 7. For the first time since the Industrial Revolution, DMs are facing serious competition from EMs. The flow of electronic information, new technologies and R&D endeavors are no longer a monopoly of the historically most powerful. The process of globalization of the past 20 years is rearranging the allocation of skilled labor, capital and productive capacity. Nevertheless, DMs remain the center of capital, specific educational concentrations, technological innovations, and R&D. While GDP growth is slowing, national debt for most hovers above 100% of GDP. Nearly all have progressed to a post-industrial economy, clearly defined by low fertility, consumerism, and excessive debt. Many nations are borrowing to consume, and, in the process, are becoming less wealthy. The new normal in DMs is a stagnant economy with near zero interest rates. 8. The 20 richest countries consume 70% of all goods and services. They consume more than they produce. For many countries, the inflation rate is higher than GDP growth and the short interest rate combined. In order for the negative elements to be reversed, concerted efforts are required: reduce unfunded liabilities, control immigration, reduce debts, raise R&D expenditures, redefine education, and increase investments in cutting-edge technologies. 9. Developed governments have not maintained the value of their fiat currencies, thus promoting inflation, an inability to balance budgets, and increased debt levels to dangerous levels. 10. For more than a century, the three largest economic blocks have been Anglo-America, Europe, and Japan, commonly referred to as the "old order," with Asia emerging as the world's economic driver.

# Emerging Market Characteristics

Those nations that have embarked on a focused program of economic development, by initiating sound economic, political, and social reforms attracting foreign investment are now referred to as "emerging nations," forming the most rapidly growing global economic block. Their economic performance over the past 15 years has been impressive as their share of global GDP, growing trade surpluses, and accumulation of foreign reserves have outperformed DMs. In the process, the world has witnessed, since 1990, the largest, internal migration in history with more than 600 million people moving into metropolitan areas. In addition, they have the prerequisites for sustained growth because they contain populations hungry for material things, a passion for saving, and a capacity to learn and innovate as fast as possible. They vary widely in terms of geographic size, population, per capita income, etc., and are therefore difficult to generalize, as it is impossible to compare such disparate economies as Brazil, China, Thailand, and Chile.

Their economies are propelled by the export sector, but increasingly by domestic demand for infrastructure and consumer goods. They are also adding to their gold reserves fearful of the long-term concern for monetary inflation. BRICS are the core of EMs; the other important countries include Korea, Taiwan, Philippines, Mexico, Singapore, Malaysia, Israel, South Africa, Vietnam, Indonesia, Pakistan, Argentina, Turkey, and Chile. All are growing rapidly, contributing more than 75% of global GDP growth. Their domestic markets are growing, rural to urban migration accelerating, and their share of global market share in secondary industries is offering considerable competition to DMs. Nearly all countries are in Rostow's third stage, with several just entering the fourth stage. BRICS hold approximately $9 trillion of reserves of which China leads the list followed by Russia, India, and Brazil. With 33% of the global economy, they are large enough to bring down the global economy. Capital flows are flowing to EMs where the expected returns are considered above average when risks are taken into consideration and where principal can be repatriated without difficulty. For the first time, the combined GDP of EMs and TWs is greater than DMs. This should not come as a surprise as present DMs have not always been dominant in terms of global GDP.

EMs have gained economic respectability since 1990 as governments revised legal systems to protect private property, instituted many reforms, strengthened their banking systems, privatized government-owned assets, and reduced bureaucratic inefficiencies, all of which helped attract capital. As a result, geopolitical strategies and historical political and economic alliances are adjusting and transforming into new patterns. Growth is highly concentrated to water transportation with hinterlands remaining backward in contrast to growing coastal regions. EMs are becoming major players in international trade, and their biggest weapons are: raw materials, secondary output, low-cost labor, a growing middle class, rising standards and levels of living, and a high saving rate. They will continue to grow because: DMs simply are unable to live without the cheap labor of EMs; historic mercantilist policies which manipulated international trade to the advantage of DMs through quotas, exchange rate controls, subsidies, tariffs, etc., and by the international flow of capital, are coming to an end; EMs, as the primary drivers of the global economy, offer excellent investing opportunities; and EM equity valuations are lower than those of DMs. Coupled with a savings rate at least ten times that of the US, these nations are emerging as primary capital markets, and when one adds the rapid growth of college education, particularly science and information technology, their productivity is increasing much faster than during the Industrial Revolution. This part of the world has benefited more from the diffusion of knowledge in the past 20 years than what took place in the previous 500.

## Third World Market Characteristics

TWs are not similar to "EMs," as all are in Rostow's first and second stages. They are home to most of the world's poorest population: two billion, mostly in Africa, and portions of Latin America and Asia, and nearly all tropical. The fact that more than 500 million live on a $2 a day and the bulk on $4 day is significant in the sense that domestic demand is limited and economic investment opportunities are highly circumscribed. They are also defined as those having 50% or more of the workforce engaged in primary activities, those that are not industrialized, and those that rank at the bottom of most economic and cultural metrics. Nearly all TWs have colonialism in common with most attaining their independence after WWII, an event that brought a recurring pattern of socialism and/or despotic rule. The initial aims were to promote nation building, not economic growth and, in nearly all instances, authoritarian rule with close military imprints with good doses of elitism, privilege, and feudal-type structures were emphasized. The road to domestic tranquility was for the state to own all major enterprises, and to distribute monopolies and trade concessions to favorites. In nearly all countries, the colonial infrastructure was not improved, but allowed to deteriorate. In addition, land distribution schemes and an anti-colonial bias promoted the exodus of skilled Europeans, further reducing the ability of embryonic nations to embark upon a sustained economic development path. As a result, nationalization of foreign property was and is a common occurrence, especially energy and mining concerns.

In addition: 1. There is a high dependency on few exports for foreign exchange. Negative terms of trade are particularly pernicious as nations merely tread water over long periods without economic progress. 2. Economic development is mainly concentrated in the capital region. 3. The financial sector is undeveloped, with many countries lacking active stock markets. 4. GDP growth is erratic as are sovereign debt defaults, endemic political corruption, trade imbalances, budgetary deficits, and high rates of inflation. 5. Ninety percent of national wealth is highly concentrated in the top 1% of the population, described as a "kleptocracy," because of the magnitude of the theft that takes place by dictators and elites. 6. There is an absence of value-added industries. 7. Due to a brain drain, the two largest shortages are entrepreneurial talent and technical expertise. 8. More than 70% of the population lacks clean running water, the sanitary disposal of polluted water, and a dominance of water-related illnesses. 9. Lacking is a national consensus of basic social and political goals, the integration of minority groups, the secularization of politics, a trained civil service, a competitive political system, civilian control of the military, and possibilities of political and economic mobility. 10. Because they borrow in foreign currencies, they remain indebted in perpetuity.11. Nearly all nations exhibit centrifugal forces (disruptive) to the detriment of centripetal forces (unifying). The fact that a country has a name, flag, and a government, and the fact that other governments recognize its sovereignty, do not produce a cohesive political unit of substance and significance. Most important, the *raison d'être* of state formation, a significant element in creating a national cultural identity and a feeling of destiny is lacking.

# The Search for Causative Factors

In an attempt to explain the concentration of economic wealth and power, academia presents a long list of factors, of which the following are the most important: geographic determinism, physical determinism, biological determinism, and cultural determinism. What is missing from the above are two essentials that have been used as causal elements—population densities, and the concept of natural resources. Throughout history people thought that there was a direct correlation between population numbers, physical resources located within a circumscribed area, and wealth.

## The Concept and Importance of Natural and Human Resources

The concept of natural resources as a factor in the unequal distribution of wealth is a fascinating topic full of contradictions and myths. The historic and most widely used definition of a resource states that resources were "tangible," "material," and "fixed" and excluded man as an essential ingredient in the calculus. Resources today are defined not as substances but as forces, institutions, and policies and, as such, are dynamic living phenomena expanding and contracting in response to human behavior. They are defined as "that upon which one relies for aid, support, or supply; the capacity to take advantage of opportunities; to extricate oneself from difficulties; and means to given ends." The concept of resources, therefore, reflects human appraisal. While coal, for example, occurs in nature, coke, tar dyes, aspirin, nylon, sulfate of ammonia, and thousands of other products do not. It is man that adds to the stock of knowledge enabling innovations and inventions. It is the dominance of human resources over the physical world that produces disparate spacial wealth. Natural resources, therefore, are always evaluated in terms of a cultures capacity to convert them to goods and services; hence, the conversion process is a function of ability, technical expertise, attitudes, abilities, and objectives. Empirical evidence, however, is replete with examples of countries that are rich in natural resources but are economically marginal. Haiti, once the richest French colony and, at one time, wealthier than the US, has succumbed to grinding poverty making the country the poorest in Latin America. The Congo, one of the richest countries in copper, diamonds, gold, and other resources, is one of the poorest. West Virginia is an immensely rich area in terms of natural resources, but it is one of the poorest states; a picture that lies in sharp contrast to New Jersey, a state that has no resources but whose per capita income is significantly higher.

Consider the unfortunate plight of Spain, which discovered so much gold and silver that it emerged as the dominant military and economic power in Europe. In 1575, Spain stood tall and practically invincible as the principal colonial nation. Nevertheless, the joys of mercantilism were rooted in one particular cancer: the importation of precious metals in a relatively short time span with government debasing its currency by running fiscal deficits. By neglecting to build an efficient infrastructure and improve its secondary sector, Spain lived beyond its means, became involved in ruinous military adventures, and thus neglected to build an efficient infrastructure and improve its secondary sector. The gold of the New World flowed not to Spain but to Western Europe, primarily the Low Countries and the UK. In less than 150 years, Spain declared bankruptcy nine times. The days of Spanish imperialism lasted less than 125 years and, along with its next-door neighbor, Portugal, languished in poverty until the post-WWII period. Another example involves the Confederate states, which accounted for more than 85% of foreign exchange prior to 1860. Exports were centered on indigo, peanuts, cotton (at one time 7/8th of global output), rice, and tobacco, all highly concentrated in a few localities. Four years of war and a naval embargo, ruined all as Europe developed and imported long-staple cotton from Egypt, Turkish tobacco from the eastern Mediterranean, rice from Southeast Asia, peanuts from the Guinea coast of Africa, and synthetic dyes replaced indigo. In four years, the "unique" geography of the Confederacy and its products were replaced by alternatives, making the South the poorest region in the US. In contrast, Iceland, straddling the Arctic Circle, has absolutely no resource base, save that of hot geyser water used for bathing and home heating. Agriculture is practically non-existent necessitating the importation of nearly its entire food supply, and yet this austere physical environment maintains a standard of living of $45,000 per capita, a remarkable number given the fact that it amassed its wealth not through plunder. Its people are obsessively clean, orderly, and civil to each other, and its crime rate may well be the lowest on the planet. It developed human resources along with very progressive attitudes in a hostile environment where the sun shines no more than two weeks a year and for no more than six hours at a time. How do we explain this anomaly with the historic notion that the physical environment determines a regions economic prosperity? The notion that a resource is something that is fixed, material, and tangible is discarded to the academic wasteland. People matter, for it is they that have provided the stimulus to develop the wheel and the concepts of rent, leasing, and derivatives. A country's standard of living is a function of both physical and human resources, with the human dominating.

# The Demographic Transformation

The demographic transformation seeks to explain the historical evolution of birth and death rates, and hence, the growth, stability, or decline of population. It consists of five stages, each one affected by cultural elements and similar to the Rostov model:

Stage 1: With energy solely based on solar resources, people lived to population limits determined by food supply. Population numbers, therefore, vacillated within a narrow band without significant increases for 99% of human existence. With high fertility and death rates, population numbers were remarkably stable until the Neolithic Revolution.

Stage 2: This stage refers to a commercial-based agricultural economy beginning with the Neolithic Revolution that produced the first urban units in the Tigris Euphrates. It is noted for revolutionary technological innovations and discoveries, a rising saving rate, and the beginnings of exchange economies. The shift(s) mark watershed events that have changed the course of economic history in which the fertility and mortality gap widened to accelerate the growth of population. While the hydraulic civilizations of the Fertile Crescent were impressive, the technological innovations that produced the ancient thalassic cultures were revolutionary for the times, as the primary population was reduced from 97% to 90%, thus increasing the size and number of urban places.

Stage 3. This stage coincides with the Industrial Revolution and associated, medical advances. It reduced the birth rate dramatically and the death rate only marginally. Nevertheless, the divergence increased the population growth rate greater than 2.5% annually. This stage promulgates the most rapid population growth due to the diverging fertility and mortality trends mirroring rural to urban population migrations. The first country to reach this stage was the UK in 1800 when London became the first city to attain a population of 1 million, and the world 1 billion, a figure that rose to 2.5 billion in 1950, and 7.5 billion in 2012. Current global population growth is 2.2% and falling, as the concomitancy of urbanization and industrialization intensifies. For the bulk of global population in 1900, infant mortality was 80%, average lifespan 40, and more than 20% of all women died at childbirth. The youthful population comprises more than 50% of total and hence produces a highly unstable social, political, and economic environment. Two percent of global population was urbanized.

Stage 4: This stage is noted for the rapid decline in the rate of population growth and the further decline of birth and death rates, which produced zero and negative population growth in the latter stages. It coincides with rising urbanization and the dominance of tertiary activities over primary and secondary for the first time in world history. In Western Europe, Japan and Scandinavia, the old-age dependency ratio more than tripled. While children are an asset on a farm, urbanization renders them liabilities, and since the bulk of global population today is urban, the fertility rate will decelerate in the coming decades to 2%, while mortality rates decline further. It is significant to note that global urbanization, which was 5% in 1800, is expected to grow to 75% by 2030. At the time of this writing, the aging aspects of this stage attracts a lot of attention as it conjures a number of interesting features covering a wide spectrum of political, economic and cultural factors: a. Consumption patterns change. b. The economic demands of the aging population results in reduced investment and increased deflation. c. Interest rates decline due to a moderation in the rate of GDP growth. d. Investment strategies change as adults in an environment of less than zero population growth promote a more conservative asset allocation. The US is aging rapidly as the number of Americans aged 50-plus now total 100 million with 80% of all financial assets owned by people over the age of 57. The 65-plus cohorts rose from less than 1% in 1900 to 8% in 1945, 14% in 2000 and, by 2030, are expected to rise to 33%. The ever-aging population in this stage continually produces more retirees than new workers, affecting healthcare and pension liabilities. e. The gap between the aged (65-plus) and the youthful cohort (under 15) is greater at this stage than any other, thus producing a more stable political, economic and social environment. Europe and Japan are at historic low levels of GDP growth, but many argue the following: If the retirees are wealthy enough to support themselves, where is the harm? The infrastructure is in place (schools, streets, sidewalks, etc.) so that a stable or slightly growing population would not place undo pressures for capital expenditures. The fact that DMs are experiencing zero population growth features does not imply that a deterioration of wealth production or a diminution of quality of life is imminent. A young, growing, and working population that was needed in former years is not necessary, as working careers are extended beyond 70. In 1950, 31% of the global population was urbanized; in 2000, 48%, and in 1913, 57%. Developed countries, with more than 85% of the population, are the most urbanized, and the least urbanized, TWs, with less than 40% are the least urbanized.

Stage 5: This stage affects mature economies, and known as a "post-demographic tertiary economy." It is characterized by medical technology that is able to prolong life by an even larger margin than what took place over the course of the past one hundred years. By growing tissue, diseased organs would simply be replaced by the new, and hence, extend life to unimaginable levels, all of which will have a profound economic impact. Along with increased longevity is the associated cultural phenomenon of a falling birthrate to below *population zero* levels. The historically defined "family," of daddy, mommy, and two children will become a historical relic, replaced mainly by the single head of household. These circumstances will reshape the leisure, furnishing, toy industries, and the *ekistical* nature of humankind in the 21st century. The redefinition of "retirement" will present a picture of the gentrification of urban America thus prompting a huge migration from the isolation of a childless suburban environment to a more vibrant and gregarious urban lifestyle of high population densities. Moreover, a young, growing, and working population that was needed in former years is not necessary as longevity continues to increase and working careers are extended beyond 80 years.

In the final analysis: 1. Despite the fact that world population will rise to 8 billion by 2030, it is aging and longevity means longer retirements. Aging populations are deflationary as individuals demand less, consume less, and spend less. 2. Attempts to increase fertility have started in most DMs with a number of incentives offered to those of childbearing age. 3. A new sociology has emerged for those beyond the age of 65. The nest is empty, assuming that mommy and daddy will live into their 90s, the remaining life will essentially be without children; therefore, a new social order will be born. 4. Investment strategies and asset allocations become highly conservative and defensive in an environment of zero population growth. 5. Once baby boomers retire, the demographic complexion of the US will change dramatically exerting a profound impact on the consumerism that first appeared after World War II. The number of people in the maximum spending ages of 20-50 will decline, and this will redirect financial and labor resources away from several sectors into others.

## The Concept of Entrepreneurial Talent: "Creative Alphas"

When one compares developed and undeveloped regions, the critical distinguishing ingredients to development are not natural resources and capital, but the percentage of "alphas," or creative entrepreneurial talent. The alphas of the world are unusual personalities characterized by the following: 1. They have experienced adversity and overcame failure at an early age, and as a result, look at the entopic world differently. In the words of ancient Chinese philosophers: "If you have not passed through the bitterness of starvation, you know not the blessings of abundance." 2. Alphas originate from all occupations, and are not exclusively a product of the privileged. 3. They create, not because of innate talent, but because of desire; they are driven, and never satisfied. They are not born with an innate ability to succeed, but acquire this trait at an early age. 4. They are passionate, patient, disciplined, and independent thinkers, and they recognize and seize opportunities. 5. They reside in high-density venues, as the high degree of interaction acts as a stimulus for greater innovations and discoveries. 6. They place importance to the travails of working through problems. 7. The quality of peer friendships and associations is vital to success. 8. They have close contacts with scientific information sources; they are highly interactive with innovators; and they are blessed with the widest information field possible. 9. They are competitive as they consider spirited contests, rivalries, and struggle the lifeblood to innovation and discovery and the principal driving forces behind progress. 10. They are the entrepreneurs and innovators of society; people with sufficient drive, discipline, patience, a willingness to take risk (and to sustain a sub-par standard of living) while struggling to succeed. They have the mental fortitude to tolerate temporary failure and a propensity to build wealth. 11. They sacrifice all manner of daily pleasures in order to save and invest. They are, therefore, different from ordinary mortals; they are in short supply; and they gravitate to those cultural regions that allow their talents to maximize personal achievement. 12. When their numbers are limited, they become the principal limiting element in GDP growth. 13. They understand the differences between utopic and entopic concepts; they adapt, improvise, and overcome.

## Variations on the WW Rostow Model of Economic Growth

WW Rostow's notion of how nations evolve economically is simple and concise. If one is contemplating investing in a foreign country, make sure you are aware of the particular economic growth stage the country lies in. According to W.W. Rostow, countries evolve through five stages, all mirroring the infinite variation of a nation's economy: The nature of the central government, monetary system, demographics, institutional framework, and cultural character of the population. Each element shapes, defines, and develops a composite that offers similarities and differences between one country and another. No stage is static as all indicate evolutionary trends at varying rates and all conform to the demographic cycle. With considerable literary license on my part, they are:

## Figure 1

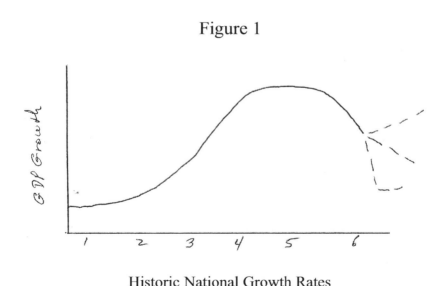

Historic National Growth Rates

Stage 1. Traditional Society: This stage is characterized by no long-term savings, capital accumulation, and technological progress, and not able to improve productivity for most of human history. Subsistent in nature with pre-Newtonian science dominating, the entire population is agricultural with the lowest life expectancies. The governing technological base is *eotechnic*, or that which is dominated by muscle, wood, wind, and solar power, and where population limits were determined by food supply.

Stage 2. Preconditions for Take-Off: A 90%-97% primary population with a low but rising national savings rate characterizes this stage; therefore, sustained incipient economic growth makes its appearance. The driver for the growth is based on societal changes and new technologies. This was the picture in central and Southern Europe and the Mediterranean until the Dark Ages. The latter, called feudalism, was a society based on a symbiotic trilogy of clergy, aristocrats, and serfs, all of whom produced little wealth of consequence. Feudalism, a form of slavery discouraged social, political, and economic mobility. In the latter stage, foremost developments were the transformation of the English Isles into the United Kingdom, the breakdown of feudalism, and the formation of a parliamentary form of government. Additional elements included the accumulation of capital, "enclosure laws," the migration of French Huguenots, and maritime improvements to promote commerce. In addition, a series of key agricultural developments took place in central and Northern Europe that enabled agricultural workers to leave farms. The production of large horses to pull plows in clay-dominant soils; the production of the Norfolk (four-field) rotational system; and the horseshoe, collar, and harness improved tuberous crops, and hardy winter vegetables increased productivity. Primogeniture in the Protestant central and northern European regions enabled the enlargement of the family farm, and although encumbered by a short growing season, a new agricultural system developed around the dairy cow, with ancillary pig and truck farming. By the end of the 1600s, the saving rate accelerated 5%-10%. These developments spread to Scandinavian Europe, the Low Countries, France, Germany, and Switzerland. What made the evolutionary developments of Western Europe distinct from previous history was the rise of capitalism, which dictated the superiority of capital over land and labor.

Stage 3: The Take-Off. The national savings rate exceeds 10% and growth becomes self-sustaining. Historically, the UK entered this stage in 1725, France in 1820, the United States in 1845, Germany in 1850, Japan in 1880, Russia in 1890, and China in 1990s. This is the stage of a declining primary population and a rapidly accelerating urban population. As the post-medieval societies of Western Europe evolved along the path of nation building and evolving demographic changes, a middle class emerged. Because of rising capital formation, disposable income, and commercial interactions, the Industrial Revolution had global implications as central governments exhibited an active interest in economic development as a national priority. The technological base, which defines this stage, is *paleotechnic*, or that dominated by coal and iron. The Industrial Revolution, therefore, based on mass production, mass marketing, and large-scale transportation produced the wealth that made modern society possible.

The Industrial Revolution was a long-term economic, political, and social revolution through which an agrarian society was transformed into an urban-dominated culture. It was a revolution in which secondary output was transformed into factory production by the application of power-driven machines, thus making the cottage-system obsolete. The localization of secondary activities occurred near coal mining regions because of the reduction of bulk and weight in the process of smelting. Political, labor, and capital were increasingly concentrated in national capitals producing primate cities. It led to dramatic population increases, rural to urban migration, the explosive rise of a middle class, and an equally rapid acceleration in the levels and standards of living. The second Industrial Revolution dominated by *neotechnic* (electric) technologies offered greater dimensions during the second half of the 19th century due to the technological progress of anthracite and bituminous coal utilization and the production of large-scale rail facilities reducing land distances, followed by the automobile and airplane. In short order, the wealthiest, blue-collar population in history emerged. By WWII, the secondary sector dominated the American economy, and by 1960, one in seven workers directly or indirectly worked for the automobile industry. Within a generation, service oriented industries came to dominate the labor force with equally historic consequences. Once introduced industrialization altered the structure of traditional, subsistence societies. The elements of change were many of which modern systems of accounting, the preponderance of capital and labor as the driving forces instead of land, and the increased importance of secondary and tertiary activities replaced agriculture as percent of GDP. Most significantly, for two centuries following 1800, global per capita income rose ten-fold while population growth grew six-fold. Economic Colonialism, over time created two different economies: the European model and the Colonial model—the latter exporting raw materials and the former importing raw materials and exporting secondary goods. It was also a period of monumental inventions and no income taxes.

Stage 4: Drive to Maturity. In this stage, the slope of the curve steepens, the savings rate increases to about 20%, production and productivity rise faster than population growth, service industries increase and manufacturing peaks. The US became the world's dominant economy, Wall Street supplanted "the city," the $US replaced sterling as the dominant currency, New York emerged as the most vibrant city of the 20th century, and the US became the recipient of the "brain drain." The US stood as the shinning beacon for opportunity and ultimate success. By 1946, while the whole world lay prostate, America was the home to 90% of all millionaires, produced 85% of all vehicles, possessed nearly all the world's gold, and 90% of all aircraft.

Stage 5. Mass Consumption: In this stage, the curve flattens and begins to decline, indicating that consumption exceeds productive capacity, and the economy stagnates and/or declines for a considerable period. The stage is characterized by the highest percentage of population urbanized, zero population growth, and sophisticated *biotechnic* and nuclear technologies dominating. A number of features present themselves: nations dissipate their wealth through profligate behavior, governmental entitlements, a failure to innovate and maintain market share, and productivity declines. In this stage, where tertiary activities dominate, diminishing returns become common, corruption at all levels increase in intensity, and the economy stagnates as the former forces contributing to economic development are debased. This negative stage is similar to Stage 1 in terms of a low savings rate and GDP growth. The UK was the first country to fall victim to this malaise after WWI. The unsustainable Bacchanalian consumption, excessive government spending, and the accumulation of ever-larger governmental debt, exaggerated the depression and kept the UK in this stage for the next three generations. Japan entered this stage in the late 1980s and the US in the 1990s. The structural changes necessary to overcome the negative cultural elements are not easy to overcome, require time and bold actions. This stage represents another salient point. "*Schaffendes* capital" (creative capital) has been replaced by "*raffendes* capital" (unproductive capital), thus the distinctions between "wealth creation" and "wealth extraction."

Stage 6. Beyond Consumption: This stage introduces several scenarios for DMs: further decline, stability or recovery. Few wish a continuation of the malaise, but the inertia of "bread and circus" begs strong and affirmative political and economic action for the good of the majority. Reversal of the flat and/or declining trend to an upward trajectory will be a function of producing new technological innovations to increase productivity and reverse profligate behavior. The effort to extend life to new, unheard of limits requires leadership, vision, and a strong dose of urgency. This stage will be defined by a varying period of painful adjustments, and will be called *wirtschaftswunder*, or economic miracle, characterized by post-*biotechnic* technologies producing the Third Industrial Revolution, which is characterized by robotics, 3-D printing and scanning, harnessing hydrogen, wireless transmission of energy, etc. In the final analysis, the broad concept of economic progress rests on six assertions: 1. A definite pattern of change exists. 2. This pattern of change manifested throughout history is known. 3. The existence and known examples of change, in the end, are irreversible in direction. 4. The direction of the known and irreversible blueprints of change in history is progressive. 5. Economic progress is not linear. 6. Economic progress must be promulgated by entrepreneurial will. Economic progress authors maintain that progress is necessary because it is willed; hence, assured by providence. Contingent progress authors, on the other hand, maintain that economic progress is a product of man's desire, or willingness to bring it about. Therefore, economic progress will pulsate and exhibit cyclical activity commensurate with the nature of the prevailing national cohesiveness, determination, and the ability to sacrifice. The next Industrial Revolution, currently under development in DMs, is centered on niche-oriented "cottage" industries that will be noted for their cutting-edge technologies in the fields of biotechnology and pharmaceuticals, nanotechnology, wireless energy transmission, etc. 7. Countries must be willing to augment capital stock, a necessary ingredient in raising productive capacity.

A number of generalizations are in order: 1. No country has skipped stages, and countries do not evolve at the same rate in a clear and orderly fashion. Economic progress is never a "linear" progression or a natural phenomenon. 2. The elements propelling economic growth are technological discovery and innovation, encouragement of an entrepreneurial spirit, saving, and capital accumulation. 3. Until the dawn of the Industrial Revolution in 1725, economic growth was negligible, a rate that began to increase gradually until the 1820s, when it began to accelerate. Historically, what took centuries is now being abridged into decades. 4. Technological progress in each stage altered the factors of economic location. The factors that localized cigar production in Tampa, rubber in Akron, shirt production in Troy, NY, car production in Detroit, etc., no longer apply. 5. All revolutions have ideological components. The Industrial Revolution was influenced by the "Protestant Ethic," "the spirit of capitalism," and the psychological force of "progress."

## The Importance of Technology

The US, for more than 130 years, has been looked upon as the premier nation for economic innovation and the accelerator/incubator for new enterprises. America stood for innovative technology and unbridled entrepreneurship; therefore, the world's brainpower flowed in an uninterrupted stream to the US. The combination of a lack of opportunities abroad and stable and appealing institutional and cultural features in the US compelled this one-way flow pattern of the world's greatest minds. However, relative to other countries, the US is not innovating fast enough to reverse the current economic malaise. The gap is closing and unless trends reverse, the US will no longer lead the world as it has in the past. Technological leadership in pharmaceuticals, medicine, drilling bits, and a few other fields are narrowing rapidly. Like all economic activity, these industries have reached strategic inflection points requiring massive infusions of capital, infrastructure, and human resources. America's historic advantage of enticing quality scientific and entrepreneurial labor has dimmed, and a counter brain drain flow has emerged. As the competition for creative talent intensifies globally, many "creative alphas" are leaving the US for what they consider greener pastures. Not only is the competition coming from the other side of the "pond," but also both sides of the Atlantic are losing ground to the frenetic production of highly skilled technocrats and committed entrepreneurial individuals from Asia. The US has about 20% of global individuals referred to as "creative alphas," Europe has 34%, and the rest lie mainly in Asia, a region that had less than 15% 25 years ago. Everyone forgets that the competition for quality talent is far more important than the global competition for natural resources.

R&D is economic activity that is capital, technological, and labor intensive and, essentially, a monopoly of the wealthiest nations since the resources for such activities exist there, and include such industries as pharmaceutical, electronic, computer oriented, telecommunications, etc. Today, comparative advantage is a factor of one country inventing and innovating faster than another in order to benefit. Over the years, these activities have created "techno poles," or regions of concentration associated with universities and research facilities. In the US, there are seven such regions responsible for more than 90% of all innovation and invention: 1. The region from Southern Maine to Northern Virginia is the largest and most important. 2. Greater Chicago to Minneapolis 3. Greater Atlanta 4. Greater Houston to Dallas and Austin 5. The region between greater San Francisco to San Diego 6. Greater Seattle from Bellingham to Portland 7. The "research triangle" of North Carolina. The second largest technopole region is Western Europe including all Scandinavian capitals. In Asia, the largest center for R&D is Japan, coastal China, Taiwan, Korea, Singapore, and India. The number and size of technopoles with their concentration of exceptional talent, have both increased in size and number in recent history, and are key real estate investment regions.

### Technology Defined

Technology is defined as the social pool of knowledge of the industrial arts, and it plays a major role in explaining the spacial distribution of wealth. The causes of technological invention are knowledge-induced. The rate of technological progress is the rate at which new technology is produced in any given period, and it is a function of education and GDP, plus a willingness by the political and economic leadership to make "potential" technology "kinetic." The rate of replication refers to the rate at which technology is disseminated. Technological capacity is that portion of existing technology that a nation has distributed among the labor force. Technological progress is measured by cutting-tool efficiency, acceleration of physical power, acceleration of human speeds, acceleration of longevity, and the acceleration of diffusion. The rate of technological progress has accelerated to the point that the advances of the past five years have exceeded all that occurred in history. In the aggregate, all technological revolutions free people from restrictions. Unfortunately, contemporary ideological opinions trump scientific evidence.

Although figures expressing pure R&D expenditures are difficult to define, the US spends less than 2% of GDP on R&D when it should be spending 4% and more. Since there is no exception to the correlation of R&D and GDP growth, the US is losing the battle of maintaining its century-old supremacy in technological innovation, and the decline in patents by 30% is a testament to the degree of deterioration over the past 30 years. These elements are significant because technological growth does not occur naturally. The cause and effect of technological growth are the result of variables and not constants, the critical variant being the presence of entrepreneurial talent. Therefore, as income discrepancies narrow between DMs and EMs, one can expect the brain drain, once monopolized by North Atlantic nations to decline further as productivity is rising faster in EMs. During the 1800s, productivity increased by 1.5%, and in the 20th century the percentage nearly doubled. In the 21st century, information-based technology is expected to increase to new heights. Scientists and engineers in the US make up less than 2% of the adult population but are responsible for creating more than 70% of GDP growth. The trends, however, are disturbing: China is producing 30 times more engineers than the US, and foreign students are no longer arriving to the US as they did in prior decades. In addition:

1. Globalization is intensifying *cultural convergence,* the latter, a reference to the integration and homogenization of human behavior. Its convergence has exploded in recent history, and with it the engine of change, as languages, ideas, and goods are transported and integrated at breathtaking paces. In addition, the accumulated knowledge currently available is far greater than at any time in human history as nine out of ten scientists that have ever lived are alive today. If all the technical achievements of humankind were divided in half and placed on a balanced beam, the fulcrum would occur in 1995. Ninety percent of all PhD's have been issued since 1965, and 95% of prescription drugs available today did not exist prior to 1985. More than 95% of all scientific discoveries ever made were the product of the 20th century. The first printed book–the "Gutenberg"–was instrumental in the dissemination of knowledge, and within a 50-year span, more than 40 million books were printed. Eighty-six percent of all books were printed after 1990, with three million-plus new titles printed annually today. It is now possible for the average person to receive more information by reading the daily edition of a large newspaper than in an entire lifetime during the middle Ages. Technological growth and innovation, according to Joseph Schumpeter are the prime movers in GDP growth because the introduction of a new good, the introduction of a new method of production, and new structural business techniques, all combine to redefine economic markets through "creative destruction," as in newspaper, line telephone, photography, travel agencies, bookstores, etc. Technological rewards, therefore, always flowed to those regions and cultures that invented and innovated in order to increase productivity, and the next centers for futuristic travel will involve those regions that implement "hyperloop" systems (ultra-high speed pneumatic vacuum tubes).

2. Technology continues to miniaturize, get faster, and cheaper. In the 1950s, computers were made with thousands of vacuum tubes occupying hundreds of square feet of space and encumbered by high temperatures. However, with the advent of innovations, one could now have more capability on one's desk. In 1970, about 100,000 computers were in use in the US, most of which were located in universities, government offices and businesses. In the 1980s, personal computers became affordable. Today there are more computers than people. Most importantly, constant innovation and discovery are keys to competing in a global economy. Engineering creativity, pharmaceutical advances, scientific discoveries, and miniaturization of data and applications are critical in outperforming competitors. It is possible that a more powerful chip that would be invisible to the human eye will replace the microprocessor, and wireless transmission of energy is no longer a foreign concept. All of the above indicate that man has increased its mastery of

the physical environment, that human knowledge is doubling every six years, and in many areas, every six months. As the pace of technology progresses unabated, so will the velocity of global economic growth. The latest medical revolution involves genetic engineering (limb regeneration, transplant brain cells, etc.), and the ability to increase the productivity of both animals and biotic matter. Longevity of animals will be lengthened, protein production increased, diseases reduced, and the production of multiple products from one animal a real possibility. In addition to increased yields, resistance to disease and drought, the ability to absorb existing nutrients without commercial fertilizer, etc., will have the effect of reducing agricultural land by half while quadrupling output. The medical miracles of the next 20 years will dwarf all others. The major advances will focus on ways to facilitate organ rejuvenation, thus reducing surgical procedures. The re-growth of cartilage, more potent vaccines and anti-infection medications intended to reduce hospital visits, will reduce medical costs by 50%. Human genome advances will accelerate, as will discoveries relating to photonics. Wireless technology, and in particular, Long Term Evolution, will revolutionize the dissemination of data to unheard of levels. The geography of technopoles will also change. "Blueseed," a floating city for entrepreneurs has attracted nearly 1,200 firms from 60 countries to a venue located in international waters, off the coast of central California. The purpose is to create a competitive working environment, be close to investors, facilitate talent recruitment, reduce legal regulations, etc.

3. The desktop computer and the internet over the past 20 or so years have produced a number of revolutionary changes in the securities industry. With the click of a button, commissions have been slashed, the speed of executing a trade has been reduced to nanoseconds, and information is now online and not in a library twenty miles from home. The World Economic Forum, reported (2008) that for the first time in modern history, the country ranking number one in their network readiness index was Singapore followed by Finland and Denmark, with the US, Korea, Japan, and Hong Kong, among the top 12.

4. "Disruptive" technologies are those that produce less expensive, more complicated, smaller, and more productive products and services that displace older, less efficient technologies. The word processor displaced the typewriter, and the internet, many a library. Technological rewards always flowed to those societies, regions, and cultures that invented and innovated in order to increase productivity. Technology that drives economic performance, but since innovations and inventions historically did not evolve at regular and predictable rates, economic performance was erratic and difficult to perceive in a single lifetime. However, with the evolution of the modern laboratory and the self-financing corporation, innovations and inventions have combined to reduce the gaps in peak to trough and degree of amplitude. Today, computer technology is doubling every five months, but the production of thin circuits is revolutionizing "imperceptible electronics," especially in healthcare applications.

All of the foregoing is of immense significance if one accepts the premise that economic growth is not a natural phenomenon, but a product of will, desire, and determination by extraordinary people. The concept of the atom is not a common topic of conversation, innovations do not derive from space, and economic progress is not a by-product of indolence. "Alphas," a small percentage of the entire population, dominate every aspect of the modern economy in a dimension that is infinitely greater than their small number suggests. The economic impact, however, can only be realized when the creative sector is rewarded, encouraged, and stimulated, and this occurred in very few places in the past. Many economists are worried about the pace of technological competitive erosion, maintaining that America has lost its historic edge to produce new and better products. Only the production of high quality military weaponry, selected pharmaceuticals, drilling bit equipment and related products, remain. Over the past 25 years, foreign nations have carefully picked the best from America and are flooding the world with a myriad of economic niches. Countries like China, Taiwan, Japan, Korea, Singapore, Germany, Netherlands, Sweden, Switzerland, and others, are increasing the growth of their human talent by 3%-7% annually. While the US still leads the world in innovation, scientific publications, technology, and patents, the signs that all have peaked are evident. While subject to heated discussion, many in the profession maintain that the US is no longer the innovator it once was and that, in relation to other countries, is falling behind as the competition for global talent accelerates and spreads over all occupational groups. Human talent will gravitate to those areas where abilities are rewarded to maximum levels.

# International Trends

The world is evolving rapidly: a generation ago, the international economy consisted of the US, its major European allies, Canada, and Japan. This is no longer the case. The geographic diffusion of industrial, technological, and financial power is shifting rapidly with significant ramifications. The global economy is now in unchartered waters as it is about to transfer the largest amount of assets from DMs to EMs in human history. This will not be a smooth transition as cultural, economic, and the possibility of military conflict raise serious concerns. It will definitely alter the US-centric world as geopolitical tensions, speculative financial activities, increasing national debts, and global monetary inflation offer the world new challenges. Many, therefore, see a troubled future: 1. A global crash in real estate is underway, and the meltdown in the US in recent years has reduced household net worth by more than 25%. 2. The international monetary system is engulfed by rising inflation. 3. Economic and geopolitical events have hastened the decline of the $US and propelled commodities to higher levels. 4. The BRICS will continue their relentless economic growth pace. 5. The current US secular bear market will last much longer than expected. 6. Despite the flight to "privatization" and "free markets," state etatism of the past century will make a comeback. 7. The drive for world government will intensify. James Warburg in 1950 said, "We shall have world government whether or not you like it…by conquest or consent." The political, social, and economic elites of the US are of the opinion that the nation-state is obsolete and that, eventually, international institutions will supplant national sovereignty. 8. As fiat currencies fail, economic dominance will shift toward those nations holding large gold reserves, and few debts.

## Globalization

Contemporary globalization is the transfer of capital, secondary output, R&D facilities, and expert talent from DMs to EMs on a scale never witnessed in all previous history. Past descriptions of the *pays* and *lays* of indolent, self-sufficient communities, largely cut off from the rest of the world, are no longer, as they are forced to engage in real social and economic intercourse. Globalization has facilitated the growth of trade, the flow of financial resources, people, and ideas. In the 1990s, global trade doubled, and it doubled again in the first six years of this century.

1. Cheap labor, the instantaneous transfer of capital, and the rapid transfer of technology are the key drivers of globalization. Inexpensive labor, a major constituent to the new paradigm is determining the prospects of economic dominance in redistributing economic wealth. The export of secondary activities from DMs to EMs will continue because the historic capital/labor relationships between developed and developing countries have been dismantled. In Asia, globalization has been so successful; it has produced overcapacity, and unleashed fierce competition for the finest intellectual minds. The emphasis on secondary sectors where capital and skilled labor are highly intensive such as electronics, aircraft, pharmaceuticals, information technology, precision base metal products and luxury good production. High-end employment and R&D activities are being relocated as capital flows from DMs to EMs intensify and increasingly lie beyond the realm of *pax dollarum*. a. High-end employment and R&D are increasingly becoming more important in EMs. b. EMs have become the world's main manufacturing centers. c. The new "global" growth is highly concentrated in no more than 50 metropolitan areas, mainly in Asia. d. As secondary employment is shifted overseas, the overwhelming amount of new employment in DMs is in tertiary activities. e. Real income growth is slowing in DMs, and growing rapidly in EMs. f. Due to technological innovations, global interconnectivity has skyrocketed, thereby enabling economic activities to be transferred rapidly around the world in a fraction of former times, giving EMs a comparative advantage. g. The fastest growing middle class is occurring in EMs. h. The principal global commodities are fuel, electrical components, machinery, vehicles, plastics, optical, pharmaceutical, and iron and steel.

2. Globalization is not a system where everybody benefits equally: not every country is able to deploy capital, labor, physical resources and technology at competitive levels. The benefits accrue to those who have a comparative advantage in productivity, the latter a function of R&D and national commitment. Other elements that complicate the picture are sufficient capital, overcapacity, and technological progress. Reality dictates that this system simply will not be allowed to work in perpetuity as it will negatively impact DMs. Reactions are already surfacing in the US and Europe, and in the words of Otto von Bismarck: "Free trade is the weapon of the dominant economy anxious to prevent others from following in its path." For the US, the picture is clear: as long as it misallocates capital for the construction of sports stadiums and not for crucial R&D, other countries will seize opportunities.

3. Evidence of EMs decoupling with the US is everywhere. The bulk of Chinese trade is not with the US, but with the rest of Asia, the bulk of Japanese trade is with China and not the US, and the bulk of BRICS trade is with the rest of

the world. Globalization is an apoplectic condition for the US, as it exhibits vulnerability when foreign companies gain a foothold in the US economy. Therefore, The US is not benefitting from globalization as the US is currently experiencing a contraction in standards and levels of living, and as the *Daily Reckoning* has so aptly put it: "They make, we take. They save, we spend. They lend, we borrow. They sell, we buy." Obviously, the system only works as long as America borrows to buy. The question is for how long, as no major nation in history has been able to sustain a negative current account deficit indefinitely. The domestic picture is disturbing as the population ages, the middle class shrinks and the work ethic shunned and ridiculed. Short-term benefits from globalization arise when the US takes advantage of its managerial and technical abilities through its multinational corporations who enjoy a history of market penetration. However, the above is not enough as it benefits a small portion of the working population. Many state that other jobs are created in the US, but how many are paying upwards of $40 an hour? Since 2000, the US lost 30% of all computer equipment employment, 40% of all jobs in semiconductors, and 43% in communications equipment. Since 1995, one of four manufacturing plants has been torn down. At present, the determination of what is produced in the US is "the China price." In the future, the latter will be affected by domestic, inexpensive energy and higher foreign wages.

4. Global economic systems are changing. In the past, EMs exported raw materials and DMs manufactured goods for export. For nearly 400 years, the structure operated under elaborate quota systems with mature countries promoting the system and developing countries wishing its destruction. Quotas represent managed trade that has remained a major obstacle to free trade. These trading patterns, however, have reversed, but not on a uniform level. The global economy is dominated and regulated by the geography of money, which is overwhelmingly concentrated in the G-20 nations. Important events in the globalization imbroglio have seen the transfer of technology from DMs to EMs, the transfer of capital from DMs to EMs, a reduction of the brain drain from EMs to DMs, slower rates of economic growth in DMs and much more rapid GDP growth in EMs, and growth of capital and labor-intensive activities in EMs.

5. As globalization progresses, protectionist policies are colliding with free markets. Politicians wishing to reverse the outsourcing of jobs by blaming other nations introduce "protective" measures to garner votes, and, as a result, protectionist hyperbole has surfaced in nearly all DMs. In its basic form, protectionism seeks to confine trade through tariffs, quotas, etc., in order to offer advantages to domestic industries. The agricultural subsidies of DMs depress prices in poor countries, tariffs depress value added activities in TWs, quotas create economic dislocations and are a barrier to free economies, and protection of secondary activities inhibit exports while promoting instability. Bound to inflame passions are cross-border mergers and acquisitions.

## The Global Financial Crisis Will Intensify

The world is entering a period of sustained financial instability that will witness the end of the "golden age" of both public financing and consumer spending. Globally, there is too much money, too much debt, too much credit, too much speculation, and not enough saving in the US. In addition, because no currency is convertible to a fixed quantity of any commodity, the manipulation of currencies by central banks to gain a competitive advantage is accelerating due to their reactive policies. The obvious result of these currency devaluations is the rise of inflation and commodity prices. Monetary inflation will eventually stifle GDP growth and reduce real income. While no one knows what will precipitate the next international financial crisis, the signs of financial instability are everywhere:

1. Nearly all countries are in debt greater than 120% of GDP and a drag on the national economy when the GDP to debt ratio exceeds 90%. Japan and the US spend 28% of revenues on interest payments, a percentage that would increase beyond 90%, should interest rates double from present levels. Global sovereign debt exceeds $165 trillion, the highest in history. As the process of fiat inflation continues, currencies lose their value leading to inflation. If "tightening" occurs, markets will crash leading to depression, and hence the dilemma facing central banks. 2. The citizenry is in debt, the degree varies with country, but the debt disease is universal. 3. The global real estate bubble has yet to bottom. 4. Rising protectionism may act as a brake to global economic expansion. 5. Derivatives exceed $700 trillion, or 43 times the size of US GDP. 6. Central banks have supplanted and distorted free markets in order to prevent the collapse of fiat currencies. Central governments owe more than $82 trillion not counting unfunded liabilities. 7. History has shown that fiat money throughout history has become worthless. No country has been spared the humiliation of a financial debacle. 8. Global central bankers appear to be more worried about deflation than inflation, and inflating the money supply is an effort to prevent the former and be damned with the latter. 9. When one country seeks to better its economic performance by worsening the economic problems of other countries, the practice is called "beggar-thy-neighbor," and one of the easiest policies is to lower the value of currency in order to boost exports. The problem is that all countries are unable to accomplish this feat at the same time, and sooner, rather than later, the policy angers public officials: President Francois Hollande said, "We can't let the euro fluctuate according to the mood of the market." Since 2011, all countries have reduced interest rates, and because there are no vacuums in nature, the countries that accumulate gold will outperform in the looming currency wars. In times of crisis, fiat money is not accepted–but gold is. The day will arrive when the US and other nations are expected to pay with gold or a currency totally or partially backed by precious metals. In fact, the EU parliament recommends gold-backed bonds. 10. Current low interest, high indebted policies of the currency cartel (US, UK, EU, and Japan) are destabilizing global trade patterns and promoting inflation.

Currency manipulation has led to capital, wage, trade and price controls on a scale unprecedented in global history.

Financial crises are endemic with hundreds of fiat currencies having gone out of the money business by acts of war, hyperinflation, and other means. Nearly 1000 years ago, the world's first paper monetary crisis occurred in China, and in recent decades, financial crises have occurred with increasing frequency, the number exceeding 45 since 1980. The necropolis of failed fiat currencies, in fact, lies in plain view. Because there are more than 100 countries on the verge of national bankruptcy, all financial crises have the potential to create instability, and are thus viewed with alacrity. In past decades, currencies were backed by gold, offering monetary stability and discipline. The situation changed after WWI with debt and spending running out of control in most countries, it began to accelerate after 1971, first gradually, and then after 1982 with a vengeance. In the past 10 years, the $US has fallen by 82% in value when priced to gold, and as central bankers inject liquidity global markets are being set up for many more bubbles. In the meantime, the purchasing power of gold continues to improve. In 1970, it took 68 ounces of gold to buy a compact car, and now just 10 ounces. In 1970, it took 23 ounces to buy the Dow, and now 8 ounces. If one looks at the events leading to the Great Depression, a similar scenario has unfolded in recent decades. Travel to any corner of the globe, and the result is the same–huge bubbles fed by easy money, ostensibly creating "wealth." Moreover, because no currency is convertible to a fixed quantity of any commodity, the manipulation of currencies by central governments to gain a competitive advantage by keeping their currencies weak is accelerating. In this regard, it is necessary to consider the words of Henry Morgenthau, US Treasury Secretary in 1939: "We are spending more money than we have ever spent before, and it does not work. After eight years, we have just as much unemployment as when we started, and an enormous debt to boot." Since then, central planning policies have continued to fail.

Two related elements that signal the true causes of the global financial cliff are debt and excessive money creation. For the first time in history, the world is entirely unconstrained in the production of fiat currency. The orgy of monetary creation is unprecedented as the amount since 2008 exceeds $19 trillion, or 23% of global GDP. The result has been a torrent of bubbles in real estate, bonds, equities, and entitlements; collectively resulting in an astonishing flood of debt at all levels. The situation is not new but a product of post-1980 policies to inflate the money supply and extend credit beyond normal market parameters. Governments and central banks are not inclined to reduce the money supply, cease the manipulation of interest rates, and lower governmental spending. The plan is more intervention with no policy to ameliorate the trend. That means that there is no way to avoid the final collapse of financial markets and national economies. The twenty largest central banks have become major economies, controlling their national financial markets and thus replicating the American model. In the process, free markets have been debased, along with national currencies. They cannot raise interest because the action would plunge the global economy in a depression that would be infinitely worse than that of the 1930s. The process of monetary inflation, therefore, continues and eventually inflation will turn to hyperinflation before markets correct. The current global financial arrangements in place are not sustainable (the US wishing to inflate the globe and the rest of the world wishing to deflate the US). The US consumes more than it produces, imports more than it exports, saves next to nothing, has become addicted to debt, and has produced a climate of hedonistic desires, all of which is made possible through the concerted efforts of manipulated data. In the delusional world of financialization, everything is adjusted, manipulated, retooled, and recalibrated. Additional elements accelerating the international financial crisis are the tolerance of fractional reserve lending, the manipulation of interest rates by central banks, dangerous central planning schemes, and the proclivity of printing money for military purposes. Global money supply is rising faster than 12% annually.

"Bread and circus" is currently the financial plum that represents the *soziale marktwirtschaft,* the good life that has become universal. The combination of small, but intentional measures have produced a perfect storm: central bank interventionist policies and prolonged low interest rates have produced the equity bubble, the dot.com bubble, housing bubble, credit bubble, and sovereign debt bubble since the 1980s. The various stimulus packages enacted in nearly every country merely expanded the money supply, have not curtailed expenditures and raised the saving rate, all of which indicate that a global correction is lurking. This is only part of the problem: a system addicted to debt requires massive and constant liquidity, hence the need to print additional sums. Globally, more fiat money has been created in the past fifteen years than in all history. Influenced by Keynesian principles, central banks have become very adept at increasing the supply of money during economic contractions to stimulate economic growth and are less enthusiastic to contract the supply of money during growth periods. Their history is replete with major mistakes precipitating considerable national misery and igniting contagions. Furthermore, currency wars have arrived due to global dependence, historic debt levels, and untamed monetary policies. The main culprits are DMs who have generated financial repression by manipulating foreign exchange markets, and have gained the most by exporting inflation. It is they who dominate global currencies and who perpetuate the greatest rates of currency defilement, an evil practice as they lead to military conflict, social and economic unrest, and the diminution of competiveness; the race to debase among DMs has begun as sound monetary systems are lacking. Globally, nearly every nation is racing to destroy their currencies relative to gold. A senior Obama official said in late January 2013, "We are going to kill the dollar."

Capital is highly concentrated and sensitive to geopolitical events. Until the 20th century, it was stationary and, as such, it was clustered in relatively few areas. Because of its immobility, capital had an extremely high cost, and hence, its availability circumscribed. The 20th century with its technological advances had permanently altered these historic elements, and even more so in this century. Not only is investment capital highly mobile, but it can be instantly transferred around the world with ease and no risk, and since money has no odor (*pecunia non-olet*); it flows to areas where returns are highest relative to risk, and in regions with capital-intensive industries. In addition, never forget Gresham's Law, that bad money will chase good money away, which always applies to governments debasing their currency. At the moment, nearly all major countries are doing so. Many mention that since economic conditions are so precarious a prudent investor should "internationalize" by having a home in a second country, a bank account in a third country, a business in a fourth, and a second passport.

The $US for nearly a century has been the primary currency employed in more than 90% of all international trade transactions. Since 1998, global $US reserves have declined from 90% to 61%, and the forces that will help burst the *pax-dollarum* bubble are many: 1. A continued lowering of confidence in the American economy 2. Increased inflation eroding the value of the dollar 3. The continuing expansion of current account deficits (EMs are outperforming the US and will be attracting ever-increasing capital.) 4. The US exported credit scandal affected many foreign banks, pension plans, and governmental units in excess of $8 trillion. Given the fact that America's economic system rests on trust within the international community, the packaging and selling of fraudulent financial instruments does not inspire trust. 5. One dramatic innovation that will revolutionize the global economy is the resurrection of the old Keynesian idea of "Bancor," a supranational currency to settle international trade accounts. In this regard, the IMF suggests that a modified global gold standard be implemented to "guide" currency rates, and several governments have suggested that the Muslim dinar be used to settle regional trade imbalances for 1.5 billion Muslims. Inevitably, the devaluation of the dollar creates a number of problems for the international economy. Since all commodities are priced in dollars, the importation of such goods, particularly energy, becomes more expensive. For commodity exporting nations, the depreciated dollars buy less and if a cabal develops to sell dollars, stop buying dollars, or replace the dollar, the economic consequences for the US are incalculable. 6. Ever since 1971, the economic driving force has been "creditism".

The end game, therefore, sits in Washington where the world's largest debtor can no longer pay what it owes except by rolling debt with more borrowed money. Jim Rogers said in February 2008, "The dollar is a terribly flawed currency and its days are numbered," and Marc Faber states that, "…the monetary policies of the U.S. will destroy the world." A weak dollar places upward pressure on commodities, which are paid for in dollars; hence, stimulating price inflation. A declining dollar also reduces the purchasing power of those who hold dollar reserves. Nevertheless, there are several reasons why the $US remains the premier global reserve currency: safety due to America's military dominance; global acceptance; the largest economy; and inertia that perpetuates the global trading system. The rewards for the US have been immense, resulting in lower borrowing costs. Over consumption, borrowing, and the decimation of the industrial base have resulted in the current blight. The trend, however, is disturbing: when the € was established it accounted for about 16% of global reserves, a figure that has since increased to 29%. Note that while the US is encouraging foreign governments to hold $US reserves, America is the only country with 72% of all its reserves in gold while the world holds 90% paper and 10% gold reserves. The movement to diversify out of dollar assets is underway and the hegemony of the $US appears to be on a declining trajectory. The world sends more than $3.5 billion daily to the US in order for Asian nations to continue their exports and bolster the $US. At the same time, the demand and price for gold is increasing, anxieties increasing, inflation increasing, disposable income decreasing, and the fear factor is rearing its ugly head.

As DMs are drowning in debt, economic options point to depression, inflation, or stagflation, and since the first two appear to be too extreme for voters accustomed to "bread and circus," central banks will opt for the last option, as it is considered less painful. Take the world's largest economy–the US–with $125 trillion (perhaps $200-plus trillion) of real and unfunded obligations. How is it possible to deleverage when the average wage is $45,000? Add also $1 trillion in state deficits. There is a mathematical limit on how much debt can be serviced by this income while preserving a traditional lifestyle. There is also a diversity of opinion concerning the future of global financial markets. One theory posits a disorderly decline in the $US. The opposing view maintains that the world's central bankers, having much to lose by this event, and will do anything and everything to prevent a sudden decline in the $US. Nevertheless, the need to circumvent the dollar is on the rise and the movement away from dollars has begun: Australia and China have agreed to direct currency convertibility without $US intervention, a most significant development as Australia is the first major DM to engage. RMD and rubles are also freely traded on the Moscow Interbank Currency Exchange. The substance of the arrangement involves tens of billions of dollars, that the RMD is now officially accepted (the fifth most-used global currency), that Shanghai and Beijing have emerged as major financial centers, and it portends major RMD *dim sum* bond sales in direct competition with Treasuries. In addition, gold reserves are expected to rise six-fold by 2014 in order to make the RMD convertible. Qatar announced in early 2007 that it would begin accepting euros and other currencies as payment for oil and natural gas exports. Other energy exporting countries have announced similar plans to reduce $US holdings. Brazil and Argentina announced that they would replace the dollar with local currencies for bilateral trade. In December 2009, the Gulf Co-operation Council (GCC), announced that an agreement has been reached to launch a single currency modeled on the €. While the idea has been floating for some time, this is the first time that concrete steps have been taken to create a currency that would replace the dollar in oil transactions from the Gulf region. The head of the IMF, in February 2010 called for a new reserve currency to replace the dollar. China will have the RMB included in the International Monetary Fund's special drawing rights basket, to be used as payment in multilateral trade. When made convertible, the RMB will be accepted as a reserve currency. It has already emerged as a "reserve," as nearly all East Asia nations track the RMB more closely than the $US. Japan and China engage in direct trading of the RMD, without the use of dollars. Malaysia has ceased the purchase of dollars and switched to RMB-denominated bonds. As gold and silver moves from DMs to EMs, rising precious metal reserves will force the abandonment of the $US reserve system. The BRICS, in fact, wish their own equivalent of a World Bank and IMF. Therefore, the reserve status of the dollar is ending. The reserve status for specific currencies has not lasted long: for Portugal it was less than 60 years, for Spain about 150 years, the Netherlands for less than 50 years, France 100 years, UK for 150 years, and thus far, the $US less than 70 years. One thing is certain: a new currency order is in the making.

The most credit-worthy nations are Australia, Norway, Switzerland, Germany, China, Singapore, Sweden, Luxembourg, Finland, the Netherlands, New Zealand, and Denmark. A small number indeed, and important to note the following: global monetary inflation exceeds GDP growth in nearly all countries. The International Bank of Settlements, therefore, is calling for radical changes in the international financial system, as it exists now before a financial crisis erupts. The world, in fact, is witnessing one of the greatest reflation promotions in history in which three forces (money creation, currency manipulation, and deficit spending) are about to produce a perfect storm. The international financial crisis will be partly induced by the International Swaps and Derivative Association because it is the sole arbiter of default. Of course, many things can enter to upset the wobbly apple cart. Protectionism is one significant arrow in the quiver of all DMs and military adventure is another. All, or a combination within a relatively short period, will provide the spark to unravel the "economic globalism" paradigm of the past 30 years. To prevent a total crash with international consequences, the strategy in Washington is to unwind the structural imbalances in the American economy by stages. A "managed" approach to the current account deficit, domestic budgets, savings, and the dollar will shift in stages until the economy falls into a "normal," historical rhythm. The only item that will have to be skewed is inflation. It will rise because that is the surest, fastest, and easiest way to unwind debts. The worst possible scenario is for foreigners to begin liquidating their dollar holdings. However, one thing is certain, the inertia generated over the course of the past 30 years simply cannot continue indefinitely. As aggregate debts continue to soar beyond $125 trillion, the trade gap widens, the dollar continues to fall, 89 governments pursue a zero or negative interest rate policy, and as defaults and bankruptcies increase in number, standards, and levels of living plummet, the greatest credit bubble in history will begin to deflate. Central banks have embarked upon an unprecedented monetary experiment to spend with wild abandon until economic health is re-established. The global economy has entered the era of a permanent, fiscal calamity because printing fiat has never worked, and there are no schools of thought that advocate otherwise. Only the magnitude and intensity of the impending crisis is questioned.

## Economic Dislocations and Resource Nationalism Will Intensify

All manner of dislocations are to be found under the guise of quotas, embargoes, tariffs, sanctions, bilateral agreements, etc., by various nations against each other that have produced and radically altered normal trade relations and are a good example of the hypocrisy of "free trade" policies. The absurd nature of economic dislocations is rooted in historical and political notions of extreme nationalism preventing the rational flow of labor, capital, and information technology. Bolivia, a country with 8 million impoverished people sits on 100 trillion cubic feet of natural gas adjacent to four wealthy, but energy deficient countries–Chile, Argentina, Uruguay and Brazil–but politics prevents the development of this resource to the betterment of everyone. A Pacific LNG pipeline is also scrapped, as bitterness over the 1879-80 war between Bolivia and its archenemy Chile still harbors disharmony. To overcome Ukrainian intransigence, Russia has constructed a pipeline across the Baltic to ship natural gas to Western Europe thus bypassing Ukraine. Canada has passed a "buy Canada resolution," and US stimulus packages contain "buy American" provisions.

In a crisis, narrow national interests trump rational behavior. Tensions are rising between the US, Russia, China, Iran, and the former Soviet Republics for the control of energy from central Asia. There are serious title issues in the Caspian Sea where its territorial division among Azerbaijan, Russia, Iran, Turkmenistan, and Kazakhstan are in dispute. The fact that 80% of conventional global energy reserves are located in Russia, the Middle East and central Asia is the basis of potential conflict. Additional territorial disputes involve the flow of Russian energy to Japan, Korea, and China, the Falkland Islands, the South China Sea, and East Timor. The Persian Gulf is the site of island and border controversies and slanted wells involving many parties. Political boundaries in the Middle East are very artificial, as are all political units in Africa, and Latin America, exacerbating the complicated issue of scarce natural resources.

A typical policy of EMs is the assumption sovereignty over exportable natural resources. Evo Morales, on May 1, 2006, nationalized Bolivia's energy industry by proclaiming, "The pillage of our natural resources by foreign companies is over," and many other nations have come to embrace this nationalist fervor of nationalization. Modernizing infrastructure, increasing capital investment and production, however, present formidable obstacles. When TWs nationalize foreign property, especially energy and mining concerns, their cost of production rises, and capital spending declines. Controlling the destiny of one or two sectors might placate domestic concerns, but nationalization for the sake of nationalization, is never a good policy. Nevertheless, future economic wars was mentioned as distinct possibilities by Condoleezza Rice in early 2008 when she said, "I will appoint a special US energy envoy to monitor the use of oil and gas for political ends, because the politics of energy were "warping diplomacy in certain parts of the world." Energy, however, is only one facet of the overall issue of resource competitiveness. After blocking shipments of rare earths and other critical raw materials to Japan, China had stopped shipments for a short time to the US. Since China controls 95% of rare earth output, this "economic warfare" threatened commercial and political harmony. One can slice and dice a myriad of additional factors, but in the final analysis, control of certain resources will lead to ideological discussions that are often expressed with military compulsions.

## The Role of Sovereign Wealth Funds (SWFs) Will Intensify

An SWF is an investment vehicle funded by foreign exchange assets managed separately from official national monetary reserves. It is owned by countries whose capital has been accumulated mainly through the export of commodities and other trading activities. The purpose is to provide current growth as a hedge to negative, future, economic conditions and to act as national legacies. The total amount currently outstanding is said to exceed $4 trillion, with some estimates placing the figure as high as $6 trillion and expected to rise to $10 trillion by 2019, or 10% of global GDP. Although there are 30-plus SWFs, the principal SWFs emanate from Abu Dhabi, Saudi Arabia, China, Singapore, Norway, Kuwait, Russia, Korea, United Arab Emirates, Qatar, Libya, Russia, Brunei, and Kazakhstan. While many governments refuse to divulge information and others offer false data, numbers vary from the $1-plus trillion $100 billion. They are manifestations of state capitalism in sharp contrast to free market capitalism, and nearly all operate in a secretive, non-transparent environment. The motives for their creation vary by nation, of which the preservation and accumulation of wealth for the common good is of paramount importance. They are growing rapidly in total assets, and becoming a focus for international investment. They have already invested hundreds of billions of dollars overseas, and the pace is expected to accelerate in the future. As the tempo of foreign investments increase, their influence and political ramifications will also affect geopolitical alliances as these SWFs are investing from positions of strength. They will be instrumental in the formation of new capital centers, dominating precious and base metals, timber and energy, as well as other commodities, and increasingly play a dominant economic role in determining the flow of global investment capital.

# The Anglo-American Market

## Unique Themes That Distinguish the US From the Rest of the World

1. The US is a nation of 310 million people whose *non-pareil* economy of $16 trillion is responsible for 21% of global GDP. Not to be forgotten is the fact that France sold nearly half of continental US for less than $0.03 an acre, Russia sold Alaska for a mere $6 million, and the US-Canadian border has never been fortified. To all blessed by intelligence, boundless energy and vision, America has been the proverbial "street paved with gold." The growth of the US economy since 1800 has been without parallel in global financial history. With compounding and reinvestment of dividends, equity markets grew by 5%-8% annually. It became the largest consumer, most formidable military power, collected within its political borders more scientific talent than have lived throughout global history, and during the period 1945-2000, the US produced the largest and wealthiest middle class ever. It came to the aid of Western Europe in World War I and II, defeated fascism in the Pacific, overcame the threat of communism under Reagan, and was the pillar of everything that was good in the world. People with ambition and talent came to the US and made what this country eventually became–the pantheon of the ideal life. For more than 100 years, America has dominated, like no other country, invention, innovation and science–the only constant in America's history is change.

This prosperity of human achievement is new, not old, and certainly not a product of inheritance. When America declared its independence from England in 1776, less than 3% of the population was urban with Philadelphia and Boston the largest cities, none of which had more than 30,000 people, and as recently as 1820 more than 80% of the population was rural. In 1850, wood heated space and boiled water for 95% of the population. The US in 1900, had a life expectancy of 45 years, fewer than 5% of all homes had a telephone, 11% had a bathtub, and there were fewer than 6,000 cars and 130 miles of paved roads with speed limits of 10 mph. The average pay was 18 cents per hour, the average wage was $365 annually, and the leading causes of death were influenza, tuberculosis, diarrhea and pneumonia.

The population of Las Vegas was 19, fewer than 9% had reading and writing ability, 5% graduated high school, and there were fewer than 220 murders. Interestingly, one could legally buy heroin, marijuana and morphine without prescription in any pharmacy, and Coca Cola contained cocaine. California had but 1.2 million people, or fewer people than Brooklyn, NY. You were in the upper 10% of the income spectrum if you earned more than $1,000, and the annual wage of the highest paid professionals was rarely greater than $5,000. Ninety-five percent of all births took place in the home, 90% of all doctors had no formal college education, most people washed their hair once a month with borax and egg yolks, men shaved, and changed shirt collars and cuffs once a week, and the shirt twice a month. One of the most expensive household items was soap. America became an urban nation in 1920, when tractors replaced 22 million draft horses. It took 18 farmers to feed one person in 1776, and 1 to feed 1,500 today.

Each generation has not only been different from previous, but during the period of 1945-1980, 10% of the population changed its residence annually. Therefore, America has become a nation of strangers–people who are rootless, isolated, and indifferent to neighborly associations as reflected by the "boomer" generation. The nation is inundated by more than 3,000 "pseudo towns," which are located on interstate on/off ramps with proximity to shopping malls. The current population is scattered in suburbia, reliant on horizontal mobility, and to the wasteful aspects of this existence is the rise of anonymity, aggressive and anti-social behavior. In addition, the population is aging. The median age in the US in 1950 was 30, now it has risen to 38, and the number of Americans aged 65-plus years is growing. The average American has become comfortable, spoiled, and delusional about the nature of the economic world and America's role in it. Prior to 1950, a small number of women worked, self-directed retirement accounts did not exist, socks were darned, retail establishments were limited in number and size, and people did without the myriad of "gadgets" and "things" considered vital and necessary. The US since World War II has had the enviable position to buy whatever it wanted by just printing additional quantities of money to the point that more dollars are to be found overseas than in the homeland. In 1959, secondary employment represented 29% of GDP, and today 11%. As recently as 2000, the US ranked number one in average household wealth; it now ranks ninth.

2. The US is a politically, economically, and culturally a fragmented nation with its citizens unaware of its "exceptionalism." In the annals of history, America is not a nation-state, inhabited by common culture, blood, and language. English is spoken only by sheer accident and, save for Thanksgiving, the US celebrates no other unique holiday. The US is the only nation with established, domestic, political borders that proceeded to fill them with people; hence, absurd and disastrous economic consequences. The country is also politically fragmented in ways that confound sensible minds. The Detroit metropolitan area contains 1,172 separate governmental units distributed among 37 counties, 128 cities, 260 villages, 635 townships, and 52 disparate districts. The state of New Jersey has 578

municipalities, of which nearly 400 have less than 10,000 residents. Equally important is that nothing is standardized, including the fact that mayor-council, commission, or council-manager forms govern cities. Indian reservations have assumed the role of extraterritorial regions with special privileges. The US has become a nation of 52 governments with a similar number of legal systems, thousands of educational systems and disparate governmental structures. Lacking a significant pre and post-medieval history, the US is devoid of cultural continuity, and hence, a Balkanized nation.

3. The US faces serious foreign policy issues as it struggles to remain the world's only imperial power. It entered the empire business with the founding of Jamestown, received an impetus with "manifest destiny" and now considers itself as the planets "epicenter," a civilization second to none. The delusion of "superiority" has induced a belief that "democracy" should be imposed on other cultures because the US knows better. Therefore, "what is America's appeal and charismatic nature?" Interstate highways with wide shoulders? Suburban homes? Efficient kitchens and functional bathrooms? All features say nothing about poor bread and diet, the world's highest incarceration rate, and all manner of social dysfunctions. Americans think that their brand of democracy is superior, their lifestyle enviable, and their economy and government exceptional to any other. Everything American is "best," including professional wrestling.

The Iraq, Afghanistan, Syria, Iran, Libya, Pakistan, "terror" wars, and interventions in Somalia, Kuwait, Yugoslavia, Bosnia, and Haiti have dealt America colossal and ever-mounting expenses. In terms of direct, military outlays of equipment, indirect aid for reconstruction, physical rehabilitation of injured troops, and the cost of resources diverted to military activities are estimated to have consumed more than $7 trillion since 9/11. America, the world's largest debtor, and bankrupt, borrowed to fund these conflicts. The cost of the Vietnam War varied 1.5% to 2% of GDP for each of eight years, but that was when the budget and trade deficits minor, household debt low and the average American saved money. The direct and indirect cost of the American empire is 10%-plus of GDP, something that is unsustainable. The US has been in a state of perpetual war since WWII and Leon Panetta states that "We are within one inch of war almost every day." The US built the world's largest embassy at a cost of $1 billion in Iraq. It maintains fifty military bases in the region, the largest such concentration of military power anywhere. According to Pat Buchanan, "The United States is strategically overextended worldwide. What are we doing borrowing money from Japan to defend Japan? Borrow money from Europe to defend Europe. Borrow money from the Persian Gulf to defend the Persian Gulf. This country is overextended. It is an empire and the empire is coming down." The US also borrows from China to "contain" China. While no one questions American superiority in the military realm, its cultural dominance is not what it once was. This is a critical issue as cultural power makes military power either successful or a dismal failure. In the end, the appeal of US power lies in its ideas and values, but in the meantime, it has garrisoned the globe. Maintaining an empire on a credit card is not sound policy. The US has spent more than $5 trillion is defense spending during the period 1994-2013–all of it nonproductive consumption. The Pentagon plan is to attack six countries by 2019, and that, according to the *Economist*, makes US democracy dysfunctional. Signs of US global decline are mounting with China becoming America's default antagonist.

4. Evidence of corruption is everywhere: dead people have been voting in Chicago for 200 years, Goldman Sachs bet against their clients, and the financial crisis of 2008 produced few prosecutions. Phantom zip codes were found in many states through which millions of dollars were earmarked for "stimulus," and dozens of counties, hundreds of municipalities, and nearly every state had been sold bogus financial instruments facilitated by phony AAA ratings. Regulators turned their head aside when subprime borrowers with no income, no job, and no documentation approved "liar loans" by the millions. They also turn their heads when investigating fraudulent disability claims. In recent years, four Illinois governors have been jailed for corruption, and a cablevision company awarded options to a dead executive. America's two largest banks, dozens of corporations, and many investment houses have paid tens of billions of dollars in fines, all pleading "innocent and promise never to repeat the offenses," and let us not forget the words of Lucky Luciano, who remarked on a tour of the floor of the New York Stock Exchange: "I joined the wrong mob." Criminal activity is rewarded, mediocrity is encouraged, and savers are punished. These are not accidents, but premeditated policies aimed to increase dependency, and in the words of Barney Frank: "We are trying on every front to increase the role of government." In the words of Neil Barofsky: "We have a financial system that concentrates risk in just a handful of large institutions, incentivizes them to take risks, guarantees that they will never be allowed to fail and ensures that the executives will never be held accountable for their actions. We should not be surprised when there is another massive financial crisis and another massive bailout. It would be naïve to expect a different result." Yet, corruption continues unabated, even after one of the worst financial scandals in US history: the theft of segregated client accounts at MF Global–and the fact that former senator and governor of New Jersey, did not know what happened to $1.2 billion in client brokerage accounts. Corruption is ignored, and fraud has become a way of life.

5. A major American problem is the poor state of its educational system. At least 80% of all adult Americans have a high school education, and 16% have a college education, with 47% of all 18- to 25-year-olds currently enrolled in colleges. Impressed? Do not be. The figures are highly misleading when you factor the element of quality, especially when you compare American educational achievement with those in the Euro Zone, Japan and another 20 nations. Consider the following: a. Science in the US has been politicized, especially environmental and energy issues. b. In one Ivy League university, 46% of all grades were "A." c. While competition encourages students to strive harder, affirmative action,

retention policies, etc., have accelerated grade inflation. d. America's infatuation with "liberal arts" has raised the cost of higher education, made the country less competitive and lowered standards to critical levels. Since the 1950s when General Education courses gained in popularity and now account for about 50% of all taken, the quality, integrity, and practical use of these courses are useless. e. In New York City, 80% of all High School graduates cannot read and write at grade level. The outcome, for parents paying high tuition, is simple: instructors pass everyone–even those described as "7-ups" (never had it and never will). Instant educational gratification has now become an entitlement. Everyone must feel good; have a huge high-esteem quotient, and thus the debasement of the educational "entitlement." The best of the best are not allowed to excel in public unless they insult or hurt the feelings of the less-gifted. In the process, the bar is lowered to the point that distraction and propaganda shifts priorities to under-achievement. f. There are nearly 22 million students enrolled in higher education, half of which do not complete, and for those who receive a degree 50%-plus are either unemployed or underemployed.

For the US to remain competitive, the economic future of the nation rests squarely on a trained labor force, and "dorm sensitivity" classes do nothing to further this goal. University presidents proudly announce to graduates and the audience that the university has increased its "retention rate." What the president is not saying is that it now takes a college student, not eight semesters to graduate but 10 or 12, and only with the facility of grade inflation. Few are taking notice that as the quality of education has declined, the political rhetoric that promotes the myth of a superior US education. It might have been superior at one time, but not now as the marginal returns of a higher education degree have declined. The situation is worse than it seems because the nation must confront the huge educational student loan bubble of $1-plus trillion (more than sub-prime loans in 2007), in effect placing college graduates into an environment of debt peonage. Forty percent of college graduates work in jobs requiring no degree; annual college tuition increases are twice that of medical care, three times higher than the cost of a new car, and four times higher than the cost of food and energy. Yet Duke University has raised fees to pay for sex change surgeries. The gravity of being economically illiterate hardly ever becomes a worthy academic topic for consideration.

6. While anti-Americanism is nothing new, current perceptions are. Foreigners historically disliked the US because of envy, but events over the past 30 years have come to present a new anti-Americanism, and it boils down to an inconsistent foreign policy of arrogance, and hypocrisy. The world is annoyed and frustrated; they fear the US, and the number of people who have a favorable view of the US has consistently been eroded to dismal levels. The reasons are not hard to find. The US has constructed alliances with various unsavory regimes: we have befriended the largest drug dealers in Europe (Albanians), the largest drug smugglers to the US (Mexicans), the producers and traffickers of cocaine

(Colombians), the largest producers of heroin (Afghans), all manner of dictators, and at least a dozen countries that launder money with US blessing. Foreign perceptions of a delusional nation, however, are something to ponder. American form of government, fashions, sports, political resolve, and consumptive economy are not superior to all others. Moreover, the list of delusions enveloped in mythology is long. It is a myth to think that the federal government has the inclination and power to dictate the course of the national economy; that the federal government has the ability or the mechanisms to guarantee that all the safety nets will allow all that has been promised; that the federal government is in a position to prevent deflation by monetary or fiscal policies; that the introduction of massive credit is a "desired" economic goal; that inflation is "under control"; that profligate behavior will continue forever; that the total wealth of the nation continues to climb; that the expansion of money and credit is something that is of no concern; that deficits do not matter (but do impede GDP growth); and that the nation's economy is on the "right track." The entopic world, however, refutes all of the above. The debt to wealth ratio is the highest it has ever been since the founding of the republic, and yet, Chicago clamors for "Jerry beads." Voltaire said it best: "Illusion is the first of all pleasures."

7. US secondary production has declined for the past 30 years at a rate of loss greater than that of the Great Depression. In 1914, the US accounted for 34% of the value of global industrial output, and 100 years later, it had fallen to 11%. Since the 1970s, the decline in machine tool and related industries that made America the world's premier manufacturing nation has accelerated–rolling mill machinery by -60%, textile machinery -48%, ball and roller bearings -38%, and office machines -76%. Nine of the 10 largest appliance manufacturers, 8 of the 10 largest metals companies, 8 of the 10 largest vehicle manufacturers, and 7 of the 10 largest electronics companies are headquartered overseas. The US, furthermore, has lost 45,000 factories since 2000 and more than 35% of all secondary employment. Today the secondary sector employs the same number of workers as it did in 1940. Globalization has cost the US millions of jobs, not all low-wage as secondary employment rewards more than services. The US emerged from World War II as the only major country with a secondary base that was not damaged by war. It produced more than 78% of all vehicles and controlled more than 85% of global gold reserves, with similar percentages in practically all spheres of economic endeavor. In addition, the US has run a trade deficit since 1974.

# Figure 2

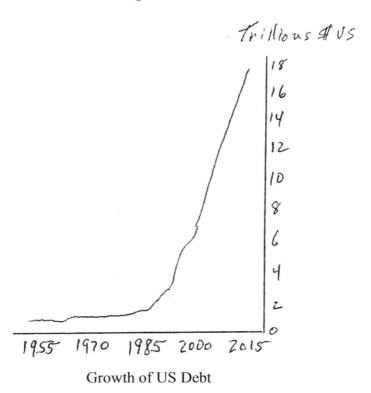

Growth of US Debt

8. Over the course of 125 years, the US has rapidly metamorphosed from an agrarian to an industrial to a tertiary, and finally, a debt-ridden society, often described as "debtocracy." At the time of this writing, and according to the Federal Government Debt Report, total federal debt stands at $17 trillion, state and local debt $3 trillion, household, debt $18 trillion. When unfunded liabilities are included, the sum rises to $125 trillion (some estimates are as high as $220 trillion), more than $400,000 per capita, and 700%-plus GDP. Never before has America exhibited such huge debt levels relative to net worth. The US government spends $4.9 trillion and collects only $2.5 trillion in taxes leaving a deficit of $2.4 trillion annually. Profligate cultures rarely offer quality leadership and an optimistic future, and history has never been kind to such societies. Foreigners own more than $9 billion of US financial assets, 17% of the stock market, 20% of corporate debt, and 28% of the US Treasury and agency market. Paul Volcker in 2005 cogitated: "At some point, both central banks and private institutions will have their fill of dollars...I don't know whether change will come with a bang or a whimper, whether sooner or later...it is more likely that it will be financial crises...that will force the change." Not only is the federal debt growing the most, but each

succeeding stimulus is producing diminishing returns. By 2016 the Fed balance sheet is expect to exceed $6 trillion. Of course, there is nothing wrong with debt as long as it is used to generate additional growth. Unfortunately, this has not been the case for the past two decades.

Governmental debt is not an American tradition. In 1791, the national debt stood as $75 million. During the Jefferson administration, the governmental debt rose to $83 million, only to rise to $100-plus during the War or 1812 and $127 million in 1816. In 1848, the debt stood at $63 million, was $65 million in 1860, and quickly jumped to $524 million in 1862, only to rise further to $2.8 billion in 1866 due to the Civil War. In 1899, the debt was $1.2 billion; dropped slightly to $1.1 trillion by 1910, at the end of WWI, it stood at $26 billion; in 1937, it was $72 billion; rose to $260 billion in 1945; and by 1960, it stood at $284 billion. In 1968, the federal debt rose to $348 billion, it more than doubled to $930 billion by 1980, and in 1989, it rose to $2.9 trillion. It sprinted to $6.9 trillion in 2000, $9 trillion in 2006; and $17 trillion today, with many stating that it may be as high as $30 trillion. Never forget that Glenn Hubbard advised President Bush to cut taxes in 2001 and 2003 and to finance two wars with a credit card, only to be succeeded by a president that spends even more. The US, therefore, like many other nations, is bankrupt (the IMF said so), and unless Congress reforms the financial system, healthcare, and retirement systems, simplifies tax regulations, enforces economic regulations, and takes control of all entitlements, the economic situation will only worsen. In addition, the nation's pension plans are underfunded by $2.3 trillion. In the words of Ron Paul: "We're so far gone. We're over the cliff." America has feasted on borrowed money for too long. How can the aggregate debt be paid when the average household net wealth is but $116,000 and disposable income at $38,000? It should also be noted that per capita US governmental debt is worse than Ireland, Italy, Greece, France, Portugal, and Spain.

Aggregate debt is at least seven times the size of the American economy, and the consequences of continued national debts are serious and long lasting. a. As American deficits increase in size requiring additional sums, and once confidence in the $US declines, the importation of money will prove difficult and will disrupt global financial institutions. b. Because of the sheer weight of the national debt, the dollar will decline and the US will experience serious inflation. c. Loses to foreigners holding Treasuries are mounting and their desire to stem declines drives them to gold and silver. In the end, international markets will prove more powerful than the American Treasury, the White House, Wall Street, or the Fed. d. State and local debt mirrors that of the federal government because a good deal of the "social" burdens have been pushed on to state and local governments by Washington. Nearly all states have a negative current account and depend on tobacco, casino, and lottery sales to balance books. e. It now takes more than $400 billion to service the national debt, and by 2020, interest will be the second largest component of the federal budget. What makes the current debt more vexing and dangerous is the fact that it was accumulated for unproductive purposes. f. Can a

"Greek style" austerity solution be forced on the average American? In the words of Thomas Jefferson: "A government big enough to give you all you want is strong enough to take everything you have." g. The US is now a debtor country, and will remain so for a considerable time. Therefore, debt obligations will have a severe impact on domestic capital investment, and a serious blow to future GDP growth. Among the many realities confronting the nation, the inability to manage the mountain of debt obligations remains a top priority as each dollar of additional debt leads to lower GDP growth.

Therefore, what can the US do to alleviate this debt predicament? a. It can tax. All governmental units have already implemented this option, but taxes can never eliminate the entire debt. b. It can reduce spending. This option is anathema to the anointed, as spending is the mother's milk of Congressional existence. When Washington uses the word "cut," they refer to a decrease in the projected increase. The most important component of the national debt problem is the "entitlement cliff" as most of the borrowing is to provide liquidity to "entitlements." c. It can go to war. While this option worked superbly in the past, the nation is currently stretched, and the American people are tired of war. d. It can devalue the dollar through inflation, the most viable option. This is an old, tried and true method of paying debts with worthless currency, and while it worked in the past, it will be very difficult to expect China, Japan, Russia, Brazil, India, UK, oil exporting nations and Canada to accept with pleasure, trillions of devalued dollars. Since all commodities are priced in dollars, the importation of such goods becomes more expensive. For commodity exporting nations, the depreciated dollars buy less and these nations will seek alternatives. Moreover, if a cabal develops to sell dollars, stop buying dollars, or replace the dollar, the economic consequences for the US are incalculable. e. Sell gold reserves. The 8,000 tons that the US holds are insufficient, and there is the possibility that they may not exist. f. It can default (not honoring outstanding obligations, also referred to as restructuring). The US is in technical bankruptcy as its outstanding debts are larger than revenue. While it occurred in the past, true sovereign default is not likely to happen, but a sharp devaluation of the dollar will have the same effect. Both inflation and the possibility of default are $US negative. In the end, it is only a matter of time before the US experiences a financial shock, as the drip, drip nature of economic problems compound. It is wise to remember the sage words of Cicero (55 B.C.): "The budget should be balanced, the Treasury should be refilled, public debt should be reduced, the arrogance of officialdom should be tempered and controlled, and the assistance to foreign lands should be curtailed lest Rome become bankrupt." The US has not balanced its budget for 35 years. Imagine what would happen if the US was compelled to pay for imports with gold rather than digital dollars. In the final analysis, the dangerous mix of low interest rates, rising debt levels, increased spending, and money creation will remain in place for a protracted period. Any attempt to raise interest rates and reduce federal spending will annihilate the economy, equities, housing and the consumer. As long as the government is bellicose and imperial in character, the US economy will remain in crisis as the endless cycle of spending, borrowing and printing is unsustainable. In the end, the only beneficiaries are gold and silver.

9. The financial instability of the US is characterized as "too much": too much gambling, too much eating, too much spending, too much debt, too much monetary inflation, too much everything, and not enough production, exports, and savings. There are too many colleges, sports stadiums, parking lots, malls, etc. There are three million storage lockers filled to capacity with household goods that remain unutilized. The future of the US economy does not rest with the consumer but by increasing the saving rate beyond 15%, investing in capital goods, tripling the nation's investment in R&D, reducing debt to bare minimums, and increasing output of basic industries. According to Ludwig von Mises, "There is no means of avoiding the final collapse of a boom brought about by credit (debt) expansion. The alternative is only whether the crisis should come sooner as the result of a voluntary abandonment of further credit expansion, or later as a final and total catastrophe of the currency system involved." Axel Merk has succinctly captured the contagion: "After the tech bubble burst in 2000, policy makers in the U.S. and Asia set a train in motion they have now lost control over. In an effort to preserve U.S. consumer spending, the Federal Reserve lowered interest rates; the Administration lowered taxes; and Asian policymakers kept their currencies artificially weak to subsidize exports to American consumers." The collapse of Enron in 2002 was in many ways, a mirror of the American economy. Like the federal government, Enron borrowed excessively, lied notoriously, and was mired in a culture of fraud and deception. It is amazing how many Nobel Prize winners and famous economists accepted money as Enron advisors. Examples of financial uncertainty are illustrated by Texas and Germany, both of whom wish the return of gold bullion stored as "unallocated gold accounts" in the New York Federal Reserve. The latter states that the transfer will take up to seven years.

10. The US is in decline: The tallest buildings, secondary output, rapid GDP growth, consumer discretionary growth, etc., all occur and are found outside US borders. The high-debt, high-cost economy is bankrupt. Therefore, a number of immediate concerns remain. 1. Wealth destruction will continue and big government will continue to expand. More people are now working for the public sector than at any time in history. 2. Real wages have not risen in 30-plus years, with another "lost decade" to follow. 3. GDP figures are overstated. Cooking belongs in the kitchen and not in the hallowed halls of the Treasury Dept. Peter Schiff states that "Unfortunately one of the few things still made in America is inflation. In fact, it now ranks as our greatest export." 4. Fifty million Americans are "living in poverty" and never in the history of the republic have so many citizens been so dependent on the government for assistance. 5. Be careful of the following black swan—world government. James Warburg, the Rothschild Group, Franklin D. Roosevelt, Henry Kissinger, etc., all have praised its virtues and inevitability. William Fulbright, in 1963, said, "The case for government by elites is irrefutable." 6. The prevalence of *ineptocracy,* defined as "A system of

government where the least capable to lead are elected by the least capable of producing." Currently, the economy is growing its unproductive sectors, and essentially living off yesterday's savings. The misery index (an index of unemployment and inflation) in December 2011 was the highest since the Great Depression. No American will like austerity, as everyone has been conditioned like a Pavlovian dog to consume and consume even more. Seventy percent of the current generation will not enjoy higher standards of living than its parents. 7. America is no longer a creditor nation, no longer self-sufficient in manufacturing and capital, and no longer the world's most vibrant economy. Kurt Richebacher warned, "Instead of accumulating foreign assets, America is accumulating foreign debts. And internally, instead of expanding its capital stock for higher future output and income growth, there is a record accumulation of unproductive debt collateralized by inflating asset prices." Yet the US cannot be sold short, offering enormous investment opportunities once the current secular bear ends. 8. The US finds itself in a *zugzwang* situation where every move the Fed and government make worsens economic conditions. This is reflected in the fact that average Americans no longer think that they will become rich, own a business, become financially secure, and that their children will be a part of the middle class. 9. "Statism" is the nation's fastest growing religion.

## Canada

Canada, with a population of 32 million, is not only the world's second largest country in land area, but also one of the richest in natural resources, especially in non-conventional oil, and a country still in the making. The population is growing, the development of the national resource base is intensifying, its spirit of independence from the US expressed more openly than ever, the problems of divided national jurisdiction are being resolved, and its balance sheet is better than most DMs. Despite the fact about 50% of temperate land area is forested, it is an incredible nation for the production of wheat, oats, barley, rich fishing grounds, and is one of a few nations with ample water supplies. Nevertheless, as rich as the nation is, mineral matter makes Canada important. The nation ranks among the top five producers of aluminum, asbestos, barite, zinc, silver, gold, selenium, natural gas, cadmium, copper, gypsum, iron ore, lead, magnesium, molybdenum, oil and uranium reserves. It ranks among the top nations in the potential use of alternative energy like wind and hydropower. Canada's economic dependency with the US represents more than 33% of its GDP, and nearly 50% of the nation's total trade. Therefore, Canada is highly vulnerable to sudden and severe economic changes in the US. Furthermore, Canada holds as many euros in reserve as dollars, and it is the only G-8 country with both a fiscal and current account surplus and unlike the US, consumer indebtedness is contained. Most important, Canada has experienced seven straight years of budget surpluses due to draconian spending cuts, and the strongest economy among the G8. Canada remains an excellent place to invest.

# The European Market

## Western Europe

Europe stretches from the Urals to the Atlantic and is divided economically and culturally into the following segments: Scandinavia (the northernmost and wealthiest); the UK (the origin of the Industrial Revolution) and Ireland; the Low Countries (economically developed and politically stable); the DMs of Germany, Austria, and Switzerland; Slavic Europe; and the four Mediterranean climatic nations of Portugal, Spain, Italy, and Greece. Europe, ex-Slavic portion, has a larger population than the US, a larger GDP, a more diversified economy, and in terms of geography, this region is small in land area, but high in population density, particularly as manifested by its northerly location. The latter is further subdivided into the 17-member European Monetary Union (the "paella" coalition), all of which is in Rostow's fifth stage. It is responsible for 35% of world exports, is the world's largest importer and fabricator of food, and with 28% of world GDP, it is the world's largest economy. Along with Japan, Europe's population is aging, and the old steel-oriented industries have given way to new information-oriented, electronics, engineering, financial, and pharmaceutical sectors. It leads the world in luxury good output, quality infrastructure and education.

Beyond the usual cultural generalizations, the differences between the US and Europe are enormous. 1. Europe has a longer and more complicated history resulting in excessive local and civic pride. 2. It is composed of small political units, thus limiting the extent of the natural resource base and size of market. 3 All economic and cultural elements are non-conforming in cuisine, legal systems, music, etc. 4. It exhibits a high propensity to import and export. 5. There is a prevalence of smaller farm sizes with farmers mostly living in villages. 6. Europeans, because of their historical connections with the rest of the world, have a larger market share and particular niches for a large number of products. 7. Europe emphasizes high quality, high labor, and capital-intensive exports. 8. Unlike the US, Europe went through one thousand years of near continuous religious and military conflict, with hunger and misery as common as a soccer match. 9. In addition to cultural fragmentation, Europe exhibits similar physical disparities, as it is a region surrounded by water on three sides with countless peninsulas, like no other area. 10. The economic dislocations of the past are disappearing, as a citizen in any country can migrate to another, have a bank account in any member country and buy real property without difficulty. 11. During the formative stages of the emergence of the European nation-state and in the centuries since then, Europe became the world's wealthiest, most powerful and technologically advanced region. It was comparatively stable as it was in political/military equilibrium between the British, French, Russian, Hapsburg, and Ottoman Empires, but it all came to a dramatic conclusion with World War I with the devolution of Eastern Europe and the Ottoman Empire. The losses in human life, treasure, and national pride and dignity contributed to the Great Depression and World War II. Therefore, Europe thinks and behaves differently from most Americans who never experienced occupation, political ignominies, extreme hunger, and total and complete destruction of infrastructure.

Europe is the birthplace of incipient developments during the medieval period that laid the seeds for capitalism, and the concomitancy of industrialization and urbanization. With the end of feudalism, it emerged with superior maritime, industrial and manufacturing technologies, boasted superior capabilities in metallurgy, transportation, and chemical industries by 1800, and maintained a global superiority until the 20th century. 1. The economic burden of colonialism severely weakened the UK and France. 2. The emergence of communism in Russia, the devolution of European Turkey and Slavic Europe, the global depression of the 1930s, and the rise of fascism all combined to further autocratic developments thus increasing the negative effects of economic dislocation. 3. Europe's dominance in world trade and manufacturing declined and took a back seat to the US after WWI. 4. World War II further exacerbated previous developments with the spread of communism in Eastern Europe, and the Cold War reinforced existing hard positions between communist and NATO Europe. 5. The growth of the European Union is a remarkable achievement given historical economic, political, religious and sectarian conflicts. The Treaty of Rome in 1957 paved the way for the Inner 6 (Italy, France, Luxembourg, Belgium, Netherlands, Germany), and over the next 47 years, another 17 countries joined. Large-scale privatization and the integration of Eastern Europe are key to a revitalized EU in the hope that historic economic dislocations will be overcome, and strengthen European competiveness with the US and Asia. The specter of an enlarged unified market and currency will increase consumer participation in the equity market rather than investments in real estate. A further review reveals the following:

1. The Daily Reckoning states: "The Old World is the best part of the world to live in. The food is good. There are few police officers. You can still smoke in most places. You can drive fast. Avoiding taxes is not a crime. Women are pretty. The towns are charming. The scenery is attractive. And you don't have to take your shoes off in order to get on a plane." Trains are better in Europe in terms of cleanliness, timeliness, and comfort than any other area. Streets are cleaner,

properties tidier, and people are better dressed. The quality of life in Western Europe cannot be minimized. Not only are more tourist dollars spent in Europe, but the number of dollars spent per capita is the largest. The EU enjoys a longer life span, is better educated, does not carry excessive household debt, saves more, maintains a smaller incidence of poverty, and has fewer social disorders. It also has a smaller incarceration rate, high per capita wealth, and the highest propensity to trade of any other comparable area and population size. The EU appears to be at parity with the US in the brain drain, as the brightest and finest minds from around the world arrive with minimal immigration impediments. Nordic countries are the richest, healthiest, and ranking as the best places to live.

2. The €, disparagingly referred to as an "*esperanto* currency" has surprised many by its stability relative to others despite the fact that it is a stateless currency. It is the official currency of 17 nations, and accepted by everyone. In a span of 24 years, it has become the world's second reserve currency and as a major rival to the $US. It has had its share of difficulties, and despite recent controversies concerning the possibility of sovereign defaults by six of its members, it has remained far more durable than most had expected. Moreover its fundamentals appear to be significantly seasoned as the European community has a strong trade balance and its budgetary deficits are lower than the US, Japan and UK. Unlike the US, consumer spending in the Eurozone accounts for less than 58% of GDP.

3. The elaborate welfare state, endemic throughout Europe, is a product of pressure groups, political struggles and an egalitarian spirit with considerable history. Welfare dependency consumes a huge proportion of GDP, and faced with high taxes, those with means have developed a lucrative hobby–tax dodging. A heavy blanket of social legislation, economic regulation and high taxes reduce gross wages by 50%-plus for many countries. For economists the "Finland model" has emerged. A country with few natural resources, an intemperate climate, isolated in terms of location close to the Arctic, with a small population of five million and a limited, agricultural base is the quintessence of "development and stability." While most of the world's nations are characterized by rampant corruption, the *Economist* in 2004 noted that Finland is the least corrupt, followed by New Zealand and Singapore. Similarly, Germany, with an aging population, and by US standards, an economy burdened with union regulations, a socialistic mentality whose sclerosis is supposed to be the bane of a modern economy supports a vibrant export sector. In addition, Switzerland continues to make money by producing precision tools for export, and France is the premier exporting nation of "luxury." The practical Scandinavians observed potential conflicts, and self-corrected in various stages over the past 30 years. State involvement from birth to death has been reduced and many benefits like state "engagement," and marriage" presents, etc., have been eliminated. A number of thorny issues, however, plague Europe:

1. Despite formidable accomplishments, Europe suffered much in the 20th century. It had spent itself in countless military conflicts, became Balkanized,

culturally swollen with animosities, and mired with cottage industries. It lacked a common electrical and transportation grid and standardization of sizes and measurements. Multiple political borders prevented the efficient exchange of economic talent and money, and the inertia of tradition maintained a drag on innovation. In terms of technology, economic growth and political power, the United States emerged as the world's principal driver early in the 20th century. The $US came forward as the premier reserve currency and world's principal market during the second half of the last century. Yet, Europe looked at the U.S. with disdain: America lacked refinement and it remained for Europe to "educate" the US with the finer aspects of sophisticated cuisine, perfume, fine wine, ideological literature, and superior fashion. Mass culture belonged to the US, and not Europe. In the meantime, a. Economic sclerosis was brought about by a rigid welfare system burdened by protective and inflexible labor laws. b. While globalization exhibits debilitating effects in the US, Western Europe continues its high rate of export growth. c. The fact that Western Europe has embarked upon a political platform of "federalism" in a world that admires "devolution," is noteworthy and significant. d. It has the highest labor costs in the world. e. Fertility rates throughout Europe are falling rapidly, particularly in the more developed areas, and over the next 50 years, the population is expected to remain below replacement levels. f. The recent strains between the debt-burdened Mediterranean countries highlight the basic differences with the more economically conservative, low-inflation, disciplined, and prudent economies of the north. g. Europe, by $US standards, is expensive. In Luxembourg movie tickets for two cost $35; cappuccino is $14; dinner for two in a "classy" restaurant without drinks is more than $325; and the rent on a two-bedroom apartment is $6,000 a month in a middle class neighborhood. h. The history of Europe is remarkable for its preoccupation with the issue of social, economic, political and technological progress. It has been obsessed by these forces for more than 500 years, and if economic progress is to continue, the urgency on technology will intensify in order to remain competitive.

2. EU financial problems revolve around the lack of a single budget, fiscal integration, uniform taxation, and standardization of most economic functions. The amalgamation of 30 different cultures and languages with distinct political and economic histories, pose serious challenges. Expulsion from the union is not allowed, but sovereign nations can choose to secede, but with painful consequences. The outcome of present financial difficulties will be a combination of sovereign defaults, and a possible collapse of banking systems. Nevertheless, with the formation of the €, commodities can now be traded in a currency other than the $US and, hence, used to settle regional accounts. The fact that the € is now legal tender in a region that contains more people and produces more per capita than the US is a dramatic phenomenon, yet the transfer of development capital to poorer countries, and the formation of supranational political and economic structures remain primary concerns. Despite weaknesses, the EU has a larger slice of world trade, is Islam's largest trading partner, imports more oil, LNG, and more commodities than the US. All of the foregoing confirm and

encourage faith in the €, and as a result, Russia, China, Canada, and other nations have converted a portion of their reserves to the €.

3. It is said that the Eurozone is characterized by *soziale marktwirtschaf,*" or an unproductive welfare state that promotes a spoiled leisure society, high taxes, superb benefits, and no motivation for furthering the work ethic. West Europeans consume more leisure, work shorter hours, but save more than the average American. Workers in Germany earn $30/hour, in the US/$22, and $19 in France and UK while workers in Eastern Europe earn less than $8/hour. Furthermore, Germany has a 35-hour workweek and six weeks of paid vacation. It worked fine for the past 60 years, but is finally unraveling as the disincentives are promulgating a host of inefficiencies of which runaway profligate behavior by public sectors have strained budgets leading to a financial crisis. Despite the above, there are a number of positive developments: a. Former economic dislocations have largely disappeared. b. Europe, unlike America, believes in a much higher level of state intervention in the daily lives of its citizenry, and the suffocating aspects of state "paternalism" are slowly being dismantled. c. Corporate taxes to stimulate growth have been reduced, bankruptcy legislation reformed, labor unions have become more flexible on pay, extending the workweek, and reducing vacation length. d. The graying of Europe is different from what is occurring in the US because European retirees are not encumbered with debt and have a much larger asset base to keep the economies vibrant. e. The geography of wealth is highly concentrated in four countries–Germany, UK, France, and Italy–that collectively make up about 75% of the entire Euro Community. f. Offering incentives to raise fertility rates, limiting public spending, privatizing public companies, and increasing the retirement age, are all constructive policies. g. When the € was established it made possible for poorer countries to borrow money at the same rates as the wealthy, and they did so with impunity and without collateral. The Eurozone, therefore, requires a common fiscal union, and a central government. The biggest threat to the EU is a Greek exit, and should that occur interest rates would rise to double digits, the drachmae would be reintroduced, financial chaos will precipitate a contagion within Europe and across the Atlantic. A spike in precious metal prices is a certainty, and a major injury to European banks. On the other hand, separation from the € would make Greece more competitive, stimulate tourism, and begin with a fresh slate as is the case with all bankruptcies. It should also be emphasized that Germany (and the other wealthy nations) cannot leave the community, as it would destroy its export-driven economy and financial system. It is France and Germany that have benefitted the most from the €, and Germany in particular who prospered from exports.

## Slavic Europe

Slavic Europe (Albania and the three Baltic nations are included), the most backward economic region of Europe is a huge area that spreads from the Baltic, east to the Urals, and southward to Bulgaria, Macedonia and Albania, and forms two distinct political and economic units. Former communist satellites, commonly referred to as the "Shatterbelt," are unusual because they were a product of political devolution after WWI, and again after the fall of the Soviet Union. The vast majority are small in population and very dependent on other nations for their economic existence. Russia has an active stock market, the world's third largest energy exchange, and is in Rostow's fourth stage. The ruble is convertible and rising energy prices have made the 1989 default a distant memory. The Russian Trading System created a commodity exchange that is based on the payment of rubles, euros, and other currencies. For the first time in history, Russia has emerged as a creditor nation, and has reduced taxes, thus attracting capital. Moscow is home to more billionaires than any other European city. In recent years, Russia has repaid foreign loans ahead of schedule, is running a trade surplus, and its bond rating has been raised to AA. Because of numerous reforms, the most notable involving private property, Russia is rapidly moving closer to Europe, socially, economically, and politically.

Russia was a feudal society under the Czars, and transition to communism was merely an economic system of stylistic fine-tuning. Throughout its tormented history, it had produced neither a capitalistic economy nor a strong middle class, and its short history since the end of communism in 1989 has been impressive, but incomplete. Historically claustrophobic, it has embarked upon an active program to cement new economic arrangements with its immediate neighbors, as well as nations outside its traditional sphere of engagement. Post-communist Russia emerged with a weak president that gave the most lucrative assets to a new elite, the *siloviki*, who exercised crippling economic control over the whole country. The Yeltzin excesses have largely been corrected and, as a result, the economy has been revived and real disposable incomes have risen over the course of the past ten years faster than at any time in history. Its infrastructure is steadily being improved, and primary activities are becoming more efficient. As a result, Russia is a fulcrum in the geopolitical game of the new millennium. Japan and China are lusting its oil and natural gas, Iran requires protection, and Western Europe needs energy. However, an old, worn, and incomplete transportation grid remains the nation's Achilles heel. Russia, with eleven time zones, is vast in an east-west direction while the rivers flow to either the frozen north or the desert south.

Russia's economic potential is centered on energy resources, base and precious metals, tourism, and improvements of the primary and secondary sectors. It is increasing its base metal output by more than 15% and gold reserves by more than 5% annually. Russia has the fourth largest oil reserves. It has the largest conventional natural gas reserves; it controls more than 75% of global palladium; it has the second largest coal reserves; it is the largest nickel producer, the second largest platinum miner, and the fourth largest iron ore miner; and it and ranks among the top five in at least fifteen other metals. In recent years,

Russia has emerged as the world's largest oil producer and exporter, as well as a major gold buyer.

Flushed with wealth like no other time in history, Russia is keenly aware of its geography and EM status. Culturally and economically, it has been eclipsed by Western Europe in the West, and Japan and Korea in the East. With the rise of China as the world's economic driver to the southeast, there is a determined drive to accelerate development. Nevertheless, a good deal of Russia looks like its past: poor in relation to the rest of Western Europe, corrupt, and institutionally deprived. Russia requires a generation of rapid, conscientious and focused infrastructure development and massive foreign capital inputs. The latter has begun, but is currently insufficient to redress decades of communist misrule and infrastructure degradation. Recent reforms, however, have contributed to a rapidly expanding economy, the emergence of a middle class, and have become Europe's second largest car consumer. Russia remains highly vulnerable as oil and natural gas accounts for 50% of exports and more than 60% of government revenue.

The "Shatterbelt" emerged after the devolution of communist Russia completely devastated and pregnant with a myriad of problems: governmental deficits, a high level of political corruption unimaginable to West Europeans, and mismanaged national economies. Nevertheless, starting from a lower economic base, this region offers a much higher rate of economic growth than the older, more mature nations to the west. The most progressive countries–the Czech Republic and Slovenia, and to a smaller extent Poland, will outperform in coming years. Except for Russia the former communist satellites lack R&D facilities, and are hard pressed to overcome former communist neglect. There are a number of bright spots. The most significant are large exploitable Albanian oil reserves estimated to represent 15% of global sweet oil. Slavic Europe has low labor costs, and the prospects of EU integration for some have introduced a good measure of political stability. All countries have adopted a pro-growth stance that will continue to attract investments, primarily in secondary activities. The entire region is revolutionizing tax codes, and this has promoted industrial infrastructure as tax rates are the lowest in Europe. Privatization has produced a flood of small and large companies that are poised for exceptional growth, and, hence, will narrow the economic disparities with the older, more established countries of Western Europe.

The investment community recognizes only four main developed markets: Anglo-America, Western Europe, Japan, and Australia/New Zealand. In terms of economic inertia and the force of history, the most mature and sophisticated capital market is Europe, and at the time of this writing, valuations are fully 25% lower than US counterparts. While many make the case for slow, or no growth at all for Europe, it should be noted that due to an excellent existing infrastructure, skilled labor, the availability of capital, and governments committed to the export of quality goods, Europe remains an excellent area for investment. As long as governmental stability and reforms progress, Slavic Europe is also an excellent area to invest through mutual fund exposure. Russia has emerged as America's fourth largest trading partner; the ruble is cheap, and the stock market undervalued. The other Slavic nations with investment possibilities are Poland, the Czech Republic, Hungary, and Slovenia. Non-Slavic Europe, however, is the place to invest as it offers excellent value, particularly in the financial sector, hospitality, high-tech, basic metals, and specialty niches.

# Asia

Asia is the world's largest continent that encompasses a huge region east and south of the Ural Mountains and nearly the entire Middle East. It not only contains 65% of global population, and the entire climatic spectrum, it is home to 75% of world conventional energy as well as other physical resources. It contains three of the five BRICS, has become the world's main economic driver accounting for 70%-plus of global GDP growth, and banker to the world. The aggregate GDP exceeds $37 trillion, or more than 55% of world total, holds in excess of $4 trillion in reserves, home to 240 billionaires, contains the world's fastest growing economies, the highest savings rate, and the bulk of its foreign trade is intra-regional. The recent GDP growth has increased the pace of rural to urban migration, stimulated the construction of a neglected infrastructure and produced a rising middle class with spending power. Today Asia is the leading region for innovation, discovery, and growth, and it is accelerating rapidly through the second and fifth stages of the Rostow growth model.

Historically, the first Asian nation to emerge and compete in the global economy was Japan. Hong-Kong, Singapore, Taiwan and Korea, grew rapidly since the 1970s, and the emergence of China and India have come to dominate global GDP growth in recent years. US corporations are expanding everywhere and nearly all countries appear to be accommodating the needs of globalization, as low-cost labor will continue to deflate import-oriented developed markets. Pacific-Rim nations are producing more than 55% of the world's secondary output, and Asia's share of world trade increased from less than $400 billion in the 1980s, to $20 trillion in 2011. Furthermore, Asia holds a disproportionate amount of the world's reserves, is able to amass the bulk of productive capacity, is increasing GDP at thrice the rate of DMs, and the brain drain has reversed direction. There is nothing trivial about these events. The 21st century belongs to Asia, and particularly to China and India. Modernity is exploding everywhere. Rural to urban migration is rapid and beneficial, political stability is spreading, and Asian brands are becoming commonplace.

The geographically diverse region contains a number of economically and politically important components: 1. Japan is the most mature economic and political nation, and the first Asian nation to compete in the global economy. 2. China is the current economic dynamo and the world's most populous nation. 3. India is the world's second most populous nation and the largest English-speaking nation with an economic growth rate second to China. 4. A number of nations with unique economic niches like Korea, Taiwan, Thailand, Singapore, Australia, New Zealand, Vietnam, Indonesia, and Pakistan contribute substantially to Asia's economic complexion. 5. The emergence of an urban and industrialized Asia with all its political and economic ramifications will alter international economic patterns. 6. An absence of major military action (ex-Iraq and Afghanistan); economic liberalism and privatization of national industries; a preoccupation with export-led industries; focused quality education; a series of reforms to improve economic niches, protection of infant industries and reduced taxes have helped improve the economic ascendancy of Asia in recent decades. 7. The western Pacific Rim is the world's leader in the construction of ships, cars, consumer electronics, textiles and 50-plus other industrial products. It is the world's main region of personal savings and capital investment. Japan invests 30% of GDP, Korea 29%, Singapore 36%, and China 40%. 8. Asia's population is about 10 times larger than Europe's, but by 2050, it will be 20 times larger, and as Asia becomes more prosperous, it will demand huge amounts of raw materials in order to provide a modern urban infrastructure. 9. Mongolia is a large country that contains fewer than three million people and one that has not left its mark on society since the days of Genghis Khan. Despite its backwater nature, there is extreme speculation in an effort to develop its resources, and in particular, gold, coal, potash, natural gas, uranium, iron ore, copper, and rare earths. It stands to become one of the richest countries.

## The "Great Game" and the "Geographical Pivot"

The "Great Game" is a term first used in the 19th century to describe the rivalry between Russia and the UK for control of heroin and the political dominance of Central Asia. The notion was revived by Sir Halford Mackinder, in "The Geographical Pivot of History" (1904), in which he outlined how the control of Central Asia would enable the UK to dominate the rimland that surrounds it and, hence, the rest of the world. This landmark idea influenced the conduct of WWI, the interwar years, WWII, and the post WWII period. Despite the fact that no one accepts a "single pole" world, and since all major and aspiring powers wish to preserve privileged interests, the geopolitical focus on Central Asia will intensify as *weltanschauung* is interpreted differently by the principal players. Therefore, the "Great Game," today is a significant geopolitical strategy played by the US, Russia, China, the "Stans," India, and Iran. The Great Game also involves control of the vast energy resources of the Caspian Sea and peripheral areas; hence, the geopolitical posturing among many nations for control of energy out of the region. The Caspian Sea, surrounded by Russia, Kazakhstan, Iran, Turkmenistan, and

Azerbaijan, is controlled by Russia. The US wishes energy to flow westward through Turkey while Russia desires a northerly route, and China an easterly route. The fact that six major pipelines flow west east and north south, is clear evidence as to who is winning the "Great Game." The chessboard is set: American military might with imperialistic ambitions of complete domination of the "Pivot" is firmly in place; Iran, Russia, China, and the "Stan" nations wish American military presence to disappear. Because Afghanistan borders Iran, Russia, Turkmenistan, Uzbekistan, Tajikistan, Pakistan, India and China, its strategic value in the Great Game is obvious. Because all who invaded and occupied had failed, Afghanistan has been described as the "graveyard" of foreigners.

The Great Game has become a *cause célèbre* for Russia and China, and, consequently, they are forging new political, economic and military alliances considered beneficial to both nations. Not only are they cooperating in the expansion of Russia's oil and natural gas industries, but also the newly found friendship has extended to joint military exercises, Russian electricity exports, military arms sales, and a common front in the United Nations. Both countries have recently embraced Iran as an ally to be protected, both of which are expending considerable resources to further economic development. China's strategic interests are to secure access to oil, natural gas, coal, cotton, precious metals, zinc, molybdenum, uranium, etc. The final objective is to partition Pakistan, Iran, and Afghanistan. Tajikistan has also become strategically important to the "Great Game" as there are more Tajiks living in Afghanistan than in Tajikistan. In the final analysis, this hitherto insignificant nation has become a "big deal" in the geopolitical game of central Asia. "Tulip" type revolutions inspired by the US in central Asia are viewed as something beyond meddling by neighboring countries, who consider the "Great Game" a serious threat to their security and interests. There are many moving and constantly alternating parts to this portion of the world with uncertain consequences: China, Russia, Kazakhstan, Kyrgyzstan, Tajikistan, Uzbekistan, and Iran founded The Shanghai Cooperation Organization (SCO) in 2001. SCO objectives are to change existing geopolitical realities, foremost of which is the end of US Afghan occupation and the control of energy. This organization also seeks to thwart all American attempts to wean central Asian states from Russia and China.

## China and India (Chindia)

Chindia, with 2.7 billion people, or 38% of the world's population, has surfaced with sudden aggressiveness onto the global economic scene as the two dominant global growth engines, especially for industrial, consumer goods, and information services. China is currently in the fourth stage, and India lies in the third stage of the Rostow model. Incomes are rising and a middle class is emerging that will consume huge quantities of natural resources. China ranks second to the US in GDP, India fifth, and both are expected to produce an annual growth rate of 4%-8% annually for the next 20 years. It is interesting to note that China and India were the world's largest economies in 1400, and seven centuries later, they may once again attain this distinction. Both countries are transforming their societies from primary subsistence to industrial/tertiary at a pace hitherto unknown in human history. China's GDP and saving metrics are larger by 2%-plus, it has a better infrastructure, a larger export sector, larger capital reserves, and receives five times the amount of foreign capital than India. Agricultural reforms in China are more progressive leading to larger field units and, hence, greater efficiencies. While China has given priority to an industrial export economy, India has emphasized technology, pharmaceutical and service industries. In addition, India has a better business culture and a longer history of protecting private property rights, plus a younger and less expensive labor force.

Chindia will emerge as the dominant, global, economic power. Its combined middle class will exceed that of the US and Europe; its currencies will rise against the dollar; it will produce about twenty times the number of engineers than the US; more than 50% of all people in cities larger than two million will be living in Chindia; and the economies of Chindia will switch from an export-oriented to a domestic-oriented character. Because government authorities are committed to a path of accelerating the *"la dolce vita"* climate, Chindia offers extraordinary investment opportunities, including a huge and growing market and a will to build efficient national infrastructures. Dozens of companies may be purchased directly in major exchanges, but for the tyro, mutual fund exposure is suggested.

China, a nation of 1.5 billion people, is the fourth largest country in land area, has about 8% of world arable land, 7% of fresh water, and less than 2% of global forests and crude oil. More than 80% of the population lives in the more humid eastern portion, the north-central portion of the country is cold and barren, and the western portion arid. Wealth is overwhelmingly concentrated in 100 cities, of which 56 contain more than 3 million. During the past 25 years, it has lifted half a billion people out of poverty, and has produced current account surpluses for more than 35 years. It has metamorphosed from a pathetically poor country into the world's lowest-cost goods producer. Its PPP output is $12-plus trillion, a remarkable achievement given its xenophobic and colonial history. Since World War II China has experienced several earth-shaking revolutions: the rise of communism and its dramatic alteration of the economic landscape; the failure of the "Cultural Revolution"; embracement of Western economic principles, the development of the world's largest export-oriented economy; and encouragement of the world's largest and most profound transfer of knowledge. No matter how one arranges numbers about the Chinese economic miracle, the transition from state ownership to a modern market economy has been astonishing. China has become the most rapidly growing economy; it is the world's largest consumer and importer of energy; it holds more than $3.5 trillion in foreign reserves; it builds a city the size of Orlando, Florida, every two years; per capita incomes are doubling every eight years and the demand for electricity every nine years; it ranks first in a large number of secondary activities: textiles, clothing, refrigerators, cement, copper, footwear, steel, TVs, cell phones, laptops, cars, toys, office products, etc.; it is the world's leading producer of rice, fruits, cotton, and vegetables; and it ranks third in the world after the US and the EU community in scientific research. Compared with the US, GDP is growing four times faster and the median income six times faster.

The "Great Leap Forward," resulted in famine that cost an estimated 30-plus million lives, the "Cultural Revolution" resulted in extreme misery, but beginning in 1979, with a series of economic reforms, the Chinese economy has outstripped the economic growth performance of DMs. Communism, decided that it was a good thing to become rich and behave like capitalists. All systems turned green to industrialize in the shortest possible time for the express purpose to export and accumulate foreign reserves. Since 2000, China has been responsible for more than 40% of world GDP growth, and accounts for more than 60% of global trade growth. It is the world's largest consumer and producer of nearly everything, the largest importer of nearly every natural resource, and has overtaken the US and Japan as the world's largest exporter of electronic goods. In addition, China is currently building the nation's infrastructure at fever pitch, unlike anything that the world has ever seen. By 2025, it will have constructed 71 new airports, and by 2030, 10 hydroelectric facilities, 45 nuclear electric generating plants, and will construct 60,000 miles of national highways to connect each city with a population of 200,000. The country had but 6 million cars in 2000, a number that increased to 80 million in 2013.

The reasons for the post-1973 economic miracle are not hard to find. 1. China invests a high percentage of fixed capital. It does not tax savings and offers preferential investment incentives in an effort to encourage a sustainable work ethic. 2. China is undergoing sweeping economic and social reforms, the most important being the protection of property rights, and expanding financial markets. The prime drivers for growth are the introduction of reform measures to undo former colonial restraints. 3. There are more than 100 million educated and wealthy Chinese living around the globe who speak Chinese at home and continue relationships with China. They are investing and returning to China not only with money, but also with vigor, expertise, and with a sense of nationalism to see their historically poverty-plagued country develop into the world's largest economy. Chinese dominate Singapore, and the wealth of Myanmar, Thailand, Indonesia, Malaysia, and the Philippines. The population of Taiwan is Chinese, and 1.2 million inhabit California, as well as 500,000 in Canada. 4. The middle class grew from 3% in 1975 to more than 30% today. 5. Therefore, China will continue to expand global market share, particularly in value-added goods; to maintain a strong RMB; increase its stock of precious metals; and stimulate domestic demand. It wishes to be considered the equal of all DMs, which means that it craves to be a permanent member of elitist, global associations. China is neither happy nor content with the World Bank and IMF policies, and wishes to create similar financial organizations.

Despite the above economic accomplishments, a huge litany of "Achilles heels" remains: 1. China is not a democracy but a communist dictatorship with a corrupt bureaucracy that lacks a free market economy. It is estimated that $3.8 trillion has left China illicitly due to political issues in recent years. 2. Its financial sector is extremely fragile due to a large basket of non-performing loans, and lacks the sophistication of more mature systems capable of competing globally. 3. Air and water pollution remain serious concerns. Of the 20 most polluted cities, 16 are in China. Water is getting scarce, as 40% of surface fresh water is not potable, and for those cities getting their water from underground sources, water tables are dropping. 4. Chinese official statistics are suspect, and transparency of its listed stocks equally so. 5. It is inefficient in energy consumption. 6. Geographically, the growth of the past generation has occurred in selected coastal areas and Beijing while 20% of the country remains under semi-feudal conditions. 7. A collapse of the economy remains a distinct possibility, as the torrid pace of the past 33 years cannot continue without a major correction. In addition, aggregate debt is increasing, as is inflation, and unless corrected, it could provoke a national financial crisis with a severe global contagion. The current economic landscape embraces the following:

1. China has progressed from a "low-wage" to a low-cost producing country, and has become the site of 30% of all global patents. Of interest is the rapid evolution of the information/scientific component of China's exports. Once known for "cheap" goods, China is now exporting electronic and biotech articles of greater sophistication and value added. It is rapidly becoming a "hi-tech" exporting nation rivaling the US, Japan, Korea, Taiwan, and Europe. The emphasis now rests on originality and resourcefulness in electronics, and, in this regard, China now leads the world in scientific research growth.

2. China has devised an interesting method of gaining commodities for its rapidly expanding industrial base–building infrastructure in Latin America, Asia and Africa. Host nations find the arrangement irresistible as they gain income and employment. Most significantly, these nations do not feel threatened by China as it lacks a history for colonial adventures. In addition, China has eliminated tariffs on nearly 200 imported goods from 30 African nations and has cancelled foreign debts. China, therefore, is on a mission to assure an uninterrupted stream of natural resources to maintain its development program, and as a result, it has managed to acquire the largest percentage of energy of any other country. Over the past 15 years, it has invested $1 trillion in more than 30 countries in industries ranging from natural resources to pharmaceuticals and electronics. In the process, China has invested in the refurbishment of 20-plus ports and terminals in all continents to facilitate trade.

3. Not only is China experiencing a major economic transformation, but a demographic revolution that will have profound economic implications. The nation's birth rate is falling, the average age increasing, and its labor force will

peak by 2025. With rising savings and wages, the pent-up demand for homes, furnishings, and durable goods is staggering as the economy switches from its export orientation to domestic output. China ranked 31st in competiveness among the 60 largest economies in 2005 and now ranks 8th. The number of millionaires in China rose from zero in 1979 to more than 50,000 in 2011, and the number of billionaires grew from zero to 140. According to Jim Rogers, "China will ultimately be the largest consumer of everything."

4. China has emerged as the world's largest gold producer, and has tripled its gold reserves since 2008. The national gold strategy is to buy and hoard domestic gold mine output, and to purchase in the open market. Rare earth elements are essential ingredients in such technologies as wind turbines, high tech magnets, communication systems, etc. Tungsten, one of the hardest metals critical in the production of specialty steel, is another virtual monopoly responsible for more than 75% of world output. How quickly the Chinese innovate and attract market share is illustrated by the production of laptops, which rose from zero output in 2002, to 65% of global sales by 2011. China is also becoming a significant banker to the world. It is signing bilateral currency swap agreements to reduce dependency on the dollar and raise the RMB to respectable international levels. More than 25% of all its trade agreements, especially with Russia, Brazil, Argentina and others are replacing $billions in global trade transactions. China in 2009 began selling RMD-denominated bonds to foreigners, thus reducing the necessity of holding $US reserves, and made the RMD freely convertible in nearly all neighboring countries.

5. The growth of national and multinational corporations is impressive. In 2000, it had one, a number that rose to 115, ranging from telecom, banking, insurance, base metals, auto, energy, petrochemicals, and household appliances and trading companies. All, highly aggressive and armed with billions of $US, they are competing worldwide for increased market share. One-third of the world's 20 largest companies are Chinese.

6. China's entry into the international energy arena has been swift and decisive. It has become an active international explorer, shipper, developer, refiner, and aggressive in the construction of terminal facilities and pipelines. In Latin America, China is becoming the second largest trading partner, committing hundreds of $billion in various investments. In Africa, China is particularly active in Sudan, Congo, Angola, and along the Guinea Coast. In Asia, it has forged energy arrangements with nearly all producing nations including Australia, and Pakistan by offering lucrative energy and mineral contracts. It is in the Muslim realm that China is making a concentrated effort to gain access. China imports 15% of Saudi Oil, but its largest investments are in Iran where it is developing the largest oil field, constructing a large LNG facility, pipeline construction, subways, fiber-optic networks, ports, and factories.

7. China has a mission: to attract as much capital in the shortest time to build the largest industrial complex. Therefore, all surplus monies are invested in housing and national infrastructure. In the meantime, China is willing to assume losses in the value of American Treasuries to continue momentum. It has become the largest luxury market, and the gambling capital of the world.

Launching economic reforms in 1991, 23 years after China took unprecedented measures to modernize the economy India has been rapidly evolving as a major trading nation, making remarkable strides in transitioning a medieval economy into the 21st century. In this regard, it has become a large magnet for foreign investment, and the recipient of 300,000 IT employment positions. In addition to information technology concentration, India's pharma industry is growing by more than 20% annually, controls 21% of global generic drug production, and there are more engineers in Bangalore than in the State of California. For the first time since independence, India is no longer a debtor nation, its foreign reserves are increasing, its college graduates doubling every seven years, the growth of urbanization outpacing all others with the exception of China, and its currency upgraded to investment grade. GDP is growing 6% annually, and the Mumbai stock exchange rivals Tokyo, Shanghai, Singapore, and Hong Kong. The torrid pace of economic growth shows no signs of slowing, as its economy expected to become the world is third largest before 2025. India has 65 billionaires, remarkable, as it had none 10 years ago. It is currently in Rostow's third stage, and future prospects for rapid economic growth look bright because India has chosen a different growth model than other EMs. Instead of concentrating on the export of inexpensive goods, the plan concentrated on high quality human resources, IT, and primarily in the computer software, commercial, pharmaceutical, medical, and financial sectors. Equally important is the fact that its birth rate is stabilizing, an event that is contributing to its rising per capita income.

The reasons for India's success since the middle 1970s are not hard to find. 1. Government is led by the architect of numerous, financial reforms who restructured financial markets. As a result, the country is experiencing a huge boom in fixed capital investment. 2. Privatization is accelerating, as is governmental willingness to de-emphasize the most inefficient features of socialism. Its currency is convertible, infrastructure improvements proceeding at a record-breaking pace, and there is a national priority to increase R&D. The government has made a determined desire to emphasize high-tech economic activity. 2. With the fifth largest scientific pool in the world it is effectively competing with the US, China, Europe and Japan in high quality services and technology. 3. India is quickly changing its patent laws, thus placing pressures on its ability to continue to replicate western pharmaceuticals, high-tech goods and other products. 4. A return movement of Indian technocrats from the US and the UK stimulated a significant number of industries, many of which have morphed into multinational companies. 5. Reforms have eliminated the worst bureaucratic restrictions on trade and investment, and import quotas have been gradually reduced. 6. The poverty rate as defined by the percentage of population living on $2 per day was reduced by more than 50% during the past 10 years, and the middle class has more than doubled. 7. Gandhi economic myths have been replaced. For more than one generation after independence, antiquated notions of self-sufficiency, hostility towards foreign investment, pro-agrarian policies, plagued India and the notion "machines were the work of the devil were pervasive." 8. Flushed with newfound wealth and the need for energy and investment outlets, India has been very active in overseas investments. Indian companies since 2005 have purchased more than 100 foreign corporations, particularly hotel chains, information companies, pharmaceuticals, and energy.

While India is a fast growing economy, all figures must be tempered by reality: 10% of its population sleep outdoors, average per capita income is less than $4,500 a year, and half the population is subjected to unsanitary water. The problems abound further in this country of 100-plus languages, and 50-plus ethnic groups: huge agricultural subsidies, high rural illiteracy, poor nutrition, and grinding poverty are endemic. With 60% of the population engaged in primary activities, India has a long road to travel to achieve economic maturity, but recent reforms and GDP growth appear to be on a sustained course. On the other hand, the national scenograph is being altered with new transportation, research parks, industrial facilities, and high-rise residential construction at a pace never experienced in its history. It is the world's sixth largest generator of electricity and, along with China, will collectively account for about 60% of global energy growth. India is the site of the world's largest petro-chemical facility that will produce 5% of global gasoline. By 2019, India will become the fourth largest consumer market.

## Japan

Japan, the world's third, largest economy, represents a nation with an extraordinary economic history that reversed the course of isolationism in the 19th century and became the first non-occidental country to lower birth rates to 25 per thousand (1960), industrialized rapidly and, eventually, without any domestic physical resources, became the world's second largest economy. By discarding its xenophobic tendencies, it transformed itself from feudalism to a tertiary society and became the first non-European nation to reach Rostow's fifth stage. When measured by its civility, the lack of social aberrations and superb infrastructure, Japan is wealthier than most nations. The astonishing speed with which Japan assimilated western technology had long puzzled economists, but has been first among non-western nations "catch up" with the West, and has served as the model for nearly all Asian nations. It was the only major non-occidental country to escape colonialism, and the first to embrace westernization. After WWII, it introduced massive quality control mechanisms to their secondary sector and thereby increased exports. In addition, it strengthened the character of *zaibatsu* (large vertically and horizontally integrated industrial and financial conglomerates), as well as *keiritsu*, a group of companies that transact business with each other in order to promote the interest of the whole. What made economic progress possible is tenacious nationalism, frugality, hard work, a culturally homogeneous and resolute *espirit d'corps* imbued with an unusual ethos of sacrifice for the common good. It is driven by a single mindedness that rarely exhibits significant public economic, cultural, and economic discords.

Japan, however, is not without serious issues. Extreme conformity may have been necessary when Japan was industrializing rapidly after 1860, but excessive convention with inflexible features is antithetical in an urban-dominated, post-industrial society. Perhaps this element of cultural inertia explains why Japan entered a secular bear market in 1989 and has been unable to reverse course. Japan is also highly protectionist by maintaining high tariffs on rice, the nation's staple, and a host of other products. It also holds too many dollars and too little gold, the banking system is burdened with underperforming loans, and the avalanche of political and financial scandals continue. Not only is Japan burdened by low fertility rates and the highest median age in the world, but its old-age dependency issue is compounded by a huge, internal debt. Japan's public debt is 230% of GDP, a malaise referred to as the "Japanese Disease." The only positive element in this statistic is that Japan owns its debt with little foreign participation. Nevertheless, while it has experienced deflation since 1989, the Nikkei declined 70% from its high 22 years ago. Real estate values have been cut in half, and the central bank has been printing money. Furthermore, the population lives four years longer than in the US, the export economy is vibrant, it saves and invests a larger percentage of its disposable income than any DM, and R&D efforts in electronics, pharmaceuticals, and other fields is very progressive. Despite the stream of negatives concerning the aging of the nation, it should be noted that the Japanese are capable of working far into their seventies, as they are extremely healthy and have a strong work ethic, thus giving them an excellent opportunity to deal with their "demographic problem." The country sits on a large pile of currency reserves, has a low unemployment rate, and its export-oriented economy is quickly shifting to higher capital and labor intensiveness.

Nevertheless, standards and levels of living continue to increase, and the nation continues to invest heavily on infrastructure, and in secondary employment. Its economy is not only capital-intensive, but also Japanese companies supply the world with the most sophisticated components for many industries. Japan is spending incredible amounts of money on bio/healthcare, technology, information technology, and high quality, value-added secondary production. Japan invests a larger share of GDP on R&D than any other nation. Although amongst the highest, the base level of education and technical skills continue to improve thus giving Japan a major competitive advantage among DMs. Some interesting economic features to consider: 1. Japan has experienced 24 years of a secular bear market, the longest such stretch of any DM in recent history. 2. The government encourages high population densities, and as a result, Japan is energy efficient. 3. At the time of this writing, Japanese equities are oversold. 4. For the past 21 years, Japan has encouraged a zero interest policy amounting to free money, and a lucrative carry trade that has supported the Treasury market. 5. While Japan has no natural resources, it has a large, well educated, dedicated, resourceful and technologically advanced population. 6. Japan is a high-tech machine, known for high quality consumer and industrial goods.7. As the population ages, savings will be drawn down and the proceeds used to fund retirement.

## The Asian Tigers and Australia

The moniker "Asian Tigers" originally referred to Korea, Taiwan, Hong Kong, and Singapore describing rapid, focused, and export-dominated economies. Within recent decades, Thailand, Malaysia, Vietnam, Indonesia, Philippines, and Bangladesh have been added to the list. All have emulated the key economic features of Japan and China becoming vital to globalization. They are in the third to fifth Rostow stages and therefore have solid, economic niches and contribute a significant role in EM mutual funds.

Korea, overshadowed by its two larger neighbors, China and Japan, has a GDP that is 30 times that of North Korea. It is one the most robust economies whose success is based on focused national policies that favor niche industries and solid technological advances. Nearly all-economic activity is capital and labor intensive, particularly in electronics, transportation, shipbuilding, and medical. In the quest to maintain innovative leadership, it has spent billions to make the nation the most wired on the planet and the 15th largest global economy. Singapore, a modern-day city-state that was not much more than a mosquito-infested tropical rain forest with a population of less than 100 prior to the British, now contains a population of 5 million, and is the wealthiest country in Asia. Strategically situated in the Strait of Malacca, it has become the world's largest container *entrepot* and the locus of a major global financial and high-tech center. Politically stable, the well-educated population has a saving rate of 40%. Its Chinese population stands in sharp contrast to its neighbors in terms of devising an economy that is the most capital-intensive in the entire region. Taiwan is emerging as one of the world's major, technopole centers, as it is high in chip services, notebook PCs, and LCD monitors and is the second largest in the production of servers and digital cameras. GDP per capita exceeds $39,000, and it holds thousands of patents in the US. Thailand, Indonesia, the Philippines, and Vietnam are the second fastest growing global economies. Australia is the world's largest producer of iron ore, uranium, zinc, and lead, and it is a major producer of gold and nickel and a major exporter of raw materials to China and India. About two-thirds of Australian exports are commodities, with coal leading the list followed by metals and agricultural products. New Zealand, similar to Australia in terms of history and culture, also exhibits many related economic features. Both, along with the Asian Tigers, offer above-average investment opportunities.

## The Islamic World

The Muslim cultural realm is a huge, geographical region that stretches from Northwest Africa to the Western Pacific and south to the tropical areas of Africa, encompassing about 1.5 billion people, with nearly all nations in the second through the fourth Rostow stages. Contrary to popular images, the most populous Muslim nation is Indonesia, followed by India, Pakistan, Bangladesh, Egypt, Turkey, and Iran, collectively responsible for more than 80% of all Muslims. Due to geography, the Muslim cultural region is neither homogeneous nor easily defined, and while not all Muslims are Arab, the core of the religion goes back to the Arabian Peninsula. Historically Islam expressed the geography of aridity with only Indonesia and small portions of Southeast Asia and Africa south of the Sahara not entirely arid. The desert portion, however, formed a unique cultural "tripod" of extensive nomadic, scattered urban, and localized "oasis"-based food production. Of the three distinct and highly competitive societies, the nomad had shaped religious and political institutions, while the urban produced the cultural elites and the primary sector employed the bulk of the population. At the time of this writing, North Africa and the Middle East are engulfed in social and political unrest, representing a major tipping point in reversing centuries of nomad domination over progressive, urban, secular forces. When one includes the negative elements of Balkanization perpetrated by colonial powers, the above have produced a cultural realm with a list of extraordinary challenges:

1. Despite the wealth produced by energy in the Muslim Realm, nearly all of it has been wasted, and, as a result, the region has been dependent upon the US and Europe for all its technical needs. Hospitals, airports, and nearly every technical structure related to oil were built mainly by Americans and Europeans, a sign that the chasm between the very wealthy and the impoverished is greater in the Muslim world than in Latin America and Asia. The medieval monarchy of Saudi Arabia, for example, with more than 4,000 princes, has plundered a good deal of the nation's wealth. A strong middle class eludes all Muslim nations save Turkey, Iran and Israel, the only non-Arab nations in the region.

2. A decisive secular war has yet to be fought that would allow complete freedom of religion, press, and equal rights for every citizen. The region has one foot in the 8th century and the other in the 21st. This is illustrated by the Ayatollah Khomeini, who wished to recreate an 8th century Islamic Republic in Iran after the expulsion of the Shah. He burned "Western books," banned all alcoholic beverages, instituted religious law, and referred to all things "Western" as "works of the devil." However, when he suffered a heart attack, US-trained doctors, a US-built hospital, and US equipment brought him back to life. With few exceptions, political parties and trade unions are outlawed, church and state are not separated, and the process of westernization has yet to produce the desired effects. It is hard, therefore, to alter and even accommodate the dichotomy of a feudal society under present conditions without conflict. Progress is inevitable but uneven, as the seeds of

secularization were not evenly sown. The Mediterranean fringe of North Africa and the Eastern Mediterranean will be the centers of secular progress, but failed states like Afghanistan will take time. Those that export energy are accumulating foreign reserves, but the vast majorities that have little to export are falling behind world trend levels. Saudi Arabia, among others, suffers from a number of cultural peculiarities. The Wahhabi religious sect and royal family control the oil industry and all facets of Saudi life. The population of 35 million is spoiled in terms of the pleasures of an extreme welfare system, and the realities of earning a living once energy revenues decline. That which has not been squandered on expensive arms purchases is wasted on unproductive social programs. This nation exhibits a history of foregoing opportunity on a mammoth scale.

3. The Muslim world, however, does have a model to copy, and that is Turkey, the most secularized state, and curiously, the only one where the day of rest is Sunday and not Friday, and a member of NATO. It is the world's 16th largest economy, the most diversified economically, and the strongest military power in the Muslim cultural realm. Progressive elements are rooted in the basic principles Mustapha Kemal and his doctrine of "etatism," or the application of reformism, republicanism, statism, secularism, modernism, and nationalism—a revolution by the elite to speed up the process of westernization. Therefore, women received the right to vote, civil marriages and divorces are allowed, the Latin alphabet is applied, the Islamic dress code and Islamic titles are banned, the Western calendar is adopted, and religion is separated from legal, educational, and military affairs. These developments escaped every other Muslim nation.

4. A large portion of the Muslim world is part of the "Great Game." The British disembowelment of the region in order to divide and rule the various populations and to play "the game" that would benefit their interests produced two economic dislocations: "artificial" political boundaries and the denial of an ethnic state, despite the fact that more than 20 countries share the same religion, language, diet, and lifestyle. In recent decades, a new round of nationalism and control of the region's major resource–energy–has radically altered the game. Another important consideration is that the Persian Gulf region has become a strategic geopolitical obsession to the US, centered on five burning issues: The war against terror, the preservation of Persian Gulf medieval monarchies, the control of heroin from Afghanistan, the Palestinian issue, and the slow pace of westernization.

5. Incipient progressive efforts are emerging. After 100-plus years of Western political domination, many nations are seriously considering regional cooperation on a scale once thought unthinkable. The Gulf Cooperation Council (GCC), consisting of Saudi Arabia, Kuwait, Oman, UAE, Qatar, and Bahrain are combining forces to create regional financial, oil and natural gas, real estate and resource markets. All are expected to de-peg from the $US, thus undermining the petro-dollar standard. They are also entertaining notions of creating a common currency much like the €. Given the fact that Persian Gulf states hold more than

$2 trillion of foreign assets, the parties involved wish to preserve their purchasing power. It should also be remembered that the biggest winners in the recent rise in energy prices are the Persian Gulf energy exporters, who have surfaced as major, geopolitical strategists for keeping the peace in the Gulf, as they all have a stake in keeping the region as tranquil as possible. Certain parts of the Muslim realm are growing rapidly such as Dubai, which has built the tallest building and largest shopping center in the world. Saudi Arabia is spending more than $13 billion on a new research center in an effort to reduce its dependency on the US. Dubai, with 20% of global gold trades, is becoming a major gold *entrepot* in which 100 countries maintain deposits. While the Muslim realm offers investment opportunities, caution, and due diligence are in order as opportunities are limited to mutual fund investing, with only Israel and Turkey offering equity selections.

## Latin America

Latin America, a region of many faces, stretches south of the U.S. border (including the Caribbean) to Tierra del Fuego. Consisting of nearly 40 nations and 600-plus million people, it is a resource-rich, rapidly developing cultural realm with nearly all countries in the 2nd–4rd stages of the Rostow model. It contains the largest tropical forest in Brazil to a cold and drizzly West Coast Marine climate in southern Chile. Its most distinctive features are the Southern Rockies to Panama, and the Andes from Columbia to the extreme south. With few exceptions, these two mountain chains have created three distinct climatic regions arranged from sea level upwards–*tierra calliente* refers to the lower, more tropical, least developed portion mostly in the Caribbean, eastern Central America, and Northern, and North-eastern South America; *tierra templada*, the more developed area, containing the capital; and *tierra fria*, the coldest and inhabited by Indians. All three hypsometric regions have a distinct climate, with dissimilar economic bases, and are culturally diverse from each other. Until recently, with the population concentrated in the *tierra templada* and coastal regions, the rest of Latin America presented a scenograph of an arrested frontier as nearly the entire population (with the sole exception of the capitals in the *tierra templada*) was water-oriented. Each ethnic and racial group has its own economy with no national economic integration. Central America emerged as mestizo, self-sufficient, built on a corn-based economy, and centered in the more humid regions. African Americans and mulatto dominated the historic sugar growing regions of the *tierra calliente*, and the Europeans inhabit the capital region and all other major urban areas. Throughout its history, national economies, based on commodities, reflected the classic patterns of "boom and bust." The Caribbean is a collection of small island nations, tropical, and undeveloped save those with a lucrative tourist industry, offshore banking, and a few natural resources. Other characteristics include:

1. Capital and human talent are highly concentrated in primate cities. 2. "Social dualism" exhibits a profound variation among all cultural groups. 3. The usual economic malaise of debt, default, dependence on one or two exports for

foreign exchange, political instability, and dependence on the World Bank and IMF for assistance are major economic impediments to sustained economic growth. 4. Close economic ties with the US did not offer long-term economic benefits for most nations. 5. Bartering has become fashionable with Venezuela engaged in oil for Argentinean beef and cereals, and has participated with this type of medieval behavior with Mali for bauxite, cotton, gold and other materials. 6. Historic regional trade agreements have all failed. 7. Nationalization of foreign assets is continuing. 8. With Mexico City and other capitals located in the *tierra templada*, the population of Latin America is peripheral with no adequate transportation system to integrate *tierra calliente*, with *tierra templada, tierra fria,* and one country with another. Due to the above conditions, Latin America has exhibited an "arrested frontier" where vast interior regions have remained undeveloped. 9. Latin America, long under America's sphere of influence and financial domination, is now exerting considerable independence. Venezuela is signing energy agreements with China; Bolivia is planning a number of natural gas pipelines to Brazil, Argentina, Uruguay, and Chile without western participation, and has asked China to develop its natural gas resources. Brazil and other nations are exporting more to China. Venezuela has convinced many Latin American leaders to pay off their debts to the IMF and World Bank, and to remain clear of any future entanglements. 10. Despite recent improvements in levels of living, the vast majority remain extremely poor. Haiti is the poorest nation in the region, and 60% of Bolivia's population lives in an environment of no running water or electricity. 11. For most countries, China has emerged as either the primary, or the second largest trading partner.

Historically, all of Latin America was colonized by Spain, Portugal, the UK, the Netherlands, France, and the US. It exhibited typical, mercantilist, economic features of an economy dominated by foreign investment, the export of commodities, and the importation of finished goods. The dependency on one or two single raw material exports has been extremely high, with oil from Venezuela accounting 90% of its wealth; coffee and bananas dominate more than 80% of the economies of Central America; tin in Bolivia, copper in Chile and Peru; sugar and tobacco in selected areas. The dominance on one or two commodities to sustain government produced an economic environment of negative terms of trade. Today, the most robust and economically diverse economies are Brazil, Mexico, Argentina, Colombia, Uruguay and Chile. Most of the Caribbean, save for tourism remain undeveloped. Economic prospects, however, are improving. Latin America over the course of the past 10 years has reduced inflation, currencies have strengthened, productivity and exports have risen, balance sheets upgraded as commodity prices continue to improve, and consumer spending is increasing. While more than one hundred Latin American companies may be purchased directly, the prudent investor should limit purchases to fund instruments.

Brazil, the largest country in Latin America in terms of land area, is the region's largest economy, as it contains about 40% of total, regional population. Its economy has been growing faster than 5% annually for many years. It has entered the fourth Rostow stage, and is about to harness the power of the Amazon. Its drainage area, with a population of less than 15 million, is 75% of America's continental size. Mainly a commodity export-oriented nation, it is increasingly diversifying its economy in the secondary and tertiary sectors. Mexico is the leading country in Central America, and remains economically separated from the rest of its neighbors to the south. Within sixty years, Mexico progressed from the first Rostow stage to the third, but in recent years, its export sector has suffered from Chinese competition. Despite the explosive growth since NAFTA, declining oil revenues, mismanagement of the national economy, and falling foreign investment, Mexico appears to be troubled.

An immensely rich nation in terms of natural resources, Argentina is testimony to how government and bad policies can wreck an economy. It was once considered a rival to the US and, at one time, wealthier than the UK. In 1900, its stock exchange was comparable in size to New York. It had a robust economy, wages were nearly equal to those in the US, and it was one of the world's ten richest countries. It had a large, educated middle class, and it boasted the largest opera house in Latin America. It is resource rich, and contains the Pampas, a grassland region not unlike the American Midwest that grows considerable corn and wheat and produces the bulk of the commercial beef output of Latin America. Buenos Aires became a mecca for venture capital in the 19th century when life was considered better than good. However, the Great Depression, a series of misguided socialist policies, excessive debt, inflation, and a number of political coups resulted in the mismanagement of the economy and bankrupted the country several times. The wealthy, educated, and brightest minds left, and the country languished to TW status during the period 1930-1999. To the west lies Chile, pencil thin with three climatic zones that stretch the equivalent distance from Northwest Europe to the Sahara, but in reverse order. In recent years, Chile, like Argentina has reformed its political and economic system, and remains one of the most rapidly growing economies. Fiscally prudent, economically pro-market, and politically responsible, Chile, since 1990, grew its GDP by 5%.

## Black Africa

Africa, a continent that is nearly four times the size of the US, contains the world's largest desert and savanna and is divided into two, major sections. The north and northeast is Muslim, and areas to the south animistic and Christian. It has the bulk of the world's landlocked countries. The population is not evenly distributed, but mainly found along rivers, the Rift Valley, the Guinea Coast, and South Africa. It is mired in grinding poverty as it contains the bulk of the world's failed states. It is also the least urbanized and has the largest negative economic metrics. Full time, organized stock exchanges are found in only seven countries. An indication of the economic backwardness is highlighted by the fact that the GDP of Germany is larger than the regions aggregate.

Independence from European colonial powers arrived after WWII, and it was characterized by a process of Africanization: the replacement of European administrative personnel and bureaucrats with inept domestic civil servants. The expropriation and nationalization of property did much to discourage foreign investment. Agricultural output plummeted everywhere, the infrastructure was neglected, civil war, and the alteration of one dictator with another all combined to reduce economic growth. In addition, Black Africa lacks the existence of a single nation-state. Carved up for the convenience of European colonial powers, the present political borders and ethnic patterns do not coincide, and are a potential source of friction once these nations begin to develop economically. Along the Guinea Coast, for example, political borders run at right angles to the coast while ethnic groups run in the opposite direction. Nigeria is not one country but three: an arid (and Muslim) region to the north, the dominant Yoruba in the southwest, and the Ibo to the southeast (both areas Christian and animist). Between the Yoruba and Ibo is oil, and the whole country is embroiled in a civil war that is fostering corruption, preventing national unity, and because of military conflict oil exports are held hostage. The Movement for the Emancipation of the Niger Delta has made it known that it wishes to destroy the central government. In the meantime, foreign oil companies pay for "protection" and ransom for kidnapped workers, pipelines are destroyed, oil is stolen from violated pipes, and *baksheesh* reigns along the landscape of Black Africa's most populous country.

Black Africa is positioned in the first and third Rostow stages and requires $50 billion in annual aid to maintain present poverty levels, with estimates rising to more than $1 trillion in order to sustain GDP growth to population growth levels. The region has remained the most backward and has benefited the least from globalization. A good portion of the region subsists on less than $1,000 per person annually, and real incomes have declined in most countries since 1980. Secondary activities remain less than 15% of the adult working population, and most countries have a GDP that is below the capitalization of a large American corporation. Nevertheless, the regions immense physical resources offer considerable potential. Africa holds about 10%-plus of global oil reserves, and accounts for a third of new reserves discovered since 2000. It is the world's primary region for diamonds, gold, chrome, vanadium, and platinum.

Black Africa is burdened with a number of unique elements: 1.With few exceptions, its economy are dominated by primary activities; hence, the largest cultural realm with the lowest arithmetic, settlement, and physiological population densities. 2. Secondary activities are not capital intensive, and non-competitive. 3. The region is hampered with a primitive infrastructure, as the road connectivity index is the poorest of any continent. 4. Economic dependency is on one or two mineral and agricultural exports per country, and, as a result, national economies suffer from the boom and bust nature of the commodity markets, the persistency of negative terms of trade, and the lack of domestic capital hampers economic growth. 5. With South Africa the sole exception, black Africa remains a geographical region with limited investments to the average investor. 6. The lack of ethnic statehood has fostered economic dislocations. 7. The region is plagued with a primitive social structure based on tribalism and displaced loyalties. 8. There is a pervasive "brain drain," primarily to the US and Europe. 9. Despite the above, Africa is poised for an economic transformation. At the time of writing, frenetic energy exploration is occurring in the Guinea Coast, Angola, Kenya, Namibia, Zambia, and Mozambique. Finally:

1. The re-distribution of wealth away from both sides of the Atlantic to Asia and emerging economic regions will continue. 2. With sustained economic growth, EMs are generating the fastest growing middle class. 3. The pace of technological growth will increase in strength, and as technological growth intensifies, knowledge-intensive industries will explode from present levels, fueled by millions of new university graduates from EMs. 4. Access to knowledge has become universal with profound implications. What took thousands of years to diffuse is now abridged to *milliseconds*. What once took two days in the Library of Congress, an overnight stay in a hotel, and a 500-mile round trip by car, now takes place in one hour with the convenience of a computer. 6. The global, geopolitical complexion has been altered, China emerged as the new, global, economic driver; the sick dollar will be replaced by a basket of currencies including precious metals; financial crises will redefine political and economic power; interest rates and inflation will rise; and global overcapacity will generate a number of crises.

# CHAPTER 2

# ASSEMBLING KEY CONSTITUENTS AND ESSENTIAL INGREDIENTS

*"There are people who know the price of everything and the value of nothing."* - Oscar Wilde

*"If you torture the numbers long enough, they will confess to anything."* - Statisticians

*"The Only Thing That Gives Me Pleasure Is To See My Dividend Coming In."* - John D. Rockefeller

*"Everyone wants to live at the expense of the state. They forget that the state wants to live at the expense of everyone."* - Frederic Bastiat

# The Ingredients

## Cash, Bonds, Government Bonds, Corporate Bonds, and Municipal Bonds

The basic ingredients of a well-diversified portfolio is a judicious mix of cash, bonds, equities, real estate, and commodities, and while all asset prices are capable of moving in the same direction, they rarely do, and when they do so, it is at different rates. All asset classes vary in terms of liquidity, price stability, tax shelter advantages or disadvantages, and as inflation or deflation hedges. In addition, all asset classes compete with each other for investor dollars, and each exhibits its own specific cyclical and secular cycles. The "value" of cash, in relation to other assets, will vary with interest rates. Bonds will behave in similar fashion, and the degree of variability will be a function of their maturities and whether they are municipals, Treasuries, corporate, or foreign. The value of equities will be a function of interest rates, the economic cycle and the quality of management. Real estate prices will also vary with economic conditions, the cost of money, monetary and fiscal policies, and precious metals respond to geopolitical problems, the value of the $US and inflation. All asset classes move in a rhythm, most are not correlating and the prudent investor should move money accordingly. For example, gold and utilities are non-correlating; REITs exhibit no correlation to technology or healthcare stocks; rising interest rates and utility stocks are negatively correlated; financial assets respond negatively to rising interest rates; commodities and bonds are negatively correlated; bonds respond positively to declining interest rates, etc.

The Vanguard Group reports the following annual returns for the three principal asset classes for the period 1926-2003: Cash had total annual returns of 3.9%, all of which was derived from income; bonds returned 5.8%, nearly all of which was income; and equities returned 10.4%, of which dividends comprised 4.5% and capital gains 5.9%. The above are extremely long-term averages with annual fluctuations exhibiting significant variations. Note also the risk-free returns of 3.9% for cash, and the risk-laden capital gain return of 5.9% for equities, the latter nearly identical to the total returns of bonds. The difference lies in the income portion for equities, and in order to gain advantage in equity investing, dividends should exceed 5% at the time of purchase. Therefore, the superiority of the equity market throughout history is quite impressive. There has been no 20-year period of negative equity prices, and only two 10-year periods where the equity market declined. In addition, up markets outnumber down markets by seven to three, and returns are at least one-third higher than bonds and nearly triple for cash. Based on historical evidence, equities, over time, are the vehicle to wealth creation. The Center for Research in Security Prices (CRSP), maintains the most inclusive database for stocks, mutual funds, and bonds, all indispensable for financial research.

Cash as an investment includes Certificates of Deposit (CDs), and other instruments that hold ready money. While the least volatile of all asset classes, cash investments provide safety but have lower total returns than bonds and stocks. Although all of the returns from cash are derived from interest, there are times when cash is a great investment, particularly during depressions when it is described as the "king" of all assets. Commonly defined as "opportunistic capital," one always requires a certain portion of total assets in cash for emergencies. However, there are times when cash is not as safe as one might think, particularly during periods of rising inflation. At maturity, you get your principle back from a CD plus interest, but when inflation is higher than the interest rate, you experience a negative real rate of return; hence the term "Certificate of Depreciation." Not only do CDs yield less than other investments, but the loss of "opportunity" can often be substantial. Nevertheless, because markets are emotional, the wise investor always has cash reserves to buy what others are throwing away. Nevertheless, cash has no intrinsic value and can be printed forever.

Bonds are debt obligations where the investor lends money for a certain period at a specified rate of interest. Bonds are issued by corporations, states, counties, municipalities, and special agencies, all of which are extremely important investment vehicles that are misunderstood, scorned by many, ridiculed by others, and overlooked by most. However, in the world of investing, bonds are a major tectonic plate, as the global value is said to approximate $90 trillion, and the US market is valued at $33 trillion. Their main advantage is a steady stream of income no matter what the nature of the financial markets. Four factors play a critical role in determining the merits of bond investing: the flow of money, the business cycle, interest rates, and inflation. The flow of money refers to how capital is flowing through the economy and the amount that might be borrowed. During an economic recovery, corporations and small businesses begin to borrow money to increase productive capacity and, in the process, compete with others for available funds driving up the cost of money. To attract money, banks increase interest rates and bond yields rise because bond prices fall opposite to the direction of interest rates. High inflation and interest rates combine to reduce the demand for money, bond prices decline and their yield increases. When buying individual bonds, be aware of duration, credit quality, and maturity. Duration refers to a bond's sensitivity to interest rates; credit quality refers to the credit-worthiness of the bond issuer; and maturity refers to the number of years remaining until the face value of the bond is repaid. In addition:

1. Foreign bonds are poorly correlated with US equivalents and, hence, offer opportunities. 2. The income that is produced by bonds provides seed money for new investments. 3. Bond investors wish to be paid a higher premium for holding debt for long periods. 4. Over time, income and safety dominate the attraction of the bond market. 5. The US bond market is double the size of the equity market. 6. The bond market will experience greater than normal volatility because never in the history of the American bond market have foreigners and the Fed owned so much. 7. Bonds offer steady income, the propensity to grow capital when interest is reinvested, and a mechanism to preserve wealth, achieve some capital appreciation, and enhance total returns. 8. Bonds offer stability and ballast to a portfolio because they behave counter to the equity market. For example, while equities declined by 19%, 11% and 21% in 2000, 2001, and 2002, bonds rose 12%, 8%, and 10% respectively for the same years. 9. Because bonds produce a higher yield than stocks, they are the preferred income-generating instruments. 10. There is an old adage on Wall Street that says, "You only have to get rich once." And when that occurs, "You preserve wealth by holding bonds." 11. Unless large sums of money are involved, bond fund investing is the preferred avenue as individual date-certain bond investing is costly. 12. Corporate bonds are the most speculative, and pay the highest interest. Bonds should be purchased at discount and at the height of interest rate cycles when bond prices are depressed. 13. Bond trading is a treacherous business and is best left to professionals. When considering a bond investment of $500,000 or more, seek professional advice. 14. Bond diversification refers to the purchase of a basket of different bonds such as high-yield, short- to long-term corporate and treasuries, TIPS, agencies, municipals, etc. 15. The percentage of your portfolio that would be allocated to bonds depends on age, investment objectives, sensitivity to risk, income, total net worth, the presence of an inflation-adjusted pension, etc. 18. If you are a holder of bonds, you are speculating that inflation will average less than historical norms. 19. Bond prices follow secular trends. Bond yields declined from 1865 to the end of 19th century; they rose for the first 20 years of the 20th century; fell between 1920 and 1946, and again during 1982-2012. Bond yields are rising as this is written, meaning that bond prices will fall for a very long time. They underperformed prior to 1982, outperformed the Total Market since 2000, and are about to enter a long cycle of underperformance. They will be the latest in a series of bubbles.

Bonds are rated by ability to pay interest and repay principal by four, bond-rating companies, of which Moody's and Standard & Poor's are the most important. For the sake of brevity, investment grade bonds rated in descending order are AAA (the highest quality), AA (high quality), A (upper medium grade), and BBB (medium grade). Also in descending order, the following are considered below investment grade: BB (lower medium grade), B (low grade), CCC (poor quality), CC (most speculative), and C (no interest being paid, or bankruptcy petition filed). The symbol "D" stands for default. When purchasing bonds, two, dominant issues determine portfolio composition: maturity and quality. For supreme safety, one should concentrate on short-term corporate investment grade, Treasuries, I-bonds, and Ginnie Maes. High-yield or "junk bonds" offer the highest risks.

There are many Treasury debt instruments of interest:

1. Bills (T-bills) that mature in less than a year, offer high liquidity, negligible price volatility, and offer low total returns. Notes mature between 1 to 10 years, and carry a higher yield. Long bonds carry the highest yield. The principal advantages of Treasuries rests on the issue of safety of principal and interest, availability in a wide range of maturity dates, no credit risk, but are affected by interest and inflation risk, and the fact that they carry no call provisions make them indispensable for individuals who have a low risk tolerance. A good sign of how good Treasuries really are is indicated by the fact that central banks, domestic banks, insurance companies, and other financial institutions hold more than 70%. Because they are exempt from state and local taxes, Treasuries offer better returns than CD accounts. Serious attention should be paid to the Treasury bill/equity ratio. When the bill yield is higher than the yield of the S&P 500, the equity market is considered to be overbought, and vice versa.

2. Zero-coupon ("strips") bonds are issued at a deep discount to their face value, with the interest paid at maturity. A main advantage is that they offer exceptional capital gains. A major disadvantage is that taxes (called imputed) must be paid annually, despite the fact that the owner of the bond does not receive the interest. Zero-coupon bonds are ideal for those who are not in need of current income and for tax-deferred accounts. They are to be purchased when interest rates are high; hence, for most investors, they are bonds to buy and hold.

3. TIPS are Treasury securities whose coupon and principal are indexed to inflation as measured by the CPI. The problem lies in the fact that the CPI is controlled by federal authorities that have a stake keeping the CPI as low as possible.

4. US savings bonds are grounded in safety of interest and principal, and they come in two flavors: EE and I. They can be purchased for as little as $50 and, despite their apparent simplicity, are riddled with qualifiers. Saving bonds have all the advantages of Treasuries. They have no local and state taxes and no default or call risk, and they offer competitive rates, they outperform CDs, and they can be used as collateral. While they appear to be identical, there are differences. EE bonds are attached to interest rates, and I bonds are pegged to inflation. EE bonds have their interest compounded semi–annually and are sold at half their face value.

I Bonds are sold at face value and grow in value with inflation-indexed provisions, with interest added monthly but paid when the bond is sold or matures.

5. Government-sponsored enterprise bonds (GSEs), first promulgated in the depths of the Great Depression to stimulate home construction, are debt obligations issued by agencies that are owned, backed, or sponsored by the American government. The most popular and important are Government National Mortgage Association (Ginnie Mae), Federal National Mortgage Association (Fannie Mae), and the Federal Home Loan Mortgage Corporation (Freddie Mac). There are significant differences among them, the most important being that GNMA bonds are guaranteed by the federal government, while the other two are not.

Treasuries are important because of higher yield, to preserve principal, seek a guaranteed source of income, and wish tax advantages. Although there are critical interest rate and opportunity risks, the compulsion to preserve principal is so overwhelming that individuals are often willing to sacrifice total return for safety. With corporate bonds, the investor is primarily seeking higher yields. In between these two extremes are municipal bonds, which offer safety, predictability, and tax advantages. When deciding where to invest either for the intermediate or long-term among cash, bonds, or equities, it is wise to remember the "5.8% solution." Over the course of the past 100 years, the average yield on the long Treasury has been 5.8% with no risk. Investors consider this an important benchmark when attempting to decide where to invest for the long run.

Corporate bonds are the most volatile, carry considerable credit and call risk, and pay the highest interest. Despite the fact that corporate bonds yield more than Treasuries and municipal bonds, many investors, who buy individual date-certain bonds, find that they are not liquid. They should be purchased only at a discount when interest rates have risen substantially and are held to maturity. These opportunities come two to three times in the course of a lifetime, so pick your moments carefully. There are many choices. 1. Investment-grade are the highest rated corporate bonds and compelling when their prices are depressed in an atmosphere of high interest rates, and particularly when their yield is at least 2% higher than the 30-year Treasury. 2. The allure of high-yield bonds rests with a higher yield and, hence, their name and popularity, but the risk factors (particularly liquidity and credit risk considerations) mitigate potential total returns as the majority are rated B or below, making them highly speculative, particularly in times of crisis. The margin of safety is dramatically improved when buying a good, no-load, high-yield mutual fund. 3. Corporate zero coupon bonds produce spectacular total returns when purchased during periods of high interest rates. 4. Preferred stock exhibits features of both bonds and stocks. It pays a fixed dividend, has a preferred claim over common stock shareholders, and trades like a bond as it responds inversely to interest rates. When purchased carefully, considerable capital gains can accrue in addition to the income stream. To compensate for their subordination to senior debt, they often offer a higher yield than high-yield bonds.

5. Convertible securities are hybrid investments whose advantage rests with high yield, plus expectations of a stock price rise that would produce capital gains when conversion takes place. 6. Foreign bonds have a long history of default, and because of higher risk and difficulty in purchasing, they offer a higher yield and require a considerable sum to purchase; hence, entry through a bond fund becomes a necessity. 7. Despite the fact that corporate bonds yield more than Treasuries and municipal bonds, many investors, who buy individually date-certain bonds find that they are not liquid, highly prone to credit risk, issuer risk and sector risk, and if bought to trade, market forces may turn the tide against investors for a prolonged period. They should be purchased only at bond market lows and held to maturity. For most investors, purchasing corporate bonds within a no-load fund family is the best course of action.

Municipal bonds are issued by states, cities, counties, and special governmental authorities that build and maintain public facilities like hospitals and infrastructure. There are three, major types with significant distinctions: 1. General obligation (GO) bonds are backed by the full faith and credit of the state and, because of taxing power, GO bonds are considered the safest. 2. Special purpose bonds include hospitals, colleges, healthcare facilities, etc. 3. Revenue bonds are those where revenue pays interest and principal to bond holders. Municipals often outperform taxable bonds and, if one lives in high tax states like New York or California and lie in a high tax bracket, tax savings can be substantial. The formula determining whether you are a potential beneficiary of municipal bond investing compares the tax-equivalent yield with that offered by the taxable bond. When a corporate bond yields 7%, and a municipal bond yields 5%, subtract your federal and state tax rate from 1. (If you are in the 35% tax bracket: 1-.35 = .65). Divide 5% tax-exempt yield by .65 and you get 7.6, a far better yield than the corporate, and with less risk. The municipal bond market, with aggregate valuations of $4 trillion, is large and popular. The fact that the wealthiest 20% hold more than three times the dollar amount of Treasuries attests to their popularity, safety, and tax advantages.

The risk and rewards of the "muni" market are considerably better than corporate bonds because they offer investors credit worthiness and considered second to Treasuries in risk. There are a number of compelling reasons why munis should be purchased by investors: 1. They are less volatile and much safer than corporate. 2. Munis have higher after-tax returns than other bonds of comparable maturity and credit quality, and often outperform taxable bonds in high tax states. 3. Munis trigger alternative minimum tax obligations, and are less transparent than Treasuries. 4. There are many reasons why investors invest in munis: to preserve wealth, to receive income, to reduce taxes, and to diversify. Note the fact that a 7% after tax return enables capital, with interest compounding, to double in less than 9 years making municipal bonds an extraordinary investment. 5. The ideal time to buy municipals is when their yield exceeds the 10-year Treasury, something that occurs frequently.

Buying individual, date–certain, munis takes plenty of skill, large dollars, and a good relationship with a broker who would offer good terms. Therefore, while it is beneficial to purchase municipals in the primary market, individuals rarely have the ability to purchase in competition with institutions. Similarly, purchasing in the secondary market is quite expensive since favorable, real time pricing and execution are beyond the scope of the small investor. A further problem is the lack of liquidity in a large universe of fragmented individual issues. Therefore, a municipal bond fund is the preferred entry to the municipal market because it provides diversification in terms of issuers, duration, low costs, diversification, and compounding of re-invested interest. For those with mixed emotions concerning municipal and high-yield, the first offers tax advantages in a taxable account and the second offers higher yields in a tax-sheltered account. Finally, Detroit, Michigan has defaulted for the second time in history, and joins another 39 cities, counties and special districts in bankruptcy.

# The Federal Reserve, Inflation, Interest Rates

## The Federal Reserve (FED)

The nation's financial health is regulated by monetary and fiscal policies. The latter, promulgated by Congress, refers to government spending and its influence on the budget, including the use of surpluses, and Byzantine tax legislation. The former refers to policies that affect the money supply, interest rates, margin requirements, buying and selling government securities, and changing bank reserve requirements, etc., all of which have a profound economic effect. By adjusting interest rates, the Fed is able to influence lending standards, equity prices, short-term bond yields, the rate of capital formation, and the value of the dollar. The above notwithstanding, current monetary policy is based on rising money creation and debt. The Fed is the "big Bertha," "the" most effective form of government as it has more control of the national economy than Congress, and is the most profitable financial institution in the country. The Fed creates money from nothing, loans it and charges interest. It also buys Treasuries with zero-cost money and charges the taxpayer interest. In addition, its policies often induce capital consumption and mal-investments, encourage consumption and debt, reward corruption, and help to exaggerate business cycles. The Fed is Prometheus unbound and biased in favor of institutions.

The Fed was established in 1914 as a private corporation registered in the State of Delaware by a group of domestic and foreign banks. The US taxpayer owns no stock in the corporation and its decisions are made in secret. According to Ben Bernanke, "Our mission, as set forth by Congress, is a critical one; to preserve price stability, to foster maximum sustainable growth in output and employment, and to promote a stable and efficient financial system that serves all Americans well and fairly." In the process, the Fed has become the largest private for-profit US enterprise. Since its founding, the Fed has functioned without audit, scrutiny and oversight. Its budget is unknown, the remuneration of its chairperson is not disclosed, and all security purchase programs, credit facilities, and gold reserves remain hidden from public view. The Fed regulates thousands of financial companies, banks, thrifts, and exercises direct oversight of all. It also provides financial services to domestic and foreign depository institutions. Furthermore, the Fed is incapable of letting the "invisible hand" operate. Alan Greenspan, for example, constantly intervened to reward Wall Street, and to appease the White House and Congress. At every opportunity, he slashed interest rates, bailed out banks that made risky loans to Latin America and elsewhere, and lowered interest rates for prolonged periods fueling housing bubbles. In addition, his successor is exhibiting more aggressive "easing" proclivities, which encourages consumption and additional debt. Thus far, Ben Bernanke's tenure at the Fed indicates that he is no student of history. He refuses to note that more debt does not extinguish insolvency, that it cannot force businesses to expand operations, and banks to lend. The public is also unaware of "hidden powers"–a clause in the Fed Charter calls for action to be taken during periods of "exigent circumstances." In the main, the Fed is a financial purveyor to the largest banks. It seeks power and exercises enormous control over the government. It has failed in the fulfillment of its two historic mandates–maximum employment and price stability–since its establishment.

Fed monetary policy, therefore, is important. A "loose" policy means that there will be sufficient liquidity, lower interest rates, uncompromising lending, uninhibited consumption and borrowing until inflation rears its ugly head. The Fed has had a zero interest policy since 2005. The Fed, in essence, is saying to the American people, and especially retirees, "We will pay you nothing for CDs, nothing for Treasuries, and nothing for money market funds." The only alternatives open are malls, casinos, and the stock market, all of which impoverish 80% of the population. The Fed is supposed to even the peaks and troughs of the business cycle and never allow "panics." Yet the Fed has been central to all financial disasters with its accommodating "easy credit" policies. The flaw in the ointment is that it often introduces mechanisms where resources are misallocated leading to reduced saving, trade and budgetary deficits, consumer indebtedness, lack of capital investment, etc. When it wishes to tighten, the process is reversed, leading to increased interest rates, credit contraction, recession, and additional negative, long-term elements. While the "boom and bust" nature of markets is inevitable, Fed interference has exaggerated the amplitude and duration of these events. The Fed is the only private institution in the nation that manages monetary policy by producing money out of thin air and receives interest for the privilege. Thomas Jefferson had it right when he said, "...banking establishments are more dangerous than standing armies." In a similar vain, Paul Volcker stated that, "The truly unique power of a central bank, after all, is the power to create money, and ultimately the power to create is the power to destroy." Faced with the fact that the $US is not backed by anything entails no monetary discipline. Therefore, under Bernanke's leadership, gold has risen by more than 400%, inflation rose by 19%, equities returned 6%, employment has risen, and the dollar and home prices declined.

The issue of a strong Fed, or no Fed, is defined clearly by the following contrasting points of view. Mayer Amschel Rothschild said, "Permit me to issue and control the money of the nation and I care not who makes its laws," and Joseph Stiglitz, in 2010, said that the Fed is so fraught with conflicts that it is "corrupt" and "undermines" democracy. Although the Fed is supposed to be apolitical, it is obsessed with expanding its powers. Ben Bernanke, before Congress, attempted to make a case that the Fed should not only keep all regulatory banking duties and instead add others. This comes from the chairperson who would not regulate before and after the collapse of the financial sector in 2007. What is good for the Fed is not necessarily good for the nation. In the words of President James Garfield: "Whoever controls the volume of money in any country is absolute master of all industry and commerce…and when you realize that the entire system is very easily controlled, one way or another, by a few powerful men at the top, you will not have to be told how periods of inflation and depression originate." Writing in the 1930s, Rep. Louis T. McFadden had this to say about the Fed: "Every effort has been made by the Federal Reserve Board to conceal its powers, but the truth is the Fed has usurped the government. It controls everything here (in Congress) and controls all our foreign relations. It makes and breaks governments at will…When the FED was passed, the people of the United States did not perceive that a world system was being set up here…A super-state controlled by international bankers, and international industrialists acting together to enslave the world for their own pleasure." It is obvious that since inception, the Fed has shamelessly sacrificed America's future in order to curry political favor; it has debased the currency, rewarded its allies, and has manipulated markets. Beginning with Alan Greenspan and accelerating under Ben Bernanke, the credibility of the Fed has eroded to dangerous levels. Three months before the global credit crunch and subprime losses were revealed, Ben Bernanke said, "We do not expect significant spillovers from the subprime market to the rest of the economy or to the financial system."

The overt and covert Fed activities are increasingly intrusive and highly disruptive of free market forces. Not only do Fed activities interfere with markets cleansing unsuccessful firms, but also its actions exaggerate business cycles, postpone economic recoveries, strengthen Plunge Group activities, introduce a good dose of public fear, and make the public more reliant on federal stimulus programs. Moreover, its chairperson repeatedly expresses the thought in front of Congressional Committees that it will retain its right to operate in secrecy and that it is protected by "Rule 16." The causes for the financial crisis are laid square on the steps of the Fed as its manipulation of credit, interest rates, money supply, involvement with Congress, and its incestuous relationship with Wall Street encourage bubbles to form. In addition, the Fed has been characterized as a cartel, and for good reason. It is neither federal, a reserve of anything, and operates with no fiduciary responsibilities to the taxpayer. It is not a federal agency, nor mentioned in the Constitution. It is a "private corporation" owned by an international cartel that exists to make profits and whose membership and loyalty is unknown to US taxpayers. It is also insolvent, as it owns more than $1.2 trillion mortgage-backed securities that no one else wants, as they are nearly worthless, has increased its balance sheet to more than $3.4 trillion, and overreached along a dangerous path when it nationalized 80% of AIG without shareholder approval. It also has a dismal record in regulating banks, and encouraging corruption. The Fed has not made attempts at financial reform in the wake of the 2007 financial debacle, nor has it called for criminal prosecution of the major culprits. Alan Blinder, former Vice Chairman of the Fed, said, "The last duty of a Central Banker is to tell the public the truth." Furthermore, the Fed is guilty of what Friedrich Hayek called the "fatal conceit," or the arrogant belief that someone knows everything at any one time to plan and manage an economy without mistakes. The Fed is of the opinion that state intervention is compulsory, that free markets are unable to correct cyclical behavior, and that it has the ability to eliminate business cycles. "Too big to fail" has become the operative expression by which taxpayers are forced to accept corporate losses.

Fed actions affect the value of the dollar in many significant ways. Currently, the $US is falling because the Fed wishes it to fall, and over the long-term, the objective is to debase the dollar to the point where the US can pay its obligations with monopoly money. A weak dollar raises equity prices, helps exports, discourages tourism, and imports become more expensive, thus promoting inflation. If the decline in the $US is sustained, the cost of capital will rise for manufacturers as well as the cost of credit for consumers. It is hard to imagine that the so-called finest minds at the Fed are unable to understand that the nation cannot spend its way out of debt, that the nation cannot live beyond its means forever, and that you cannot debase the currency without making it worthless. Ben Bernanke's career has been based on the notion that printing money will eventually reverse any negative economic condition.

The case for Fed policies is based on Keynesian ideas, many of which are outdated. Lord Keynes was writing at a time when more than 70% of a DMs population was employed in secondary activities, mining, and agriculture–all wealth creating in reference to service industries that consume wealth. Today, DMs are overwhelmingly tertiary, and the basic tenets of Keynes are no longer relevant. The US is suffering from a lack of structural reforms; something that quantitative easing will not cure. What the Fed is doing is buying time by postponing the day of reckoning. Another disturbing element is that the government's share of the economy grew by 12% during the years 2007-2009. Now with QE3, it is slated to grow even faster. In 2011, "Operation Twist" was initiated in which short-term debt was exchanged for long-term debt, increasing Treasury holdings to $1.6 trillion. QE3, the most aggressive stimulus in history, is characterized as open-ended with zero-interest rates pushed to 2015, thus promoting the process of "financial repression" through negative interest rates. The Fed will be purchasing $85-plus billion each month. To date, while no QE program has worked to expectations, it is threatening to introduce QE-infinity. Marc Faber is of the opinion that it will rise to $1 trillion monthly. Because foreigners are not purchasing Treasuries in sufficient amounts, QE will continue, as the Fed is the buyer of last resort. To date, it is the most bizarre monetary experiment in US history, as it is willfully promoting uncontaminated inflation. Therefore, markets in recent history have been distorted and no longer "true" and "honest," as the Fed encouraged speculation by offering incentives for institutions to borrow at 0.20%. The idea that the government can stimulate GDP growth with historic spending of money it borrows is unique. Making matters worse are governmental pronouncements that spending cuts are similar to debt reduction and consistent with a zero interest rate policy, something that has prolonged the addiction of cheap money. In the meantime, the fraud is methodically devaluing the $US, and the nation's credit worthiness has recently been downgraded from AAA to AA. Apparently, Fed-induced credit is good, and more Fed credit is that much better. Given the fact that the present chairman of the Fed is an academician who has never worked in the real world, and assumes to be an "expert" on the Great Depression, will continue to provide liquidity until he kills the economy and $US. The stagnant economic picture is described by the Fed Chairman as being "transitory," and not all existing economic problems are the fault of the Fed." It appears that QE will never end unless a *Kobayashi Maru* (pressure cooker) event occurs.

## Inflation

There are various explanations for the causes of inflation. Money creation-push inflation, a common explanation, refers to excess printing of fiat currency, and the excess credit that accompanies it. In the words of Milton Friedman, "Inflation is always and everywhere a monetary phenomenon." Monetary debasement, therefore, has always led to inflation. When a government prints excess quantities of money several things happen: interest rates, energy and food prices rise immediately, the saving rate declines, capital investment falls, unemployment rises, "real" wages decline, and an inflationary climate develops ruining the national economy. Crisis-push inflation, or those caused by physical disasters. War-push inflation caused by military conflict, disruption of normal economic conditions, loss of life and property, and the longer it lasts the worse it gets. Cost-push inflation is caused by high labor costs often induced by strong union demands, but also in geographical regions where labor is scarce and where little or no substitutions are available. Many economists are of the belief that as long as labor inflation remains benign, the general inflation rate will be restrained. Do not believe it! As long as excess money creation is taking place, inflation will rise to dangerous levels. Profit-push inflation is caused by arbitrary corporate price increases by monopolies, cartels, etc. Keynes thought that spending was the key to economic growth. If the economy is sluggish, the solution is simple: print money to induce spending, and vice versa. The problem is that politicians rarely wish to squeeze the public dole, and when they do, they over do, inducing recessions.

Inflation is widely accepted in its early stages by just about everybody as it stimulates economic activity, government spending, stock prices and wages. Unfortunately, this early euphoria turns to economic bitterness as purchasing power erodes. The relationship between the production of fiat money and price escalation is obvious to the blind, is not natural in the Aristotelian sense, but something created intentionally by man. When allowed to continue, it is sophisticated theft, and nothing more than embezzlement, done legally and creatively. Politicians, who love to spend money and not raise taxes, create a perfect symbiotic relationship that can last a surprisingly long time. Eventually, the piper must be paid, and it is usually through a massive transfer of wealth. Inflation is a deadly drug, a furtive sedative whose lethal effects take time to be realized. Inflation, therefore, encourages and exaggerates the inevitable boom and bust nature of business cycles; reduces investment capital by discouraging savings and frugality; it prevents the accumulation of wealth, encourages waste; discourages efficiency; decreases the supply of investment capital; increases the cost of production; encourages speculation, erodes purchasing power, degrades currencies, and creates economic dislocations. It introduces a large element of uncertainty and, hence, dissuades investment and saving. It devalues income on interest-bearing securities; encourages the output of substandard goods (*ersatz* products, like watered-down beer, cardboard shoes, etc.) and spawns social and political turmoil. Credit expansion is the Fed's principal means to ameliorate all problems. To the Fed, "inflate" is the most significant operative word in the lexicon. No matter what the exigency might be, the solution is always "inflate"–post-haste. In late 2000, oil was $22 the barrel, the euro was $.90 per dollar, and gold sold for less than $280 per ounce. Within a few years oil has risen to $145 the barrel, the euro is $1.35 per dollar, gold stands over $1,600 an ounce, and the annual cost of housing an inmate in a New York City jail exceeds $167,000. In the end, *cui bono:* who benefits from inflation? Political elites and those in the top 10% of the income ladder receive access to new money first and benefit first through asset appreciation. Those who occupy the lower 80%, suffer the most because they lack access to credit and are most subject to rising prices. Since the biggest debtor in the world is the US, it is also the biggest beneficiary. It was Ronald Reagan who said it best: "Inflation is as violent as a mugger, as frightening as an armed robber, and as deadly as a hit man." The "Great Inflation" is coming because it is inevitable when the national debt and monetary growth are increasing faster than GDP. Inflation also means the decline of the $US. The government means to destroy it in order to pay debts, to improve the economy, to wage currency war, hide depression, and to enhance political interests of those in power.

## Austrians and Keynesians

The Austrian Economics School believes in limited government, a gold standard, sound money policies, free markets, protection of property and personal freedom. With minor modifications, this school is the antithesis of the "Keynesian School," the most fashionable guiding economic policy prevailing for three generations. It is commonly referred to as "statism," where the central bank and government conspire to reduce the peaks and troughs of the business cycle through aggressive monetary and fiscal policies. The Greenspan/Bernanke strategy of not wasting opportunity: when a crisis arises flood the market with money! Where implemented, this policy has always promoted inflation.

## Inflation Characteristics

1. Rising inflation causes a decline in financial markets. 2. It destroys a national economy, promotes civil strife, decimates retirement plans, discourages saving and thrift, encourages gambling, class warfare, and expands debt. 3. Inflation compounds making its erosive force that much more lethal. 4. In 1966, Alan Greenspan wrote, "In the absence of the gold standard, there is no way to protect savings from confiscation through inflation. There is no safe store of value. If there were, the government would have to make its holding illegal, as was done in the case of gold…Deficit spending is simply a scheme for the confiscation of wealth. Gold stands in the way of this insidious process. It stands as a protector of property rights, and in the words of J.P. Morgan: "Only gold is money and nothing else." If one grasps this, one has no difficulty in understanding the statists' antagonism toward the gold standard." Hemingway is alleged to have said, "The first panacea for a mismanaged nation is inflation of the currency; the second is war. Both bring a temporary prosperity; both bring a permanent ruin. Both are the refuge of political and economic opportunists." 5. Today every impediment to inflation has been removed. The new mantra is "inflation is good" and, according to Bill Gross in 2009, "Inflation is the only way out of the crisis." Recently Ben Bernanke said, "The economy cannot grow its way out of its fiscal problems." 6. History reveals two major, global, super- inflationary spikes. The first began in the early 1500s and lasted until the mid-1600s; the second began during World War I. The largest period of no inflation began in the mid-1600s and continued until World War I, with only one significant exception: the period of the French Revolution to Waterloo. The relationships between war, monetary expansion and inflation are ever-present. Domestically, it is important to note that between 1775 and 1779, when Congress issued "Continentals," it ushered the worst inflation in US history. Inflation was low throughout the 19th century due to the gold standard, but sustained inflation is a phenomenon of the 20th century. 7. In the words of Ludwig von Misses: "Government is the only institution that can take a valuable commodity like paper, and make it worthless by applying ink…There is no reason to be proud of deficit spending or to call it progress." 8. The association of inflation to equity market performance is illustrated thusly: Inflation in 1971 was 3.5%, 3.4% in 1972, 8.8% in 1973, and 12.2% in 1974. The S&P 500 index for the same years was 14.3%, 18.9%, -14.7%, and -26.5%. Since 2006 the dollar's purchasing power has declined by 18%, 24% since 2002, 86% since 1971, and 97% since 1914, not much for purchasing power and price stability. 9. Since the government is the world's largest issuer of debt, it has a stake in promoting inflation. In the words of Ben Bernanke: "The US government has a technology, called a printing press that allows it to produce as many US dollars as it wishes at essentially no cost." 10. All inflations end with rising asset prices, debased currencies, and a flight to "tangibles." 11. High inflation begets higher interest rates. 12. The rate of

inflation is accelerating and that means that Treasuries and the $US will fall. The new Fed chairperson, Janet Yellen, has announced that inflation will rise in an effort to stimulate economic growth, and would not do anything to restrict fractional reserve lending. 13. The government benefits from low interest rates and high inflation. At the time of this writing, savers are losing 4% and the government gaining $600 billion through the hidden tax of inflation.

The relationship between government and military actions highlight the fact that without the production of fiat, the wars that the US has engaged in have been unrelenting in destroying the value of the dollar. No other country spends as much on the military as the US, no other country has troops in 70-plus countries, and no other nation has committed so much money to an ill-defined, unformulated war called "terror." "War is a racket," said General Smedley Butler, describing the redistribution of money as a direct cause. As long as the preemptive military option is alive and well implemented, the debasement of the dollar will continue. Inflation caused by conditions of scarcity occurred in 1776, 1812, the Civil War, the Spanish-American War, and during the periods of World War I, WWII, Vietnam, and the post 2000 period. Usually, these inflationary periods are of short duration because they disappear immediately after the conclusion of military conflict, but the post-9/11 period is different. The present unofficial inflationary figure of 2.5% is neither benign, innocent, or low, but a figure large enough with which to be reckoned. The degree of propaganda has been so effective that most Americans accept 3% inflation as normal. As this is written, the present inflationary cycle is about to heave like a horst that threatens to dwarf those of the past.

A few related clarifications: 1. Hyperinflation is uncontrolled inflation, eventually leading to a major breakdown of the bond market. It is more common than one realizes, mostly in TWs where it causes devastating social upheaval as it underscores government insolvency, and promotes economic chaos. Few escape the disastrous effects as standards and levels of living are depressed, and basic prevailing cultural values are destroyed. Hyperinflation of post-World War II Hungary reached a figure of 41 followed by 15 zeroes. Turkey in the 1970s issued a 20 million Lira note that would buy a cup of coffee. Zimbabwe recently printed a $100 trillion bill that would not even buy a loaf of bread. Globally, there have been 87 episodes of hyperinflation in the past 100 years. 2. Stagflation: this is a combination of inflation and deflation, characterized by weak economic activity, rising unemployment and inflation, a declining equity market, and rising interest rates and commodity prices. The incongruence of rising inflation in combination with slow economic growth and rising unemployment means that sooner or later, a severe economic crisis will envelope the nation. The very policies that produced stagflation in the 1970s are occurring now, the only major differences being that the magnitude of the problem now is infinitely worse. For corporations, stagflation translates to increased costs and reduced sales, and for consumers rising prices and stagnant and/or falling incomes reduces consumption, and, if prolonged, it generates Verdun-type attrition patterns as the devastation in purchasing power becomes unrelenting. Stagflation will continue because the nation is borrowing $4 billion daily; debt is growing at 7% annually, inflation rising at 5% annually, and GDP at 1.5%. Either inflation destroys bonds or deflation destroys stock prices; in periods of stagflation both are destroyed. The US is currently in the fifth inning of the "Great Stagflation," "Greater Depression," or "Great Correction." The number of factors that are needed to be "corrected" is historic. 3. Deflation. The cycle of deflation is characterized by a decline in the money supply, excess capacity generating reduced pricing power resulting in competitive devaluation, prompting tariffs and protectionist policies, beggar-thy-neighbor tactics, etc. While the Fed considers deflation anathema, it remains a likely scenario for several reasons. First, due to wage differentials between DMs and EMs, the price of basic manufactured goods will continue their downward spiral. Second, nominal salaries will remain flat. Third, with 65% unable to afford a median-priced home, the housing bubble will decline further. Fourth, consumption will decline further due to reduced discretionary income.

In the final analysis, George Bernard Shaw said it best: "The most important thing about money is to maintain its stability. You have to choose between trusting the natural stability of gold and the honesty and intelligence of members of the government. With due respect for these gentlemen, I advise you, as long as the capitalist system lasts, to vote for gold." Joshua Stamp, Director of the Bank of England in 1928, said "But if you wish to remain slaves of bankers and pay the cost of your own slavery, let them create money." Today, the illusion of prosperity is everywhere. The Fed is printing $120 million an hour, and, eventually, that will translate to inflation. QE stimulus packages are keeping the equity and bond markets elevated, creating the illusion of a "wealth effect," all necessary features to prevent a meltdown of the national economy.

From birth, inflation is your shadow, a steady companion, and you must invest accordingly to avoid it. What to do? 1. Taking Will Roger's advice, invest in inflation because it is rising. Buy and hold quality dividend-rich stocks whose dividends grow faster or keep pace with inflation, and reinvest all dividends. 2. Do not trust Fed propaganda. 3. Stay clear of dollar-denominated debt. 4. Since Treasuries and CDs offer no protection against inflation, invest in real tangible assets. 5. Be prepared for price controls and government imposed import restrictions. 6. Reduce expenses, assume extra work and start a business.

## Measuring Inflation

1. The Consumer Price Index (CPI) measures the price of selected goods: food and beverages; housing; apparel; transportation; medical care; recreation; services purchased by an average consumer, etc. 2. The Producers Price Index (PPI) is a broad index that measures the cost of raw materials and services to producers of physical goods from the seller's perspective. 3. Wholesale Price Index (WPI) measures the price of goods at the wholesale level and is said to be an advance

warning of the direction of inflation. Because the government controls the definition of the CPI and manipulates the PPI, the latter is not as accurate as the WPI. 4. The Employment Cost Index (ECI) measures aggregate employee costs from wages to benefits and all manner of intangibles, and, therefore, is usually a highly critical metric about the health and direction of the national economy. 5. The Dow Jones Commodity Spot Price Index seeks to track raw material price movements and is considered an important indicator as the index offers direction of both deflationary and inflationary tendencies. 6. While there are many other esoteric and hard to find indexes, the CPI is widely accepted as "the" most important measure of inflation.

The CPI metric is flawed from several perspectives. In its simplest form, the CPI refers to a basket of goods and services, numbering in the thousands, of which about 450 are considered important. The figure is published monthly and has huge implications affecting all aspects of the investment arena. The cost of a basket in broad terms consists of housing (44%), food (17%), transportation (17%), healthcare (7%), recreation (6%), clothing (4%), and education (3%), other (2%). It has become over the years the single most important statistic for retired people, the employed, and those on public assistance because the CPI is the benchmark for cost of living increases, labor contracts, etc. The Bureau of Labor Statistics, which compiles and publishes CPI statistics, underestimates the rate of inflation in order to reduce the above obligations to a bare minimum. A high figure fosters public outrage, and, therefore, the federal government prefers to cook the books as it camouflages unpalatable realities. A low CPI indicates a lower inflation rate, and inflates the magnitude of GDP, a figure that federal authorities constantly like to boast. Mark Twain reported that the British Prime Minister uttered the following. "There are three kinds of lies: lies, damn lies, and statistics." In the main, the nation is systematically misled and swindled.

The CPI is understated because historic measures of price changes in the magical, fixed basket allow for substitutions. The problem is that once you embark on the substitution road to measuring the CPI, the metrics change radically as substitutions do not necessarily measure a constant standard of living. Furthermore, the problems created by hedonistic metrics are compounded by the fact that once the price of anything increases, it automatically receives a lower weight, thus lowering the CPI. However, if the price of a particular item declines, it automatically gets a higher weight. Therefore, if the same CPI were used today as in 1970, S.S. checks would be 73% higher. With inflation "massaged," the government doesn't pay as much in S.S. COLA increases, and it cheats TIPs holders of their due. It molds public opinion by repeating the big lie that inflation is under control, and mollifies public dissent. Most important, it fails to consider the cost of government, and fails to compute tax increases, all manner of subsidies, tariffs, fees, regulatory costs, etc. Published CPI figures, therefore, are fraudulent. The most egregious distortions in the CPI involve "intervention analysis," "geometric weightings," "hedonistic regressions," and "imputations." In addition,

Arthur Burns first introduced the concept of a CPI "core" in 1973-1974 in order to reduce the importance of food and energy, the very items that are used each day. A lower CPI saves local, state, federal governments and private industry an enormous sum of money. The Fed wishes through inflation to reduce debt and promote more spending. A high figure necessitates tax increases, and therefore, the federal government prefers to cook the books as it camouflages unpalatable realities. Despite the disharmony about its measurement, the CPI is mainly a metric unique to every household, as they are circumscribed by unique purchasing elements. The CPI tracks consumer spending and not the cost of living, the latter greater than 5% in 2013. It does not reflect reality, as it fails to accurately measure the purchasing power of earned income. Since 1980, the cost of a medium-sized car has risen by 187%, food by 490%, energy by 722%, medical care by 1222%, and college tuition by 1339%.

## The Importance of Interest Rates

1. Interest rates are considered the single most important determinant of market behavior, affecting everything and anything of economic significance. They influence the direction of bond movements and since the bond market is more important than equities in terms of total valuation, interest rates are central to broad market fundamental impacts. Therefore, interest is the most important price in any economy. Interest rates are the principal drivers of bonds, stocks and commodities, and, as interest rates fluctuate so do, the underlying values of all assets, particularly interest-sensitive assets. Since interest rates and inflationary patterns involve cyclical behavior, the investor must be diligent and patient to make the necessary entry and exit decisions. Interest rates fell to 1.93% in 1946, rose to 16.4% in 1982, only to fall to record lows in 2013. The most important interest indicators are the movement of the 10 and 30-year Treasury yields because they influence the direction of all markets. When inflation and interest rates rise, a vicious cycle of negative, economic effects are placed in motion and reverberate throughout the economy. Not only does the cost of money increase for industry, but the general price level also rises, displacing money from uses that are more productive. A strong economy raises fears of inflation and promotes higher interest rates, and a declining economy is affected by lower Fed-induced interest rate declines to stimulate both consumption and capital good investment. During periods of falling interest rates, buy real estate, stocks and bonds. During periods of stagflation, buy commodities and real estate.

2. Interest rates fall in a weak economy and rise as the level of economic growth increases. As the pace of economic conditions improves corporations borrow money to grow, bond prices rise, and yields decline. This continues for variable periods until the economy peaks and interest rates fall increasing yields, as interest rates will always fluctuate in response to economic conditions. When the Fed creates bank deposits out of thin air making loans available at below-market rates, mal-investment and overcapacity results, setting the stage for the next

recession or depression. Many welcome the easy credit policy: stock-market investors, homebuilders, homebuyers, congressional spendthrifts, bankers, and many other consumers who enjoy borrowing at low rates and not worrying about repayment. When the cost of money approaches 0%, it produces rising asset prices, and as long as Fed policies depress interest rates, the only game in town is equities.

3. The negative real interest rates under Greenspan and Bernanke discouraged saving, encouraged borrowing and speculation, led to bubbles, misallocated resources and weakened the value of the dollar. While low interest rates stimulate asset values, high rates encourage the importation of money and promote saving. A highly leveraged economy is unable to endure a sharp rise in interest rates. With household debt above 130% of GDP, any quick upward movements in interest rates will have a negative economic impact. Rising interest rates from present levels will also trigger major financial meltdown for cities.

4. Interest rates vary more than most people realize. Over the past 40 years, they have varied more than 50 basis points over a period of six months and, hence, volatility is an unpleasant fact in the bond market. The principal driver influencing bond prices are interest rates, and important because bonds are the principal asset class that continually competes with the equity market for its share of a portfolio's composition. There is no such thing as "the ultimate, long-term investment" because at any given time the prevailing economy will have one or several investments that can be referred to as "better." Generally, the worst year in bond market returns will be better than the worst year in equity markets. Bond investing demands attention to more than one event at a time, just as a stew requires a sharp eye on temperature, time, gradual additions of ingredients, and attention to spices. Navigating the bond market requires a fast hand on interest rates, a handle on the prospects of being repaid, and an eye on inflation. For retirees, high interest rates produce plenty of interest from CDs, but rising inflation destroys purchasing power at the same time. The seesaw continues in the other extreme: low interest rates generate little income, while low inflation destroys purchasing power less. When interest rates are rising, or are high by historical standards, they stifle capital investment, reduce consumer expenditures, and decimate the bond market. Interest rates, therefore, should be constantly monitored by serious investors as they reveal how best to invest money.

5. The yield curve helps to assess risk associated with various bond maturities as it illustrates the relationship between the yields of short and long-term bonds of the same quality. When short-term rates are lower than long-term, the yield curve is said to be "positive" or "normal," and when short-term yields are higher than the long-term, they are "inverted," and prognosticate recession.

6. Interest rates are responsible for more than 80% of the movements of both stocks and bonds. Therefore, it behooves the astute investor to invest in those asset classes that respond to interest rate and inflationary fluctuations. Since interest rate

and inflationary patterns evolve gradually and over time, the investor must be diligent and patient to make entry and exit decisions. When the CPI and PPI remain flat or trend lower, bond and equity prices rise and vice versa. Utilities, banks, financials, REITs, preferred stock, and all bonds (but especially long-term) are sensitive to interest rates. In an environment of rising interest rates, it is compulsory to look for company potential to raise dividends/distributions, and those who benefit from rising rates (financials). One can boost total returns in the present low-interest environment through convertible and high-yield bonds, and dividend-paying stocks.

# Equities

Ibbotson Associates reports that the period 1926-2003 produced 10.3% returns in large-cap stocks, 12.5% in small-cap stocks, 5.9% in long-term corporate bonds, 5.4% in long-term government bonds, and 3.8% in 30-day Treasury bills. Jeremy Siegel states, "For 10-year horizons, stocks beat bonds about 80 percent of the time; for 20-year horizons, it is over 90 percent of the time; and over 30-year horizons, it is virtually 100 percent of the time. Time, therefore, is always on the side of the prudent, disciplined and patient equity investor. The odds of losing money in any one-year period are 28%, and 10% in any five-year period. The odds of beating inflation increases from a 1-year period to a 20-year period by 68% and 100%, respectively, and the chance of equities beating bonds increases from 62% to 97% for the same periods. The crucial point to remember is that over the entire investable life of an individual, time is an ally that one must embrace and nurture. The last 30-year period in which bonds beat stocks ended at the onset of the U.S. Civil War." The superiority of the equity market throughout history, therefore, is quite impressive. In addition, up markets outnumber down markets by seven to three. Equities offer high risks and high returns; cash offers low risk and low returns, and Treasury bonds fall somewhere in between these two extremes. Over the course of the past 80 years, large-cap growth stocks rose by 11% annually, large value stocks by 14%, small-cap growth by 11.8%, and small-cap value by nearly 16%. The correlation of several asset classes with the S&P 500 is significant and worthy of note. Where 1.00 indicates perfect correlation and 0.00 no correlation, commodities are the least correlating with 0.01; large-cap stocks are most with 0.94; bonds 0.23; real estate 0.52, international 0.52; small-cap growth 0.78; and mid-cap value 0.87. While equities have outperformed all other financial assets over time, not all equities are created equal. Those that have outperformed over time are the value-oriented and dividend-paying stocks that also exhibited growth characteristics. While equities are the preferred investment in the US, sovereign bonds and cash are favored in Europe, and real estate and precious metals in TW nations. Equities, real estate, and precious metals are the only asset classes that consistently outperform inflation over the long run.

## Investing Indicators

The Holy Grail of investing is to discover a flawless indicator of buying and selling assets for profit commensurate with risk. Other than reiterating the old adage of "buying low and selling high," there are no systems that can offer profit without risk to capital. However, this has not stopped people from Yale and Wall Street from attempting, and when it comes to gastronomy there is more than one recipe for making any dish, and when it comes to investing, the approaches are just as varied. In fact, history is replete with names that attempted to outfox financial markets. The nerds, considered the smartest of the smart at Long-Term Capital Management, thought that they had contrived the perfect strategy for making money. Heavily leveraged, this firm provided investors with spectacular returns for several years, but despite the fact that it employed two Nobel Prize winners, many PhDs, and brilliant mathematicians; it lost 90% of its value in just one month. In the end, they could not outsmart the market as two low probability events converged to implode the investment company in 1998. Since the brightest of the bright fail, what chance does the retail investor have in outperforming the market? There is a lesson and a moral here: always stay clear of false prophets, charlatans, glib tongues and pens, and balance your portfolio to suit the prevailing investment climate to your objectives. Nevertheless, the following approach the topic of investing differently, and all have been successful. Peter Lynch focused on growth companies and considered bonds a losing investment; Benjamin Graham was a fundamentalist with a penchant for low-risk companies; William O'Neil, the antithesis of a fundamental investor, assumed more risk and developed a disciplined disposition when it came to purchasing and selling; David Dreman is a classic value investor who holds positions for long periods; and John Bogle represents the classic buy and hold index investor.

For the retail investor, the compilation and monitoring of economic and stock indicators are beyond competency and best left to professionals. The federal government on a monthly and quarterly manner publishes a prodigious amount of economic data intended to portray the status of the American economy. Likewise, private industry also collects and publishes an incredible amount of information. Taken together, there are three basic indicator divisions: leading, coincident, and lagging. Leading indicators are the appetizers of what is in store for the economy and includes such items as consumer installment debt, corporate profits, stock prices, new unemployment claims, interest rates, weekly initial unemployment claims, new orders for manufactured goods, building permits, etc. Coincident indicators vary with the vagaries of the business cycle, and refer to long-term bond yields, retail sales, personal income, industrial production, etc. Lagging indicators include change in the CPI, commercial and industrial loans outstanding, etc. The critical metric is the Index of Leading Indicators. At the beginning of each month, the government releases figures that receive an enormous amount of market commentary as it is supposed to forecast market direction. Nevertheless, leading economic indicators are notorious for sending false signals. For the retail investor, the most significant economic indicators are the 10/30-year Treasury yield, interest rate, inflation rate, retail sales, industrial production, employment, and real disposable income.

However one defines and categorizes the above, they represent important components of the economy. The problem is that not all indicators move in the same direction at the same time, or interact with each other with the same intensity. Every economic indicator provides a small piece of information that often influences market behavior in the short term, and when several converge to reinforce each other, they generate a trend that can last decades. The above notwithstanding, equity market returns are a function of GDP growth, interest and inflation rates, earnings, and dividend yields.

## Fundamental Analysis (FA)/Value Analysis (VA)

FA attempts to reveal the value of a company by analyzing earnings, sales growth, debt, and other vital "internals" by determining the critical parameters of "undervalued" (in order to buy), and "overvalued" (in order to sell). The fundamentalist does not believe that markets are efficient citing the fact that stock prices often deviate from their intrinsic worth. FA presents formidable obstacles to the retail investor because the latter has no way of knowing what the market potential is of the company in question. He has no way of knowing the quality of the company's management, its sales organization, the *spirit de corps* of the work force, and the effectiveness of the competition. "Intrinsic value" is generally defined as the difference between stock price and the value of the underlying business of a company. Price is simply a number between the last transaction between a buyer and seller and nothing else; it is quite simple to understand. Value, however, is more complicated, and mainly an opinion of what the price of a particular asset ought to be. Therefore, while opinions on "value" are variable, price is not as it is based not on emotion, but on cold "fundamentals." During periods of euphoria and depression, the varying opinions, laden with emotion create an environment where "value" can be overpriced or underpriced. FA is complicated, laborious, highly sophisticated and beyond the scope of the ordinary investor. FA arrives, like all tomatoes, in many varieties, colors, and sizes. In the final analysis, value investing refers to buying a sound business that generates cash flow from which shareholders will be reimbursed with rising dividends or price appreciation. History has documented its success, especially when future cash flow is purchased at a discount.

Whenever investors discover a deep discount, they buy and are referred to as "value" investors. When the stock price is above what is considered intrinsic value, value investors do not buy. The advantages of such a strategy are obvious as buying at a discount is always a good idea. One problem is that the average investor is unable to determine intrinsic value, and neither can most professionals, otherwise, everyone would be wealthy. In addition, companies selling at a deep discount are risky because they might be in some type of trouble; hence, their depressed share price. The principle rewards, but after considerable patience and many nervous moments. As a result, it is best for investors with limited ability, time and effort, to engage in this strategy through a mutual fund. Despite the fact that this is an inexact science and hard to define, and even harder to recognize on a consistent basis, intrinsic value matters a lot since it is based on the notion that if you buy below intrinsic value, the risk of losing substantial sums of money during market declines is limited. It is always wise to remember the words of Robert Vishny: "You don't make money by investing in a good company…You make money by investing in a company that is better than the market thinks." Therefore, an accurate measurement is a function of quantifying both tangible and intangible assets, a process demanding considerable time and effort. The rewards are stunning as value investors outperform growth-oriented investors by 3% annually. For those with time and desire, gross profit, net income, operating income, and earnings per share are the most critical analytical measurements.

Three different types of value metrics are recognized as Level 1, Level 2, and Level 3 assets. The first can always be described with certainty because assets are liquid and portray distinct market prices. Level 2 assets are nebulous because prices are based on inactive markets, such as municipal bonds, restricted stock, derivatives, swaps, etc. Level 3 assets are illiquid; they involve unobservable inputs and assumptions in the pricing of certain assets under unusual and variable circumstances. Obviously, Level 3 assets are the most circumspect, and as recent history has shown, they are subject to fraud and are beyond the capabilities of retail investors to discover and evaluate their true "value" (the latter, not easily defined, varies from writer to writer). In the manner of Graham and Buffett, it boils down to such items as "fair market value," "intrinsic value," "book value," etc. Fair market value, common in real estate, rarely seems to satisfy the passions of common stock investors. If you are a seller, fair value, obviously, is much higher than what the buyer bids. In business, the "final price" establishes the market value of that and similar assets. This is a relative concept if one takes into consideration what dot.com stocks were selling late in 1999 in comparison to what prices were in 2001. If history teaches anything, it is that no single valuation method works consistently, and what the industry says is intrinsic value today, may not be so tomorrow.

## Why Value Investing is Important

In the main, FA breaks down into value and growth investing. It is important to breakdown the origin as reported by Ibbotson Associates of the 10.4% historical equity market returns. The largest share (4.6%) is derived from dividends, 3.1% (from inflation), 1.75% (from real earnings increases), and 1.25% (from P/E augmentation). When the prudent investor looks at the above a second time, or even a third, then there is a stark realization that dividends do matter, and over time, they obviously matter a great deal. In the final analysis, value investing is difficult to measure, and when it is, it varies widely by source. For the individual investor, it is a near impossibility no matter what the books tell you. However, several metrics such as P/E, book value, and sales to earnings, in combination will reveal an ample picture. Value fund investing cannot be dismissed because over the past 125 years, nearly 50% of total market real return has been derived from dividends. Value funds also behave differently from other market segments, do far better than growth stocks during bear markets, but can remain undervalued for prolong periods. Therefore, value stocks require considerable discipline and patience. Also, note that not all beaten down "value" stocks are valuable, as they often place the investor into what is described as a "value trap," where the stock price continues to decline. Value is subjective and varies with the age and personal circumstances of the investor, and it is never absolute or fixed. Given the fact that interest rates will remain at low levels for some time, one must add dividend-paying securities to a portfolio.

1. A value strategy emphasizes patience, discipline, and favors dividend-paying stocks. It relies on three imperatives: that value stocks outperform growth stocks and bonds, outperform inflation, and outperform non-dividend paying securities. VA investigates the true value of tangible assets like inventory, cash, property, etc., vs. "intangible" assets like intellectual property, patents and goodwill. The margin of safety is the difference between the purchase of an above-average company at below-average prices. 2. Value stocks are not traded as frequently, thus reducing expenses, and the effects of reinvestment and compounding enhance total returns. 3. VA is ideal for those who are young, for those with money, and for those with a tax-sheltered retirement account. 4. Value ignores "hot" stocks, and because many rebuke high-dividend paying stocks, the "turtle-pace" nature of these companies transcends greed and fear. Value investing is classic "cherry picking." 5. Dividends are expected to exceed inflation and because dividend-yielders are important in environments of low interest rates, the value of dividend-paying stocks as an element in wealth building becomes a crucial consideration. 6. Low PE securities outperform high PE stocks. 7. Dividend-paying stocks are evaluated by comparing the yield of the stock with the yield of the Total Market, as the dividend yield of the market is a reliable indicator of secular bear and bull inflection points. For those wishing to buy value companies paying average to above-average dividends, consult Moody's Handbook of Dividend Achievers, the S&P High Yield Dividend Aristocrats Index, and the Mergent Dividend Achievers Index. 8. Over time, value investors outperform growth investors because they are more patient and disciplined, they pay less for their value stocks, and hold them for long periods. The S&P 500 Dividend Aristocrats Index is comprised of the fifty, highest yielding companies that have raised dividends for at least twenty-five, consecutive years and consistently outperform the S&P 500 Index and the Total Market Index.

## Elements of Value Investing

1. Dividends are distributions that a corporation pays to its shareholders in the form of stock or cash. As percentage of individual income, dividends have played a varying role throughout history. They were much more fashionable prior to the 1960s, but since 1982, dividends have contributed a much smaller percentage. This is because investors during the "go-go" year's preferred stock price appreciation rather than quarterly cash distributions. Therefore, corporations increased share buybacks to boost share prices, and that kept shareholders happy. Historically, dividends represented more than 45% of total return of the S&P, but since 1982, the return has been less than 30%. In addition, more than 40% of all companies offered dividend payments, while today the figure is less than 23%. Another significant difference over the course of the past generation has been the dwindling dividend yield, currently standing at 2%, vs. 4.5% in the 1950s, and more than 6% in the 1920s. Despite the foregoing, it is important to note that dividend-paying stocks also exhibit, over long periods, significant growth in both secular bear and bull markets. For nearly 100 years, dividends have been influenced by secular trends, tax policies, and investor perceptions. Often called "wealth multipliers," dividend payers offer income, tax advantages, compound benefits, and portfolio stability. In bear markets, they contribute more than 70% of total returns. A new dividend cycle began in 2003.

2. The formula for total return is dividend plus dividend increases plus capital appreciation plus compounding minus expenses minus taxes minus inflation. During the period of the 1990s, more than 60% of the total equity return was a function of multiple expansions. PE ratios went up from the historic average of 14 to more than 30, with many dot.com issues extended beyond 100. People all of a sudden forgot history in which dividends produced about half of total returns. During market corrections, dividend-paying stocks do not decline as much as growth stocks, and have a built-in adjustment mechanism as the reinvested dividends purchase additional shares at lower prices. These effects for extended periods are very inspiring, and become key investment strategies of the wealthy as value outperforms growth; equities outperform bonds; and dividend-paying stocks outperform non-dividend payers. Among the many metrics, the most important elements for security selection includes the number of consecutive years the dividend increased; the number of consecutive years the dividend has been paid; the interest coverage ratio greater than or equal to 1.5; the positive cash flow for more than five years; a quick ratio greater than or equal to 1.0; and a debt-to-total capital less than 60%. Not to be overlooked is the significance of compound dividend investing, a practice that is able to augment long-term wealth creation by more than 30%.

3. A dividend yield is determined by dividing the dividend by the stock price. Dividend yields at the time of this writing are near generational lows, and this confuses investors, as dividend yields are higher at market bottoms than at market

highs. In addition, investors are wary, as the number of dividend reductions has exceeded increases during 1982-2008. At the time of this writing, there are many quality corporations whose dividend yield exceeds the 30-year Treasury. The dividend payout is a significant measure that reveals much: if a company earns $10 a share and pays a $1 dollar dividend, its payout rate is 10%, in sharp contrast to another that pays $8 for an 80% payout. The higher the rate, the more precarious the dividend, as the company may experience a decline in earnings and the dividend reduced or eliminated. Those companies with payout ratios of less than 50% exhibit consistency and an ability to continue to increase dividends. Elements that would place dividend yield and payout in jeopardy include rising interest rates, declining cash flow, company skullduggery, and a shift in company policy. In the final analysis, dividend-payers should be selected because of their sector yield; an S&P rating of B-plus or better; a 10-plus-year history of uninterrupted dividend increases; a PE ratio below historic norms; price-to-book below 2; price to sales under 1; return on equity above 15%; a dividend yield above the 10-year Treasury; a low debt relative to its peers in the sector; and a high cash flow. The dividend growth rate is more important than yield, as it accelerates total returns over time. Remember that high yield is not necessarily the best yield and often an outrageously high yield is a product of a falling share price. Usually, extremely high dividend yields are unsustainable, so that caution is necessary. In addition, to be remembered is the fact that, although the dividend growth rate is important, its sustainability is difficult to predict.

## Figure 3

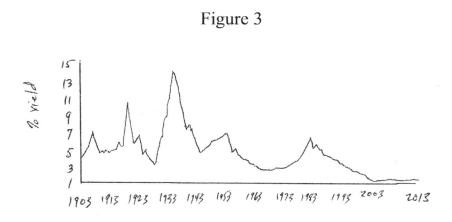

## Historic S&P 500 Dividend Yields

4. There is a big difference between investing in dividend-paying stocks and bonds. While the interest on a bond remains stable for its duration and the interest taxed as ordinary income, dividend yields vary over time, and taxed at a lower

rate. The value of the bond at maturity will be worth much less in real dollars due to inflation, while the value of stock can be higher. Never confuse dividend-paying stocks with bonds.

5. Understanding secular bull and bear markets is of immense benefit to dividend investors as dividend-payers follow cyclical patterns. The principle is simple: Buy when the S&P 500 dividend yield is rising and exceeds 5% and sell when it approaches 2%. Buy companies whose current PE is at least 20% below their historic average. By comparing the yield of a given stock with the yield of the S&P 500 and/or the Total Market, the measurement provides a relative gauge of value. When selecting dividend payers, begin with recipe 10, diversify, and adhere to important metrics like, beta, price to sales, price to book, etc. Direct Stock Plans allow investors to enroll in a company's purchasing and dividend reinvestment plan, often at a discount.

6. Because value investing is closely allied to stocks with dividend yields, many dividend-related strategies have surfaced, of which the "Dogs of the Dow" is the most celebrated. It is simple, requiring only a pittance of time, and some bookkeeping. The "Dog" approach invests equal dollar amounts in the 10 highest-yielding Dow stocks. At the end of the 12-month anniversary, those that no longer rank among the 10 highest yielders are replaced. One might also consider choosing the 10 highest yielders from the S&P 500, or the five lowest-priced stocks from the 10 highest yielders of the Dow, and trade them in similar fashion. It also pays to note that there are a seemingly infinite number of variations to this strategy.

7. While value outperforms growth, and dividend-paying stocks outperform non-dividend paying securities, risk remains ever-present. For example, during the 1972-1974 period, American Express declined 73%, Avon 87%, and Disney 86%, among many others. Moreover, companies can reduce, suspend, and eliminate dividends at any time. In 2009, 74 companies in the S&P 500 cut nearly $50 billion in dividends, the largest amount ever. While good, value-oriented companies exist, few remain "good" and "value-oriented" over the course of a lifetime, even among the prestigious Dow 30. The time to buy is when price corrections of 10% to 50% occur.

8. Pay attention to "economic moats," or to the earning attractiveness of the industry in which the company is in, and the company's competitive position within that industry. Companies that are the lowest cost producers in their industry own high quality, tangible assets and have an ability to maintain a competitive advantage, name recognition, and trademarks, while maintaining pricing power, predictability of a strong earnings stream, and characteristics that act as an impediment to competitor ability to penetrate the market. Wide moats imply a strong sustainable competitive advantage.

# Figure 4

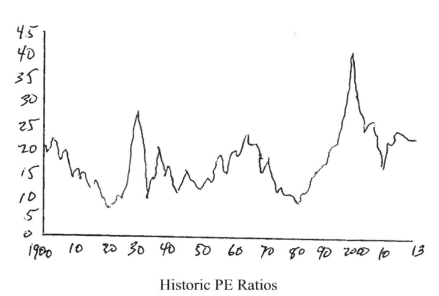

Historic PE Ratios

9. Five elements define dividend-paying stocks: capital gain component, dividend yield, dividend growth, dividend payout, and the stability of aggregate assets. Writing in 1992, Knowles and Petty had this to say, "Common investment wisdom holds that the best way to achieve capital gains is to purchase low-yield 'growth' stocks. Our research shows that just the opposite is true: *dividend investing* produces both high income and superior capital gains. The high dividend strategy is one of the most powerful investment tools available to both the individual and professional investor. For seventy years, numerous studies have shown that stocks with high dividend yields consistently outperform low-yield 'growth' stocks. Remarkably, the high-yield issues both resist decline in bear markets and appreciate faster in bull markets. The individual investor enjoys the best of all worlds–protection of capital in negative environments and superior returns in positive ones." The power of dividend growth can never be dismissed.

10. Dividend-paying stocks vary enormously throughout global equity markets. The Pacific Rim markets yield nearly 4% and Europe 3.5%, both of which also enjoy lower valuations. US dividends hover around 2%. Over the past 45 years, large-cap international value has outperformed large-cap international growth by 5%; large-cap domestic value has outperformed large-cap domestic growth by 4%; EM value has outperformed EM growth by 7%; and domestic small-cap value has outperformed domestic small-cap growth by 5%. Since value beats growth and small outperforms large, it is reasonable to include similar amounts in each portfolio with a bias for small-cap value.

11. A quality, value-oriented portfolio should contain: REITs, consumer staples, utilities, pharmaceuticals, financials, energy-related and quality-oriented foreign firms. In selecting securities add the long-term growth rate and the dividend yield, and divide by the PE. Anything above one is gravy, and anything less than one is less ideal. A more difficult selection method is Benjamin Graham's: buying at a price so low that liquidation would yield a capital return. Therefore, what are the compelling reasons for investors to resist a value strategy? Brokers do not encourage it because it is mainly a long-term strategy. It is boring, and they view dividends as unfashionable and unproductive, despite the fact that during bear markets, dividends are the only return on investment.

## Growth Investing

1. Growth investing is the Viagra of all investing strategies and a prime reason why it is so appealing. Growth securities have earnings growth exceeding 20% for years. They have high PE ratios and no dividends, and are engaged in risky, "cutting edge" activities with high R&D costs. Should all the above materialize, the investor enjoys lifelong bragging rights, a mansion, and everything else that goes with a high-wealth designation. The most important metric is the rate of growth. Therefore, the allure of growth stocks can be addictive, much like mashed potatoes, as you cannot get enough of them; on the other hand, a portfolio with an overconcentration in growth stocks can often crack like a dry Dorito. 2. They over perform during raging bull markets, underperform during range-bound markets, and experience the largest declines during both inflationary and deflationary periods. 3. Their performance with value stocks alternates, as in the 1990s when they outperformed and after 2000 when they underperformed. Nevertheless, while value investing has trumped growth over time, the two rarely correlate, meaning that, if nimble, the investor will be able to enhance total returns by holding both at different times. 4. If they remain in business long enough, they become mature companies that pay dividends. 5. A growth stock need not necessarily be in a growth industry. 6. To be successful, the growth investor requires considerable time, effort, mental and emotional fortitude.

While many growth investors are successful, the reverse side of the coin presents a number of distressing features. 1. High mortality rates and erratic earnings characterize growth stocks. They are usually companies without a long record of accomplishment, no way to evaluate intrinsic value, and no way to appraise the long-term effects of its current technology. Overexposure to this sector and close association with those that invest in this speculative fashion is a prescription for failure. 2. Highly successful growth companies are hard to find in their infancy. By the time they mature and become common names, it is too late to participate in the rapid third growth stage, thus missing maximum gains. 3. Growth companies are subject to creative destruction, a term coined by Schumpeter describing the process by which new, aggressive technologies or innovative companies obliterate older companies. They are the *prima donnas* of the market place and the bane of every careless investor as they come with exciting stories and miserable outcomes. The American market must have a hot sizzling darling on the front burner, whether is it biotech, gambling, high-tech, healthcare, railroads, dot.com, radio, television, real estate, airlines, commodities, etc. There will be at least one sector at any given time that is referred to as "hot" enough to command ever-larger sums of monies from investors. In fact, there has never been in the history of the US, a sector that has never shown brightly in the Arizona sun. There are few such companies and fewer yet that are able to sustain rapid growth without missteps. Therefore, while it is quite acceptable to "take a flyer" on the occasional growth stock, positions should be limited. 5. This sector is known for high debt levels, erratic earnings, and due to their glamour and expectations of extraordinary capital gains, investors are seduced and ensnared to overpay. 6. Growth analysis is arduous because it is difficult to forecast the future earnings of a young company in order to evaluate. Because expertise to select such companies is lacking, further problems arise when the company is compared with its peers in the sector. Small-cap companies are not terribly transparent, nearly all work within a narrow "emerging" field whose technology may become obsolete without the investor knowing it, and there is no way to appraise the long-term effects of existing technology. Institutions have exceptional access to resources, and thus the individual investor simply is not able to appraise the entire or specific portions of the market.

## Modern Portfolio Theory (MPT), Random Walk (RW), and Efficient Market Hypothesis (EMH)

MPT assumes that all investors act logically and with equal ability to evaluate all information available simultaneously. There appears to be no mountain of evidence to support these notions because if MPT were to exist markets would not behave as they do. MPT also highlights diversification as an important component of prudent investing by emphasizing the fact that risk and total returns are a function of non-correlating asset classes. RW simply posits that market direction cannot be predicted by history because stock price changes fluctuate in a random manner, and the investor is better off indexing. EMH rests on three columns: investment information is available to all; all available information is reflected by current prices; and prevailing prices are considered to be fairly valued. Hence, it is impossible for any investor to gain advantage. When new information becomes available, it is quickly digested, and prices readjust accordingly. Price changes are considered unpredictable and "random" in this environment. In the main, the theory states that, over time, no one can beat the market. However, there are dissenting views that have brought down the numerous shibboleths inherent in the notion that all markets are "efficient."

All of the above are similar, used interchangeably, and academically flawed because not all information is available uniformly in the investing universe, and individuals never evaluate or digest available information equally. Most peculiar is the fact that significant price movements occur without any news. When a company's stock declines by 11% on Monday on no news, drops a further 4% on Tuesday, on no news, and another 15% by the end of the week on no news, how can anyone say that markets are "efficient." Inside information is received by certain individuals before the public is informed, thus enabling those individuals to trade with an advantage, and since it cannot be eliminated, it runs contrary to the EMH, MPT and RW theories of investing. The number of fraud complaints to the FTC exceed half a million annually, with more than 25 million investors losing in excess of $34 billion to fraud. Moreover, efficient markets also vary on a grand cultural level, as people value industries, sectors, and companies with different metrics. Because the value aspect differs culturally, so do the inevitable reversals to the mean. This further reinforces the anti-efficient market hypothesis that available information somehow equalizes fair price. An entopic mind is able to perceive all manner of foolish and unreasonable prices based on prevailing fashion and human emotions, but EMH appears to disregard corruption, governmental manipulation, and simple "rigging" by "Scarsdale Fats." One thing is clear for average investors: index investing allows the best measure of market participation relative to risk over time. Given the inevitable negative effects of the "Tragedy of the Commons," market efficiency is a fantasy. The proof rests with the daily, weekly, and monthly financial scandals. The utopic mindsets are not based on facts, but on matters of faith, and in the process, the *illuminati* are able to propagandize the gullible. Just as there is no *Shangri La*, one must also be skeptical of the sanctity of EMH, MPT, and RW.

How can markets be "efficient" when governmental agencies since 1982 looked the other way as corporations hid dubious assets from their balance sheets in order to mislead investors? More than 35% of S&P companies habitually manipulate reported earnings, bond rating agencies have inflated bond ratings, and Fannie Mae had misstated earnings by billions, thus deceiving investors. How efficient was the market during the AIG meltdown and the Goldman Sachs bailout when Timothy Geithner, as head of the New York Fed intentionally restricted and delayed vital information from shareholders in direct violation of existing SEC guidelines? Just how efficient were markets when obscene numbers of short stock took place for major financial firms prior to the banking crisis? How can the housing markets be efficient when Freddie and Fannie, responsible for 90% of the nation's mortgages, were allowed to speculate? How can efficient theorists maintain their position in view of market manipulations that affected AIG, Lehman Brothers, Bear Stearns, Wachovia, Fannie and Freddie, Washington Mutual, and dozens more since 2000, as market losses exceeded $5 trillion? And in the words of Warren Buffet: "I'd be a bum on the street with a tin cup if the markets were always efficient." Public knowledge or "wissen," is often false, conceptual, disingenuous, and for the average investor, sheer poison. Because investors do not have equal net worth with similar volumes of money in the "market," their proficiency in gathering, understanding, and acting on "information" differs. It takes a well-read and experienced individual in the ways of financial markets to divorce the cacophony between the noise emanating out of the canyons of Wall Street and the entopic experiences of Main Street. Price movements for most stocks take place at the margin, as more than 99% of all equity owners do nothing on any given day. Moreover, "flash orders," a practice by large institutions, place the retail investor at a disadvantage.

## Market Timing (MT) and Technical Analysis (TA)

MT is a utopic investment concept that lives in the hearts and minds of all investors. It burns their inner souls to know that they have possession of a formula that tells them the ideal time to buy and sell with consistent certainty. Throughout history, no economic strategy has captivated the investor, as this notion, and no serious investor not sell his youth for such knowledge. Think about it: day after day, week after week, and year after year, you can consistently buy at market lows and sell at market peaks. Without fail! The obvious problem is that no savant knows the exact moment of the "low" and the "high," and, as a result, the "Wall Street's" of the world are littered with failed tactics and destroyed lives. Since people will lie endlessly about their sex life, dog, and money, a word of caution is necessary as many confuse occasional "luck" with skill. MT is beyond the aptitude of mortal man. It fails because it treats economic conditions as being "unique," with investors targeting the fact that "unique" elements are not subject to predictions. In the words of John Bogle: "It's one thing to get out of the market at the perfect time, and quite another to get back in at the perfect time." Therefore, market tops and bottoms are daunting to time and trade. The legendary Benjamin Graham had this to say about market timing: "We are equally sure that if he places his emphasis on timing, in the sense of forecasting, he will end up as a speculator and with a speculator's financial results. The speculator's primary interest lies in anticipating and profiting from market fluctuations. The investor's primary interest lies in acquiring and holding suitable securities at suitable prices." Market timing is definitely the antithesis of the "buy and hold" philosophy with many brokerage houses encouraging this practice. They offer seminars, and for those with a sizeable stake, provide all manner of services for the "trader" to make an endless stream of trades in the hope that by 4 p.m. he will be in the black. The failure rate is 100%, but the clueless continue to flock to this practice with the hope that they will be the exception. Similar to ancient gladiators, all eventually become slaughtered. In the words of Anonymous: "Market timers make astrologers look respectable."

A few items to ponder: 1. The Chicago Options Exchange Market Volatility Index, referred to as VIX, is the so-called "fear gauge" that seeks to measure the implied volatility of the American equity market. Experts state that any figure above 40 indicates a bear market bottom, and anything below 20, a bull top. While the two extremes have not always been timely in their indications, there is often a delayed reaction, so that the cautious or opportune investor can begin to sell or buy gradually. 2. MT is an aggressive attempt to outguess the Total Market, specific indexes, specific sectors and industries, and specific stocks–on a daily to secular basis. Before the large and rapid computerization of the industry, MT attempted to foresee future market (and sector) direction by observing past movements in a very laborious manner. Rarely did the market timer trade in *milliseconds*. However, in today's world of inexpensive, desktop computers, specialized software trading programs, reduced transaction fees, and cheap money, the speculation of "day trading," or rapid fire trading, has reached dangerous levels. Hardly an hour goes by on economic radio and television programs that one is not subjected to "day trading" commercials promising early retirement in a matter of months. Do not be fooled by the hype: in the words of Alfred Smith: "No matter how you slice it, it's still baloney." 3. Attempts to time the market end in failure. However, there is one certainty: those who are unable to time the market are often the same personages who sell MT newsletters. Charles Ellis had it right: "Market timing is a wicked idea. Don't try it—ever." Even the notorious John Maynard Keynes abandoned his market timing strategy, called "credit cycle." Never forget that timing the market is not the same as "time in the market." 4. The divining of changes in market direction in terms of seconds, minutes, weeks or months is difficult. The fact that all markets revert to their mean is not in dispute, but the ability to "time" inflection points is a significant challenge. 5. Another major issue lies in the fact that each economic cycle, though similar to those of the past, is somewhat different in terms of amplitude, duration, and impact in the overall economy. History offers a guide but one cannot use the past for market entry or exit with any degree of certainty. If you have time, go to Delphi and consult the oracle, consult Laksmi, the Hindu goddess of wealth and good fortune, select and rearrange the entrails of any animal or listen to MSNBC, but remember the wise words of Solon: "You never know what tomorrow brings."

By studying the history of price and volume fluctuations of a particular company, economic sector, or the general market, TA produces an immense amount of data in the form of tables, graphs, charts, and computer simulations that stagger the mind. In recent decades, the investment community and day traders have embraced TA with blind passion. By plotting and charting past performance, TAs maintain that it is able to discover repetitive patterns of price and volume that indicate buy and sell signals and, hence, be so accurate as to take advantage of MT capabilities. The number of variables confuses the mind necessitating the production of a significant cottage industry that feeds on itself. Trends are only recognized through hindsight and that is what makes TA dangerous. It is impossible to chart what is unseen.

It should be noted that, 1.TA is not a science. 2. There are multiple false breakouts offering false signals that promote whipsaw trades leading to major losses. 3. There is no definitive study indicating that chart reading will lead to sustained trading profits. Charts portray a clear picture of where one was, but not where one is going, thus ignoring market psychology and, in particular, the forces of greed and fear. TA professes that randomness be dismissed, and price and volume trends remain the alpha and omega of the strategy. In the meantime, the imbroglio concerning its merits continues unabated. 4. In its purest form, TA works only in the absence of market manipulation and inside information, and that means that over time it does not work because it ignores "price causation." Since market inefficiencies do not accurately reflect supply and demand, TA fails. 5. TA is plagued with unlimited gibberish such as, "It is a very risky trade to buy stock that has broken trend line support, but it can also be quite profitable." 6. Individuals who respond to advertisements of instant riches by day trading are handicapped by flawed programs, diminished capacity, and a predilection for reckless speculation. These people risk the grocery and rent money, and forget that the market is much smarter. 7. If enough investors observe the same pattern in a given moment and enter in unison, they boost prices artificially, and, in a similar fashion, when all decide to exit at the same time they pound prices to ridiculous low levels. The retail investor, lacking information, resources and expertise, is unable to assess the factors behind the "mo," fails to identify the "top" or "bottom," is so dependent on "street noise" that he is unable to make a serious, informed decision, and fails miserably. The odds are better in growing your net wealth by keeping your day job, saving money, living frugally, being patient, and investing in index funds. 8. Trading systems are ineffective and worthless. All the software, countless seminars, and books on TA have failed to consistently make money. Many during the 1990s quit their day jobs to "trade" in their pajamas, but few if any, are still trading. There are many reasons for failure, of which ingrained bad habits work against the essentials of sound money management grounded in discipline and patience. This is similar to the person in the kitchen who wishes to reduce the cooking time in half by setting the temperature setting at 500 instead of 250. The failures are dismal and predictable. Disciplined, value-oriented investors make money because they think long-term, while traders think in terms of nano seconds.

# Commodities

Commodities are in the middle stage of a secular boom. The period of 1980-2001 was one long secular bear market for all commodities characterized by low prices and no, or reduced capital investment for exploration, infrastructure construction, etc. Nevertheless, as long as the Fed and global central bank policies are committed to inflation, real tangible assets will continue their price escalation. Lower global interest rates are stimulating price increases and producing no logical reason to hold fiat currency. One thing is certain: the longer tight monetary policies are restrained, the worse the eventual pain. In the meantime, for the duration of the current secular bear market, commodities should be overweight. Therefore:

1. Fundamentals drive commodities when governments print excessive amounts of money, when they promulgate "bread and circus" policies, and when they encourage inflation, excessive debt, and hedonistic behavior. 2. Commodities provide a hedge against event risks like war, terroristic attacks on energy installations, political instability, etc. 3. Asia did not play a material role in the last commodity secular bull market in the 1970s, but today it is the principal driver. 4. Due to increasing population, rising disposable income, improved diets, and reduced arable acreage per capita, fertilizer consumption is expected to rise dramatically. 5. Given the sad state of disrepair of America's infrastructure, enormous amounts of new bridges, hydroelectric dams, roads, and rail mileage would have to be repaired and built at a cost $15 trillion by 2023. 6. Chindia's insatiable appetite for raw materials has fueled sustained price escalation in all manner of commodities. For the first time since the Industrial Revolution, the "West" is directly competing with the rest of the world for global resources. 7. Since 2000, the largest returns have been fine wines and commodities; the laggards were the $US and cash. Gold has risen in price for 11 straight years, and JP Morgan is now accepting gold bullion as collateral. Precious metals in early 2013 appear to be underpriced, and many gold companies are increasing dividends, thus making them competitive with utilities. 8. Public trust in fiat money is declining. Alan Greenspan in 1966 said that gold "is a safe store of value." And nearly half a century later, he said: "Gold is the ultimate currency" and "Gold and economic

freedom are inseparable." In the absence of a gold standard, there is no way to protect savings from confiscation through inflation. Deficit spending is simply a scheme for the confiscation of wealth. Gold stands in the way of this insidious process, and protects property. If one grasps this, one has no difficulty in understanding the statists' antagonism toward a gold standard." Given the fact, that gold's share of total financial assets is less than 1%, it has significant room for price augmentation. Furthermore, gold output is surpassed by the growth rate of fiat currency production.

Broad sector features include: 1. The CRB Index is a basket of twenty-eight different tangible assets, of which energy products, metals, water, agriculture, forest products, and real estate are the most important. Commodities constitute an impressive influence over the world's economy, as human sustenance and secondary production could not exist without them. 2. Commodities are important because they reduce portfolio risk. History has shown that the largest fortunes have been made from commodities and real estate than any other source as they offer portfolio diversification and outpace inflation. While their value can decline, it is never to zero. 3. Commodity price movement is inverse to the value of the dollar. 4. Commodities provide a hedge against event risks like war, terroristic attacks, political instability, or a climatic exigency. 5. Price fluctuations are notorious, as supply and demand elements induce either sharp spikes or sudden crashes. 6. Bonds and equities are both negatively correlated to commodities. 7. Governments use quotas to protect domestic activities, to relieve pressure on their balance of payments, and to apply political pressure against others. Often, quotas turn to outright bans on commerce save for humanitarian needs, and while public statements forbidding commerce in certain commodities, *sub rosa* trade flourishes with governmental approval. 8. Commodities, like all assets are not similar, and exhibit diverse price charts in both secular bull and bear markets as each commodity is guided by its own supply/demand patterns. The Daily Reckoning in 2004 reported that in the decade of the 1970s, stock prices increased by just 3.6%, inflation 7.7%, housing 10.2%, US farmland 14%, silver 23.7%, gold 31.6%, and oil 34.7%. 9. Urbanization is the main driving force for global commodity demand.

Unlike most other economic sectors, the following beleaguer commodities: 1. Exploration and feasibility projects may take years to complete. Funding may take another several years. Permits and environmental impact studies may last longer than five years. After discovery, it could take anywhere from five to twelve years to bring an oil field or mine on line. Investments are made during periods of rising prices, but neglect and abandonment occur when prices decline below production costs. Mining, loading, transporting facilities, milling, crushing, washing, sorting, grinding, concentrating, smelting, roasting, and converting facilities consume huge capital resources. Exporting to fabricating centers to roll, draw, extrude, refine, fabricate, etc., require expensive facilities. 2. Transportation to centers to convert the commodity to a consumer product requires a huge financial and construction undertaking. As of 2012, it takes double the time to bring a new mine into production than in 1980, and it is more than three times more expensive. While the metal price structure may support this enterprise, it is often possible that by the time, the entire complex is completed, metal prices decline and the project becomes uneconomic; the average mine lasts about 20 years; and when prices fall, mines become unprofitable, equipment rusts, mine flooding occurs, and workers depart. Therefore, governments place quotas on the importation of certain metals/minerals, tariffs to protect producers, subsidies are increased or instituted, and stockpiling occurs to even out demand/supply requirements. 3. During the past 200 years, the US has experienced six, major, secular, commodity bull markets: 1823-1838; 1847-1865; 1878-1918; 1929-1952; 1963-1980; and 2001-. Over the course of both secular commodity bull and bear markets, there were specific years in which the gap between the commodity index and the long-term Treasury diverged more than 76% in favor of commodities as in 1973, and posted more than a 53% decline relative to the S&P 500 in 2001. It is, therefore, prudent to hold a small core position in commodities, and to increase it during the depths of a secular bear commodity market. 4. Commodity prices are often volatile: in April 2006, silver fell by 15% in two days, in June it fell 22% in 9 days, in July it fell by 11% in 7 days, in September 19% in 10 days, and in December 11% in 14 days. 8. Mining industries exhibit long-term cyclical behavior. Gold peaked in 1980 and then went down for the next 21 years. Oil peaked in 1980; fell for the next 19, only to peak again in 2008.

Syndicate-type relationships characterize metal and mineral industries. For example, a *cartel* is an association of independent enterprises/nations that produce similar goods that attempt to secure monopoly in a specific market. To work, policies must be similar in both production and price, but it gets complicated if members wish to cheat and conspire with others to gain advantage. An *oligopoly* involves a market structure in which a small number of firms dominate output. A rare occurrence, *oligopsony*, refers to a market structure of few buyers. A pure *monopoly* refers to a market structure of just one seller, thus exercising total price control. Still rarer, is a *monopsony*, or a market structure with a single buyer. Americans dislike OPEC as a cartel, but forget that until 1970 the Texas Railroad Commission set the price of crude oil. OPEC was created in 1960 when Venezuela, the only non-Islamic nation and principal instigator, persuaded Iran, Iraq, Kuwait and Saudi Arabia to join together to boost oil prices.

The number of metrics used to evaluate a mineral deposit are many, complicated, laden with fraud, and something beyond the ability of an investor to discern accurately when investing in a resource company. The reserve concept is one such issue as owners of the deposit wish, for a variety of reasons, to hide or mislead actual reserves. "Indicated" or "inferred" reserves are the least accurate of all measurements in which opinions of quantity, and grade are estimated by the most simple observations such as outcrops, pits, trenches, and limited drill holes. Inferred reserves are unverified, and, therefore a guessing game at best. "Possible" or "prospective" reserves contain a margin of error in excess of 50% because they are a low confidence class, as the terms imply the "possibility" for recoverable resources. "Probable," or semi-proved, contain a margin of error twice the proved, but better than possible, and refer to the economic extraction of mineral wealth as determined by a preliminary feasibility study at minimum, including information on mining, processing, metallurgical, economic and other factors. "Proved," "measured" or "assured" reserves are those blocked in three dimensions by actual penetrations. They contain a margin of error of 20% or less, and thus exhibit maximum probability for the presence of minerals, which, with reasonable certainty can be recovered under existing economic (technological) conditions. "Potential" and commercial reserves are estimates of the quantity available under assumed conditions of improved technology and greater demand (higher prices) within the next 25 years. A further complication is the fact that each mineral industry defines the above terms differently. As of 2009, "proven reserves" are no longer constrained by "certainty," further complicating the issue of "what really exists underground." The figures are not reliable, especially for OPEC countries, but not exclusively as evidenced by Royal Dutch Shell revelations that overstated reserves by 60%. After the 1973 oil crisis, OPEC established a quota system based on country reserves and, hence, the beginning of blatant fraud, as everyone inflated reserves. As prices fell in the 1980s, each OPEC member raised their "official" reserve estimates in order to pump more oil, with most members raising their reserve figures by more than 50%. Conventional wisdom, especially textbooks, states that the Middle East sits on 66% of the world's reserves, a figure that has never been independently verified. While reserves remain unknown, inflated figures are known as "paper" or "phantom" barrels; therefore, petroleum reserves and all other mineral reserves must be viewed with a jaundiced eye. For most countries, proven reserves are no more than "expectation reserves," and it would behoove the prudent investor to question all reserves as companies and countries lie. One of the most famous episodes was that of Bre-X, a gold mining company whose share price skyrocketed to the stratosphere only to crash to zero once it was discovered that core samples were "salted" in order to falsify gold concentration.

## Importance of Energy

1. Throughout history, the relationship between energy and economic growth has been crucial, as energy resources have always separated the wealthy from the non-wealthy. Energy and GDP growth are positively related. Consider the sources of energy for the US during 1850, 1970, and 2011. In 1850, wood supplied 64% of all energy, followed by work animals (22%), wind power (7%), and coal 7%. In 1970, 41% of all energy came from petroleum, natural gas (22%), coal (21%), nuclear (10%), hydropower (4%), and 2% from other sources. In 2011, petroleum accounted for 38%, NG 26%, coal 21%, nuclear 9%, and renewable and other 6%. A good indication of America's supremacy in the world of 1946 lay in the fact that the US consumed 85% of all global natural gas and petroleum, 50% of all electrical power, and 40% of all coal. Today, China is America's strategic rival in the race for energy and commodities. Energy, like all mining operations, is a cyclical

industry, its peaks and troughs and degrees of amplitude varying throughout history with market and political conditions.

2. The first oil discovery in the small town of Titusville, Pennsylvania in 1859, produced but 25 barrels of oil from a depth of 69 feet. Since then, oil has become the dominant source of energy changing the course of global economic history. Crude oil, the world's most important traded commodity, has become the lifeblood of industrialized and urbanized nations. It is literally indispensable in every facet of daily life from transportation, food production, medicine, soap, paint, etc... It stores a tremendous amount of energy per weight and volume, and it is inexpensive and immensely versatile in today's economy to transport and manufacture an incredible array of products of which without the world is unable to live. The aggregate employment effect exceeds 10% of all secondary workers, 16% of income, and 18% of total value added. Oil is the industrial engine of modern civilization, and a main contributor to present global high standards of living. It is basic to everything accomplished: 90% of world transport and 98% of all food is oil-dependent. One barrel of oil produces in excess of 10,000 individual products. Therefore, there are few economic alternatives to oil. In 1969 the world consumed 45 million barrels per day, in 1973 55 million, in 1979, 65 million; and by 2012, 86 million.

3. The petrochemical industry is characterized by the following: a. The chemistry of refining is becoming more complicated and expensive. b. There is widespread competition of unique intensity, like no other industry. The inter-commodity competition is notorious as chlorine, an oxidizing agent and as a bactericide, competes with at least 100 additional chemicals. Inter-process competition is also highly competitive as ethylene glycol can be made by many different processes. c. The industry is a major innovator producing dozens of new products every year. d. The industry is capital and labor intensive. e. Equipment, due to high temperatures and pressure, is subject to rapid obsolescence. f. The compelling force of R&D is critical in producing new products. Economies of scale are a vital component in reducing costs. g. No other base matter is able to produce so many different products as crude oil. h. The average barrel of oil yields 41% gasoline, 21% diesel, 9% jet fuel, 4% heavy fuel oil, liquefied gases 4%, and 21% other products, the latter, responsible for the bulk of all value added in such areas as medicine, plastics, fabrics, and thousands of products from shoe polish to computer disks.

## International Energy Issues

1. An American geophysicist, M. Hubbert, in 1956 predicted that US oil production would peak by 1975. Known as "Hubbert's Peak," this event is considered a serious topic of an impending global oil shortage. When global peak occurs, the annual decline in oil production would occur at rates greater than 2% annually because new discoveries of mega oil fields are not on the horizon. Moreover, the

geologic "tipping point" (the point when the world will have used up half of all existing conventional crude in the world) will arrive before 2020 say the experts, and that means that remaining oil will be more expensive as light sweet crude peaked in the 1990s, and world class discoveries remain at 60-year lows. OECD oil production peaked in 1997, and most OPEC oil in 2007. Of the 65 oil-producing countries, 57 have reached peak levels. While the peak discovery period of oil in the US occurred in the 1930s, recent discoveries have reversed the trend. Output from Angola and West Africa, Brazil, Peru, Ecuador, Russia, and Kazakhstan more than doubled since 2000. Crude oil discovery reveals the following: In 1930, the world discovered 10 billion barrels of crude and used but 1.5 billion. By 1964 48 billion barrels were discovered, 73 billion in the 1970s, 34 billion in the 1980s, 18 billion in the 1990s, but thus far in 2000-2010, less than 15 billion. Seventy-five percent to 80% of all pumped oil originates from fields discovered more than 50 years ago, and 20% from fields discovered 57 years ago. World oil discoveries have declined for nearly 50 years, from a high of 29 in the decade of the 1950s, to fewer than nine for the period 1995-2005. The older fields are played out, and while new oil fields are being discovered, they are smaller, harder to find, and require more technology and money to extract and ship. In aggregate terms, the world is spending more to find less.

The world needs to discover the equivalent of an Iraq every year just to meet demand. a. Energy consumption per person has increased 225% since 1950. b. The energy industry employs 100-plus million people, and contributes 15% of GDP. c. Since 1990, non-OPEC oil production has outpaced OPEC production. d. In terms of "unconventional reserves," the US holds 2 trillion barrels of shale oil followed by Venezuela and Canada. No one really knows how much oil is available and how much can eventually be extracted. e. The geography of annual increase in oil demand is interesting: DMs less than 2%, China 7%, and the Middle East 4%. f. In the present world economy, few countries are entirely independent of energy resources. g. It is a myth that inexpensive energy is vital to GDP growth. Among many others, Japan and Korea import expensive energy but have developed economies. It is not necessarily the cost of energy that is important, but how an economy improves its energy efficiency over time. h. High energy prices encourage discovery, benefit exporters, make importing nations less competitive and increase the incidence of economic recessions. New technologies like fracking and enhanced oil recovery have changed the direction of global energy. For the moment, peak oil is passé, and for those countries whose economy is dependent on oil exports, their national finances are in disarray. i. From a geographic perspective, crude oil production is not evenly distributed, but highly localized. Globally there are 150,000-plus wells, but more than half of output emanate from the 120 largest fields, of which the 15 largest produce 22% of total output, and contain 70% of all discovered oil. Saudi Arabia's largest oil field, Ghawar, Mexico's Canterell, Kuwait's Burgan, and Da Qing in China have peaked.

The vast majority of world oil comes from fields discovered prior to 1973, and many geologists are of the belief that 70% of all conventional oil that has existed is currently being pumped. Whether this is accurate or not is of little consequence. In order to meet demand (barring new technological discoveries), energy costs will not only rise, but also maintain a new upper price level in order to entice companies to explore, drill and produce. Thus far, the world has not found a replacement for Ghawar, and should that field continue its downward production schedule, there will be difficulties for Saudi Arabia to meet production quotas. The world would require 126 million barrels a day by 2020, up from 86 million in 2012. The contrarian opinion to peak oil is that oil and natural gas are renewable resources, as they are a product of geothermal activity. The controversial theory, in all its forms and implications, is hotly debated. The search for gas and oil involves more expensive and sophisticated technology that drives exploration to deeper and more inhospitable environments. Many also state that this is the fifth time in recent history that the doomsayers have been making these claims and the world continues to discover oil. It is also maintained that the figures given are capricious, thus compounding unreliability. Furthermore, abandoned oil wells rejuvenate themselves after decades of neglect, with new technologies emerging to resurrect these fields. Finally, a number of new discoveries in North and Latin America, Africa, and Australia, along with new processes of extraction, have raised the possibility that no global shortage exists.

2. Control of discovery and production, transportation, processing, financing and expertise are major issues confronting the industry. Western nations, for the first time in history, fear the loss of control of energy supplies from the Middle East, Asia, Africa, and Latin America. An immediate concern is the unraveling of the petrodollar system that began in 1971. Therefore, the rest of the world began to export to the US to obtain dollars, thus ensuring a negative US trade balance. Today, the "floating" petrodollars are losing value, and those who hold them are getting irritated. The New Shanghai Cooperative Group speaks for Russia, China, India, Iran, Indonesia, the former Turkic Soviet Republics, and others, in which critical commodities are bought and sold under special arrangements outside the petrodollar system. Maintaining a global demand for dollars is a primary function of US foreign and trade policies. In addition, state oil companies own 80% of global oil reserves; hence, the energy game is changing as the grip of western oil companies has diminished. Historically, western oil companies had a monopoly on energy technology, capital, exploration, transportation, refining, and markets. Over the past generation, the BRICS have successfully challenged control over all aspects, and while they lack several critical niches, they have severely weakened western dominance. The US is no longer the controlling force in global energy, as it neither controls supply, demand and capital. After WWII, the global crude industry was centered in the US and the Persian Gulf, and dominated by the "7 sisters," but today, these companies along with other independents control less than 20% of world total reserves as the bulk of oil is owned by national entities. Therefore, the energy picture of the future will be different from that of the past,

as EMs drive global consumption growth. It is widely recognized that an international war is occurring for control of energy with China the highest bidder and India not far behind. Sixteen of the largest 20 energy companies are foreign, a major departure of the global energy status of 1980 when the situation was reversed.

3. The above is critical to the "Grand Plan," or the enforcement of the sale of energy for dollars. While easy to implement from 1971 to 2000, the "Grand Plan" is fraught with danger and of similar geopolitical importance as the "Great Game." The key player is the US who wishes to preserve the petrodollar system, a huge economic advantage as it drives the demand for dollars. Hugo Chavez was the first to break away from the petrodollar, followed by Saddam Hussein and by Omar Qaddafi, all of whom are no longer. Bashar al-Assad of Syria is accepting other sources of payment for exports, and he is presently in the crosshairs of the "Axis." If and when the time comes that the old medieval monarchies of the Arabian peninsula begin to accept other currencies for payment, a new wave of military activities will commence. The ultimate prize is Iran, and when the devolution of that country takes place, it is assumed that Middle Eastern oil will forever be dominated by the US and its allies. In this manner, all Israeli enemies will be neutralized, medieval monarchs preserved, and the petrodollar system would remain firmly in place. The US has chosen "fundamentalism" over the process of "secularization" and that is the essence of the "Great Plan." Changing events in the Middle East, however, are introducing new tactical elements, the most important being the degradation of OPEC as the swing institution in the price of oil.

4. The Russian, Iranian and Dubai oil bourses will exert an impact on global currency markets. Russia's oil exports represent 15% of world totals, and Iran accounts for 6%. If one factors Venezuela which exports 5%, these three countries, responsible for more than one-quarter of the world's global oil exports, are no longer exclusively accepting dollars as payment. If one adds an even larger percentage of natural gas exports from these countries, then the demand for dollars will fall further. Historically, oil-exporting nations shipped the raw material and DMs added processing value. Today, exporters are getting sophisticated and wish to maximize their profits by investing in refining and petrochemical industries, thus adding value and exporting the more expensive, finished product.

5. Artificial low prices deter exploration, capital investment, conservation, and R&D for alternative fuels. Equally important is that low energy prices encourage waste. Crude oil reached a low price of $10b in 1998, a particularly bad time for the industry as more than 500,000 lost employment in the US alone. This merely accelerated a climate of under investment, well abandonment, and despair; exploration was reduced, drilling companies went begging and everyone began to waste gasoline in a new suburban rush. The world is not about to run out of energy today, tomorrow, or the next decade. It is merely running out of cheap energy, and unless a "Black Swan" appears, this condition will prevail, as any strategy to

reverse the present course will require time, enormous sums of capital and political compulsion. When the price of conventional crude oil rises to new heights, the economies of scale for the efficient exploitation of "alternatives" will commence. In the words of Zaki Yamani in the 1970s: "The Stone Age did not end for lack of stone, and the Oil Age will end long before the world runs out of oil."

6. The scene for price escalation is firmly in place. a. More than 80% of energy consumption growth is in EMs. b. Since the 1990s, only four major oil fields have been discovered. c. OPEC no longer considers itself the cartel it once was because it has lost its geological ability to affect the price of oil as its spare capacity has declined from 25% in1983 to less than 3% today. d. Energy infrastructure, long neglected, is currently straining to maintain production and distribution. e. Crude oil is increasingly getting more sour and heavier, thus making products more expensive. f. The nations of yesteryear that exported the bulk of global oil are now using more domestically. g. Vehicle output is increasing by more than 3 million units annually. h. The rise in oil prices is partly the result of the fall of the $US. i. In order for oil exporters to finance government, oil prices must remain above $95 a barrel, anything less spells trouble for both fringe exporters as well as US "allies" (like Saudi Arabia) who were promised benefits since the 1971 agreement to introduce petrodollars. Gulf States have made the threat of fracking known to the US. Should the flood of newly found shale, NG, and oil reduce prices to critical levels, the prevention of geopolitical tensions will prove impossible.

7. The Iranian Oil Bourse on Kish island operating under the Iranian International Petroleum Exchange, has been established but remains largely inactive in the settlement of oil, natural gas, selected commodities and petrochemicals, but a key element in the US-Iranian political imbroglio.

## Domestic Energy Issues

1. Domestic oil and NG output, declining for nearly 40 years, has recently reversed course with the discovery of the Bakken, Eagle Ford, and other fields–a product of technological innovations that "discovered" NG and oil reserves exceeding those in the Arabian Peninsula. Oil imports are declining rapidly while domestic output of oil and NG are increasing significantly, thus reducing the current account deficit and strengthening the dollar. The American oil renaissance is bigger than first imagined and the "energy crisis" appears to be over for the moment as US oil imports are declining. US energy is not only abundant, but also widely available and affordable. However, the annual decline rates pose serious issues. The US consumes 25% of all gasoline, 30% of all fossil-based energy, produces about 36% of global electricity, but owns less than 15% of conventional world oil reserves. The US consumes four times more energy per capita than other DMs, has a propensity for long-distance driving, and allows a subsidized antiquated mass transit system to continue.

2. Lack of a coherent national energy policy has prevented exploration in Alaska, the Gulf of Mexico and other areas. Although there have been several small new refinery additions, no large facility have been built since the early 1970s. In 1981, there were 324 operating refineries in the US, a figure that declined to 124 in 2011. Low return on capital prevents rehabilitation of plant and equipment, and, as a result, the number of shutdowns, fires, and malfunctions has intensified in recent years. Since the 1860s, more than 1 million miles of pipelines were constructed, but 60% of infrastructure remains obsolete.

3. The "energy crisis" is a myth. There are a myriad of policies intended to diminish dependence on imported oil, of which reduced suburbanization belongs on the pantheon as more than 90% of the population is dependent on the automobile. By placing people in central cities emphasizing public transportation, the savings in moving people and goods for short distances along with reductions in space heating and hot water would halve gasoline and home heating consumption. Other items include increasing nuclear electrical production, raising efficiency of oil and gas use, investments in alternative energy sources, and force conservation by raising prices.

4. The price of gasoline is a major topic despite the fact that energy is not a "core" component of the CPI. Nevertheless, each $10 upward move in the price of a barrel of gasoline reduces GDP growth by 0.4% annually. Americans grumble, but the most expensive gas per gallon is in Bosnia-Herzegovina ($12), Eritrea ($10), Norway ($8.76), UK ($8.44), and Monaco ($8.37). People complain about rising gasoline costs, but continue to buy 9.5 out of every 10 cars with borrowed money, most of them gas guzzlers. Yet, people blame the "power of big oil," etc., for rising prices. Many frame the case differently by stating that coffee, bottled water, soda pop, beer, etc., are all luxuries while oil is a necessity. Nevertheless, the cacophony against recent oil price increases is unwarranted as the price of oil has never been cheaper when adjusted to inflation. Many oil exporting countries are acutely aware of this dynamic, given the fact that the purchasing value of the $US has fallen by more than 30% since 2001. For those who consider gasoline to be expensive, consider the cost of the following, all more expensive than gas per gallon: Joy perfume $102,400; Tabasco sauce $1,695; Pepto Bismol $160; and bottled water $14. The media, politicians, and the public continuously refer to energy price increases as a "tax," but why not refer to state lotteries with a similar expression? Gas is the cheapest liquid at a gas station.

5. There are huge supplies of oil far exceeding Persian Gulf reserves, but they are unconventional oil reserves, mainly tar sands and shales. In order for these sources to be developed, crude oil prices would have to remain high. Shale oil is to be found in enormous quantities in Colorado, Utah, and Wyoming, with deposits estimated to contain more than 5 trillion barrels of oil, and thus capable of providing enough energy for centuries. The oil shale is kerogen, a hydrocarbon similar to petroleum, but far more expensive to process and refine.

6. The US energy industry has entered a "renaissance" period in which lower costs produce advantages over global competitors. In addition to LNG and refined oil exports, the chemical and fertilizer industries are poised to benefit. To meet demand, unprecedented infrastructure construction is under way.

## Natural Gas (NG), Coal, and Nuclear Energy

Because people feared its explosive nature, NG was not considered a vital energy component and dismissed it from serious discussion. Today NG is easily and inexpensively transported by pipe, and it is a dominant, raw material in the production of food processing, glass, petroleum refining, chemicals, plastics, fertilizers, cement, and pulp/paper. Its costs are half as much as coal and is about 40% cheaper than nuclear power plant construction. In addition, NG is a more efficient alternative to oil and coal; 65%-plus of all buildings are heated with natural gas; 6 out of every 10 new electric generating facilities are powered by natural gas; and one-fifth of the US industry uses natural gas as a primary fuel. NG accounts for about 23% of total energy consumed in the US, of which 46% is for commercial use, 23% for electric generation, and 22% for residential use. Due to its exploration, production, processing, and distribution aspects, it is a $250 billion industry employing more than three million people. NG is the third-largest global energy source after oil and coal, the largest source of fossil fuel in terms of reserves, and it comes with many advantages: it burns cleaner than coal and crude, and is more versatile and efficient. Conventional NG reserves are highly concentrated in four countries: Russia dominates with 30%, followed by Iran with 18%, Qatar 15%, Central Asia 10%, the US 5%, and Saudi Arabia, United Arab Emirates, Nigeria, Indonesia, Venezuela, and Algeria the remainder. However, the US has discovered unconventional (shale) NG in recent years by hydraulic fracturing; producing numbers twice the equivalent of Saudi oil reserves. Large quantities of shale gas are found in the US/Canada, China, Europe, Argentina, Brazil, North Africa, and Mongolia. If Pennsylvania were an independent country, it would rank as the world's eighth largest gas-producer.

The problem of NG is not supply but that it is difficult to transport across oceans; hence, the rise in liquefied natural gas (LNG). LNG requires, in the exporting country, terminal construction involving compression and storage, and decompression facilities and pipeline construction in the importing country. For Japan, Korea, and Taiwan, NG arrives via LNG, of which Trinidad, Qatar, Egypt, Russia and Algeria are major exporters. The second largest market is Europe, primarily France, Germany, Spain, and Italy. LNG has been around for more than 40 years, but until recently, international trade has been limited to a few exporters and importers. This is about to change as more than 50 LNG ships and 34 liquefaction facilities are under construction. While pipeline costs run in the tens of $billions, it is LNG transportation technologies that impress. Tankers cost $200 million, regasification investments run upward of $2 billion, plus similar costs to construct liquefaction facilities and pipelines to transport the gas to market. The entire picture of the US modernizing its LNG facilities staggers the mind: tankers the size of three football fields, stand 12 stories high, and carry the energy of nearly 60 Hiroshima bombs.

Coal is the second largest source of energy in the world, and although rather ubiquitous in its geography, the US dominates world coal reserves, and has a monopoly on quality anthracite, and along with Germany, the finest high-quality metallurgical coal. Globally, 47% of all electricity is produced by coal, 20% by natural gas, and 17% by nuclear and 12% by hydro. From 1850-1950, coal emerged as the dominant energy source. It accounts for 45% of America's fossil fuel reserves, and the principal reason why, no matter what the environmental issues, it will not disappear as an asset class. As the base for the Industrial Revolution, the historic significance of coal cannot be understated. It employed enormous numbers of people as they converted coal into three basic substances that produced a myriad of goods–light oil, gas, and tar. Light oil produced benzene, toluene, xylene, crude naphtha, etc., which in turn produced hundreds of items such as explosives, synthetic fibers, insecticides, varnishes, etc. Coal gas produced feedstock's that included hydrogen, ethane, methane, ethylene, hydrogen sulfide and cyanide, and ammonia, all of which produced such items as fertilizer, solvents, sulfuric acid, resins, etc. Tar produced pitch, creosote, naphthalene, a large variety of phenol and pyridine bases, all of which delivered pharmaceuticals, plasticizers, dyes, wood preservatives, etc. Europe is the global leader in the processing of coal into gas, oil and numerous chemical industries. This fuel made high quality steel production possible as it created the largest economic multiplier in history until the second half of the 20th century. Coal has several major problems, of which the environmental concerns of $CO_2$, and sulfur emissions are paramount. Coal is also dangerous to mine, promotes subsidence, and is unsightly. Despite its disadvantages, coal consumption is growing, as it is 10 times cheaper than solar power, twice as cheap as wind power, and five times cheaper than biomass for electrical production.

Nuclear energy is produced (19% of global electrical energy) from 450 facilities in 31 countries: 104 are located in the US, 59 in France, 55 in Japan, 38 in China, 31 in Russia, 20 in Korea, and 18 in Canada. The number will increase by more than 140 by 2035, with China building 47 of the total, the rest by India, Russia and Europe. France, Belgium, Sweden, Russia, Ukraine and Belarus produce more than 50% from this source. The leading nations with recoverable uranium are Russia (40%), Canada (20%), Namibia (12%), and Australia and US (11% each). Although widely available, commercial uranium deposits are highly concentrated with seven mines responsible for more than 60% of global output. In addition to mine supply, a good portion of fuel is derived from stockpiles, decommissioned nuclear warheads and armaments, and reprocessing of spent uranium. The model for nuclear power is France, a country that produces the lowest cost electricity in Europe with more than 90% of its electricity emanating from nuclear and hydro sources. It is a net exporter of electricity to its neighbors, and a major exporter of nuclear technology. Despite the historical dominance of the US, Asia is emerging as the world's leading nuclear electric generating region.

Nuclear power and uranium are important investments for a many reasons. 1. One pound of uranium has the same energy content as 6,150 barrels of oil, and more than 1,300 tons of coal. 2. Nuclear electricity is clean, efficient, and reliable, requires little space, is capital intensive, cost effective and demands an expertly trained work force. If one factors environmental and health costs, nuclear is significantly cheaper and safer than coal- and oil-generated electricity. 3. Despite the advantages, nuclear power has a number of disadvantages, among which the high initial cost of construction, and the eventual disposal of waste are primary. 4. Of all possible alternatives to electrical generation, the nuclear option appears to be the most sustainable in terms of cost and environmental concerns. The next generation of reactors will be much safer, cleaner, more efficient, more powerful, less wasteful and cheaper to build. Mini nuclear reactors are efficient, cost effective, and flexible in their location. Thorium is also more common than uranium, less expensive to extract, unlimited in quantity, is much safer than conventional nuclear fuel as it is not subject to chain reactions, it does not produce weapon-grade fuel, is more plentiful, and produces far less radioactive waste. Therefore, the easiest, cleanest, and in the long-term cheapest way of meeting world electrical needs is through nuclear power, particularly through new breeder reactors and the use of thorium.

## Other Energy Sources

The most important renewable energy sources are solar, hydro, wind, geothermal, and biofuel, and while their aggregate percentage has more than doubled in the past 10 years, there is no evidence to suggest that they can replace fossil fuels and nuclear in the near or intermediate future. The "beyond petroleum" slogan is increasing, but like many faddish slogans, it is proving to be more noise than substance. So is "25 by 25," a proposition to have American agriculture provide 25% of the nation's energy by 2025. In order for alternative fuels to become important and replace oil, coal, nuclear, and natural gas, the price of oil must increase above $200b. Therefore, there is a false sense of security on renewable energy dependence as all remain expensive, and only exist through subsidies. Consider the following:

1. Hydro accounts for more electric than solar, geothermal and wind power combined. China is the world's largest producer of hydroelectricity, followed by Brazil, Canada, the US, and Russia. Also interesting is the fact that in 1920, the US generated 20% of its electrical supply from hydro, a percentage that has declined to 5%. The Congo River has the capacity to produce more hydroelectricity than in all of Africa. This is just one river with another 10 offering additional opportunities.

2. Ethanol, America's principal biofuel is a product of corn, and in Brazil and other tropical nations from sugar cane. Brazil is the world's leading producer followed by the US. With more than 80 million acres under cultivation, corn is the most widely produced feed grain in the US, of which 20% is used for ethanol production. The 110-ethanol producers are consuming a quantity of corn enough to feed 135 million people for one year. While ethanol, has become the darling of the "greens," it has a number of negatives: a. It is expensive as ethanol plants require huge amounts of water, and makes little economic sense as it takes 1.6 gallons of gas to produce one gallon of ethanol. b. Ethanol is not taxed. c. It lowers gas mileage. d. It is expensive to transport. e. The demand for corn, sugar cane, and soybeans is elevating the cost of these commodities to prohibitive levels and raising food inflation to new levels. It is neither a solution to the energy crisis or cheap, but a gargantuan misallocation of resources with enormous economic implications. f. Economically, the comparative advantage rests squarely with tropical nations with sufficient precipitation and the right soils to produce sugarcane. The latter is preferred, as it produces double the ethanol per acre than corn. Converting food to fuel is inefficient. Biomass is 40% more expensive in the generation of energy than wind, and nearly four times greater than coal. Unless there is a major technological breakthrough, its future is limited because it is subsidized.

3. Wind power is currently trendy, and positioned for huge growth prospects over the next 10 years. It is popular in Denmark where it supplies the country with 20% of its electricity, but there are many other nations and regions with sustained wind velocities greater than 18 miles an hour that can produce large volumes of electricity–Chile, Argentina, portions of Russia, Alaska, Norway, Ireland, the UK, Spain, France, etc. While there are many problems, as the price of oil exceeds $150 per barrel it will become more appealing, but the notion that 30% of global electrical energy by 2030 would come from wind power is a fantasy. Wind power in the US stands at 1% and will probably double by 2020, but it offers no panacea over the long run, despite subsidies.

4. Of all the renewable energy fuels, geothermal and solar hold the most promise because recent technology has reduced costs making production economically feasible, and safer. Trapped between the earth's crust and magma, the various forms of energy can be economically used in electric generation. The US is responsible for 29% of global output, followed by the Philippines, Mexico, Indonesia (contains the largest pool of geothermal energy), and Italy. Globally, the solar market is growing by 20% annually. Germany, Japan, and China appear to be the leaders, the latter emerging as the global leader in solar panel production.

The energy sector offers a number of compelling attractions: Valuations are low; the dollar continues to depreciate; the sector continues to consolidate, and usually underweight by most investors in favor of more glamorous sectors. It should be viewed as vital because as goes this sector goes the economy. In addition,

US energy demand over the next two decades is expected to increase faster than in the two previous decades by 2% a year with commercial energy consumption rising three times faster than residential consumption.

# The Metal and Mineral Industries

Metals are classified as: 1. Ferrous (iron) and associated ferrous alloys like manganese, chromium, cobalt, molybdenum, nickel, tungsten, etc. 2. Non-ferrous, include copper, lead, zinc, tin, etc. 3. Light metals contain aluminum, magnesium, etc. 4. Precious metals, embrace gold, silver, and the platinum group. While not all of the above are considered equally important, the most vital are referred to as base metals, and copper is considered the "king" because of its unique properties. It is the most indispensable in modern civilization due to its ability to conduct electricity and, hence, considered an excellent barometer of economic activity. 5. The importance of ferrous and non-ferrous metals is crucial to the production of machine tools, agricultural and industrial machinery, automobiles, shipbuilding, and electrical and chemical industries, among many others, as they form the backbone of the secondary sector. 6. Non-metallic minerals and building materials form a huge market, and they are used for all manner of construction, manufacturing, agriculture, monuments, glass, dam construction, brick, etc. The most important are: crushed and dimensional stone (slate, marble, sandstone, limestone, granite, etc.), sand, gravel, clay, etc. Fertilizer includes nitrates, potash, phosphates, and sulfur. In terms of tonnage, the most common construction sources are stone, gravel, sand, and clay. The aggregate quantities, value, and labor involved in mining, quarrying, etc. are highly significant to local, regional and national economies.

The significance of geography offers many insights. While well-endowed with metal/mineral resources, their distribution is highly concentrated in a small number of places. Depending on demand, areas containing those resources become political flash points. In time and place, these areas assume an aura of extreme importance. All metals and minerals are highly concentrated, and some of the largest deposits in unstable political regions. Columbrium, for example, comes from just four countries–Brazil, Thailand, Nigeria and Malaysia. Mica comes from Brazil and Malaysia; Manganese from Brazil, Gabon and South Africa; Platinum from South Africa and Russia; Chromium from Turkey, South Africa, and Russia. Furthermore, mining activities are usually located in low population and inaccessible locations such as mountains, desserts, and tropical rain forests. Nearly everywhere, there are major environmental issues dealing with pollution, ecological disruptions and water problems. The search for metals/minerals, plus additional commodities, has intensified in recent years as commodity prices have risen and EM demand accelerated.

## General Characteristics of Mining Industries

1. The mining industry is capital, technology, and labor intensive, and that means that in order for capital investments to take place, commodity prices must rise. A mine is a fixed asset requiring time to amortize a huge investment, and often, "Manhattan-type" projects are required with serious concerted governmental efforts to speed the process of sustained output. 2. Each resource has a peculiar economic geology that can be exploited by technology. Iron ore, such as hematite, magnetite, siderite, limonite, and taconite, have an unusual geography in terms of mining and processing. 3. Not all metal prices move in sync with each other, but generate their own specific cycles based on supply and demand, political, and other considerations. 4. Since 2001, all base metals have appreciated in price from 20-year lows when capital expenditures for exploration, mine development and infrastructure had left the sector in disrepair. 5. The ability of the industry revving up supply is not easy. Feasibility studies take time, and so does the construction of infrastructure. 6. The mining industry is encumbered by cost overruns, equipment, and skilled labor shortages. 7. The industry is characterized by: mining (extracting, loading, transporting, etc.); milling (crushing, washing, sorting, grinding, concentrating, etc.); smelting (roasting, converting, etc.); refining (electrolytic, etc.); fabricating (rolling, drawing, extruding, etc.); and finished product. 8. Mining and commodity companies are impacted by natural disasters like tectonic forces, hurricanes, etc. 9. Life of a mine is a function of reserves divided by annual output. All mineral and metal substances are finite as their output decreases with time. 10. Due to technological efficiencies, mining and mineral industries do not rank high in employment as compared with agriculture. 11. The sector is characterized by boom and bust features. 12. All mineral industries are influenced by geography, current technology, market conditions, political events, and operating costs.

2. A strategic metal is anything that is vital to defense and national welfare, and includes cobalt, manganese, chromium, rare earth elements, platinum group of metals, lithium, etc. What makes them politically problematical is the fact that nearly all are by-products of other metals, and, therefore, difficult to increase production, and easy for the few nations that do produce to extract political consideration. Of consequence is the fact that the largest concentration of rare earth research is China. Lithium is highly concentrated in three South American countries–Chile, Argentina and Bolivia. It is the lightest and least dense metal, and expected to grow demand by 20% annually. Cobalt is referred to as "critical" because it is vital for many cutting-edge metal technologies, such as specialty steel production. It is exported from the Congo, the world's leading supplier. Titanium

has the highest strength-to-weight ratio of any metal; hence, a critical ingredient in transportation. Molybdenum makes corrosion-proof steel, used in deep-water drilling, petroleum processing, pipelines, nuclear power plants, and shipbuilding. Two-thirds of molybdenum is used in steel and stainless steel output, 14% in the chemical industry, and an increasing percentage in super alloy and high-speed tool production. The US and China are responsible for 60% of global output followed by Chile. Beryllium is an "exotic" metal that has exceptional properties found in no other metal, and used in rocket production, semiconductors, optical systems and aircraft.

The importance of minerals throughout history cannot be understated as they shaped political, economic, and cultural landscapes. The following generalizations illustrate: a. Metals and minerals have helped to define national "core" and economic/political "pivot points," "heartlands," etc., and a crucial theme in the western political ethnic state system. b. Metals and minerals have been central to the concept of autarky. A country that could not produce a needed commodity from its own resources was considered weak in relation to its neighbors. Insufficiency posed dangerous conditions such as the possibility of blackmail in time of crisis, and the ignominy of dependency. c. From a political vantage point, metals and minerals are considered concomitant military and economic power elements. d. No country is 100% self-sufficient, but the size of the political unit enhances the possibility of more resources becoming potentially available; hence, one reason for imperial aspirations. e. Technology has a tendency to make what was once a "strategic metal/mineral" useless from an economic viewpoint, and to make others indispensable. Rare earths, a collection of seventeen rare elements, have recently emerged from complete obscurity to become major players in a host of new superconductors, magnets, wind turbines, etc. As demand rose rapidly in recent years, China has emerged as the world's leading producer with an output exceeding 95% of total. These metals are so critical in minute quantities for many cutting-edge technologies that a buying panic may ensue in the near future. Cerium produces the finest glass polish. Neodymium is a critical ingredient in the production of tiny magnets used to direct smart bombs and an important component in helicopter blades, tanks, submarines, and guided missiles. In recent years, it has experienced one of the most spectacular price increases in the history of commodities. Alternative supplies are difficult, thus crippling the defense industry, as there are no substitutes for certain applications. Scandium is an element that is 10 times more expensive than gold. 7. As the world's super military power, the US has become highly vulnerable to a number of strategic metal imports. Twenty-four metals represent 100% import dependence with another 65 compromising between 20%-80% self-sufficiency. The US imports more than 75 minerals and metals today than it did 15 years ago. The strategic, geopolitical element of metals is so important that it prompted J. Paul Getty to say, "The meek shall inherit the earth, but not the mineral rights."

Technological and strategic considerations play a heavy hand in this sector: a. Depending on the country or region, these metals are highly significant to the national or regional economy. b. With technological advances, competition from substitutes, synthetics, and the ability to switch from one to another, occur at an amazing rate, and, as a result, it becomes difficult to estimate future use and demand. c. Over time, metals and minerals have varied in their geopolitical significance, as in the case of the Persian Gulf for oil, Morocco/Algerian border for cobalt, Ruthenia for uranium, Cyprus for copper, Zimbabwe for asbestos, the Congo for copper, China for tungsten, South Africa for uranium, Sri Lanka for thorium, and Baku and Ploesti for oil. d. The evolution of metal discovery from empirical observation to geophysical exploration (magnetic, electrical, electromagnetic, single cable, gravimetric, seismic, refraction, radiometric methods, etc.) has evolved at a phenomenal pace. e. All metals are the product of specific geologic forces and thus found in specific places. When the mode of formation is correctly diagnosed, discovery is facilitated in determining depth, lateral extent, richness, etc. The geologic processes of volcanism, diastrophism, weathering, and deposition are the main factors determining the type and form of mineralization. f. Mining and mineral industries do not rank high in terms of employment when compared with secondary and tertiary industries, but are extremely important to the overall economy due to capital and skill intensiveness producing extraordinary multipliers. g. Minerals and metals often contain important national strategic components that vary with prevailing military and technological exigencies, as well as geopolitical events. h. Unlike food, minerals can be stockpiled. i. Changing world patterns of supply and demand are intensifying as industrialization has shifted from DMs to EMs. j. The speculation that the price of silver and gold are manipulated is given support by the fact that JPMorgan Bank is custodian of SLV, the largest ETF, and holds a short position in silver equivalent to 40% of global silver output.

## Precious Metals

Precious metals consist of gold, silver, and the platinum group, of which gold commands an inordinate amount of attention. Since the Neolithic Revolution, gold has been, and remains, the most important form of money as it serves as a store of value, a medium of exchange, and acts as a unit of account. It has survived war and governmental bankruptcies and remains the only means of payment free of central bank authority, As insurance against monetary inflation, it has evolved as the most hoardable commodity. In this regard, it is interesting to note that one ounce of gold buys a similar amount of goods and services as it did just prior to World War I. James Dines, writing in 1975, said that gold is "capitalism's pituitary gland." Moreover, many a writer has invoked the "Golden Rule," that "He who owns gold makes the rules." Gold, therefore, is different from any other asset as it represents the ultimate currency when all others fail. It has been accepted as payment of debt for thousands of years, and it is the basis of a store of value in agricultural societies that lack a modern financial system. In sharp contrast, politicians producing thousands of wealth-erasing bubbles and economic crashes have exploited all fiat currencies. In the words of JP Morgan: "Gold is money, and nothing else." For 5,000 years, it has been accepted by everyone and has survived all fiat currencies.

The primary producers in percent of global output are, China, South Africa, Australia, US, Russia, Peru, Canada, Indonesia, Mali, Uzbekistan, Ghana, and another 40-plus countries. The US, Germany, the IMF, France, Italy, Switzerland, Netherlands, Japan, China, and India, collectively hold 70% of all gold bullion. Equally revealing is the fact that gold represents 72% of capital reserves in the US, 68% in Germany, 67% in Italy, 65% in France, 58% in Portugal, and 55% in the Netherlands. China, Russia, Japan, Taiwan, India, and nearly all Persian Gulf nations are accumulating gold faster than DMs. All the gold mined, placered, and quarried throughout history would amount to a cube that measures 60x60x60 feet and is worth $9 trillion at current prices. Because of its unusual properties and scarcity, it is expensive, little is wasted, much is recycled, and little lost throughout history.

August 15, 1971, is an important date in the annals of gold. That's when the American government prohibited the conversion of dollars for gold, and, in an instant, the convertibility of the dollar to gold ended triggering a rise in the price of gold from the then prevailing price of $35 per ounce to more than $800 nine years later. Gold then entered a secular bear market when it bottomed at $252 per ounce in 1999. It then rose rapidly when it reached an all-time high of $1,950-plus per ounce in 2011. In an environment of rising interest rates, gold may not climb rapidly in price, but when accompanied with high rates of inflation, gold begins to soar above its historical trend line. Furthermore, a picture of negative interest rates always seems to light a fire in the value of gold and other precious metals. Bankers, who publically hate gold, are very happy to settle accounts in gold.

A number of interesting FAQS: 1. China has emerged as the world's largest and lowest-cost gold producer. 2. India and China are the world's two largest gold markets representing about 64% of total transactions. Gold reserves in EMs have more than quadrupled. The largest single central bank purchase of gold in recent history occurred in 2009 when India purchased 200 tons of gold from the IMF. 3. Gold production peaked in 2001 at 82 million ounces, and now stands at 75 million. The older mines have been exhausted, large discoveries are rare, costs have risen, lower grade mines are now the rule, and geopolitical issues do much to curtail both exploration and production. 4. Gold is extremely rare, found only in 0.002ppm, compared with iron which is 62,200ppm, and rarer than silver by a factor of 15. 5. The gold content of jewelry varies by venue: in the US, it is 58.3% gold or 14-karat, in Europe 74% gold, or 18-karat, and in many areas of the Middle East and South Asia, it is as high as 22-karat (92% gold). 6. Industrial uses for gold include electronics, missiles, computers, etc. Because of its resistance to corrosion and the fact that it is malleable, it is consumed for jewelry and for decoration. 7. Gold is immune to economic declines, currency crises, and stock market disruptions. Since gold cannot be created from nothing like fiat money, but only from work and capital investments, it retains value and simply cannot be counterfeited or replaced by a substitute. It is therefore described as the "golden constant," because of its ability to serve as a store of value and preserve purchasing power. While almonds, fishhooks, and other exotica have been used as money, gold has endured the test of time. 8. Lenin, Hitler, Mao Tse-Tung, and Franklin Roosevelt, all share an interesting commonality–they all banned the private ownership of gold. 9. Prior to World War I, inflation was practically non-existent, an extraordinary period for personal saving and wealth building. Because the gold standard imposed fiscal discipline on political and economic behavior, the dollar lost but 4% of its purchasing power during 1820-1910, only to lose 80% of its purchasing power during the period 1971-2010. 10. Eighty-five percent of all mined gold to date occurred in the past 110 years, and 50% in the past 50 years, and yet, there is less than one ounce of gold available per capita globally. 11. Gold has outperformed equities, bonds and cash since 2002 and remains the default currency. 12. Gold mirrors the rise in inflation and periods of military conflict because the latter is accompanied by rising interest rates, the destruction of property, and the loss of life, and possible reparation payments when the war ends. During the US Civil War gold nearly tripled in three and one-half years. The same thing has occurred throughout history: Whenever there is military conflict, even during periods of deflation, gold outperforms, as in the Great Depression when Homestake Mining rose from $65 a share in 1929 to $130 in 1931, $350 in 1933, and then $540 in 1936. 13. EMs are purchasing gold while DMs, in need of capital, are selling bullion.

A good measure of the value of gold is the gold/Dow ratio, or the number of ounces of gold necessary to buy the Dow industrials. For more than 100 years, the average ratio of gold to the Dow has been about 5:1. In 1980, it took but an ounce of gold to buy the Dow; in 1999, it took 44 ounces, and in 2012, it required 10 ounces. Another measure is the gold/oil ratio, which is based on the price of one ounce of gold in relation to a barrel of oil. Gold is expensive compared to oil when it takes more than 25 barrels of oil to buy an ounce of gold. That was the pattern immediately after 1980, but at the time of this writing, one can buy an ounce of gold with 13 barrels of oil. Another comparative measure is the silver/gold ratio, historically 15:1 (the same ratio found in the earth's crust) at the time of ancient Greece, 15:3 in Colonial America, 90:1 in 1991, and currently at 60:1. Silver, thus, is undervalued and likely to appreciate in price more rapidly than gold. A more important measure is the gold coverage ratio, or the amount of gold on deposit at the Fed against the total money supply. At the time of this writing, the ratio is 12%, a significant departure from its historic average of 40%. Why own gold? Banks and wealthy people own it, it is a good hedge against inflation, it diversifies a portfolio, it preserves value and used as collateral. According to Basel III, banks are allowed to hold bullion (up to 6% of bank reserves) and be counted as Tier 1 assets, just like cash or bonds.

Silver, mined since 4,000 B.C., has been one of the earliest means of exchange, and exhibited relatively stable output and prices throughout history up to 1515 when Spaniards found silver in Mexico and South America. Output rose at spectacular rates, until the 1800s when production doubled with the settlement of the western portion of the US. Since then, global output rose fifteen-fold. World production is about 600 million ounces, produced in more than 50 countries, with Peru and Mexico the leaders. Silver has been traded in London since the 1600s. The market is small, thinly traded, and its price, while volatile, tends to move parallel to gold. Very little silver is mined in pure form, as 80% is a by-product of gold, zinc, lead, and copper and the only metal whose supply is governed by the price of its primary metals. This has profound implications for the industry to meet immediate demand, as it would require the exploration and the production of the other related metals, all of which require time, money, and an effort to bring on line. In the past 90 years, the price of silver has risen dramatically. It rose from $0.25 the ounce in 1932, when $100 bought 400 ounces, to $30 today when $100 buys 3.3 ounces, and clear reflection of $US decline.

Silver is second to crude oil in the number of industrial applications, and its price inelastic in nearly all applications. In the world of commodities, silver is a tiny market in terms of the firms that mine, with the total value of the product offered for industrial use. Silver prices make parabolic moves that can be spectacular in the sense that new highs are often made in a matter of months after being depressed for decades. Global demand for silver has changed in recent years, with industrial uses accounting for 57% (increasing), jewelry and silverware, 21% (increasing), coins and investment 16% (increasing), and photography 6% (decreasing). Silver is considered the most versatile metal with many uses devoid of substitutes: It is the best conductor of electricity and heat; it is chemically stable; it is the finest reflector of light; it has high tensile strength; it is fatigue resistant; and it is used for catalytic oxidation in the plastics industry. It is a major ingredient in batteries, bearings, and silverware, water purification, and solar energy. The dramatic recent increase has been in medical applications such a burn therapy and sanitation. It is a major component in telecommunications, for silver membrane switches in computers, and to preserve lumber.

Gold and silver prices are expected to rise. 1. Stockpiles are at historic lows. 2. There are few pure silver mines in existence, and because of its secular bear market of 1980-2002, there has been little capital investment in new production facilities. 3. Production is decreasing and demand is increasing with central banks having little silver left relative to historic inventories. 4. The silver "short" position exceeds global production, something that is not found in any other commodity. 5. Each year more uses for silver are discovered than for any other metal. 6. Most gold is mined and accumulated, while silver is mined and consumed. 8. The Barron's Gold Mining Index is currently at its lowest level since 1938. 9. Central banks are buying more gold than they are selling, continued fiat creation, the lack of balanced budgets, and currency wars all fuel a price spiral. 10. Gold is the ultimate default currency and the only currency not subject to replication. 11. The combination of monetary inflation, volatile energy prices, low interest rates, and a global credit crisis will propel precious metal prices upward. 12. Gold and silver prices remain below cost of production levels. Never in history have gold prices been driven below the cost of production for an extended period of time. 13. Chindia has a middle class that is greater than the US and Eurozone combined and, hence, dominates gold and silver demand.

Less well known are the platinum group of metals (platinum, palladium, iridium, rhodium, ruthenium and osmium), all with unique properties and industrial uses, and increasingly becoming major inputs in critical industries due to their resistance to corrosion and oxidation. Platinum, in particular, has a bright future, as it is more often used in jewelry, the automobile industry, pollution control, and for coin production. With an annual production of 7 million ounces, or one ounce for 12,000 people, platinum is the rarest of all precious metals. What makes this metal an interesting investment is that central banks hold very little, thereby making market manipulations impossible. The supply is uncertain and its price erratic because more than 90% comes from two countries: South Africa and Russia. Palladium, 11 times rarer than gold, derives its value from its industrial uses due to its ductility and resistance to both oxidation and high temperature corrosion. Rhodium is rarer, six times more expensive than platinum, and has a large number of industrial uses.

## Water, Agriculture, and Collectibles

Water is the world's single most important natural resource, and, like nearly all other commodities, exhibits extreme concentration. Seventy-five percent of the planet is covered in water, 98% of which is found in oceans—salty and, hence, useless for immediate consumption. Two percent is fresh, 1.6% is frozen in polar ice caps with only .4% available for human consumption. Moreover, while global population growth is increasing by 2.2%, the amount of fresh water available for human consumption is decreasing. It, therefore, is the ultimate commodity, as people cannot live without it. In DMs, the per capita use of fresh water exceeds 100 gallons per day, a quantity that will fall as prices rise and quantities become less plentiful. For investors it is a specialty niche market that offers opportunities. More than 25% of world rainwater flows through the Amazon River and empties for 125 miles into the Atlantic, and more than 85% of all fresh lake water is found in the Great Lakes region. Two-thirds of all fresh water resources are available in regions where the people are not. Twenty percent of the world is too dry to maintain large populations, 20% is marginal to additional population growth, 20% too cold, 20% too wet, and 20% too mountainous. Eighty percent of global population lives near water, and 90% of all trade travels by water.

More than half of the world's population is experiencing and/or expected to find themselves in water-stressed conditions by the end of this decade. Naturally, most of the potential conflict will occur in marginal deserted regions, and tropical areas due to scarcity, pollution, and disease. Polluted water is the single largest cause of illness in TWs as 85% of all endemic diseases are associated with contaminated water. Furthermore, chronic water shortages affect more than 4 billion people. Clean, fresh, water is not as common and plentiful as most people think. On a per capita basis, Iceland has more fresh water than any other country, followed by Canada, Brazil, and selected countries along the Guinea Coast of Africa, Peru, New Zealand, and selected island nations in Southeast Asia. The number of water resources shared by two or more countries number in the hundreds, and their governance regulated by about 2,400 individual treaties.

1. Fresh water is one of the rarest of all natural substances vital to human existence, and unlike most other commodities, has no substitute no matter the price. 2. After oil, and electricity, water is one of the largest global commodities. The transportation of water accounts for about 6% of all global energy and 7% of all electrical production. It is an industry that does not respond to the usual business cycles, as demand exceeds production, it is guaranteed a profit, and it suffers from no competition. 3. Water requirements to produce the following stagger the mind: 500 gallons for a single pork chop, 250 gallons for 8 ounces of milk, and 25 gallons for a single helping of rice. 5. In addition to peak oil, the concept of peak water must also be considered. Water projects are getting bigger, more expensive, and complicated. One example is the $20-plus billion Great Manmade River Project to tap geologic water under the Sahara and transport it to coastal cities. 6. Major geopolitical disputes will erupt over water in coming decades, primarily in the Middle East, all the arid and semi-arid regions of Africa, Latin America, and central and south Asia. 7. Usage is increasing at twice the population growth rate, its scarcity intensifying in TWs, and it is increasingly becoming hard to meet industrial, consumer, and agricultural demand in DMs. The industries that are most water-dependent are pulp and paper, textiles, agriculture, chemical, metals, glass, and electric generation. Water is a $500 billion industry touching every segment of daily existence.

The future for water utilities is bright because of rising demand, and due to the inelastic nature of the product, the industry is essentially recession-proof. Utilities are also not affected negatively by inflation, and price stability is assured, as vast quantities of water cannot be moved over long distances easily. Opportunities include water purification, desalinization, and infrastructure construction. In reference to the latter, EMs offer huge potentials as the pace of rural to urban migration intensifies; hence, the need for water distribution and the processing of waste. China and India offer opportunities as 75% of all settlements larger than 50,000 experience water shortages. In the US, one can gain entry into this industry by buying those companies that supply essential hardware like pumps, filters, valves, pipes, and equipment unique to the industry, as well as utilities. The latter are mainly local, inefficient, and unable to modernize their infrastructure as the vast majority serves fewer than 100,000 people. In addition, all public water utilities are poorly managed, inefficient, and expensive to operate. Half of the water in their systems is lost through leakage. The estimate of upgrading the nation's water supply system is upwards of $15 billion annually. Because of the small size and spacial fragmentation of the industry, the upgrading of water systems poses Herculean challenges. The current decentralization and fragmented nature of water supply appear ready for expansion, consolidation, and privatization. Historically, water was inexpensive in the US, but prices have risen, and investors should pay attention. This means that this industry is beyond the capacity of local municipalities to handle, and eventually, the industry will restructure. Systems need to be merged, and new water treatment systems constructed. Therefore, this industry will grow and consolidate going forward. In addition, the industry is unaffected by interest and inflation rates, recession or deflation, or partisan politics, as everyone requires water.

The industry faces a number of significant problems: 1. In DMs infrastructure inefficiencies abound; London and New York are littered with 200-year-old wooden pipes. The US has one million miles of obsolete pipelines and tens of thousands of antiquated pumping stations. Furthermore, half of the nearly 30,000 water systems, 21,000 public wastewater treatment facilities, and more than 45,000 dams and reservoirs will be rebuilt within the next 20 years because of age and lack of efficiencies. 2. Many parts of the US are experiencing water shortages, primarily, but not exclusively, west of the 20" isohyet with many aquifers running dry. 3. The annual water bill for the average family has risen from $300 in 2000 to about $450 in 2010. 4. Seventy percent of all fresh water is used for irrigation, 20% for industry, and the remainder for domestic purposes.

All aspects of the agricultural sector offer promising returns in the current commodity secular bull market. This not only includes raw land, arable (about 12% of global land, or about one acre per capita), and grazing land, but agribusiness, fertilizer and equipment companies. The promising future is based on the following: 1. Global population is growing, becoming wealthier, and demanding more and better protein. 2. Scientific research is developing more efficient and friendlier environmental fertilizers, genetically engineered crops, and more efficient meat producing animals. Genetic breeding, for example, is producing rice varieties of higher yields, improved nutritional content, better resistance to disease and pests, and requiring little or no fertilization. 3. About 75% of all grains are used to feed animals, and much of the growth will be associated with EMs. 4. Global arable land is not increasing faster than the demand for food. The world, therefore, faces a major challenge in furnishing additional food for more than 7 billion people, and the most effective and easiest way of doing this is through increased yields, something that cannot be realized without capital and R&D. 5. Fertilizer is one of the top investment themes, particularly potash and nitrogen as there are no substitutes, and because they are high margin commodities, they offer excellent investment possibilities. 6. Aquaculture accounts for 50% of the global commercial fish output. 7. While prime farmland varies widely across

America, average cost per acre rose from $190 an acre in 1970, to $800 in 1982, to $3,000-plus in 2012. 10. Corporate farming will rise in intensity, as the average age of the independent farmer is 61.

Collectibles, an esoteric sector, includes such assets as *objects d'arte*, Egyptian mummies, stamps, rare coins, 250-year-old ice hooks, etc., that form a narrow market fraught with liquidity problems and fraud. Unless one is extremely knowledgeable, adroit in ferreting out bargains, and extremely lucky, the chances of making serious money are an elusive dream. As an asset class, prevailing investor psychology and/or exogenous forces mainly condition price movements in this group. No matter how exciting and enticing, these markets are not for the neophyte as deceptive practices are a veritable gauntlet. Dealers are rarely honorable, art auctions are dens of potential thievery, and buyer protection is non-existent as deceptions are common with only dealers and "experts" benefiting. For most, there are better, "more in your favor investments." Major impediments to potential profits include insurance and/or storage costs, and huge 20%-plus commissions. Collectibles, therefore, are out of the reach of nearly all investors, with gold and real estate far simpler and easier ways to protect purchasing power.

# Mutual Funds

A mutual fund is an intervening agency that pools money contributed by investors into a number of investments that have common features and objectives. There are three main types: open-end, closed-end (CEFs), and Exchange-traded (ETFs). Mutual funds, historically known as "investment trusts," went out of business in the 1930s, and those that survived changed their name. They began to grow rapidly from 150 in 1958 to thousands with the advent of the Vanguard Group in the 1970s, and the popularity of retirement accounts. In 1980, there were but 500 valued at $100 billion, a number that has grown to 7,288 in 2010, valued at $10 trillion with approximately 90-plus million owners. Mutual funds offer many advantages: 1. They take the pressure off the investor in choosing individual stocks–the fund does it automatically. Because individual stock picking is not successful for most retail investors, mutual funds homogenize risk, particularly an index fund. Because the fund owns dozens or hundreds of different companies, individual stock risk is reduced as you are buying the haystack. 2. One can participate with several hundred dollars, and one can acquire additional shares automatically. 3. No load funds reduce expenses, and distributions can be reinvested automatically at no cost. 4. When DCA occurs, the tendency of buying and selling prematurely is eliminated, as is the inclination to excessively trade. DCA, in addition, will not impel an investor to switch funds every other month or year. Other mutual fund features include:

1. Low cost diversification in investment styles, liquidity, dividend reinvestment privileges, exchange privileges, convenience, professional management, easy access to foreign markets, and simplicity with little paper work, are the main advantages.

2. Fund expenses refer to money deducted to defray operating costs. Aggregate expenses range from .05% to about 2.5%. Funds often have hidden costs that are impossible to spot. They include, among others, bid-ask spreads and commissions that are extracted out of fund assets. Redemption fees for positions held less than a specified period could amount to 2%. Exchange fees are those charged when an

investor switches from one fund to another, and account maintenance fees are those charged for the maintenance of low-balance accounts. Another significant expense is the one associated with a "load," or commission. Many funds add a penalty fee for trading within a specified period. The combination of high salaries, bonuses, sophisticated marketing, office expenses, and corporate rewards all frame a picture of potential underperformance.

3. "Style drift" refers to the fact that the original objectives of each asset class are no longer present in the fund's portfolio, thus posing a serious problem. Often as much as 50% of securities may drift from the funds stated objectives forcing investors to own inappropriate stocks.

4. A confusing element with fund performance lies in the various benchmarks used, the latter, usually an index that correlates with the compared fund to measure performance. Many funds do not replicate the benchmark entirely, and managers often take risks with client money in order to boost total returns and, in the process, bend or waiver from stated objectives. Finding a fund that has underperformed the market is easy, but discovering one that is able to outperform the market consistently is a near impossibility. Disregard all "star" recommendations; they have no predictive ability as the rating reflects former performance. "5-star" funds usually fall to the bottom quintile as often as "1-star" funds rise to the top. Indexes vary enormously over time in terms of composition and issues held.

5. Investor mistakes are common: With thousands of mutual funds, more than 600 ETFs, as well as other financial vehicles available, it is unlikely that many will be carefully scrutinized, and those that will be purchased are a result of clever advertising or as a recommendation from someone not necessarily competent to offer proper guidance. Most investors lack a foreign component, index funds, small-caps and commodities. Therefore, do your dishes thoroughly and avoid those with high expense ratios, "new-age" concepts and those not having an income-generating component. How many funds should you own? The "right" or "ultimate" number of funds is a function of many variables; foremost of which is the size of the assets in question, age of the investor, knowledge, and the propensity to expend energy and time. Therefore, there is no magic number, but one can start with one broad-based diversified index fund per asset box for each of the nine style boxes.

6. Due to mismanagement and criminal activities, funds can and do go out of business. Since 1995, more than 400 funds have ceased operations. Fewer than 60% of all funds have a 5-year record of accomplishment, and less than 700 have a 10-year history. Of those in the latter category, about 87% underperformed the S&P 500 during that period. In addition, no matter what the prospectus professes, investors may get less than desirable diversification. Therefore, mutual funds have a dark side to them, a sight not pretty to observe if one wishes to understand how sausage is made in this industry. Many mutual funds have come into serious

scrutiny in the past 20 years for poor oversight, excessively high expenses, outrageous managerial salaries, late-trading privileges to preferred clients, illegal and improper market timing, under the table payments to steer business in a given direction, etc. Remember that where there is money there is corruption, and mutual funds are not immune to the temptation of easy money. In the words of John Bogle: "When we have strong managers, weak directors, and passive owners, it's only a matter of time until the looting begins." Often, names are confusing, as in the case of "equity income" and "growth and income." Moreover, while every fund has to expense its operating costs, the range from the least cost to the highest may be greater than 4%.

7. Mutual funds come in two basic varieties: passive and active. Passively managed, or "indexing" refers to any fund that seeks to replicate an existing benchmark such as the Total Market. Its purpose is not to "beat" but to earn the "market return," minus expenses, thus eliminating manager risk. Moreover, not all funds "replicate" their target benchmark in an identical manner, and funds have the flexibility to institute "sampling" strategies. Nevertheless, over time, index funds offer the best risk/reward advantage over actively managed funds and should form the core position(s) of any diversified portfolio. According to John Bogle, over a 15-year period, the Total Market Index fund returned 86% to investors, 12% to taxes, and 2% to expenses. This is in stark contrast to the average equity fund that returns only 45% to investors, 22% to taxes, 12% to expenses, 8% to sales commissions, 7% cash drag, and 6% to transaction costs. Indexing, therefore, is a passive portfolio strategy involving minimal new inputs of information, no need for extensive research and analysis, and emotionally easy on investors: they do not have to predict the future to be successful, and that makes indexing a necessity. Make no mistake as to the value of indexing as most institutions make use of index funds. Performance is the market minus expenses. The allure of outperforming the market with an actively managed fund is the driving force for active management.

In addition: a. Index funds are cost efficient, have a low turnover rate and minimize tax liabilities. While the S&P 500 Index has a turnover rate of less than 4%, aggressive growth funds often exhibit turnover rates of 200%-plus. b. Index funds simplify the investment process by outperforming individual stock selection and managed fund performance 75% of the time. c. They eliminate style drift. d. The strategy eliminates market timing, frequent trading, and chasing performance and hot stocks. e. Index funds best capture risk and return, substantiated by the fact that more than 75% of fund managers and more than 90% of individual investors fail to outperform the market each year. If still in doubt, heed the words of Warren Buffett: "The best way to own common stocks is through an indexed mutual fund." Peter Lynch said, "Most individual investors would be better off in an index mutual fund." Charles Schwab said, "Most of the mutual fund investments I have are index funds." Jesse Livermore said, "A man may beat a stock or a group at a certain time, but no man living can beat the stock market! A man may make money out of individual deals in cotton or grain, but no man can beat the cotton market or the grain market. It is like the track. A man may beat a horse race, but he cannot beat horse racing." f. They take the element of "finding the needle in the hay stack" out of the investment equation. It is rare, if not impossible, for the individual to consistently pick winners, but an index fund will always match its benchmark performance. g. Index funds, by their very nature, do not engender high turnover; hence, a distinct advantage, because "silent partners," such as expenses, "cash drag," taxes, etc., that lower total returns are not present. h. They outperform managed funds by 3%. Buy the S&P 500 Index with $4,000 annually in a ROTH at age 25 and at 10% annual growth, you will retire a millionaire at age 65 and not pay taxes. i. While indexing works and works well. If one buys and holds forever, indexing mitigates individual stock risk as the average company lifespan is less than 20 years.

Despite the above, there are many issues confronting indexing: a. Not all index funds are alike. They differ in performance, expense ratios, sector weighing and expenses, all of which say volumes about the integrity of fund performance. b. Distortions occur because most tend to be weighted by market capitalization, thus skewing the index toward the largest companies. Equal weight indexes give each stock in the index equal weight, thus spreading risk equally among all stocks in the index with positions rebalanced periodically. c. Few hold cash, so that in market downturns, they are subject to losses due to redemptions. d. Percent composition of the Total Market, S&P 500, and other benchmarks, will vary over time. For example, financials comprised less than 1% of the S&P in 1957 and 21% today, information technology rose from 3% to 19%, healthcare from 1% to 15%, and consumer staples from 6% to 10%. In sharp contrast, materials declined from 26% to 3%; utilities from 8% to 3%, energy from 22% to 10%, and consumer discretionary from 15% to 11%. The top 50 stocks influence more than 70% of the S&P 500 Index, and thus the remaining 450 companies exert a minimal influence. e. Index funds are the classic *minestrone*–they contain everything and anything found in the garden. They also use different benchmarks and not all remain true to the percentages or the actual number of securities held. With broad-based index funds, you get homogenization of the good, the bad and the ugly.

Managed funds far exceed index funds in number, and can fulfill every investor fantasy. They come at a price in terms of higher risk and expenses, inconsistency and underperformance. In the words of Jeremy Siegel: "This lagging performance of active managers shouldn't be a surprise; it's a matter of simple arithmetic, as in the case of many mutual funds that held Enron to bankruptcy. For every investor who succeeds in beating the market, someone else has to fall short of matching the market. When the costs (time and money) of actively picking stocks are subtracted from the outcome, those who actively engage in picking stocks must, on average, lag behind the market." In the words of W. Simon: "Investing with an investment guru creates unexpected problems for investors. First, since there is no correlation between past and future performance, investors can never know when (if ever) the future will repeat the excellence of the past.

Second, investors cannot tell whether an outstanding record of accomplishment was achieved because of skill. Third, an outstanding record of accomplishment enriches relatively few investors. Fourth, in 2011, fewer than 25% of all money managers outperformed the S&P 500 index, and fewer than 20% had outperformed the index since 2000. Investors can avoid all these problems by investing in index funds." Moreover, managed funds that rank among the top quintile for one to three years, eventually drop to the bottom quintile, and the same type of performance occurs when analyzed over five and ten-year intervals. Index funds never soar, but slow steady growth commensurate with market performance rewards over the long run.

Managed funds believe that efficient markets do not exist, and that the inherent inefficiencies, which produce mispriced securities, offer opportunities to "beat the market." About three-quarters fail, and some fail miserably when compared to indexed funds. Some are successful, but they are rare, and again, expensive to own and hold. Wall Street spends tens of billions of dollars annually convincing investors that they can beat the market. Managed funds cannot beat indexed funds because of expenses, a sum that it simply too high to overcome. Active managers are able to enhance value in one of three ways: By timing the market through elaborate trading methods, by taking advantage of inside information, and by predicting the future. To accomplish this feat, the manager seeks to guess the direction of a large number of market variables in an attempt to choose those specific issues that would outperform. The fund manager is, through superior intellect and expertise able to "pick" superior stocks and avoid those that are likely to underperform. Sometimes they are correct, but their long-term record is less than stellar. By trying to outperform, individual issues are constantly "churned," and expenses remain high. Over the past 30 years, the percent of fund managers that failed to match the S&P 500 Index ranged from 28% in 1982 to 86% in 2001. The average was 74%. Even more fascinating is the fact that less than 6% of fund managers are able to outperform the S&P 500 for more than five consecutive years. Therefore, accept what the market offers, and not expose yourself to the added risk. Despite their miserable performance, they are popular, brag about extraordinary achievements, but say little about high expenses and underperformance. Benjamin Franklin said, "One man may be more cunning than another, but not more cunning than everybody else."

## Criteria in Mutual Fund Selection

1. Look for a long record of accomplishment; 10 years is good, but 20 are better. The length of time is a good indication of stability and performance as per Vanguard's Wellington Fund, a balanced fund that has a 70-year record. 2. Compare past performance with the benchmark, the latter representing a record over time. 2. Measure the expense ratio with the category average. High expenses reduce total returns. 3. Select funds with a turnover of less than 25%. 4. Low manager turnover is a good thing, as it should reflect a successful record of

accomplishment. Funds with a manager of ten or more years in office are a good sign. 5. Redemption fees, imposed to discourage market-timing activities, are a good practice.

## What is "The Market?"

Most people consider the DOW Industrials as "the market," but these large-cap stocks number 30 and account for 25% of Total Market value. The significance of the DOW Industrial Index is that since 1928, its average annual total returns over rolling 10-year periods have registered just one declining period, and that was 1928-1937. It registered gains of 18% or higher 7 of 67 times; 15% or higher 24 of 67 times, 10% or higher 38 of 67 times, and 5% or higher 57 of 67 times. Nevertheless, while nearly all of the 30 original DOW stocks have gone kaput or merged, the index endures adversity and makes new highs. The DOW is also not a true index as the editors of the Wall Street Journal choose members, and not quantitative criteria. The S&P 500 is much broader and accounts for about 70% of market value. When buying the Wilshire 5000, you are buying the "Total Market," or nearly every issue registered for sale in the principal markets, and is the world's largest index. Therefore, when "the market" is mentioned, I mean the "Total Market." Others include, the NASDAQ-100 Index, consisting of the 100 largest nonfinancial companies, and considered the tech sector proxy. The NASDAQ Composite consists of 3,000 companies. The American Stock Exchange Index is heavily weighted toward smaller and commodity-related stocks. The Lehman Brothers Aggregate Bond Index tracks the US bond market, ex-municipal and high-yield bonds. Forex is the largest global currency market. The most important foreign index is the MSCI EAFE Index (Morgan Stanley Capital International Europe, Australia, and Far East Index). The New York Stock Exchange Composite measures the performance of 1900 stocks offering breadth and accuracy.

While benchmarks are highly stable over time their sector weightings are not, and the years 1900 and 2000 illustrate the point. In terms of valuations, railroads comprised about 60% of the Dow in 1900 and less than 1% today; banks and finance 7%, and 24% today; textiles 1% and now .1%; iron and steel 5% and now .2%; technology, practically non-existent then, rivals financials today, pharmaceuticals nearly absent are now about 12%; and retailing grew from .1% to 6%. No matter what the position of US equities in this century, the sector composition of global markets by the end of this century will be as dramatically different as 2000 was from 1900, and 1900 from 1800. Of the 500 largest companies that appeared on Fortune Magazine's list in 1955, only 71 remain today, and over that span of time, about 2,000 appeared on the list. If anything, this tells a lot about the efficacy of investing in indexes, as they do homogenize risk. Nevertheless, benchmarks should always be adjusted for inflation in order to frame "real" metrics. For example, the DJI is down 8% from its 2000 high, the S&P 500 down 24%, NASDAQ down 50%, and gold up nearly 265% from the same base year. In addition, benchmarks invariably describe averages and the later are devilish mathematical concepts that distort investor perceptions. Since 1900, the Dow Jones Industrial Average has produced an annual gain of 7.1%, of which 69 years yielded positive returns, and 37 were negative. Interestingly, about 68% of the years were double (+ and -) digit returns, and only 8 years produced gains between 5% and 10%. The market, therefore, rarely produces "an average" year for the investor. For example, there are examples of areas with a 100-year flood probability experiencing two such floods within a 26-month period, while a desert region with an average of 5" of rainfall often sees no precipitation for 10 years, but can experience 55" on the eleventh year. Consider the percentage declines during the crash of 1987: S&P -33%, aggressive growth -39%, growth and income -31%, high-yield bond fund -4%, 10-year Treasury +.07. During the last three-year recession, the same five asset classes performed thusly: -47%, -62%, -27%, -13%, and +23%. The tyranny of numbers continues: in late October 2007, more than 50% NASDAQ gains were from three stocks-Apple, Research in Motion, and Google. It is also important to note that since 1970, the nominal Dow Jones Industrial Average rose by 1,840%, but only 304% in real terms.

## Capitalization Size

Many mutual funds specialize in securities according to company size, a very important consideration as capitalization presents both opportunities and caution. Large-cap stock funds usually represent 70% of market capitalization and number 500-plus companies, mid-cap funds usually contain about 2,000 stocks and account for 20% of market capitalization, and small-cap funds contain in excess of 4,200 stocks and represent 10% of the market. The reasons to hold different sized companies in a portfolio are crucial as they affect total returns, as small, medium and large-cap stocks are non-correlating. Ibbotson Associates reports that since 1926 small-cap stocks have outperformed large-cap stocks by 2% annually, 12.2% vs. 10.2%. Since 1950, the divergence has widened; small-cap value stocks have outperformed small-cap growth by 6%, mid-caps by 4.5%, and large-caps by 2.6%. Like everything else, small, medium and large-cap stocks run in cycles: 1991: large-cap stocks returned 28% and small-caps 38%; 1992: Small-cap stocks returned 16% and large-cap 7%; 1993: Small-cap returned 16% and large-cap 10%. 1994: Large-caps returned 2% and small-caps -3%; 1995: Large-caps returned 32%, small-caps 24%; 1996: Small-caps returned 15%, large-caps 21%; 1997: Small-caps returned 20%, large-caps 32%.

1. Micro-caps, capitalized under $200 million and representing the smallest companies, are speculative in nature, but they present extraordinary expectations. They attempt to find a new niche in an existing market or to exploit a market with an innovation or invention. Illiquid, they suffer from high volatility. They have no earnings and a penchant for going out of business. When successful, dreams are made of these stocks.

2. Small-cap companies, capitalized from $200 million to $1 billion, are similar to the above. Invariably, they suffer from competition, outperform in the initial stages of an economic recovery, and have the potential for above-average earnings growth. In general, price volatility is a hallmark of small-cap stocks. Their existence rests on innovation, one or two products, and trade with a high PE. Small and young companies have a proclivity for explosive growth but suffer from survival risk. They have a problem in competing with well-established firms, and suffer from irregular earnings. The problem is to find the rare gems with a future from a large stable of under performers. Because of their high volatility and tendency for underperformance for many years, small-caps should never dominate a short to intermediate portfolio. However, for those with a time horizon beyond 10 years, small-cap stocks will outperform. The reasons are varied and compelling. Due to their small size, this market sector has the ability to grow much faster than large-cap companies do. However, they are inefficiently priced, and because of their potential, they attract excellent management teams. Nearly every portfolio should have a minimum of 15% small-cap stocks and for those less than 40 years, as much as 25%.

3. Mid-cap stocks offer diversity between the stodginess of the large and the impetuous nature of small-caps. Capitalized between $1 billion and $19 billion, their appeal lies in a more proven record of accomplishment progressing from the nursery stage to the mid-level status. They exhibit greater liquidity, have narrowed the volatility and bankruptcy gap of small-caps, earnings are more consistent, and are more competitive.

4. Large-cap stocks are corporations with a history of earnings, profits, and dividend distributions. Nearly all have "brand name" recognition, a competitive global edge, pricing power, many are self-capitalizing, and their stock is liquid. In addition, they tend to be more fiscally sound, possess a seasoned management team, are more diversified, and benefit from economies of scale. Because of their size, annual growth is not as high as small and mid-sized companies. They encompass all companies above the $20 billion level, subdivided into several sub-groups: large-cap, $21-$50 billion; giant-cap, $51-$150 billion; and mega-cap, or companies with a market cap greater than $150 billion. Given the fact that these giant companies operate in a labyrinth of "state-privilege," all portfolios require at least a 10% allocation.

## Types of Mutual Funds

The best way to describe the wide range of mutual funds is to visualize a "food pyramid" divided into four levels. At the top are the aggressive, "enhanced," domestic and foreign growth, sector and hedge funds. Below is a wide variety of less dangerous domestic and foreign growth funds, followed by growth and income funds, which include a huge number of balanced and tax-exempt funds. The base includes a host of income–producing securities of which money market, CDs, and

Treasuries dominate. Within the universe of mutual funds, the number of permutations as to type is nearly infinite, but a select number are described below. All categories contain index funds offered in all sizes and varieties, of which Total Market, Total Bond and S&P 500 are the industry leaders.

## Growth Funds

Growth funds are known for above-average earnings, profit, and sales growth, usually 20% or better annually. They are known for high P/E and debt levels. Their lofty valuations are warranted as long as earnings growth remains high and they do not lose market share. Make no mistake about the allure of growth stocks when they are hot. They captivate the soul of investors and have an uncanny ability to enslave their conscious and unconscious minds.

1. Enhanced funds are those designed to outperform the market through aggressive leveraging, hedging, and other strategies. They come in many flavors, carry high expense ratios, are volatile, not regulated, expensive to own, and meant only for those with strong stomachs and a high net worth. 2. Contrarian funds seek to take the market timing aspects out of the hands of the individual investor by taking positions opposite to the prevailing direction of the herd. 3. Focus funds, characterized by few holdings, are composed of carefully selected stocks with the intent to outperform. 4. Hedge funds are unregulated limited partnerships, meaning that transparency is non-existent, as they do not disclose holdings, strategy, or performance. They have high entry point; hence, a game for the very wealthy and adventurous. By law, they cannot advertise, and only have a limited number of partners. Most important, they are very expensive as they charge fees of 20%-plus on all profits, not counting expenses. 5. Quant funds are driven by computer models whose purpose is to eliminate the element of emotion. 6. Growth funds come in all shades and flavors, from extremely aggressive to quality growth. Aggressive funds are those that seek maximum capital gain by investing in securities that do not pay dividends and expected to grow at above-average market rates. They have no or negligible earnings, are young in age, in new industries, most commonly technology, and have outrageous valuations. These funds, highly popular in the 1990s, have had their wings seriously clipped in recent years, but retain their notoriety. Taking bold initiatives in new and small companies, they often provide spectacular results. Obviously, volatility is their middle name, and are expensive to hold.

## Sector and Specialty Funds

Sector (or "theme") investing, is based on empirical observations of market behavior. Whether the market is in any stage of secular bear or bull, there is always a sector or sectors that are behaving differently. When one applies contrarian behavior, one is able to profit by selling the winners and buying underperforming sectors. The notion rests on the premise that as money flows to undervalued sectors (in any market), one or more sectors will outperform as no sector remains out of favor forever. The focus is on nine primary economic sectors: commodities, financials, consumer staples, consumer discretionary, healthcare, utilities, industrials, real estate, and technology. By paying attention to sector correlations, one can make serious money by investing appropriately. For example, REITs have an extremely low correlation with technology, healthcare, bonds and stocks; when the dollar declines, healthcare, basic materials, and energy outperform; when the dollar strengthens, financials outperform. In 2005, the S&P 500 rose 5% while utilities returned 15%, energy 34%, general retailing lost 2%, consumer discretionary lost 5%, and the automobile industry lost 30%.

The contrarian approach is based on the fact that current trends never continue forever. That is why investors must pay close attention to sector movements. For example, in the 1880s dominant industries included cotton, woolen goods, lumber, machine and foundry products, iron and steel, bricks, tile, and furniture. In the first decade of the 20th century it was machine and foundry products, and railroads. In the 1920s, it was iron and steel, cars, and electrical equipment. In the 1950s, it was bonds, cars, steel, meatpacking, and food. In the 1960s–1970s, it was cars, aircraft, steel, women's apparel, casinos, and commodities. In the 1980s, it was aircraft, communications, electrical components, newspapers and periodicals, plastics, and structural metals. In the 1990s, it was computers, bonds, communications, large-cap stocks, and retailing. In this century, entertainment, computers, communications equipment, financial services, international trade, transportation equipment, and commodities. In addition, sectors exhibit long cyclical behavior. For example, at the end of the secular bear market in 1981, the average utility yield approached 11%, and fell steadily during the ensuing bull market to about 2.5% in 2001. Since then, the yield has risen to about 3.5%, something that is expected to continue. Commit to memory the fact that excessive concentration in one area will always provide values in others areas because markets abhor vacuums. Just as water seeks its own level, money will flow to those market segments that offer the greatest returns, with market sentiment, in either direction always carrying the pendulum to extremes. At the time of this writing, precious metals offer the ultimate contrarian purchase. Sectors have also played key roles in market composition. For example, in the mid-1950s, energy and materials were the largest sectors, but 50-plus years later, among the smallest in the S&P 500. On the other hand, technology, healthcare, and financials, have switched roles, moving from the smallest sectors, to more than 55% of the S&P 500. Therefore, always look for empty trains.

What influences and drives economic sectors? Consumer Discretionary (disposable income, consumer confidence, economic growth, and interest rates); Utilities (interest rates, government regulations, environmental issues and legislation, cost of fuels); Industrial (secular economic trends, labor conditions, and government regulations); Information technology (industry competition, life expectancy of product, disposable income, national secular economic conditions, and government regulations); Healthcare (governmental regulation, industry competition, patent protection, and industrial capital expenditures in R&D); Materials (secular economic cycle, commodity prices, interest rates, and government regulations); Telecommunication Services (government regulation, industry competition, secular economic conditions, technological innovations, and discoveries); Financial (interest rates, secular economic conditions, Fed policies, government regulations, and credit losses); Energy (governmental regulation including special taxation, secular economic conditions, supply and demand conditions, and geopolitical events); Precious Metals (secular economic events, cost of production, geopolitical events, Fed policies, interest and inflation rates, and governmental regulations); and REITs (interest rates and governmental regulation, including tax policies and secular economic trends). It is necessary to note that the percentage of GDP by sector varies enormously by historical period.

When contemplating sector investing, note the following: 1. Because sector stocks have varying market cycles in terms of duration and amplitude, the tendency to trade frequently is associated with high expense ratios, often leading to inferior results. The factors that favor one sector over another vary widely over time as specific economic, social, and political circumstances generate sector-specific centripetal and centrifugal scenarios. 2. Frequently revised, sector indexes substantially alter their composition making historical comparisons difficult. 3. While contrarian investing sounds simple enough, it is difficult. Most investors find it arduous to behave in a direction opposite of prevailing opinion. It takes a brave individual with considerable fortitude, discipline and patience to buy those securities and sectors when the majority posits negative commentary. Lord Keynes described the contrarian spirit and investor as one in which "it is in the essence of his behavior that he should be eccentric, unconventional, and rash in the eyes of average opinion." 4. The safest method of buying low and selling high is to be a contrarian. Betting against the crowd rewards. The basic sectors with some overlap include:

Commodities: This sector refers to energy, paper and forest, base metals, precious metals, etc., and as a group, it is cursed by the endemic "boom and bust" cycle. Therefore, the prudent investor ought to purchase and dollar cost average (DCA) during periods when prices in this sector are depressed and characterized by low capital investment. Energy, the largest segment in the group, consists of all fossil fuels plus alternative sources for the production of electricity and other uses. It is a huge sector, usually underweight by most investors in favor of technology and financials. The sector is important because as it goes so goes the economy. A natural resource exhibits a negative correlation to equities, bonds and cash, and is one of two asset classes that have a positive relationship with inflation. Sixty years ago, when secondary production employed more people than either tertiary or primary activities, this sector was the largest in the S&P 500 Index. A neglected sub-sector is forest products, an industry that accounts for 6% of secondary output.

Consumer Discretionary: This sector refers to industries whose fortunes are based on discretionary income (cars, restaurants, etc.)

Consumer Staples: This group refers to goods such as soap, toothpaste, food, etc., sold no matter what the prevailing economic climate offers.

Financial Services: This sector includes conventional and investment banking, brokerage services, asset management firms, insurance and all manner of additional related services. Collectively, all of the above account for more than 30% of the valuation of the S&P 500. Immediately after World War II, secondary activities were responsible for 60% of all corporate profits and financial 10%, thus reflecting the enormous reversal of fortune in the character of the American economy. What used to be truly a Byzantine economic ecosystem, where all form of communication was occurring at snail pace and fraught with danger, decisions and monetary transfers are occurring at lightning speed today. It is also a sector that has undergone deregulation, and despite its recent scandals, continues to offer many opportunities. It is important to note that no broad market advance has ever occurred without financial sector participation. The importance of this sector is reflected by the fact that of the 50 super-connected global companies, 32 are financial institutions.

Healthcare: This large and complicated sector consists of giants like Merk as a proprietary drug company, biotech's, healthcare providers, equipment producers, hospital suppliers, etc. Healthcare has been the most successful economic sector, along with technology and real estate since 1982, and there is no reason to believe that with the 65-plus population increasing that it will not maintain its upward momentum. Domestic R&D as percent of drug sales rose from a 10-year low of 12% to 26% in 1995, only to fall 14% in 2004, and despite recent litigation issues, R&D is slowly increasing. Because they have high PE ratios, with most paying no dividends and experiencing bankruptcy issues, fund exposure is the easiest way for the individual investor to own this sector.

The US continues to lead the world with about 250 biotech-focused companies; Europe contains about 100 companies, and Asia has about 125. This is a sector dominated by small companies and consolidation appears to be a major reason why investors find the sector irresistible. Biotech research is highly clustered just like any other innovative technology to international technopoles. The agricultural "bio-belt," for example, is located in the greater St. Louis region, Central California, and in a few other regions with excellent agricultural universities. For big pharma, it is north-central New Jersey. In these centers, the overlap of physics, engineering, chemistry, computer science, and biology is taking place at breathtaking speed. What would usually take several hundred years to hybridize; scientists are able to do in a matter of years, or, at most, decades. That is only part of the story. The bioengineering of commercial crops is such that the new plant is more resistant to diseases, produces a higher yield, and demands no, or minimal, fertilizer. Biotech is particularly interesting as it is poised to become the next major growth sector for the coming decades as it is growing by 20-25% annually vs. 10%-plus for traditional large-cap pharmaceuticals. The emphasis in and the fields of genomics, proteomics, monoclonal antibodies, etc. is compelling, and ultimately rewarding. Taken together, the healthcare sector is highly sensitive to governmental policies and subsidies, and, as such, exhibits long stretches of growth or stagnation. What the dot.com stocks were in the 1990s, the biotech sector (especially regenerative medicine) will be for the next generation.

Industrials: Cyclical stocks, because of their "feast and famine" character, refer to companies that move in tandem with the business cycle, that include homebuilders, machine tools, etc. Not all cyclicals rhyme to the same cycle, and those that overlap with pharmaceuticals, food, and tobacco are referred to as "defensive" stocks because their sales and earnings remain more stable during economic downturns.

Real Estate: Commercial and residential real estate is important because it can provide positive cash flow, capital appreciation, depreciation advantages, residential housing tax relief, tax credits for first time buyers, and total or partial capital gain exemptions on the sale of a house, all of which are powerful motives to invest in this sector. While it is often possible for home prices to outperform the S&P 500 in the intermediate-term, as the time dimension lengthens, the best reason for owning commercial real estate is that in the history of the US since Jamestown, the most lucrative area for making money and the market sector that generated more millionaires than any other has been real estate, particularly in the central business districts of the nation's one hundred largest cities. Not only does property, over time, appreciate and surpass the tax of inflation, but also the IRS tends to treat real estate more favorably than other assets. For those in their 20s and 30s, the second real estate investment after the purchase of a REIT is residential/commercial property. Psychic and minor tax advantages of individual home ownership are one thing, but do not confuse the basic differences of residential and commercial property: commercial property outperforms residential by 30%-plus, the S&P 500 by 7%, and commercial real estate outperformed inflation by 4%-plus.

A REIT is a company that purchases, manages, and develops real estate assets. REITS are not created equal: they can be highly diversified, or specialized among residential, commercial, industrial, lodging/resort, office, healthcare, self-storage, etc. Their appeal lies in the fact that they pay no taxes as they pass 90% or more of all profits to shareholders. Besides being less volatile than other investments, they provide predictable income and growth, as real estate has grown at least 4% over inflation over time. They are particularly important to value investors because they provide a higher yield than utilities and the 30-year Treasury, capital appreciation for those with a long-term horizon, and are an efficient and economical way to own all sectors of the real estate market cheaply. REITS, therefore, are neither boring nor irrelevant in a well-diversified portfolio. When purchasing REITs, it is best to look at history and geography, diversification of holdings, and expense ratios. Real estate is important because nature is not making any more, and it is a commodity whose supply cannot grow except in a vertical direction. An acre is 43,560 square feet that you can see and build on. Unless you overpay, real estate is a safe investment. A number of features and advantages follow. 1. They are a necessary component to any well-diversified portfolio because reinvested dividends make the sector appealing. 2. Like every economic asset, the real estate market is not immune to speculative bubbles. However, while equity markets reflect the business cycle, REITs mirror the real estate market cycle. 3. Because REITs are highly sensitive to interest rates, they must be purchased and sold on a secular basis. REITs, for example, appreciated 30%-plus during 1978-79, 1986-88, and 2000-2007. 4. Real estate is a big business amounting to more than 20% of global GDP, and in most nations, real estate is responsible for about 75% of tangible capital stock. Real estate is something to take seriously.

Technology: Beginning with the discovery of fire and the invention of the wheel, history has shown that technology, as a broad category, is the world's chief driver of economic growth, and this economic segment is poised for accelerated growth in the future. Technology is a sector that ranges across a large number of subfields like computers, "soft" and "hard" material producers, telecommunications, "concept" firms, medical, electronic, etc. Companies range from small to large, with nearly all commanding high valuations, few earnings and even fewer profits, and, as a result, exhibit volatile performances and high mortality. After the debacle of 2000, technology has been out of favor, but it is not imprudent to begin to nibble at this time, keeping in mind that it is the sector that will propel economic growth in the future. Individual stock selection in this sector is particularly risky, so invest through a good mutual fund. In an era where technology guarantees obsolescence every six months, the industry is riddled with uncertainty, scandal, managerial and technological problems, and as such, most fundamental metrics simply cannot be applied with any degree of accuracy. Obviously, the industry provides, in an environment of high volatility, an opportunity for spectacular gains. Over the past 50 years, the technology sector grew from 2% of the Total Market to about 17% today.

Utilities: The classic variety refers to those corporations that provide vital services like water, electricity and natural gas to residence and business. No matter what the status of the economy, the utility sector remained relatively stable, consistently paying dividends, and, over the long run, outperformed inflation and fixed-income investments. Long scorned by "techies" as a stodgy industry not worthy of serious attention when compared to Microsoft and other *illuminati* of the 1990s, utilities lapsed into "forget land" after 1990. However, a huge portion of a nation's GDP is derived from the production of electricity, other types of energy, water, telecommunications, and their transportation. Global electric generation is a huge industry requiring vast sums of invested capital, infrastructure, and expertise. The industry is composed of both regulated and deregulated segments, and it varies as to type, location, and quality of management. Historically, the sector underperformed the S&P by about 1%, but outperformed bonds and cash by a large margin when adjusted to inflation. When one factors low volatility and high yield, utilities belong in the same category as REITs despite the fact that they are recession proof. Regulated utilities, granted a particular region of operation, are essentially monopolies that have little competition. When their costs rise, they are granted rate increases by state regulating authorities. Utilities have a dividend yield that is double that of the S&P 500 and greater than the 30-year Treasury and offer modest capital appreciation. The time to purchase is when interest rates are high and their prices low, and to then hold for the duration of the cycle. If one is optimistic about the national economy, one must be optimistic about the utility sector as the two correlate. Given the fact that the national grid, a patchwork of aging power plants and transmission lines spreading over 510,000 miles offers opportunities.

Because the industry is capital intensive it, takes billions of dollars and an enormous amount of time to construct electrical, telecommunications, water service, and natural gas networks; hence, the sector is a good indicator of economic performance. Beginning with rural electrification after World War I, and again after World War II with suburbanization, utility growth has been robust. Utilities are sensitive to negative news; hence, they offer excellent buying opportunities when prices decline as these occasions occur more frequently than one realizes. Together with REITs and financials, utilities offer, "value in the form of above-average dividends, and, as part of a balanced portfolio should be placed in a tax-sheltered account. The sector is poised for considerable growth because America's electrical infrastructure is outdated, neglected and underfunded. The telecommunications subsector has experienced amazing technological breakthroughs over the course of the past 25 years, but remains in a financial funk due to competition. Companies range from "mega" telephone companies, specialty producers of wireless technology, and a myriad of component producers. The sector is highly diverse due to the rapidity of innovation, something that occurs at "warp" speed to create new entities, bankruptcies, mergers, but, is still hampered by high valuations and often-mediocre total returns. The industry is poised for consolidation and national grid restructuring.

## Asset Allocation and Balanced Funds

A balanced fund is one which combines variable amounts of income-bearing assets and equities. Its aim is to protect principal, encourage long-term moderate growth, and provide income and a life without a "boom and bust" asset allocation. Considered "comfort food," the investor can sleep at night, as volatility is about 50% less than the S&P 500. While there are many different balanced funds the three basic flavors are a 50/50, 60/40, or 70/30 equity/bond mix. It is important to note that the name of the fund may not reflect its true asset allocation as the equity portion of holdings may contain variable amounts of large-cap, mid-cap, small-cap, and value/growth, be sector balanced or highly focused. The bond portion, along with a varying percentage of preferred and convertible bonds, can be highly diversified or concentrated.

Target Retirement (Life Cycle) Funds: These funds seek to place the investor in an automatic rebalancing environment that would involve minimum effort over an entire adult life. Once you select a fund, it automatically changes the asset allocation appropriate to your age, until retirement. Three generations ago, few people lived beyond their 65th birthday, but as longevity has steadily improved, the issues of retirement and life cycle planning have become more prominent spawning a new industry. They are effective as they copy the "one pot" dish for those that lack time, expertise, inclination, and a limited budget. They are, therefore, convenient, inexpensive, and easy to track, and provide diversification. Their simplicity is one crucial advantage, and their cost another.

Asset Allocation, the "Fund of Funds": Like the above, these funds seek to combine varying percentages of the main asset classes into a single fund, but do not do as automatically as a person ages. The Vanguard Group has five: 1. Life Strategy Growth Fund (VASGX) has 80% allocated to stocks, and 20% to bonds, intended to yield low income and high capital generation. 2. Life Strategy Moderate Growth Fund (VSMGX), less aggressive than the above, has 60% allocated to stocks, and 40% to bonds, and is intended to yield moderate income and moderate-to-high capital growth for an older population that need not assume as much risk. 3. Life Strategy Conservative Growth Fund (VSCGX), is more conservative with 60% in bonds, 40% in stocks and intended to produce moderate-to-high income and moderate amount of capital growth for a pre-retirement population. 4. Life Strategy Income Fund (VASIX), for the retiree, offers high-income growth and low-to-moderate capital growth. 5. The STAR Fund (VGSTX), is a 60/40 balanced fund composed of nine Vanguard funds that offer exceptional balance and one that can be a "core" holding.

Tax-Managed Funds: By offsetting capital gains from other transactions and maximizing unrealized gains, these funds are designed for taxable accounts whose purpose is to minimize tax liabilities. The wide diversity behooves investors to carefully research these types of funds as their asset allocations differ widely. Generally, the smorgasbord varies from tax-managed balanced, growth and income, capital appreciation, small-cap, and international.

## Dividend, Value, and Income Funds

1. Dividend Growth: The purpose of this fund is to concentrate on high-quality companies that consistently pay and increase dividends, offer capital growth, and are usually diversified across industry sectors. 2. Equity Income: A close cousin to growth and income, but overweight in dividend-paying stocks, it yields at least

1% more than growth and income funds. 3. Value: Employing widely differing objectives, these funds are certainly not monolithic as they come in many flavors, emphasizing value-oriented metrics. Overall performance suffers from investment style and manager risk, but the value index outperforms actively managed funds. Over time, they outperform growth funds, offer more protection during recessions, and are less volatile. 4. Income: These funds seek to provide income with some capital growth. They vary in terms of portfolio composition, degree of diversification, yield, and overall risk. Invariably, the highest-yielding funds are those with concentrated holdings making big bets on the movement of certain instruments. They come with many names, and the investor must pay close attention to two critical aspects: expenses and quality. 5. Convertible/Preferred: When purchased appropriately and held with DCA for secular periods with dividends reinvested, these funds offer considerable income and appreciation outperforming the 30-year Treasury. 6. Bond funds offer considerable advantages: liquidity, diversification, cost-efficiency, and a more regular stream of money than individual bonds, ease of buying and selling, professional management and reinvestment privileges. Bond fund selection, however, can be challenging as they number more than 500 and vary widely as to type, and cost. If you wish steady income and are in a high tax bracket, municipal bonds are the answer. For those in retirement with income dependency, a diversified bond portfolio is the easiest answer. For those that either do not have an inclination to buy individual bonds, diversify through a no-load Total Bond Index. International bond funds are only useful if they behave in a non-correlating manner with domestic equivalents, and/or pay a significantly higher yield to compensate for political and currency risk. Small investors are encouraged to gain exposure to these markets through bond funds. EM bond funds tend to offer between 2% and 4% greater returns than Treasuries. What makes their appeal more alluring is the fact that they are becoming liquid and, hence, the spread with Treasuries is narrowing.

## Foreign Market Funds

Foreign appellations are important because not all geographical regions are the same. Foreign investments are subdivided into the following categories: global (a mixture of domestic and foreign), international (no domestic securities), EMs (a select group of rapidly developing countries), regional (Pacific, etc.), individual country (Canada, etc.), index, small and large-cap growth and value, balanced, and bonds. EM funds offer sex appeal and exotic pleasures when they are rising. This sector is responsible for more than 60%-plus of global GDP growth. In 1970, for example, foreign issues in the MSCI World Index were about 32%, a figure that rose above 56% by 2010. During this period, America's share of world GDP dropped from 50% to about 21%. Therefore, since EMs are the fastest growing global economies in the world, this segment of foreign exposure is essential to enhance total portfolio returns.

The reasons why prudent investors should be diversified into the foreign equity and bond markets are compelling. 1. The US does not dominate global equity markets, and it is no longer the fastest growing global economy; foreign markets can and do outperform US markets. Over the past 40-plus years, international markets outperformed the US during 1974-1981, 1985-1991, and since 2003. Volatility, however, abounds as country markets are constantly shifting their leadership positions. For example, in 1990, the UK led the list; in 1991-1993, it was Hong Kong, in 1996, Spain, in 1997 Portugal, in 1998-1999 Finland, in 2001-2002 New Zealand, and in 2005 Canada. It is interesting to note that the country with the greatest total returns for the period 1900-2000 was Sweden. 2. Foreign exposure reduces systematic risk. While narrowing foreign markets exhibit non-correlating performances with DMs. The latter are growing at 2% annually, EMs between 5%-8%, and Chindia between 6% and 9%. For the past 30 years, a portfolio with 30% in foreign stocks outperformed a 100% domestic portfolio by more than 5%. In the event of a US financial crisis, a 20% foreign market position offers a good hedge against portfolio volatility. 3. The ability or inability of EMs to perform in a sustained fashion is the main risk confronting this market segment because economic performance is influenced by unresolved domestic political problems. Nevertheless, the inertia of globalization primarily from Asia is not about to reverse. With nearly 60% of all stocks and bonds found in international markets, it is inevitable that the prudent investor have a sizeable overseas position. For retirees it may range from zero to 5%, but for those with a 20-plus-year horizon, the percentage may be as large as 50%. Given the fact that EMs carry lower valuations and grow three times faster than the US economy, it is hard to consider arguments for not having at least a 20% foreign position. Since the largest creditor nations are Asian-based, it seems reasonable to be overweight in that geographical region and for those in their 20s and 30s; a 30% exposure is reasonable.

## Exchange Traded Funds (ETFs), Holders, and Closed-End Funds (CEFs)

ETFs are baskets of stocks that represent sectors, industries, and geographical regions, similar to mutual funds, but with many profound differences: shares can be traded during market hours with limit and stop orders, offer greater transparency, exhibit little if any style drift, are inexpensive, tax-efficient, can be shorted and margined with option trading available to increase investment strategies. However, unlike mutual funds, ETF dividends cannot be automatically reinvested as they are deposited in a non-interest bearing account and are distributed periodically to shareholders. Many are also less liquid, are poorly structured and esoteric in terms of their holdings and percent allocations, and many are risky. Therefore, buy broad-based ETFs, as they are safer and less expensive.

CEFs are similar to ETFs. They trade like stocks, total shares are fixed, and in reference to the NAV value, they may offer periodic discounts or premiums.

They come, like mutual funds, in all flavors and colors. Their advantage lies in the fact that when an investor sells shares, the fund's holdings are unaffected as with open-ended funds, and they never sit on a hoard of cash. They cover the complete spectrum of investment opportunities from domestic equities, and foreign exposure, to fixed-income, the latter, by far, the most popular where municipal bond funds dominate. The problem with closed-end funds is that most are noticeably smaller than most traditional funds, and lie in a "shadow" investing environment enhancing the element of mystery. Another significant problem is that since they are less liquid, the bid/ask spread is wide and volatility quite common.

# CHAPTER 3

# THE CHEF'S ADMONITIONS AND COMMENDATIONS TO WEALTH CREATION

*"The stuff that dreams are made of"* - Humphrey Bogart, The Maltese Falcon

*"If the market goes up, stays flat, or declines tomorrow, it would really surprise me."* - Anonymous Stock Broker

*"Only little people pay taxes."* - Leona Helmsly

*"Four things come not back: the spoken word, the sped arrow, the past life, and the neglected opportunity."* - Arabian Proverb

*"Savings are the indispensable precondition of investment. Plain and simple, there exists no investment that isn't financed by savings."* - Jorg G. Hulsmann

# Common Investing Mistakes

## Not Paying Attention to Risk

Webster's Dictionary describes risk as, "hazard, peril, exposure to loss or injury," and "attended with risk or danger." That is the seminal problem with investing–the possibility of loss of capital. All investments carry a degree of risk and one who is risk averse chooses the investment that will offer the greatest return with the lowest risk, something impossible to accomplish in an absolute way. However, an observation of two investment extremes will simplify the dilemma that confronts investors. A risk-free investment is one in which the investor knows what the return in the future is today, as in the case of a CD, while a risky investment is one for which the future return is unknown today. In the meantime, investors are inundated by hopeful anticipation, fearful apprehension, and greedy insatiability to the point that they sublimate their basic instincts like patience and common sense. Experimentation with highly speculative investments, hoping that mere luck would assure a solid retirement position, is fool hardy. Risk management, therefore, is one of the most important but difficult elements to be understood. Keeping risk prudent is essential to wealth creation.

What to do? 1. Risk can never be entirely avoided as it is ubiquitous, and while it cannot be abolished, it can be mitigated. 2. Eliminate excessive security concentrations. 3. Reduce, or eliminate speculative practices like option and futures trading, margin and short-term trading. 4. Minimize interest rate, market, and opportunity loss. 5. Be patient and disciplined. 6. Overweigh value-oriented companies by selecting companies rated B+ or higher. Maintain at least a 50% equity allocation to dividend-payers. 7. Risk is inseparable from return. It is zero for Treasuries and CDs, and high for Albanian real estate. 8. Emphasize index funds. 9. Pay attention to the distinctions between systematic and idiosyncratic risk. 10. Investment behavior should seek the historic return of the "Total Market." 11. There is risk in avoiding risk, as in the case of a 20-year-old leaving money in CDs for the rest of his life. 12. Risk diminishes with time. While equities are highly volatile in the short-term, they outperform all other assets over time. For 15-year periods, equities outperformed bonds and cash more than 92% of the time and never had a losing 20-year period. 13. Attempt to eliminate the risk you are able to control, and to reduce that which you cannot control. A combination of media noise, unrealistic expectations, and extreme confidence driven by relentless greed, facilitates excessive risk. The solution to most risks is diversification of non-correlating assets.

Many variables enter the calculus of risk analysis, such as age, personal history, income, net worth, gender, investment knowledge, and attitude toward risk. When greed overwhelms the emotional fabric of a person, risk is largely ignored, and when fear grips the individual, the emotional mind is inundated by risk. These two emotions when unrestrained are deadly to financial welfare. "Acceptable risk" is a relative term and varies from investor to investor and geography, as risk in Peoria, Illinois is different from that in Jakarta, Indonesia. Because risk is opposite to safety, and since variable rewards without risk are impossible, an individual's profile clearly defines the degree of risk necessary for possible gains. With that said, age appears to be the critical element that will define the degree of risk to be taken. Therefore, a person at age 25 with three or more possible secular markets before him can tolerate far more risk than a 75 year-old with limited savings and S.S.. The key element between these two individuals is short-term vs. long-term risk. The former can assume more because of time, and the latter much less because of a lack of time. Ernest Hemingway said it best: "Hesitation increases in relation to risk in equal proportion to age." Below is a partial list of risk elements:

Call Risk: The forced redemption of a bond before maturity is "call" risk. Once the bond is "called" and the investor receives his principal plus interest, it may be difficult to find a similar bond with the same yield.

Credit Risk: In the bond universe, this describes the danger that the creditor will not receive principal and interest.

Currency Risk: Currency risk has become an immediate exigency for many investors as the global economy has expanded. Given the fact that more than 58% of the financial market capitalization is foreign, currency fluctuations will exert profound influences on US investors. Emotional Investor Risk: If this sentiment is not kept under control over the course of a lifetime, it will result in underperformance at best, and ruin at worst. The risk of emotion acts contrary to rational thought processes and explains why most investors do not make money as they buy at the top and sell at the bottom. Emotion, in the absence of, discipline and patience, spells disaster, particularly in volatile markets: when prices are high, risk appears to be high, but emotional risk tends to be low; when prices are low financial risk is low, but emotional risk is high. It is never wise to let your sentiments dominate your life.

Fiscal/Monetary Risk: Since the average investor does not spend time with the Fed or the shakers and movers of policies in Washington, D.C., the ability to predict short and intermediate fiscal and monetary policies is impossible. Who would have predicted the inability of the Fed to take the speculative heat out of the tech bubble during the period 1995-2000 by not raising margin requirements? Who would have predicted 13 unprecedented rate cuts beginning in January 2001 in an attempt to avert recession and fight "deflation"? Who would have thought that while interest rates continued to decline and where historic mortgage financing and consumer spending, deficits, and government spending were running amuck, there were no spending vetoes by the Bush and Obama administrations.

Foreign Risk: Most foreign markets are plagued with political, social and economic instability, the possibility of expropriation of property, trade restrictions, etc. Over the past 100-plus years, the number of company nationalizations run into the thousands, in addition to the imposition of new taxes, export duties, fees, royalties, etc. In the fall of 2006, the Finance Minister of Canada eliminated tax benefits enjoyed by "trusts," and, as a result, more than $32 billion in value was immediately lost.

Idiosyncratic Risk: This refers to the degree of risk assumed when an investor is overweight in a particular asset class, specific company, or geography. To eliminate this risk, one has to diversify along non-correlating assets and in conformity with the nature of the secular market by limiting positions to less than 10%.

Inflation Risk: In a fiat currency universe, this risk must be faced and successfully challenged by all investors. When retirees are living on bond interest, and inflation accelerates, the fixed interest that they receive purchases less, and, should inflation continue for an extended period, the effects are devastating. For bondholders, inflation risk occurs on three fronts: bond prices decline when the rate of inflation rises; the purchasing power of the face value is reduced should you hold to maturity, and the semi-annual interest payments experience reduced purchasing power as long as inflation is progressing.

Interest Rate Risk: This risk, endemic to bonds, refers to rising interest rates that place existing bonds at a disadvantage when new bonds carry a higher coupon. To match that higher return, older bonds fall in price. You can reduce, but not totally eliminate, interest risk by investing in short-term bonds and laddering individual date-certain bonds, and the longer the bond maturity the greater the interest rate risk. Rising interest rates also affect interest-sensitive stocks by rendering their dividend yields less attractive.

Legislative Risk: This type of risk becomes important and often brutal when political legislation affects the taxability of interest, dividends, and capital gains. Consider for a moment what would happen to the price of municipal bonds if federal, state, and local tax exemptions were lifted. Corporate and personal income taxes vary by state, and have influenced over time the distribution of both economic activity and population. In addition, when governments suddenly change legislation and/or regulations affecting specific market sectors, the effects can be dramatic.

Liquidity Risk: This risk is experienced when it is difficult to trade a specific asset. This is a major problem to investors who hold individual municipal bonds that do not trade daily in the secondary market, and where the bid and ask prices can be highly divergent. In many TWs where many markets only function for a limited time, the problem compounds. "Systematic liquidity" risk occurs when the entire market losses liquidity in times of crisis, panics, national disasters, or military/terrorist activities.

Manager Risk: This refers to the value fluctuations of an asset attributable to questionable strategies of a manager that result in below average returns. Age, experience, education, and personal elements are difficult to evaluate by the common investor, and in this regard, the investor can minimize manager risk by buying an index fund.

Opportunity Risk: This refers to the possibility that the investor could have done better had he allocated funds differently thereby taking advantage of market anomalies. For example, there is a huge difference between the historic returns of equities at 10% and that of cash at 3%. Moreover, given the fact that most stocks make sudden, unexpected moves to the upside of 30% in a short period, loses through opportunity risk can be quite significant. It can also refer to the risk of doing nothing, of being ignorant of current news, indecision, not taking advantage of secular opportunities, etc. Opportunity costs are relative.

Prepayment Risk: This risk affects GNMAs and bond funds when homeowners refinance their mortgages during periods of falling interest rates. The prepayment of some or all of the principal means that proceeds are then reinvested at lower interest rates.

Random Risk: This refers to an unexpected, sudden, exogenous episode that is beyond the control of markets, as it cannot be predicted with accuracy. Once these events occur, they may be short or long-term with varying degrees of consequence, often in a chain reaction, widely known as "contagion." These events, acting as a trigger to market turmoil, are endemic in an era of instant communication. When extreme, they are referred to as "Black Swan" events. They occur and have the potential of reversing a lifetime of savings to zero. Lawyers often refer to *force majeure*, or a greater force that excuses a party from liability due to unforeseen events. On July 4, 1776, King George wrote in his diary "nothing important happened today."

Systematic risk: Systematic or "market" risk, considered one of the most important of all risk factors, refers to domestic and international economic conditions influencing broad markets. It is a risk that cannot be diversified away, the opposite of idiosyncratic risk, and the best way to mitigate this risk is by owning index funds. According to John Bogle, "Don't think you know more than the market, nor act on insights that you think are your own but are in fact shared by millions of others." "The market fluctuates," said Mr. Dow, and market volatility generates problems for the investor. Significant political and economic occurrences will make markets react violently and act to precipitate the "flight of capital" to "safe havens." The Vanguard Group reports for the period 1926-2003, the best 1, 5, 10 and 20-year Total Market return has been 54.2%, 28.6%, 19.9% and 17.8%, respectively. The worst for these periods has been, -43.1%, -12.4%, -0.8% and +3%, and the average has been 12.4%, 10.7%, 11.2% and 11.3%. Therefore, if one holds the "market" for a prolonged period, systematic risk diminishes in an appreciable manner. In addition, in times of secular bear markets, it is common for the S&P 500 Index to decline by more than 50% and for specific stocks by 100%. Under these conditions, investing with a crystal ball is a common investor frailty with many investors seeking to "time" the market in order to prevent systematic risk. Over the long run, the strategy does not work as market timing increases risk rather than reducing it.

A few closing thoughts: 1. Investors confront six degrees of risk: a. The nominal risk-free return of Treasuries and CDs. b. The average return when investing is the Total Market. c. A larger return when investors purchase specific sectors with expectations of greater returns. d. The potential of huge returns when investors purchase shares of high PE, no earnings, innovative technology companies, etc. e. Expectation of higher returns from small-cap stocks. f. The potential for spectacular returns of risk undertaken by mining concerns in foreign countries. 2. For many investors, the minimization of risk is more important than the quest to maximize total returns. 3. The most common risk measurements are, alpha, beta, R-Squared, Sharpe Ratio, and Standard Deviation. A beta of 1.0 states that the asset has experienced the same volatility as the market; a beta of 1.50 states that the asset carries 50% more volatility; a beta of .50 means it has 50% less volatility, and a safe investment like a CD has a beta of 0. 4. In recent years, the expression "moral hazard" has become popular. According to Wikipedia "Moral hazard is the prospect that a party insulated from risk may behave differently from the way it would behave it were fully exposed to the risk. Moral hazard arises because an individual or institution does not have to bear the full consequences of its actions, and therefore has a tendency to act less carefully than it will otherwise, leaving another party to bear some responsibility for the consequences of those actions." Winston Churchill, although not an astute investor in his time, accurately saw the dimensions of risk when he said, "The optimist sees opportunity in every danger; the pessimist sees danger in every opportunity." 5. Risk is a relative term since cash, bonds, equities, real estate, and "real" things like land, metals, forests, etc., all vary in a continuous manner with each other. 6. There is no such thing as a risk-free investment because there is no way to remove all uncertainty from investing. There is also no easy manner in assessing risk. Not only does it vary by individual, age, culture, and country, but by the psychological scars of history. Greece, for example, had been at war continuously from 1821 to 1952. Every 10 years, boundaries shifted, populations displaced, lives lost, property obliterated or damaged, the currency destroyed, and inflation devastated savings. Under these conditions, how would you save for retirement when from the age of 20 to 80 there was a war every 10 years? In addition, how would you allocate your assets? 7. With rising poverty levels, risk taking increases. 8. Men are prepared to stomach more risk than women, and youth more than the elderly. 9. Fed market manipulations (particularly the cost of risk) distort investor market perceptions.

## Not Avoiding Stories of "Interest" and the Illuminati

Stories of interest refer to tales, rumors, and juicy tidbits intended to tantalize, confuse, and escort investors down the proverbial garden path. They are written and/or stated by reporters, academicians, government officials, and media commentators who write in prestigious newspapers and ruminate on the radio and television. Pregnant with false information, Pulitzer prizes have been withdrawn and American universities are drained of academic integrity for the same reasons. The investor must understand this, not forget it, and always be aware of the consequences of listening to a glib pen and mouth, as the *illuminati* will say anything in order to keep you at the craps table. They all have one thing in common–a propensity and an insatiable appetite for the dissemination of propaganda.

One way of making the stories interesting is to introduce new words for old, much like putting fresh wine in an old bottle. A sampling includes "re-hypothecation," "constant proportion debt obligations," "bail in" and "bail out," "market anthropology," "Daniel" number, "super-conduit," "Biblical Money Code," "auction rate debt," etc. I recently heard a guru from a prestigious investment house describe the market's close on a particular day as "one with amazing texture." Another financial writer said: "Have the market talk to you," still another expects "the market to reach a state of uneasiness," Alan Greenspan said that "inflation is quiescent," and a money manager to the press: "I outperformed because I stayed in the present." In addition, for every Wall Street axiom that is paraded as an *a priori* principle carved in granite, there is a long list of exceptions because the "Street" is very happy to change the lock as soon as you are given the key. It also appears that the more things change, the more they remain the same. "Anarchists" are now called "terrorists," money printing is now "quantitative easing," "suspects" are now "persons of interest," "tapering" for reduction, and "increase" became "augment," then "surge," and now "stepping up." Conflicting headlines abound, of which the following are harmful: "The best funds to buy for 2013," and "A Beginner's Guide to Day Trading on Line." Within four days, a prominent advisory firm included the same company under the following headlines: "Dream Stocks for Mining Investors," and "Three Stocks in a Tailspin." It is enough to produce dyspepsia.

Savants, Indian astrologers, and others, with powers to foretell the future, are nothing new as they fill endless tomes since the development of glifths. Cassandra, the daughter of Priam in Greek mythology, possessed the aptitude to divine the future, and the citizens of countless City States made the pilgrimage to Delphi for guidance. Under the Romans, "Haruspex" was said to have the powers to foretell the future by "reading" the entrails of animals. However, the sages of time assume no risk, and that ought to tell you something. Even Yogi Berra had an opinion on the subject when he uttered, "The future ain't what it used to be." John Galbraith was not that far off when he said, "The function of economic forecasting is to make astrology look good." Moreover, despite the recent adoption of mathematical formulae intended to outfox the market, all are humbled; Nobel Laureates, brokerage house presidents, editors of financial magazines, and media gurus, all have failed in their ability to predict market behavior despite their erudition. Soothsayers never drive markets for extended periods, just as the rooster crowing does not cause the sun to rise. The *Wall Street Journal* on September 2007 reported, "A residential real estate slump is unthinkable." Bloomberg in June 2008 said, "To be sure, a crash in the oil market is not imminent." In April of 2007, Treasury Secretary Henry Paulson said, "Subprime woes likely contained." In July, he said, "This is far and away the strongest global economy I've seen in my business lifetime." In March of 2008, he said, "We've got strong financial institutions...Our markets are the envy of the world"; and in May he said, "The worst is likely to be behind us." One of television's greatest showmen recommended the purchase of Bear Stearns as a "steal" a week before its demise. In 2010, Vice President Biden said, "We misread how bad the economy was." Throughout 2008, Ben Bernanke did not consider recession as anything more than a "possibility." Despite the sloppy and erroneous economic predictions made by the *illuminati*, predictions will continue because no one trusts the figures of others, so all institutions have a large staff at the ready to crunch numbers. They do not know everything, but they do know more, and, while they make mistakes, they "homogenize" them, or seek relief from the "Fed," something that the hapless investor is unable to do. Most disturbing is the fact that the *illuminati* are not only not punished for their misdeeds, but also rewarded. Nevertheless, eventually, the "market" will correct and exert control over the corrupt, but at a price.

So what is it that makes the *illuminati* believable? They are exceedingly crafty in formulating and dispensing information; they determine what people hear and read in the mainstream media as they spoon feed lazy and gullible investors false information, and when they cannot convince, they confuse. Their purpose is to keep the public in the dark like mushrooms, and they look virtuous and speak effectively. They are either young or mature: the young are eager, beautiful and demure; the aged exude moments of wise, fatherly advice, and appear to be gentile and comforting. The most dangerous are not all packaged in "plain vanilla," but come in all sizes, shapes, and disguises. They are elitists expounding "New World Order" or other slogans, and at specific times and places, they play benign, explosive, positive or negative roles in the fortunes of common investors. By dispensing "free" advice, they remain popular; the very best act as "gatekeepers" in order to filter or exaggerate propaganda. They love to put lipstick on a pig when it suits them, but in the end, the pig remains a pig. Market gurus tend to be notorious, pathological, and incorrigible liars. The fertility of their imagination is enormous, and on rare occasions when they sweat, they do so with sincerity and able to convince you to do anything—even to eat soup with a fork. The purpose of Wall Street is to keep retail investors out of a bull market until the top, and to keep them in all the way to the bottom of a bear market. Therefore, listen and look carefully, but believe few and question all.

In addition, why should one avoid their "comments and advice?" 1. They are fallible despite their intellect and attire. A vice-president of the largest investment bank was wrong in predicting a bullish market in 2000 and again in 2001. Ben Bernanke predicted that the housing issue would not bring down real estate prices. He predicted that the housing crisis would have no long-lasting economic effect, and was wrong when he predicted a stable unemployment rate. How can one believe the former Secretary of the Treasury, Paulson when he said that the "US is committed to a strong dollar" when all Fed actions indicated contrarian behavior. Recommendations emanating from the mouths and pens of *illuminati* are much like the Platt River, a mile wide and an inch deep. This does not mean that one should not listen to diverse opinions (a belief or judgment that rests on grounds insufficient to produce absolute certainty). Just the opposite, diverse opinions are necessary just like drinking quality Bordeaux and Baco Noir from Virginia. One cannot possibly appreciate the former by not tasting plonk. Increased exposure to knowledge always makes the wise investor more astute and prudent. 2. They have no clue of "cause and effect"; hence, the need to habitually fabricate. In the name of balanced reporting, many gurus write in a style in which each successive paragraph is contradicted by the next, and couch their prognostications with "may" and "if." 3. Every vestige of this community has been convicted and/or fined, for fraud, but few have been jailed. Major mutual funds along with major banks and corporations have paid $billions in fines over the past 25 years. In fact, a scandal *de jure*, has become "common." Moreover, politicians do not fare better. In the 1990s, 84 Congressmen were stopped for drunken driving, 21 were defendants in lawsuits, 8 arrested for shoplifting, 14 arrested for drug-related offences, 29 accused for spousal abuse, 7 arrested for fraud, 19 accused for writing bad checks, 117 had bankrupted at least two businesses, and since 1980, there have been 43 sex scandals. Bad behavior in Washington and Wall Street is common and tolerated. 4. They are glib, and what makes them effective is how they interpret financial information to people and how willingly the latter accept the propaganda as they are led to the *abattoir.* Even prominent politicians are susceptible. Henry Wallace, the former Vice-President and Secretary of Agriculture told me in 1958 that he was "propagandized"; and if it could happen to him, why not the retail investor?

It appears that Wall Street's main mission is to promote sanguinity to the trusting public. Wall Street is perennially bullish on stocks–forever and always. Just as warfare is based on deception, the selling of Wall Street-by-Wall Street is no different. After all, the critical ingredients of deception, control of information and emotion-laden propaganda are all readily available for meticulous distribution. The average American has been deluded into thinking: The CPI is under control at 2.5%; ethanol will solve the gasoline dilemma; domestic deficits are minor, contained and unimportant; living standards are rising; and the $700 trillion derivative predicament is not a problem. Continued rejection of reality will hold sway for the duration of the secular bear market. The cast of characters appears to be of distinctive appearance, and are adept at repeating the big lie in an attempt to mask the truth. In the words of Agatha Christie: "The truth is so difficult to tell." They admit nothing and deny everything. The public has been led to believe that Global Crossing, Enron, Bear Stearns, and others were mere aberrations. Do not believe it! Read old issues of major newspapers and magazines, and you will be amazed at the regularity of criminal behavior in American financial history. Voltaire said it best: "Those who can make you believe absurdities can make you commit atrocities." *Alithea* is a foreign concept on Wall Street. According to Plato, "Honesty is for the most part less profitable than dishonesty."

Wall Street has many weapons of mass manipulation. One of the most important is to parade "experts" in an endless manner before the unsuspected, hesitant and fearful public in matters of finance. The common definition of an expert is one who has singular knowledge in a particular subject. This may be true for metallurgy, chemistry, and a few other subjects, but not in finance as persuasive metaphor and a good-looking face manage to seduce. Therefore, never act on media speculation concerning mergers, takeovers, and market and company predictions. "Whisper" numbers, and information out of the tender mouths of the "expert" should be ignored. After all, why advertise crucial information for free? Wall Street is not transparent despite all pronouncements. The "Street" may say that it is becoming more so, that it wishes to be more so, but in the end; it is not in the business of being transparent. They are the "house" in gaming parlance; therefore, the wish is to maintain an advantage, and the best way to accomplish that feat is not to be transparent, and it is a rare occasion when Wall Street goes to the confessional. One thing is certain: professional degrees, titles, and metaphor do not an expert make. The *illuminati* are not experts, but individuals who are paper pushers and in the business of generating fees, commissions and notoriety. Understand that experts are not that "expert." They put their pants on one leg at a time, just like everyone else. The nation's economic leadership did not know that a depression was about to befall the nation in the fall of 1929; John Maynard Keynes and Irving Fisher both guessed wrong. Keynes lost his capital in 1929 and once again in 1937, and Irving Fischer, not only lost everything, but also became a charity case to his employer–Yale University. If the best can misread the market in such a pitiful manner, what chance has the little person? In March 2000, 95% of American economists polled stated that there would be no recession. In the end, experts are known for their mendacity and deception. Explanations of causality are also complicated affairs in the world of finance. Consider the range of explanations for the price of crude oil per barrel at $107 in March of 2012. Economists suggested that its price was simply a question of supply and demand. Politicians maintained that large oil companies had conspired to rig prices. Wall Street maintained that "speculators" were to blame. Financiers blamed the falling $US. The motorist thought that gas stations were "gouging." The anti-OPEC group suggested that OPEC members had conspired to rig prices. Democrats blamed the oil industry. Political scientists and university activists held the view that "geopolitical" events were largely to blame. Oil analysts maintained that the demand from EMs and major oil exporters were consuming more oil than at any time in history and at rates faster than DMs. And accountants maintained that governmental subsidies were to blame.

Human knowledge is divided into two main areas–*chorographic* and *nomothetic*. The former refers to the social sciences of which economics is a part, and the latter refers to the hard sciences of mathematics, chemistry and physics. The chorographic disciplines study individual entities, reality, make use of inductive reasoning, and lack the ability to predict. The *nomothetic* (law-giving) disciplines exclude man as a variable and have the power to predict primarily because of their ability to apply deductive reasoning and the scientific method. Not only are the social sciences hampered by the use of inductive reasoning (proceeding from the specific to the general) and things "unique," but the use of generic data are also non-predictable. The *nomothetic* disciplines make use of teleological explanations (natural processes), something that cannot be applied to the social sciences. Nevertheless, this does not inhibit economists. One Ph.D. interviewed on TV recently said that, "stocks will continue to rise because I and others believe that they will." In general, economists cannot predict, are big on guesswork, are silent about the "dismal science" and list to the left. The social sciences, therefore, are very different from the unpolluted character of mathematics, physics and chemistry. The field of economics is messy, subject to prejudice and political favor. There are no scientific laws in investing! The *illuminati* would have you believe that risk and recessions have been abolished. In this regard, always remember the famous words of Joseph Goebbels: "Make the lie big enough, and tell it often enough, and people will believe it." Never underestimate the powers of an efficient propaganda machine, as it has convinced many that zero saving is a rational growth strategy. Most deceptions depend on your not knowing what is being done to you. Washington and Wall Street, therefore, endlessly talk of transparency, efficient markets, and new technologies that are facilitating a "true market." Both are much like the Black Sea, the later named for a specific reason. The color is extremely dark because of restricted oxygen exchange between upper and lower layers. That is what Wall Street does–keeps things in the dark.

Alchemy is a pseudoscience that sought to convert base metals into gold and silver, and discover an elixir for eternal youth. The powerful motives consumed entire cultures and even the legendary Sir Isaac Newton experimented. The contemporary use of the word is negative, intonating false promises, ideas, and trading practices that vow to produce prodigious amounts of wealth. In short, organized and focused propaganda is best clarified by Tom Clancy, who said, "The difference between fiction and reality? Fiction has to make sense." And no one was better at fabricating than rating agencies who dispensed with impunity sub-B quality as AAA to clients. In recent years, the long history morphed into Structured Investment Vehicles, Residential Mortgage Backed Securities, Collaterized Debt Obligations, Asset Backed Securities, and other sliced and diced engineered products. The alchemists have always found ways to find suckers to buy assets less than they were worth. I even heard a TV weather person say, "Potent storms are powering lots of clouds this afternoon, but other than that, plenty of sunshine."

The exploits of Michael Milken's junk bonds are legendary where billions of dollars in sales resulted in scandal and jail time for its architect. Backed by mirrors and plenty of smoke, millions of individual investors and institutions lost money in schemes to buy "assets" where none existed. Guru advice is like oleander on a Mediterranean hillside. It is beautiful in appearance, inviting and alluring in shape and odor, easy to grow as it is drought-resistant, but poisonous. The main products from Wall Street in recent years have been fraud, mispriced securities, corruption, and even a "Great Salad Oil Swindle." Consider what George Soros had to say, "All of economic history is one lie and deceit after another. Your job as a speculator is to get on when the lie is being propagated and then get off before it is discovered." After 2001, stock option back dating became an endemic activity. The shameless housing debacle, credit crisis, and bank insolvencies highlight all the nastiness that exists in the canyons of lower Manhattan, and is best illustrated by "noble rot," a mold that desiccates grapes and in the process concentrates sugar and flavor to produce sweet Sauternes and Barsac wines. But the "noble rot" of Wall Street is a pool of sharks that try to make the "bitter" "sweet." Paul Gibson states "...Michael Milken and his cohorts had used more than four hundred partnerships to manipulate, bribe, and coerce the thrifts into buying junk bonds that ended up costing them billions." Gibson also elaborates on how easy it is to trade on inside information, thus lending a good deal of doubt to MPT. Never forget that Wall Street institutions, mired in corruption, offer recommendations about specific stocks, much like a philanderer offering marriage counseling; Merrill Lynch in 2000 recommended Cisco at $82 per share for the long-term. The "Gnomes of Zurich," a derogatory term for Swiss bankers exhibiting a vindictive streak, also reside on Wall Street.

The Washington *illuminati* cannot be trusted because they dominate public opinion by controlling the money supply, security, education, and the flow of information. Once they acquire power, they can switch positions at will and betray their former principles that brought them to power, as in the case of Alan

Greenspan. In his previous life, he was for gold and a strong currency, but once he became chairperson of the Fed, he created more fiat money than all who preceded him. Worse, he corrupted central bankers around the world with disastrous consequences. He is not alone. Consider the goblygook of the former Secretary of Defense who said at NATO headquarters in Brussels in June 2006, "Now what is the message there? The message is that there are known "knowns." There are things we know that we know. There are known unknowns. That is to say, there are things that we now know we do not know. But there are also unknown unknowns. There are things we don't know we don't know. So when we do the best we can and we pull all this information together, and we then say well that's basically what we see as the situation, that is really only the known knowns and the known unknowns. And each year, we discover a few more of those unknown unknowns." Under President Clinton, the massive income tax increase was referred to as an "investment." The Bush administration stated publically that the trade deficit is not bad as it enables Americans to import more; hence, augmenting their wealth. For many investors, scandalous revelations about Wall Street come as a surprise. After all, bears "do potty" in the woods.

The government, with the complicity of mainstream media, redefines and changes how things are measured. According to George Orwell when he wrote *1984*–"black is white." Now what was once up is now down, what was down is up, what was outside is now in, and what was in is now out. The following comments are beyond the pale of common sense and professional expectation from "trusted leaders": Joe Biden: "We have to spend money to keep from going bankrupt." (These pronouncements are as authentic as the "letters of transit" of "Casablanca" fame.) Nancy Pelosi, "We have to pass the healthcare bill to see what's in it." Larry Summers, "The central irony of financial crisis is that while it is caused by too much confidence, too much borrowing and lending and too much spending, it can only be resolved with more confidence, more borrowing and lending, and more spending." It is hard to believe that George W. Bush, just a month prior to leaving the Oval Office, said, "I've abandoned free market principles to save the free market system." "Savings are no longer necessary" because Americans have S.S., said the former Chairman of the President's economic inner circle. The government massages negative statistics until they become positive, and "if you torture the numbers and words long enough, they will confess to anything," so say statisticians. Madoff clearly illustrates the incestuous arrangements in place between Wall Street and federal regulatory agencies. While the whistleblower presented proof of illegal activities, the SEC turned a blind eye and the whistleblower threatened. It is interesting to note that from prison, Madoff stated, "banks had to know of fraud," but not his friends at the SEC, the Fed, and Congress. One individual who invested with Madoff said, "I knew Bernie Madoff was cheating; that's why I invested with him." Moreover, just when you knew everything about Madoff, consider these juicy words from the master manipulator: "The whole new regulatory reform is a joke. The whole government is a *Ponzi* scheme." "Some animals are more equal than others," said George Orwell in *Animal Farm.*

Financial advisors are another breed of professionals not created equal. They travel under a large number of monikers: Certified Financial Planner, Chartered Financial Analyst, Chartered Financial Consultant, Certified Fund Specialist, etc. The biggest problem with advisors is that eventually they will steer you to commission generated instruments. In addition, many offer "wrap accounts," in which all aspects of portfolio management consisting of transaction expenses, advice, and legal services are provided under one umbrella. Many large brokerage and mutual fund families offer professional portfolio guidance for a set fee, often without a face-to-face meeting. No matter how friendly, your "advisor" is rarely your friend. In the words of Warren Buffett: "Wall Street is the only place that people ride to in a Rolls Royce to get advice from those who take the subway." A word about newsletters: there are dozens, all differing in substance, quality of information, and advice. They lack consistency in terms of reliable recommendations, and worse, they mislead, and at best, they are good contrarians. Remember the words of Mark Twain: "if you don't read the newspaper, you are uninformed. If you do read the newspaper, you are misinformed." You don't need a weatherman to know which way the wind is blowing. Newsletters and financial magazines are similar except for the *Dow Theory Forecasts,* and *Journal of the American Association of Individual Investors.*

## Not Recognizing the Destructive Force of Hedonism

Hedonism refers to irresponsible behavior, and if prolonged in duration, it leads to irreversible catastrophic financial events. A hedonistic lifestyle simply warps and misplaces rational thought and action; it propels delusional thoughts of hope and greed beyond the pale as it emphasizes a notion that living for today trumps anything that is forthcoming. Hedonistic lifestyles are not only reckless, but those who embrace this genre are constantly torn between expectation and despair, a combination that spells ruin over the long run because reasonable behavior has been high-jacked by the "moment." He observes all manner of individual and collective behavior, yet remains in denial. He observes, but does not see. The hedonist throws all caution to the wind, lacks an investment strategy, does not think long-term, loves volatility, does not persevere, trades constantly, and ignores investment risks. He is not motivated by logic, is argumentative, learns little from successful investors and is always in pursuit of the "inside straight." In the end, hedonistic individuals make rash decisions to satisfy immediate passions. They always spend more than they earn and frequently borrow from friends and family in order to pay Peter and then Paul in an endless manner. Hedonism is synonymous with selfishness and solipsism as a way of life. In the end, hedonists become a primary burden to society. There is more:

1. Negative life styles infer and involve behaviors that exemplify destructive features to both individual and family. Instead of saving and not spending, the hedonist glorifies a sloppy, shiftless, lifestyle devoid of achievement, drive, aspiration and the production of anything remotely approaching progress. Einstein said, "Only two things are infinite–the universe and human stupidity, and I'm not sure about the former." The "t-shirt and jean" have become the most common male attire for practically every age group and occasion. Personal grooming and personal appearance matter not, and the inability to "spread commonsense on bread" is particularly disturbing as hedonists are highly vulnerable to capricious behavior. They live in an "I want things now" environment in which the "I wish items" vary from tattoos to "weed," and where "tomorrow" does not matter. Instant gratification is a main reason why they have few assets. Therefore, hedonistic behavior lacks the mental discipline to "stay the course," to save, to invest, and to sacrifice.

2. The indebted hedonist never creates wealth. He lacks the ability to distinguish between consumption, leverage, and production. In 2000, I had a 55-year old high school counselor in class who should have been paying down his mortgage, but instead took out a home equity loan for $77,000, and immediately consumed his newly found "wealth" on a family cruise, a car, and a deck on his house. He said that he acted in a manner that furthered his interests. I reminded him that his net debt increased, but he thought he became "wealthier." I further told him that he stole from his children; the deck will have added, over time, a tiny fraction to the total net worth of his house, and the car and cruise represented consumption. "I gambled on the cruise because I felt lucky, and the booze on international water, was less expensive," he said. Like so many, he lived for today, not tomorrow, felt wealthier by borrowing, and failed to appreciate Democritus who said: "One of the great differences between a wise man and a fool: the former only wishes for what he may possibly obtain, the latter desires impossibilities." Warren Buffett calls this type of behavior "squanderville."

## Not Recognizing and Understanding the Tyranny of Debt

The choice of two opposing evils–Scylla or Charybdis faced by Odysseus is alive and well. US households face massive household debt, a lack of savings, and hedonistic lifestyles at the expense of an old-fashioned work ethic. Americans have always been plagued by the hallucinogenic drug called debt. Because of low interest rates, the US has become the most indebted generation in its history with debt payments consuming more than 30% of disposable income. Before 1920, Americans ran household deficits for short periods at a stretch, but the interval 1982 to the present, has been the longest continuous debt expanse since statistics have tracked this metric. The compulsive debtor has become a significant demographic cohort and an important part of the American economy. Debt enables the enjoyment of lifestyles that emulate the wealthy without the necessary income to justify such behavior. Consumer propaganda states, "Start living the good life," but it never says, "Start working and saving for the good life." The historical cultural contempt for debt is no longer rejected. At one time debt was a dirty word, but no longer. Furthermore, the nation has been conditioned to believe that it is entitled to whatever it wishes. If it craves $1 billion-plus sports stadiums over structures that make products for export, it must pay a bitter price; if it chooses to waste time and resources in the production of ineffective schools, it will pay a bitter price; if government is obsessed with imperial designs and wastes treasure and lives, it will pay a bitter price; if US households borrow money to buy expensive, depreciating assets, it will pay a bitter price; and if the citizenry continue to vote corrupt and incompetent politicians to office who squander the nation's resources, all will pay the bitter price of impoverishment. The Fed has aggravated events: the only way to fuel consumption is through debt expansion, savings liquidation, or rising disposable income, and at the time of this writing, we have two of the three. The real median household income is $82,000, and the individual income is $47,000, while 55% of the working population earns less than $30,000.

The signs of excessive debt are everywhere: 1. Total household debt exceeds $18 trillion. Debt service as a percentage of income is at a historic high with household debt the new *zeitgeist,* increasing by 70% since 1999. One hundred years ago household debt was nearly zero, and now nearly $200,000. 2. Since 2003, homeowners have withdrawn $5 trillion in equity from their homes. Fifty years ago, homeowner equity stood at 80%, a figure that has been reduced to 28%. In addition, 65% of households are insolvent. 3. Most people live above their means, and their ability to reduce and get out of debt is hindered by declining real income, higher energy costs, higher mortgage payments as percent of income and higher food prices. 4. Seventy-eight percent of all credit card holders do not pay their monthly balance. 5. With 4.8% of global population, the US accounts for 20% of world consumption, and about 40% of consumer debt. In the words of Pete Petersen: The US is "running on empty." 6. Consumption as percent of GDP rose from 52% in the early 1952s to 71% in 2012. 7. The old adage of saving now to spend later has been discarded.

There are two types of debt: productive and consumptive, and the sooner one learns the difference the better, as it will guide decision-making faculties. The former refers to capital good investment that, over time, increases output. Consumptive debt involves borrowing money in order to purchase a depreciating asset, like a vacation or car—representing, nothing but instant gratification with no enduring benefits other than quickly raising psychic pleasures. In addition, consumption consists of two parts: induced and autonomous. Induced occurs when disposable income rises, and autonomous consumption occurs as part of long-term habits related to familial behavior. Over the long run, bad debt prevents wealth creation, and is a habit difficult to extricate. In short, debt is undesirable: 1. For every dollar that the US exports, it imports $1.40 worth of consumer goods with borrowed money. This behavior purchases goods or services with debt, usually at high interest for long periods. 2. Because Americans are conditioned to "spend" immediately, to "wish" foolishly, and to "want" hedonistically, they lose control over their ability to manage money. 3. Consumption debt is inevitably inflationary over the intermediate term, and deflationary in the long-term. 4. At the national level, a system addicted to debt needs massive and constant liquidity; hence, the need to print additional money. In the words of Bill Gross of PIMCO: "We are witnessing the death of abundance for a long time." The sad part is that the average citizen is unable to observe the salient fact that the greater the debt, the less able to pay.

## How to Avoid Bad Debt

1. Limit yourself to one credit card and use it only for emergencies. The single most important plastic card to own is a library card. Millions look at their credit card as disposable income pretending to be rich. They buy things they cannot afford, and maintain destructive personal behavioral patterns. The catharsis lies in the fact that people will no longer be borrowing from the future to enjoy an unnecessary contemporary lifestyle. 2. Before purchasing an item, ask yourself if you really need it today or tomorrow, and why it was not needed yesterday. Understand the difference between "I want," "I need," "I can afford," and "I can't afford." 4. Eat less and order fewer alcoholic beverages when dining out. 5. If possible, move to a less expensive venue. 6. Increase your deductibles. 7. Shop wisely and replace goods less frequently. 8. Become frugal. 8. Associate with a support group to highlight the realities of what you make, spend and what you owe.

## The Underlying Causes of Indebtedness

1. With Greenspan lowering the Fed rate to 1%, and Bernanke to 0.20%, people were encouraged to borrow and go deeper in debt. Consumption is not allowed to fall below 70% of GDP, at all costs. The government does not want the consumer to stop spending, and has offered inducements to prolong profligate behavior. Juvenal, the Roman poet, is credited with the expression "bread and circus" to describe emperors placating the population with "candy" and "distractions." It has become common policy ever since and perfected by the Fed, Congress, and Wall Street. There is nothing wrong with moderate consumption, but when the savings rate is near zero and the individual has negative wealth and little to nothing for retirement, then excess consumption becomes a serious disorder. 2. The Production of the household debt helix frames the issue: high and rising consumption leads to high debt levels, rising interest payments as percent of disposable income, low savings, lower rates of investment for the future, declining total net wealth, lower productivity, and real income stagnation and/or decline. 3. Total national debt as a percentage of GDP has become a leading economic problem. 4. The US does not like making economic sacrifices. It wants things yesterday! I have known undergraduates, who borrowed money to go to college; do not work part-time, but who must go to Cancun during spring break, only to remain drunk for five days on

borrowed money. In the words of Adam Hamilton of zealllc.com: "There is nothing like debt to destroy prosperity and lead to poverty." A good prescription for financial ruin by the youth of America is to hold on to the illusions that one can spend as much as they please, borrow as much as they can, and live as hedonistically as possible, and in the end, all will be well and good. 5. The contemporary mantra supports the notion for one generation to borrow and the next to pay the bill; that the world will lend money forever; that house prices will always rise; that the nation can afford a "guns and butter" economy forever; and that saving is no longer required to produce a sustained rate of economic growth. Personages in Washington also believe that a boundless ocean of money exists to be spent on endless public entitlements. And the public looks upon government as a source of many subsidies and financial assistance from cradle to grave. 6. Debt is associated with the romantic notion of happiness and success, both of which are not easily defined. For example, doubling the size of the bathroom, the wardrobe, the car, the size of the kitchen, etc., does not double the degree of happiness because borrowed money must be paid back with interest. Eventually the day of reckoning arrives and pain becomes universal as houses decline in value, unemployment rises, interest rates and inflation rise, and people begin to burn the furniture in order to keep warm. 7. The concept of the "Hygeia Bowl" was supposed to be the alpha and omega of the welfare state, but is unable to provide the complete wish basket.

## A Number of Realities

1. Borrowed money is never the same as saved money. Debt is what the future pays to the past with interest. When you save and invest without acquiring debt your net worth will grow. Those under the age of 45 are condemned to work the rest of their lives repaying parental debt. Debt is a form of self-afflicted slavery, so endemic it has been institutionalized as "debt peonage." The future, therefore, is grim as all solutions of the consumer debt bubble have few, non-painful options. 2. History does not reward spendthrifts. It punishes them. The profligate "Starbucks" and the "ATM" consumer-driven behavior of the past will come to a sad end as lower standards and levels of living will be the order of the day. Among the more dominant behavioral modifications will be the adoption of, "I will postpone consumption." "The New Era Economy" is consumption and debt driven. Real disposable incomes continue to decline, yet the consumer continues to accumulate debt because of the belief that "debts do not matter." 3. One aspect of American life—waste—will come under assault. 4. Americans exhibit no fear of debt. Credit has become the mainstay of the American economy as it stimulates spending, tax revenues, offers incentives for business expansion, maintains high employment levels, and most important, boosts consumer confidence. Most credit, however, is bad credit, as it induces people to forgo current savings for consumption. 5. Commercial retail space illustrates the cause of profligate behavior. The US leads the world, with 21 sq. feet of retail floor space per person, followed by Sweden with 3.2, the UK 2.5, France 2.3, and Italy 1.5. No matter

how one looks at the general market, nearly all retailers in the US are considering store closings of 20%-plus by 2015. 6. You cannot gamble your way out of debt, but many people attempt to do so. They go to the races hoping that the long shot will get them out of debt, and they spend much needed money on lottery tickets each week hoping to do the same. 7. The estimate for the number of debt collectors is said to be 146,000 and if true, an incredible number. 8. Given the existence of cheap money, the average American is not motivated to save for anything.

## Not Recognizing and Understanding the Tyranny of Gambling

Gambling (gaming) refers to individuals placing bets where the mathematical probability of gain is against them. There may be a temporary random gain accompanied with an adrenalin rush, but that is all it is–temporary. Gaming is popular because of the instant gratification that it can deliver, the conversation that it generates, the elevation of the winner to celebrity status, and the ability to spend the winnings–instantly. Gaming, therefore, reinforces America's definition of success and happiness. It makes everyone feel good without realizing long-term consequences. Obviously, it is particularly destructive to the very young and pathetically stupid for the elderly who flock to casinos. This behavior is accepted, encouraged, and considered innocent. The geography of gambling offers an interesting spacial pattern: North America and Asia are responsible for 62% of all revenues followed by Europe (28%), Latin America (7%), and Oceania (3%). There are no reliable figures for cruise ship gambling. Globally, the gaming industry is doubling every seven years with Macao, the largest gaming city. The biggest multi-state jackpot, Powerball, exceeds $300 million, with 15% of the adult population participating.

Rarely has a nation embraced gambling like America. Prior to the 1970s, Las Vegas was the only state that legally allowed gambling, but since then the "gambling fever" has spread throughout the fruited plain. About 74% of all adult Americans indulge in some form of legal gambling with 70% buying lottery tickets, and another 37% gambling in casinos. The most disturbing element of America's obsession with gambling is that while incomes adjusted for inflation in the past 30 years have declined, the growth of the gaming industry has risen sevenfold, and all but six states have legalized gaming in order to raise revenue. This is quite disturbing if the citizenry truly believes that this is a proper way to fund necessary state obligations. Gaming constitutes a cancer of the gravest degree, and it should be viewed as a national illness. The American Gaming Association states that more than 110 million Americans frequent the more than 350 casinos. These gamblers make more than 320 million trips, spending more money than in ballparks, amusement parks, and movie theatres. Lottery ticket sales, according to the National Center for Policy Analysis, amount to $120 billion. It is no longer a rarity for people to lose fortunes in casinos, but the number of addicted gamblers with incomes less than $70,000 a year represents a national illness. If one begins to dissect the pathology, one discovers that gambling, which was once thought to be a sin shrouded in shame and guilt, has not only emerged as a growth industry, but one that has become respectable and is referred to as "recreational gaming." While states love casinos for the revenue, politicians for the campaign donations, the public at large emerges as the biggest loser. The gaming fascination has become the fastest growing addiction with major ramifications. It destroys traditional family life through impoverishment, augments crime, insurance fraud, arson, poses a threat to traditional values, and in the end, it costs the taxpayer dearly. Gambling, in short, has become a way of life in America. College students' gamble; celebrities gamble; political figures gamble; senior citizens gamble. The only segment of the population that does not gamble is babies and casino owners.

A number of parallels exist between investing and gaming as both expose psychological frailties. Just as the odds are stacked against the casino gambler, so are the innumerable potholes found everywhere on Wall Street. However, there is one crucial difference between gaming in Las Vegas and gambling on Wall Street. In casino gambling, loses are guaranteed as the laws of probability erode dwindling resources. Gambling underperforms relative to the Total Market. Always! The prudent investor wishing to invest does so with the knowledge that large returns will not occur in the short-term, while the speculator thinks in terms of large returns over the short-term. Resist the temptation to leverage, to buy the "hot tip," and do not respond to advertisements promising to make you a "billionaire in your spare time." In the final analysis, it is important to remember the following: 1. Gambling is a huge tax. 2. The only way to win in Las Vegas is not to play at all. Casinos are not places of "entertainment." 3. Nothing has helped the pawnshop business like gambling. 4. About 85% of gamblers in casinos are aged 40-plus, precisely the age that should be saving for their golden years. 5. Internet gambling is a $90-plus billion business and growing faster than income and GDP. 6. The $9 billion-plus City Center Las Vegas casino is the most expensive private construction project in US history. 7. Refuse enticements to become a participant. Say no to junkets, the free "chips," the free dinner and room, and the enticing advertisement, "you have to be in it to win it." 8. In the end, the gambler has a huge probability of loss coupled with a very low probability of gain.

# Keys To Success

## Why Saving is Important

Saving is that portion of your income that is not spent. Few people, however, have the inner drive to pursue such a strategy throughout their lifetime, a major difference between those who are wealthy and those who are not. For decades, many Americans came to believe that home prices would continuously rise, that interest rates will always remain low, that the welfare state will take care of every wish and need, that the nation does not have to export, that saving is no longer necessary, and that all will continue on the present course forever and ever. These delusions are ending. Standards and levels of living are declining, taxes rising, and considerable pain is being inflicted as the country reverses the many fiscal, monetary, and political policy blunders that have drained the national treasury. The more you save the more you have to invest, and saving should be viewed as an immutable mechanical force that is not subject to debate, but something that should occur 24 hours a day, 365 days a year, forever. At the national level, a low saving rate reduces capital investment, exaggerates trade imbalances, widens the divide between the very wealthy and the rest of society, makes the nation less competitive, and places an undue burden on the taxpayer who subsidizes hedonistic lifestyles. The fact that America consumes more than 35% of all commercial global advertising goes a long way to explain this condition.

For most of America's history, the saving rate had remained around 12%, but over the course of the past two generations, the rate has steadily declined. In the 1960s, it was 11%, in the 1970s it fell to 8%, in the 1980s it dropped to 6.5%, in the 1990s it fell below 4%, and it declined to 0% in recent years. This has had serious consequences that cannot be overlooked or minimized. In sharp contrast, Asians save more than 20% of their income and lend to Americans so that they may purchase their products, while Americans borrow from Asians, and, in so doing, employ Asians. Therefore, if the 11th commandment is "save" and the 12th is "invest wisely," the 13th is to practice the 11th and 12th as frequently as possible. When the dot.com bubble burst in 2000, it was expected that consumers would begin saving more. However, they did not, and for the next 13 years the longest and most impressive profligate behavior in history bankrupted the nation and its saving rate has been culturally abolished, a circumstance unique among DMs. What makes this condition precarious is that America has no defenses against severe stagflation. With massive international and domestic debts and a bankrupt consumer, capital investment will be insufficient to grow GDP. What America needs is less consumption and more capital formation, and as long as the official Fed policy is based on unrestrained money and credit creation, existing structural imbalances will worsen, thus creating an atmosphere that saving will not be easier going forward.

Knowing the difference between saving and speculation is fundamental to prudent investors. Saving money in secure investments such as CDs and Treasuries constitute minimum risk for ultra-conservatives, while the prudent investors strive for the historical Total Market average of 10.5%. The sensible investor should resist temptations of 15%-plus total returns, and that means to stay away from the myriad of "enhancement" strategies seen on television, heard on the radio and read in the print media. Note the following: 1. Saving refers to not wasting, and not just money, but time, the soles of your shoes, gasoline, the way you wash your clothes, and how you conduct daily activities. Unless you begin to save early and often, "critical mass" (current levels of living produced from former investments) will elude you, and unhappiness and discontent will make you cynical, and consume you with envy. Wealth building requires work, and while there are few circuitous routes to this objective, assiduousness and sacrifice for extended, periods are essential in reaching critical mass. The engines that drive the locomotive include a cluster of human behaviors that seem to have gotten lost from the contemporary lexicon: a sensible life style, endurance to make sacrifices possible, audacity to resist temptation and weakness, and astuteness to achieve lofty accomplishments in the future.

The distinction between flagrant profligate behavior and prudent saving and investment behavior is illustrated thusly: two identical truck drivers in terms of age, familial circumstances, and income. They both win a $250,000 lottery, and within a year, "A" spends the entire amount on family vacations, new clothing, cars, presents, etc. "B" does not spend but buys a new truck that augments his income over the course of the next 15 years. That is the difference between wanton "spending," and saving and investing for the future. 2. When you begin, saving is important. The individual, who saves $3,600 annually for 10 years, beginning at age 25, winds up with $772,926 at age 65. The individual who begins saving at age 35 and saves to age 65 accumulates only $315,024. The 25-year-old, by investing but $36,000, has $457,902 more dollars than the 35-year-old does. Time, therefore, is an investor's biggest ally in the accumulation of wealth. It is important to remember that: saving equals accumulation; spending is tantamount to a depletion of current and future assets; investing is equal to long-term wealth building; mistakes are learning experiences; habits are both good and bad; a focused mindset is much better than one that can only be described as "scattered"; consumer borrowing and paying interest is an impoverishing experience; a long-range plan implies current actions in order to realize long-term returns; and living below your means refers to long-term wealth creation possibilities. 3. Pay yourself first, and although the percentage is critical, any "percent solution" is better than a "zero-percent solution." You must crave its "accumulation," and as the Chinese are fond of saying, "Even the blind can see money."

To understand who saves, consider the following: The very affluent (10% of the population) have a good financial education, are professionals, creators of successful businesses, know how to protect their money, and participate in limited partnerships. These are people who know how to save and invest wisely and successfully. Household net wealth exceeds $20 million. The dwindling middle class is characterized by a second tier education, and a disproportionate percentage of employment positions in education and government. A high percentage has a home, some savings and retirement programs. Household net wealth is $100,000, with nearly all living beyond their means and struggling with heavy debt burdens. This cohort lost heavily during market declines in 2000 and 2008, is heavily taxed, wedged between higher living costs and stagnant wages, and will be struggling with retirement. At the bottom is a large and ever growing dependent class that has the lowest educational levels, practically no savings, minimal retirement monies, and the highest fertility rates. It has a negative household net wealth of more than $30,000, is the object of targeted lottery advertisements, excessive hedonistic behaviors and subject to the bulk of governmental entitlement programs. Although the federal tax rate is minimal for this group, it actually pays a higher percentage of disposable income in sales taxes and fees than the first two groups, and is the cohort that will suffer the most as stagflation worsens. In the final analysis, 20% of the nation is getting richer, 25% is treading water, and 55% are falling behind.

Levels of saving, spending habits, investing practices, and lifestyle patterns will be key elements determining the level of wealth that will be attained over the course of a lifetime. Contemporary society, however, permits those with lower incomes (in particular, immigrants) to accumulate greater percent wealth than those who earn more. No matter what their country of origin, they have the highest savings rate relative to income. Consider this experience at a convenience store in Miami in the mid-1990s. My family and I saw a construction worker buy $5 worth of lottery tickets and a "six pack" of beer, the salesperson stating that this occurred every Monday through Friday, without fail. Later that evening on a local TV news program, there was a story of an immigrant Cuban who arrived to the US with only the clothes on his back and who worked a myriad of menial jobs before becoming a millionaire—a huge difference between the two: One born in the US, while the other, risking life and limb, remained focused to the ultimate goals. He did not gamble but saved, he did not drink a "six pack" each evening, but went to a second job, and on weekends a third job, and over 12 years, he saved and invested, eventually becoming the owner of the hotel where he once parked cars. The other fellow, who saved nothing, was mired in a life of alcohol and excessive gambling. He consumed all he earned, speculated on fantasies, and accepted the bare minimum that society offered. This is not an isolated story, as there are many of humble means who are millionaires and all sharing a singular similarity–the propensity to save. In the final analysis: 1. Saving is the product of acquired, not innate, behavior. Saving is unnatural in today's hedonistic economy, and, therefore, the act of saving requires commitment and a sense of purpose. 2. With few exceptions, the saving rate rises and falls with inflation and interest rates. 3. Excessive consumption prevents saving and wealth accumulation. 4. In order to save one must differentiate between "essential" and "want," and spend accordingly. 5. In addition to marrying a wealthy person, inheriting money, or winning the lottery, the only road to amassing wealth is to work hard, save money and to invest wisely.

## Saving Impediments

1. Since the 1970s, saving is becoming harder to accomplish because of declining real disposable income. The Bureau of Labor Statistics reported in 2009 that 80% of all wage earners experienced a cut in take home pay. Another report states that 53% of all Americans experienced a net wealth decline of 55% since 2007, and still another indicates that only 47% of all adults have a full-time job. Officially, 19 million have no jobs, baby boomers are working longer hours and earning less, and contrary to official proclamations, inflation is eroding the ability to save. Fifty percent of the population earns less than $35,000 annually and the American middle class ranks 27th globally. As a result, "American reliance on government at all-time high," reads the headline, as Americans took more aid from the government than they paid in taxes. Fifty million Americans use food stamps, governmental assistance programs rose by 11% since 2007, and foreclosures remain the highest in history. Bankruptcies are at historic highs, personal debt is at record highs, and all manner of taxes and "fees" are rising faster than income. Median savings per person is but $22,000, an incredibly low figure for the world's largest economy. Obviously, income from savings has remained stagnant throughout this century due to the zero interest rate policy. About 60% of all Americans have negative wealth today than in 1995 and 60% work in jobs with no benefits and pensions. Since 2000, more than $20 trillion has been removed from the economy through declining real estate and other asset price declines. Since 1973, the average income has declined in real terms, and 72% of real income growth has gone to the top 5% of the population; 55% of all workers make less than $15 per hour; 57% of all new jobs are temporary, or "adjunct"; and 75% of the fastest growing occupations (waiters, retail sales, food preparers, etc.) are all low-paid service jobs. Saving, under these conditions, is nearly impossible. For the first time in more than 15 years, the net worth of the middle class has declined from $130,000 in 1998 to $93,000 in 2011. There is little to save after one subtracts the cost of housing, food, transport and interest from the average salary. A nation that historically rewarded investors and savers now punishes them by encouraging

consumption and debt. The solution? "Forced austerity." For the US, this dose of medicine, after centuries of comfort, is difficult. The combination of the misery and the poverty indexes represent the highest readings in more than seven decades. In addition, as much as 70% of all spending during 2002-2008 was a result of home equity extraction. Sixty percent of all households are "house poor," as 50%-plus of disposable income is devoted to home maintenance, with only the top 20% of the population can afford a "home" without serious problems. Furthermore, 80% over the age of 40 took a new position at a lower salary. For the past 10 years, more than 55% of all jobs have been non-permanent, which academia calls "adjunct." They are part of the "99ers," in reference to the 99 weeks of unemployed benefits. Since 57% have incomes below $30,000, saving becomes an impossibility. When one in five households receives food stamps, how is it possible to save? And it gets worse: 44% of all households spend 60% of their income on food and energy. The middle class, once the epitome of American life and the core savers of the nation, are no more. As their numbers and the "American dream" dwindle, they are poised to form the nucleus for civil unrest as frustration, and the lack of opportunities for social and economic mobility remain circumscribed. Since 2007, the number working has declined by more than 8 million, and those classified as "disabled" has doubled since 2009. It gets worse: in most states, welfare pays more than work.

2. The belief that *la dolce vita* embodies the spirit of America (that spending is good and saving bad), now and forever is a major saving hurdle. Rare is the individual that saves in order to buy, and atypical the person who consciously denies current consumption in order to leave children a legacy. Rather, the average American borrows to spend, and over the course of a lifetime spends the cost of his home in interest charges. Lifestyle behavior is the key ingredient to this calculus–the persistency of an anti-saving mentality. Income derived from dividends and interest is at an all-time low for 80% of the population as Americans have succumbed to federal efforts to keep spending. Yet, of all industrial nations, Americans work longer and with fewer and shorter vacations. I have colleagues, trained professionals who maintain that debt is good, that spending is good, and that the failsafe mechanisms of the Fed and Congress will protect everyone. This nonsense is dispensed in university classes across the nation as fact. What they do not understand is that everyone in the family working and borrowing to live is an impractical lifestyle. The result is that 70% of all Americans do not save sufficiently or not at all for retirement, the highest such percentage of any DM. Household savings outside retirement accounts have almost disappeared, and for the youth of America the concept of saving sounds like a life sentence at Chateau Dif. Over the course of a lifetime, the largest mistake is not saving enough, something that will cost at least $1 million. The mismanagement of risk, chasing performance, failure to allocate assets, failure to reduce expenses, and overtrading can, collectively, cost an additional $1-plus million.

3. Given the existence of cheap money for the past 30 years, the average American was not motivated to save. The official policy of the Fed for the past generation has been to provide high liquidity driving interest rates to historic low levels. This action has discouraged savings and encouraged borrowing producing the so called "wealth effect," something that is differentiated from real wealth brought about through work, saving and capital investments. The government has also become the collective parent and that progress and wealth are defined by the nature and quantity of governmental largesse. Since the tax code discourages savings and rewards debt and consumption, why save when the nation is inundated with entitlements and near zero interest rates? Under these conditions, impoverishment is assured.

4. An inability to sacrifice. Saving always involves sacrificing current consumption for much larger rewards years later, a behavioral practice that runs counter to today's hedonistic culture. It takes discipline not to yield to temptation, but that is the difference between those that have later in life vs. those that squander early and forever. The use of credit by the young, in particular, is irresistible because credit "gets you things" sooner, but at a price, and that is the payment of interest. Part of this behavior lies in the fact that the youth are myopic. They rarely project into the future and have no awareness of the benefits of saving and long-term investing. American youth have been conditioned to think of "now" and never "later"; conditioned to "spend" and not "save"; and to "squander" and not be "thrifty." The temptation to consume now and not save is a deadly combination. Saving, therefore, requires sacrifice and the re-scheduling of indulgence.

5. High household debt levels are another factor. With "Joe six-pack running on empty" and disposable income shrinking, he lives paycheck to paycheck and saves nothing. If the average price of a home were to fall 20% from current levels, about 80% of all homeowners with a mortgage would have negative equity. The freshman of 2012 will graduate in 2017 with a debt of $45,000-plus, and will not be able to save a dime for the next 15 years. Home equity has collapsed, real net worth has declined by 48% since 1999, college graduate unemployment sits at 30%, and 40% of all college graduates are living at home. Household debt levels are greater in 2014 than in 2007.

6. America, over the course of the past 30-plus years, has steadily reduced the size of its central cities, expanded suburban development, reduced family size, increased house size, more cars, lawns, larger air conditioning and heating systems, etc.—all of which are built and purchased on the theory that low energy costs and continuously rising disposable incomes would remain favorable to the maintenance of this lifestyle. The problem with suburbia is that it relies on horizontal movement for everything, but rising energy costs and declining real incomes are changing the calculus so the lifestyle driven by cheap credit and energy is not only threatened, but will terminate in impoverishment. Once having made the move, the new suburbanites have come to realize they are now captives of their own

fantasies with no way to reduce their rising fixed costs. Since 2006, property taxes have risen 31%, home prices have declined 34%, and state taxes rose by 19%. In addition, with the decline in housing prices, homes can no longer be used as ATM machines. The financial landscape becomes worse once interest rates and inflation rise further. All of the above have produced an environment of dependency and entitlements. Americans are hopelessly dependent–on sugar, drugs, sex, television, gasoline, salt, social entitlements, worthless education, gambling, over-eating, sports, celebrities, etc. In fact, the word entitlement has come to mean "rights," or something that every American not only requires but also insists and depends on, and be provided in an unrestricted manner. The Senate Budget Committee reported that in 2011 economic welfare for the poorest 20% of American households amounted to $168 a day, thus becoming a career path for many. America, therefore, has become very dependent on its government for nearly every aspect of its daily existence–and not motivated to save.

7. The decline in real wealth for 70% of the population since the 1960s prevents saving. According to G. William Domhoff, the bottom 80% of the population has but 7% of financial wealth, the next 10% have 10% of all wealth, the next 5% have 11%, the next 4% have 29%, and the top 1% has 43% of total wealth. Only 20% of the population has the ability to save. According to the Federal Reserve for the year 2007: the bottom 25% of all households had a net worth of $4,600, the next quartile $21,700, the next quartile $78,900, and the top quartile $242,800, of which the top 10% had a net worth of $1,606,600. The prognosis for improvement remains poor as the median household income declined by 9% since 2000. The Associated Press, in 2013, reported that four out of five adults "struggle with joblessness, near-poverty, or reliance on welfare for at least parts of their lives–signs of deteriorating economic security and the American dream. Furthermore, the cost of the food basket has more than doubled in the past generation, further reducing disposable income.

## How to Save and Improve Your Saving Habits

1. Eat a healthy and filling breakfast at home and not in the local coffee shop and save $4. Do not buy a mid-morning coffee or snack and save $3. Brown bag your lunch and save $5. Bring fruit for an afternoon snack and save $2. Cook a nutritious meal for dinner and save $10. Eliminate the second and third beer after dinner, along with potato chips, and save $7. At the end of the day, you have saved $31 or $620 for the month and $7,440 for year. Now compound this annually for the next 40 years at 10%, and you have just paid for your home, furnishings, and your retirement. In the words of Sir John Templeton: "The best time to invest is when you have money," and the only way money becomes available is by saving. 2. Reduce waste. People waste more than 35% of the food they buy. If this amounts to $5 a day, $150 a month, or $1,800 a year, one has a problem. 3. Resist debt; pay cash for everything and bargain for the lowest possible price, as many retailers will discount for cash. 4. Be a value conscious consumer. This means that

sometimes paying more for an item is often a better value than the one that has to be replaced frequently. 5. Delay gratification as long as possible. 6. Pay off the mortgage in the shortest possible time. 7. A penny saved is a penny earned and not subject to federal, state and local taxes. 8. Don't buy, rent, or maintain more house than you can afford. 9. Condition yourself to separate the important from the unimportant things in life. Prioritize spending by surgically reducing discretionary expenditures. John Bogle in 2012 said: "Don't spend money unless you absolutely have to. I last bought a suit in 1995. If you don't want to stay in style, you can save a lot." 10. Learn to cook and save thousands of dollars each year and at least $1 million when savings compound over a lifetime. In addition, walk short distances instead of driving, buy a $10 bottle of wine instead of one costing $25. 11. The pattern of habit improvement begins with the embracement of frugality in order to increase savings, because without frugality it is nearly impossible to save or invest. Saving becomes, in time, a cathartic habit that enables many options to become available.

# Time, Value of Money, Compounding, and Reinvestment

Just as it is wise and prudent for investors to allocate financial assets, another allocation is just as important–time–a resource that cannot be retrieved after it is abused, wasted, or neglected. What an individual does with his time will not only define his character, but also his wealth-building efforts. Wealth accumulation begins at birth with contributions to a savings/brokerage account every year. At 22 years of age, the individual, with college completed, will have a minimum of 48 working years, and with the passing of each year, time, like sand in an hourglass, is lost and will never be retrieved. A five-year-old hardly notices sand affected by gravity. At age 10, it becomes more noticeable, at 20, the pace of sand removal is more obvious, and at age 40, more than half has been removed. At 75, there is little sand left, as you have lived most of your years. At 85, you need glasses to see the few traces of sand in the upper part of the hourglass, and at 95, you need a magnifying glass to find any sand particles at all. Time, therefore, is an essential ingredient in the production of wealth and important as the purchase of Vintage Porto. In order for fine Porto to mature, you require at least 25 years, and if you are 80, the chances are that if you buy this wine for your personal consumption, you will not be around to enjoy it. But if you wish to leave your children an interesting legacy, purchase Porto when they are young, and 25-plus years later when they are established in their careers and their taste buds have not deteriorated, they will enjoy your thoughtfulness. In this manner, your two most important assets–time and money will be put to good use. Think about investing in like manner.

The "time value of money," refers to the fact that the value of money changes all the time. It is certainly worth more during deflation, less during inflation, and a certainty that a prevailing tax rate will affect its worth in real time. Not only should investors base all financial decisions on this concept, but they should also be aware of advantages that accrue when compounding dividends and interest over time. There are two ways of computing interest–simple and compound. The first is computed by attaching an interest rate to the original figure, while the latter is computed by applying an interest to the original figure plus the interest on the interest. The "rule of 72" will divulge the amount of time necessary to double money. Divide the rate of return into 72: and at 3% growth, it would take approximately 24 years, at 4%, 18 years, at 5% 14.5 years, at 6% 12 years, at 7%, 10.2 years, and at 8%, 9 years. The "rule of 115" will inform the investor how long it will take to triple money at various rates of return. At 10%, money will triple in 11.5 years (115 divided by 10). Time exponentially swells the effect of compounding. The value of money is determined by time, and while the concept of compound growth is simple, most people fail to grasp its power and significance over the course of a lifetime. For example, if $1 is invested each year at 10% annual compound growth, the dollar amount after 5 years would be $6.11, in 10 years $15.94, in 20 years $57.27, and in 40 years $442.59, much like kudzu. The time value of money also refers to the fact that $1 today is worth more than $1 in the future due to inflation, and the fact that the sooner one saves and invests the greater the chances that time will increase its value. The ability to amass $1 million at four different age groups, all achieving 8% annual returns, by age 65 is revealing: a 25 year-old would have to save $290 a month, a 35 year-old, $670 a month, a 45 year-old, $1,700 a month, and a 55 year-old, $5,500 a month. Time makes a difference, and the prudent investor would be best served by early and consistent saving. In addition:

1. Buy, sell, or hold are decisions that are time-based. The interest on the interest, monthly, quarterly, semi-annually, or annually, over the course of a working lifetime, will reap huge benefits. When capital gains and stock splits are factored, the results are even better; hence, the words of Baron Rothschild, who referred to compound interest as the "eighth wonder of the world," and Einstein, who said that the "biggest force is the power of compounding." 2. Even for modest gains, compounding only works for long periods; hence, the need for patience and discipline. Added to the mix is the fact that the process is so boring that it offers little interest to nearly all investors despite its huge advantages. 3. The compounding of dividends and dividend growth are crucial elements in value investing. Not only is the investor getting a healthy return with a dividend, but when it increases on a regular basis, the stock also rises in price, and when a "buy and hold" philosophy is maintained, the results after 20-plus years become exceptional. 4. A portfolio that is predominantly dividend-oriented, and where the dividends are compounded, is one that outperforms inflation and growth stocks over time. Here are a number of imperatives: take advantage of compounding in all tax-deferred accounts, particularly a ROTH; invest in quality dividend-payers for the long-term; and for compounding to work, the investor never consumes interest and dividends, but reinvests forever.

## Dollar Cost Averaging

Investing the same amount of money on a regular interval is a strategy called DCA. It is based on the fact that the market rises more than 70% of the time. Without realizing, DCA occurs on every payday no matter what the character of the market to holders of retirement accounts. DCA is neither exciting, scintillating, nor that imposing on the ego. It is mechanical and methodical, a boring investing approach, and to succeed, you must be disciplined, patient, and never doubt the strategy. It is important because it removes emotion from the investment equation, works particularly well with index funds, becomes particularly rewarding for those who begin investing early and continue until retirement, and reduces turnover, cost basis, instills discipline and patience, and rebalances the portfolio automatically over time. By DCA, you buy more cheap shares when prices are declining and fewer when rising, and if practiced for the long-term, you will never miss those sudden spurts of upward movements. Interestingly, the difference between buying at the top and buying at the bottom over periods exceeding 20 years, is less than you think. If you wish to wait for those elusive market bottoms, the investor stands to lose opportunity aggravated by the issue of time. Therefore, continue to invest with nerves of steel, and you will not increase your blood pressure like many other strategies. This approach allows you to emphasize consistency and continuity, encourages long-term investing, eliminates market-timing urges, yields excellent results over time and eliminates the nagging question of when to buy. As a result, DCA is heavily promoted by mutual fund companies and works well with dividend-paying stocks. Among the countless DCA variations, is "value averaging," in which the target is not based on a set dollar figure, but on asset price. If share prices drop, and your net value drops by $100, the next month you increase your contribution by $100, thus forcing you to invest more during down markets leading to lower costs and higher growth rates. DCA succeeds because it is a disciplined way to save and invest, eliminating guesswork and market timing.

## The Importance of Retirement Planning

Since standards and levels of living are declining, the wise investor must adjust to changing economic circumstances and reposition retirement strategies to avoid perilous rapids. For example, over the past generation real wages have not risen, the net worth of the average household declined by 31%, inflation has eroded purchasing power by 60%, and more than 40% of all aged between 40-65 lack a pension. This gruesome portrait of impending retirement is further compounded by the fact that 70% of the 45-55 age cohort has less than $90,000 in total net assets. Clearly, a substantial number of Americans are unprepared for retirement, and because of the age of this cohort, it is mathematically impossible to reach critical mass in the remaining 15-20 years to age 65. Under these conditions, retirement will be postponed indefinitely, and if this does not impress you, consider this singular statistic: two in five workers earns less than $30,000 annually, with few if any retirement benefits. The typical, but highly variable, five-legged retirement stool consists of savings, retirement accounts, pensions, passive income, and S.S. According to the S.S. Administration for 1999, the four sources of retirement income for a person with a retirement income of $33,777 were savings (55%), S.S. (21%), pensions and related (21%), and other (3%). That was then. Recent figures indicate that S.S. has become the primary source (48%) of retirement income for more than 50% of all retirees. This is a cause of concern as S.S. benefits are insufficient and do not keep up with inflation despite periodic COLA increases. Another distressing element is that 25% of all adult Americans have raided their tax-sheltered accounts to pay current bills.

Pension programs are essentially of two types–Defined Benefit (DB) and Defined Contribution (DC). A DB plan pays the employee a steady income for life based on years of service and salary. Should you fall in this category, consider yourself fortunate because this plan is being scaled down or eliminated. Blue chip corporations and others have frozen DBs, and many eliminated or reduced benefits. About 84% of all full-time workers had DB plans prior to 1990, a figure that has been reduced to 15%. In addition, 19 million are owed retirement pension money. Total shortfall from all pension benefits exceeds $2.3 trillion. More than 900 corporations have defaulted on their pension plans and the Pension Benefit Guaranty Corp is running a $33 billion deficit. State governments have few alternatives but to reduce benefits for the newly hired, reduce benefits for those already in the system, remove COLA provisions, and raise the retirement age. In an attempt to reduce expenses, corporations have replaced DBs with a wide variety of DC alternatives, mostly 401(k) with liability for investing shifted to the employee. For the vast majority of poorly educated workers in the ways of investing, these "do it yourself retirement plans," have become a nightmare with long-term consequences. Because of inadequate investment options and inexperience, portfolio under performance has become endemic. There is a proposal for DB and DC accounts to be managed by the S.S. Administration. Tax-sheltered plans include: 1. The traditional IRA (the simplest and most common) 2. The 401(k) account is a plan that the employer arranges with an insurance company, mutual fund, etc., to offer select investments and to handle paper work. The employee makes regular contributions, receives tax-sheltered advantages until the time of withdrawal, with contributions reducing taxable income. Many companies match employee contributions with all manner of percentages, and it would behoove the investor to maximize contributions. 3. The ROTH IRA, funded with after-tax dollars, is superior to a traditional IRA, and it should be funded first before anything else. It can be willed to heirs, with no requirements to withdraw at 70½. Individuals who qualify are permitted to convert to a ROTH account, and are entitled to extra time to pay the taxes due on the conversion. While traditional IRA contributions are tax-deferred, those of a ROTH are tax-deferred and tax-free forever. 4. A ROTH 401(k) is an employer-sponsored retirement plan that offers the same advantages as other retirement plans, but has no income-related eligibility limitations. 5. A 403(b) retirement plan applies to employees of non-profit organizations. 6. SEP-IRA and Keogh accounts are for self-employed individuals. Almost all of the above follow a clear and simple process in which a certain percentage of your gross pay may be placed into an account. Unfortunately, despite the compelling reasons why every worker should participate to maximum levels, fewer than 50% contribute at the maximum, 40% contribute nothing, and the average 401(k) is worth less than $40,000. These are important retirement instruments and investors need to pay attention as all are in a perpetual state of flux in terms of contribution limits and other provisions.

Items to ponder include: 1. Of the $10 trillion-plus in retirement assets, the single largest holding is in various IRAs, followed by government pension plans and annuities. 2. Should you be changing employment or retiring, individuals have the following options: Roll over the monies to an IRA, transfer to an income annuity, withdraw as a lump sum, move the monies to a new employer plan, or leave the monies in the existing plan. In all instances, there are short- and long-term consequences and, in some instances, serious tax liabilities. 3. IRAs are necessary for several reasons: there are few alternatives; they lower taxes; money is shielded from creditors; and you maintain control. 4. Troublesome issues include: "Day trading" in these accounts usually lowers instead of augmenting wealth; many fail to contribute the maximum thus lowering total funds available at retirement; and many overweigh in cash and bonds. 5. DC account holders are poor investors, earning less than 3% over time. 6. The typical asset allocation of 401(k) retirement plans is equities 46%, bonds 37%, balanced funds 11%, and other 7%. 8. Never consider your pension to be entirely safe. The problem with safety is that individual contributions have declined, and the aggregate value of these plans has deteriorated dramatically due to poor management and market declines. Despite the fact that they are legal contracts, pensions can be amended under certain conditions. 9. Fifty percent of all adults have saved less than $25,000, about 75% of all aged 50 and over have savings of less than $50,000, and only 10% of all aged 50 and over have saved more than $250,000. Sixty percent of all workers have no retirement savings. Only 20% of the working population has savings greater than their income. 10. The future American crisis is not terrorism and nuclear proliferation, but the lack of "critical mass." Most Americans never think about this concept until it is too late, and, therefore, America has a "retirement cliff," as a good portion of the population does not have sufficient funds saved for retirement. Remember, state pension gaps exceeds $4.2 trillion. 11. More than 60% of all US households have zero or negative net worth and 48% are very dependent on S.S. 13. For those earning $35,000 or less, 10% contribute to 401(k) accounts, but for those earning more than $150,000, the percent contributing increases to 95%. The latter also saved 15% of their income, while the former group saved less than 2%. Excluding S.S. and pension distributions, it takes more than $2 million to generate $40,000 annually. 14. Remember: budget for life; save as much as possible; manage debt; invest with a plan; augment your earning ability; and emphasize tax-sheltered accounts as they generate 20%-plus more wealth than taxable accounts.

## How to Maximize Your Retirement Investments

1. Remain committed to a healthy existence and behave sensibly. 2. Live beneath your means. 3. Eliminate all unnecessary debt. 4. Save as much as possible. 5. Invest regularly and wisely. 6. Do not engage in speculative enterprises. 7. Never borrow from your retirement account because missed opportunities will be heart wrenching, as fees, interest, and other costs will prove to be extremely high. 8. One of the most common myths is that a $1 million net worth will guarantee a comfortable retirement. If we suppose that a retired couple have 25 remaining years, the erosive effects of inflation during the duration of the current secular bear market can reduce the purchasing power of the original nest egg by 90%. 9. It is crucial for re-retirees to examine their final retirement destination as state and local taxes vary enormously and may take a huge bite out of retirement expenditures. Among the factors to be considered are state and local income, sales, pension, S.S., property, inheritance, and estate taxes. Not every state treats the above equally. Only the following states do not tax earned and unearned income–Alaska, Florida, Nevada, South Dakota, Texas, Washington, and Wyoming. New Hampshire and Tennessee only tax dividends and interest. States that do not tax pension income are Pennsylvania, Mississippi, and Illinois. Also to be configured are state and local taxes, particularly property and sales taxes, and estate taxes. More than 24 states do not tax S.S., and Alaska, Montana, New Hampshire and Oregon have no sales tax. Unfriendly retirement states include all of New England, New York, New Jersey, Maryland, California, Iowa, Nebraska, Wisconsin, and Oregon. Even car expenses vary widely by state. 10. Retirement is not entitlement. The individual must work hard, save, and invest to maximum levels to attain and preserve a comfortable retirement. Recent surveys indicate that fewer people are attempting to save for their "rusty" years. One survey states that 60% of all working individuals have not saved money at all for retirement, and those between the ages of 45-55 have a net wealth of less than $70,000, ex-house. 11. Dividend reinvesting is a wealth-building plan.

## Creating and Preserving Wealth

There are no secrets about creating and preserving wealth: you save as much as possible, invest prudently, emphasize frugality, and never spend more than you earn. That is what makes one individual wealthier than another. If your long-term goal is to build a retirement account that will be at least twenty-five times the amount you need at retirement, then a written plan is required, and it must be filed and reviewed every year. This is hard to do and even harder to project far into the future when you are eighteen, but it is a goal that should be ingrained and never forgotten. A workable plan involves a large number of variables of which marriage, career, children and their education, and life style are paramount. Only human frailties interfere with this goal. For example: 1. Frugality encourages, promotes, and enhances wealth formation, but a contemporary, hedonistic lifestyle interferes with this objective. 2. Discipline encourages, promotes, and enhances wealth formation, but chaos discourages this behavior. 3. Patience encourages, promotes, and enhances wealth formation, but impatience generates many unnecessary trades, boosts expenses, and forces many poor decisions. 4. Being master of your emotions encourages, promotes, and enhances wealth formation. This means understanding and managing fear, greed, and the character of your information field. Choose your friends carefully and doubt everything you hear and read concerning money matters. Yet, investors lose money because they are not resolute in their convictions, confused by conflicting information on network news, fall into debt to impress their friends, and associate with the wrong people. 5. Sacrifice current consumption for future consumption. 6. Never surrender assets to anyone. 7. A buy and hold strategy outperforms the notion that fast and loose trading is better. 8. Concentrate on index and tax-efficient funds. 9. Buy fundamentals. 10. Never overreach or extend your capabilities. Investors have always sought *elixir vitae*, but the ultimate alchemy—making a fortune on Wall Street is just as elusive. 11. Keep cash and not credit cards in your pocket. 12. Never place a $40 saddle on a $10 horse. Always buy within your income level. Understand that a salary of $25,000 never buys a $40,000 car, or a $400,000 home, no matter how easy it is to do so with creative financing schemes. You can also live without $550 designer sunglasses and $250 sneakers. 13. Save at least 20% of your gross salary. 14. Practice Benjamin Franklin's advice of life's important virtue's: "thrift, industry, and prudence." Over time he accumulated wealth by saving, avoiding debt, being frugal, and investing in real estate. He avoided "noise" by keeping his eye on the long-term. In the end, he said, "Nothing but money is sweeter than honey." 15. Appreciate *erfahrung*–practical lessons learned through the minefield of "hard knocks." 16. Temptation is all-encompassing, but resistance to it is far more rewarding and less stressful than accumulating debt. 17. "Sequence-of-returns risk" refers to the timing of your retirement and the amount of money withdrawn from retirement accounts. The commencement of retirement in 2006 would have had serious portfolio and total returns, in contrast to one retiring in 1982. 18. Outliving your retirement funds is referred to as longevity risk. It takes a lot of effort to produce enough retirement money to live 30%-plus of your life in retirement. 19. The fact that the median figure of household net wealth is but $120,000 is an indication that a comfortable retirement is out of reach for the median citizen. 20. Reasons for not saving for retirement include: fear of financial markets; investing is just too difficult; and not having sufficient funds. They are all stupid excuses. However, taking advantage of tax breaks, investing in a ROTH, reducing costs, eliminating debt, insure your earnings, do not chase yield, and automating your savings will do much to enhance aggregate wealth.

21. Place assets in a Trust to avoid probate, and protect beneficiaries. 22. Pay attention to the newly proposed MyRA retirement account. There is more:

### The Wealth Effect

The "wealth effect" refers to an increase in spending based on perceived increase in wealth. The official policy of the Fed since 1990 has been to provide liquidity and drive interest rates to historic low levels. This action has discouraged savings and encouraged borrowing producing the so called "wealth effect," something that is relative and differentiated from genuine, authentic, real wealth, the latter brought about through discipline and hard work. It is a peculiar concept with serious economic implications, as it refers to consumer behavior and associated misallocation of resources, which make people feel good by spending more than they can afford with borrowed money. Only productive work leads to wealth creation.

The preservation of financial assets means that you should not lose principal. For most people, retirement means that one will no longer be adding additional funds to one's stock of financial assets. The ability to augment significant amounts of wealth has ceased and, hence, the importance of preserving what remains. In this regard, never forget the sage words of Will Rogers who said, "I'm not so much interested in the return on my money as I am the return of my capital." Useful, homespun, sage advice on the subject includes: 1. Markets move in cycles, and the prudent investor recognizes and understands them. 2. Recognize your limitations and never attempt to be something you are not. 3. Insure what you cannot control. 4. Never place retirement money at risk. I paraphrase Henry Kissinger to emphasize the point: "There are no permanent friends, only permanent interests." 5. Create a *bastide* portfolio, or one that is "balanced." Often, less is more. 6. Emphasize passive income. 7. Gambling and all manner of speculations is *verboten*. 8. Become an "ox," the Chinese symbol of wealth, perseverance, hard work, discipline, and vigor. 9. Withdraw the minimum amount from retirement accounts. 10. Never forget the fact that protecting your wealth is much harder than making it. 11. To make sure that you will never underperform markets, invest in index funds. 12. To protect large dollars engage in an irrevocable trust, buy bullion, and maintain offshore accounts. 13. Among DMs, the US ranks near the bottom in the provision of secure retirement accounts for its aging citizens. The safety net has been lowered and fully 80%-plus of the population eventually become wards of the state.

## The Importance of Budgeting

The creation and maintenance of a budget makes sense because it forces the individual to "manage" money better. For most people, this means every month, but I once had a retired Mobil oil executive in 1976 relate the following scenario to my class. Each Monday he and his wife would account for every weekly expenditure, to the cent. They were worth in excess of $15 million in 1976 dollars. This is not an old-fashioned point of view but a practical, methodical, and highly rewarding behavior, and something that separates the successful from the unsuccessful. They wore good clothes, ate well, lived in a comfortable well-landscaped home, drove a medium-priced car, went on vacations, and more. What they did not do, was to buy foolishly, and to buy or do things that impressed their neighbors. In their words: "What we eliminated was "emotional social spending." Therefore, budget for life, manage your debt, and eliminate buyer's remorse.

Few people maintain a budget, fewer yet contemplate its establishment, and of those that begin the process on January 1, fail to persevere past March. Budgets, like everything else in life, vary by individual circumstances. The more simple the budget the better, and one of the better ways is to pay yourself first, and then place all other monies in separate envelopes like home maintenance, food, car, etc., and never exceed what is in each envelope. At the end of the month, whatever money is left should be saved. The mechanics of maintaining a budget requires consistency, and no cheating. While many investors keep a mental goal, those that are committed to paper are more effective. A budget is a road map of your future, and in the words of Yogi Bear: "If you don't know where you're going, you'll end up somewhere else." Therefore, to know how you spend money, keep a log of daily expenses. If diligence becomes ingrained in your conscious level, you will appreciate the philosophical Buddhist principle of denial: "If you did without it yesterday, you can get by without it today." Once you establish a budget, stick to it. A strict budget adherence avoids unnecessary travel, entertainment and associated expenditures, and prevents impulse buying. What it requires is a resolute spirit shrouded by discipline. No matter what your age, keep a mental note between discretionary and nondiscretionary expenditures. The latter refers to "fixed" expenses like a mortgage, the cost of going to work, and the like, and as strange as this appears, very few of your expenditures are nondiscretionary. Discretionary expenses are entirely under your control because they include travel, hobbies, gifts, and daily expenditures that can add up. The "latte factor" is an example. At $3.75 per day, that translates to $26.25 per week, $105 a month, or $1,260 per year. Should this continue for 40 years, that is $50,400 without compounding. Discretionary spending as in fancy cars, clothes, "hanging" in chic restaurants and bars, and other lifestyle manifestations, reduce disposable income for saving and investing. It might make you feel good to be "in," to be "cool," and to be surrounded by sycophants when you buy a round of drinks, but sooner, rather than later, this type of behavior, in the critical years of 25-40, prevents the accumulation of wealth. The opposite of course, is to live simply, to be frugal, and to be sensible and prudent.

## The Importance of Frugality

What does it mean to be frugal? It is "acquiring goods and services in a restrained manner." The antonym "waste" expresses extravagance, and lavishness, or behavior defined as profligate with no parameters concerning "abundant." Frugality, the antithesis of hedonism and irresponsibility, is the foundation for wealth creation, and must rank among the top concerns because without it, you could not implement the second–to save as much as possible–in order to invest. This human trait is not innate, but acquired behavior, and empirical evidence indicates a direct correlation between frugal behavior and total wealth. Wealthy people not only spend less than they earn and reduce impulse purchases, but also seek bargains at every opportunity. Unless debt is business related, it is reduced to nearly zero, and when contemplating a durable household good, they rely on its longevity relative to its price to determine value. Frugality also implies that you take care of clothes and other physical goods in order to postpone their replacement. It also does not imply excessive miserliness, as depravation is not the norm. Frugality is not a sin, but a habit that should be practiced with sincerity. Note the following:

1. Frugal individuals always think about diminishing returns when it comes to consumption. The first cup of coffee in the morning offers 100% satisfaction, but the second cup offers 80%, the third 50%, and the fourth 20%. If so, reduce consumption, emphasize "quality of life," and do not attempt to "follow the Joneses" because the post-consumer oriented society will arrive with vengeance. The only alternative to absolute ruin is to reestablish values that helped the US achieve middle-class prominence. The behavior of the spendthrift citizen will have to change by emphasizing such virtues as thrift, hard work, self-reliance, and saving for emergencies and retirement. If the national ethos does not change, the "invisible hand of the market" will make it happen.

2. As the current secular bear market takes its toll in reducing household wealth, people will find ways to reduce spending. Frugality will become more common, something that economists say, is causing a harmful effect on the economy, by "the paradox of thrift." This interesting phrase, rooted in less spending and self-sufficiency reduces the velocity of money and, hence, creates a situation that can cause a depression. Do not believe it! Frugality, in its very essence, refers to less waste and increased efficiency–and that cannot be bad for any economy. Replacing a car every 12 years instead of four will save, from the age of 20 to 70, $500,000. In its finest moments, frugality is the opposite of the American mantra of you can have it all "now." Frugality is the "golden mean," and sooner, rather than later, it will become the new normal.

3. Being frugal is difficult, as it requires a strong character to deflect charges of "miserly" epithets and to go against the grain of contemporary hedonistic behavior. It involves sufficient discipline to minimize repetitive expenditures by maximizing the longevity of goods. Moreover, when one magnifies an individual action by the total population, then frugal behavior becomes a huge deal for society as a whole. For American values to change, frugality once again, must become a pillar in the American ethos. As a result, thriftiness and parsimony will become

admired behaviors because frugality results in less consumption and more saving. Many believe that parsimony never leads to wealth. Well, what does? Buying a lottery ticket? Frugality is not the only contributing factor in accumulating wealth, but it is a significant part. The practice of frugality is both honorable and rewarding in an age where hedonism has gone berserk. It places you on guard, resists temptation, encourages caution, and reduces stress. Most important, I have found that frugal individuals to be happier than those who cannot resist self-indulgence. They also have fewer bad habits.

## The Importance of Patience, Discipline, Common Sense, and Perseverance

"Patience," defined by Wikipedia, is "the state of endurance under difficult circumstances persevering in the face of delay or provocation; or exhibiting forbearance when under strain, especially when faced with longer-term difficulties." Patience tends to lower blood pressure, anxieties, and allows the investor to pause, reflect and weigh alternatives to arrive at better decisions. Instead of panicking during bear markets, the patient investor, will take advantage of opportunities offered, unlike the hedonistic investor, who feels that staying out of the action is psychologically a foreign concept, and throws common sense and discipline to the wind. The patient investor maintains emotional balance and remains focused. Patience is necessary for those buying for the duration of a secular bull market. Because without it, the powerful effects of compounding will be lost, never to be retrieved. Patience also helps to control expenses and the cost of sleepless nights.

While the young benefit the most from patience, they are the least patient when it comes to investing. Imbued with a personality of "I want immediate gratification now," few have the temperament to look far on the horizon, and the myopic perspective costs them dearly. To be patient, therefore, is not easy, but all would agree that it is essential. One way to appreciate this emotion is to emulate the very wealthy, who resist risk and who sit and wait for opportunities. The patient investor seeks a long-term, secular, bear market cycle and avoids the eddies of potential cyclical dangers. Patience, therefore, is to an investor what physical conditioning is to an athlete. A sound mental attitude is necessary for investing, as patience and discipline are front and center to a successful "investment psychological profile." In China, patience is considered one of the seven heavenly virtues, and best to remember the old proverb, "One moment of patience may ward off great disaster. One moment of impatience may ruin a whole life." Cato the Elder said it best more than 1800 years ago: "Patience is the greatest of all virtues." In addition, never forget the words of Jesse Livermore: "It was never my trading that made the big money, it was always the waiting." "Be right and sit tight" and, "The market does not beat the common investor. They beat themselves as they are unable to sit tight." Always remember Othello's advice to Iago: "patience."

Patience is an overlooked, neglected and underrated investor emotion. It is irritable, but in the end, it rewards.

Not only is patience a virtue, but so is discipline as both prevent instant gratification. Most important, the attributes of patience, discipline, and perseverance are the complete antithesis of the basic features of hedonistic behavior. As such, this type of investor speculates less, and ultimately prevails due to a more sensible approach to investing. Furthermore, he does not overpay and has fewer disappointments. Therefore, patience and discipline, over time, combine to produce a discriminating investor, or one who develops a jaundiced eye for "noise," and does not allow emotions to reach deep in the pocket when conditions are not favorable.

Perseverance refers to the maintenance of a steady course despite obstacles. In almost any context, it refers to commitment, endurance, and hard work. In the words of Thomas Edison: "I have not failed 700 times. I have not failed once. I have succeeded in proving that those 700 ways will not work. When I have eliminated the ways that will not work, I will find the way that will work." Calvin Coolidge had this to say, "Nothing in the world can take the place of persistence. Talent will not, and nothing is more common than unsuccessful men with talent. Genius will not; unrewarded genius is almost a proverb. Education will not; the world is full of educated derelicts. Persistence and determination alone are omnipotent. The slogan 'Press on' has solved and always will solve the problems of the human race." It is perseverance, not income that determines your ability to save–it overwhelms and trumps temptation. A lack of discipline prompts doubt, creates indecisiveness, and invariably, bad choices. One thing is certain: discipline is destroyed in an atmosphere of loose credit policies.

Of the approximately 250 trading days available to the investor in a year, fewer than 30 will provide the vast majority of total returns, the remainder would essentially provide no, or slight returns. Therefore, the prudent investor must exercise patience and discipline in holding once a position is taken since the investor does not know when positive days occur. The average holding period for non-retirement accounts is minutes, a period of time too short to make serious money. The prudent investor must think long-term, and that means secular periods as few people think that patience and discipline are important. However, they are. Emphasizing discipline enables the investor to control those elements that are not random: a. Debt. If you do not borrow, you will not spend as much. b. Frugality. To reduce spending, resist the temptation to splurge. c. Addiction. Overcome urges that underline excesses and bad habits. d. Cultural environment. If your friends "hang out" in bars, borrow excessively, and gamble–so will you.

## The Importance of Diversification and Rebalancing

The importance of diversification hinges on the two aspects of risk that confront all investors: systematic and idiosyncratic. Wall Street is of the opinion that systematic risk represents 30% and idiosyncratic risk, 70%. Most investors, and especially those who consistently underperform, hold undiversified portfolios. Numerous studies indicate that the vast majority of investors hold fewer than seven individual stocks and those who hold more do so usually in the same asset class. Diversify, therefore, in a prudent manner; absolute diversification, for the sake of diversification, is never a good strategy. For matters of diversification, investors wish non-correlating securities to be part of a portfolio so that when one asset, sector, or security moves down, other moves in an opposite direction. On the other hand, a "concentrated" asset allocation places a large bet on a single security, or sector. Should the value of the concentrated portfolio rise, the investor believes that he is a sage when all others failed. The other side of this imbroglio states that diversification is fundamental because short and intermediate market swings are difficult to predict, thus "spreading" market risk becomes an imperative by broadening the universe of non-correlating assets, something that can be accomplished by indexing. Stock picking is out, and broad index diversification is quick, efficient, and for the common investor, quite productive. Industry and non-industry celebrities also have something to say on the subject of diversification. Warren Buffet said, "To get rich, accumulate. To stay rich, diversify." Bob Prechter maintains that, "Diversification for its own sake means you don't know what you're doing. If that is true, you might as well hold Treasury bills or a savings account." Diversification Balkanizes assets, so that no issue-specific shock mortally wounds the whole.

While everyone recognizes the value of diversification, few agree on the actual composition of a specific portfolio. The most common diversification strategy is to buy the Total Market, or divide asset allocation between major sectors, foreign securities, and bonds. Nevertheless, diversification is an exaggerated and overblown concept that mainly seeks to protect financial planners, brokers, etc., from litigation. Therefore, the only concern that "diversification" offers is the "diversification penalty," or that which is derived by the fact that the mass of stocks held by the Total Market, will never outperform the best performing stock. Therefore, the easiest way to diversify with minimum discomfort in terms of time, expertise and a huge stash of cash is through a balanced fund and/or several broad index funds. When buying individual stocks, be diversified among all economic sectors reflecting the current secular market. Diversification in the international arena is more important than in the domestic arena as the number of permutations increase immensely by continent, region, country size, and political, cultural, and economic complexions; hence, the need to homogenize risk through an index fund. The degree and type of diversification depends on personal elements, and mainly three categories: the young, middle-aged, and retirees. The young have a long-term time horizon, and, as a result, they can be very aggressive with a preponderance of equities over income producing securities. The middle-aged individual has to be concerned about the safety of the core retirement position because in less than a generation retirement will be a mandatory life-altering event. The retiree has to be concerned about not outliving retirement funds.

Rebalancing, or "constant-ratio investing," is the practice of keeping the percentages, or ratios, of all assets in balance in order that they not deviate much over time. Rebalancing is also referred to as "closet market timing" because when investors sell winners and buy those assets that are underperforming; they attempt to "time the market." Rebalancing depends on a large number of factors; the most important are market and sector-specific trends. While frequent rebalancing usually lowers total returns, so does the notion of not rebalancing at all. When exercising patience and discipline, rebalancing should mainly occur during major market inflection points, and never be overdone. No matter what the percentage, the practice should be held to a minimum as trading costs will erode gains as selling also begets buying. One should also not rebalance if the fundamentals are favorable for winning assets. Since nothing is fixed in concrete in regards to investing, the crucial element when contemplating rebalancing is prudence, and unadulterated common sense. Despite the counter intuitive nature of this practice, rebalancing is necessary because it works in the end. Remember the following: 1. Because tax liabilities are avoided, rebalancing is much easier and cheaper in tax-sheltered accounts. Unless peculiar circumstances are present, annual rebalancing in taxable accounts is not recommended because of tax disincentives. Tactical rebalancing, based on "noise," is particularly dangerous and should be avoided. 2. Rebalancing is easily accomplished when new money is placed on underperformers, thus increasing their percentage to targeted levels. 3. Because rebalancing exerts varying degrees of anxiety among investors when forced to sell "winners" in order to buy "losers," many refuse to exercise this important function. 4. Rebalancing is imperative in reaction to changing life events like family size, divorce, employment, domicile changes, illnesses and other personal considerations.

## Paying Attention to Tax-Mitigation

Tax considerations are vital to total portfolio returns as every aspect of life is taxed. One hundred ten years ago, income and payroll taxes were absent with federal revenue originating from a tax on imported goods. Today, every individual activity is subject to a tax or "fee." The question of tax mitigation is one that simply cannot be underestimated because more than 40%-plus of wealth, over the course of a lifetime, is eroded by all manner of taxes. Federal *spin maesters* expound, "Your taxes have decreased," but reality tells a different story. Federal tax rates have increased and augmented by local and state taxes. In this connection, the following should be kept in mind: 1. In the words of John Templeton: "For all long-term investors, there is only one objective—maximum total real return after taxes." 2. The most significant tax benefits are derived from annuities, dividends, Treasuries, life insurance, partnerships, municipals, equities and real estate. 401(k) and related retirement plan contributions, charitable contributions, qualified dividends, index and tax-advantaged funds, and long-term capital gains, help reduce tax liability. 3. The higher the net worth of the individual, the greater the propensity to buy and hold. 4. Tax legislation affects investment decisions in many different ways. When corporations are taxed heavily, they assume debt because they can deduct interest charges, and when dividends are taxed as ordinary income, investors shun those companies. 5. The IRS does not recognize inflation in its tax tables, just nominal dollars. The US tax rate may not be the worst among DMs, but it certainly has plenty of negatives, of which complexity, double taxation of dividends, and the way capital gains and losses are calculated lead the list. The American tax code contains more than nine million words, and it is said to constitute the largest source of lobbying in Washington D.C. 6. The month of December is usually the desirable time to engage in swaps to take advantage of tax loses. 7. Over the course of a working lifetime, tax-sheltered accounts deliver twice the performance of taxable accounts. 8. Do not base your financial plan on current tax laws, as they are repealed and/or modified constantly.

There are various types of income. Ordinary income includes wages and interest, a capital gain is the profit when you sell, and tax-free income is anything that allows you to avoid paying taxes as in the case of interest derived from municipal bonds. Ordinary income is taxed according to your marginal tax bracket, but capital gains are significantly better because you can control when you pay taxes, which means that you determine when the asset is sold. In addition to controlling the gain (or loss), capital gains are taxed at lower rates than ordinary income, when the gain is termed long-term, or longer than 12 months. Any capital gain of less than 12 months is termed short-term and is taxed as ordinary income. Moreover, a capital gain realized early in a calendar year would postpone a tax payment until April 15 of the following year. An investor may also sell a profitable stock to counterbalance the loss in another. It should be remembered that money grows faster when it's tax-deferred. Tax-sheltered accounts should include, dividend-payers, actively managed securities, convertible securities, REITS, funds that have a history of large distributions, and all other income-bearing instruments. If you actively trade stocks, do so inside a tax-sheltered account to avoid tax liability. Broad indexes like the S&P 500, Total Market, and others can be placed in both taxable and sheltered accounts. Taxable accounts include municipal bonds, growth stocks, limited partnerships, and tax-managed funds.

While there are many things an investor cannot control there are many things that he may do to mitigate the tax bite, and thus, increase total returns: 1. Avoid expensive tax shelters. 2. Take advantage of tax-swaps in your taxable account. 3. Always factor inflation in your calculations. 4. Take advantage of capital gains and dividends. 5. Buy index, ETFs and tax-managed funds, as they are more tax-efficient. 6. Allocate assets rationally and prudently among taxable and tax-sheltered accounts. 7. Start or become a partner in a business. 8. Buy real estate. 9. Move to a region with lower taxes. 10. Contribute to every tax-deferred account that is available to you. 11. Not all income and distributions are treated equally by the IRS. The difference between tax-free and tax-deferred is important and crucial, with the former referring to the non-payment of taxes of interest from municipal bonds and sales from a ROTH account. Tax-deferred refers to money that grows unaffected by taxes, as in a retirement account, with taxes due as regular income when money is withdrawn after the age of 70½. 12. Tax-free compounding over the course of a lifetime is an important consideration not to be neglected.13. Resist the temptation to trade excessively. 14. Pay attention to the tax benefits offered by municipal, Treasury, "EE" and "I" bonds. 15. Establish a trust to avoid probate, save money, and protect beneficiaries. 16. To summarize: Taxable accounts are appropriate for municipals, long-term equity, tax-managed funds, and capital gains. Tax-exempt and deferred are appropriate for taxable bonds, positive short trades, REITS, dividend-payers and other income capital gains, long-term equities, and income-paying index funds.

## Characteristics of the Wealthy and Successful

Let me tell you what rich are not. "Marty" is aged 60 living in a $4 million dollar condo with a $3 million mortgage; he spends more than $88,000 annually in restaurants and bars; drives a $100,000 leased sport car; takes two, expensive vacations a year; has $23,000 in credit card debt; $400,000 in a 401(k); $50,000 in a savings account; and he pays alimony. He is a flashy dresser, smells of expensive colognes, buys $1000 shoes, earns $535,000 annually, and saves virtually nothing. "Joey," age 60, is a waiter who lives in a $155,000, no-mortgage home. He drives a $15,000 car; is free of debt; stays away from bars; has $165,000 in CDs; has no credit card debt; takes no or one short vacation annually; buys $70 shoes; spends far less on fancy haberdashery accoutrements; and has been married to the same woman for 30 years. He earns $60,000 a year and has $450,000 in his 401(k). Should you see both in a public arena, Marty and Joey are separated by light years. One is "urbane and sophisticated," while the other is "common." However, Joey is the more successful investor because he saved more and spent less, while earning millions fewer dollars. Joey, dear investor, darned his socks, and Marty threw them away. Joey is healthier because he eats better food and consumes fewer bottles of Scotch and does not smoke $20 cigars. The philosophy behind the strategy of getting rich or at least comfortable at retirement is simple: A high salary is no guarantee of wealth. The requirement is discipline, frugality, perseverance, and patience in order to cultivate and nurture a lifelong policy of living within your means. The rich get wealthier for the following reasons:

1. They are creatures of habit and discipline. They begin the work day early, work during lunch, and are committed to goals that achieve financial *nirvana* by baking the "retirement cake" in the shortest possible time, and with the fewest possible mistakes. They follow the recipe to the letter, and when critical mass is reached, they protect this sum, no matter the countless inducements that fly their way. Attention is paid to small details, because a penny here and a nickel there add

up over a period of a lifetime into hundreds of thousands of dollars. In the words of Sherlock Holmes: "There is nothing as important as trifles." They prize time as one of the most valuable resources that they can control, and seek to manage forces that compress time by managing those elements that boost saving and compound interest and dividends. They do not waste time on frivolous pursuits, but rely on good sense. They follow a daily "to-do" list and set long-term goals.

2. They control spending and understand the meaning of "value." Which is cheaper, the $20 shirt that lasts nine months, or the $90 shirt that lasts nine years? They rarely succumb to the "whims" and "impulses" of the moment; clear distinctions are drawn between "wants" and "needs," and seldom do they spend in order to "feel good." It is a myth to think that they are cavalier about their spending habits. Even more significant, few engage in frivolous expenditures like exotic boats, vacation homes and cars.

3. They are confident and aware of the 10% rule: That 10% of all human effort, or capital, is responsible for producing 90% of all gains. Therefore, they concentrate their energies into those activities that will produce the highest possible gain. They also recognize the fact that 10% controls 90% of all patents, scientific expertise, and critical skills. The top 10% remain the largest wealth multipliers because they constantly, invest their money in investments that produce a steady cash flow. Wealthy individuals are optimistic; they not only look around the corner but over the next hill, they do not depend on "luck," they measure financial success not by their income but by total wealth, treat money with respect, and they tend to be *entopic* and not *utopic*. By being forward looking, and constantly monitoring financial progress they never burden themselves with consumer debt, knowing the difference between it, and investment debt. Their motto appears to be "adapt," "improvise," and "overcome." They are not troglodytes; they never ignore the "outside" world: they think about the future as it helps their careers, prepare for change, formulate strategies and helps them take advantage of opportunities.

4. They understand the long-term effects of saving, investing and patience. They also understand the value of doing "nothing" and are not rattled by short-term market movements. They have learned to sit and wait, something that most people, especially the hedonists, find excruciatingly difficult. They hold positions longer than most investors; they do not day trade; they are rarely short; they reduce their transaction costs to a bare minimum; and they always attempt to mitigate taxes. They emphasize income-bearing investments and change asset allocations in conformity with secular trends. Unlike those who harbor innate tendencies to consistently pick stocks that are not priced "right" by the market, they rarely, if ever, attempt to buy stocks that are expected to hit home runs. They invariably buy company fundamentals and tend to think and act independently and manage risk. The two most important metrics in their financial universe are interest and inflation rates. Less than 1% of all millionaires consider themselves active traders, and more than 90% make fewer than 15 trades annually. Investment decisions are made

mechanically after due diligence and they buy with specific objectives. Gamblers they are not. Although 64% frequented a casino, few are habitual gamblers, and few buy lottery tickets. They consider the process of becoming wealthy a "state of mind." If you do not perceive yourself as being wealthy or seek to be wealthy, you will never become affluent. Most emphasize professional careers, business, and real estate to produce the bulk of their income, with fewer than 30% acquiring their wealth through stock market transactions. About 10% of their portfolio is in cash, 20% in bonds, 20% each in equities and real estate, and 30% in business ventures. They receive 80% of all disbursed dividends in the US.

5. The ultra-successful tend to be conscientious and are imbued with confidence. They exhibit a penchant for detail. They plan, are ambitious to a fault, and are acutely aware of the formation of positive individual traits that produce character that sustain self-worth. The personal elements of veracity, discipline, fortitude, determination, and empathy stand on the pantheon of self-achievement. They value a strong "work ethic," practice frugality, and save religiously, viewing them as core elements to success. They also do everything possible to postpone retirement. They love their work, take charge of their lives, tend to be doers, and when something goes wrong they blame themselves, and do everything possible not to repeat mistakes. They are serious people who behave responsibly and keep mentally alert and physically fit. They associate with work-driven individuals and never entertain defeatist beliefs.

6. They never neglect education, whether formal or informal, as they consider it the most rewarding investment that they can ever make. They are rapacious readers, have been taught never to say, "I don't want to learn that," and value, and nurture "human capital," and that means constantly acquiring additional skills. They do not pretend to be an expert of everything because they know their limitations. They admire others who are more successful than they are. Most important, children are taught how to think and communicate.

7. Personal and familial spending habits are quite revealing as they involve the use of one credit card, $75,000 for an automobile, $25 for a haircut, and about $750,000 for a home. They buy clothes from high-end retailers but only on sale, and frequent small, specialty discounters. More than 80% purchased older homes, 40% own a vacation home, less than 10% own a boat and spend about $20 for a bottle of wine. Seventy four percent of all spouses work or worked, and about 90% were college graduates with 40% having either Master/Doctoral degrees. They appear non-descript because they live modestly without flaunting wealth. Nearly all seem to be fixated on what it would take in life to be successful in their vocation. They buy quality and maintain it to reduce replacements. Most significantly, they eat well, watch their weight and overall health, exercise regularly, and make a concerted habit to work productively.

8. There is a greater emphasis on survival than getting rich, as they are overly concerned with preservation of capital. While well aware of the benefits of capital growth, risks, and the disadvantages of excessive speculation, they are most realistic on how one goes about to achieve financial success. They understand the sage words of Bernard Baruch: "The main reason why money is lost in stock speculation is not because Wall Street is dishonest, but because so many people persist in thinking that you can make money without working for it, and that the stock exchange is the place where this miracle can be performed." Financial success is measured by net worth, not by income. Wealth is what they amass over time through hard work, frugality, a sensible lifestyle with a minimum of waste, and never about spending. They also understand risk, and attempt to manage it, and do so by being content with 10% total returns. They pay attention to passive income assets, which they consider the cornerstone of wealth creation.

9. A look of who earns and who pays taxes reveals the following. The top 1% of the population earns 21% of all income and pays 40% of all federal taxes. The top 5% earn 35% of all income and pay 56.5% of all taxes. The top 10% earn 66% of all income and pay 67% of all taxes. The top 25% pay 84% of all taxes. The top 50% pay 96.5% of all taxes. The bottom 50% pay 3.5% of all taxes. The top 1% owns about 40% of all wealth. The top 5% own about 52% of all wealth. The top 20% own 70% of all wealth. Over the past, generation income for the top 1% has more than doubled.

10. The rich get richer because a number of carefully crafted strategies: a. by investing in passive income assets, b. by buying and holding for future generations, c. by understanding risk and reward, d. by emphasizing income-bearing financial instruments such as equities and bonds, and changing their allocation depending on secular conditions, and e. by emphasizing and concentrating on business and real estate to produce the bulk of their income. More than 95% state that hard work is the reason for their success, followed by education, prudent investing, and frugality. The key elements to wealth creation are summed up as attitudes, objectives, and skills. The latter is the easiest to explain, as most people understand that knowledge is nearly always translated to higher productivity and higher income. Attitudes and objectives are culturally induced and manipulated and are important because the husbanding of knowledge stimulates skill development. They emulate each other, a major driving force for success.

## Moving Closer To Work/Central Cities

For the next generation, the path to wealth accumulation is the move out of suburbia and back to central cities. That is where the wealthiest 1% lives, and if it is good enough for them, it should be good enough for you. The high cost of suburban living and the enormous amount of financial, labor, material, and energy waste that it generates simply cannot continue amidst a failing economy. The peak of suburban existence, currently about 57%, will decline for decades. About 175 million Americans are living in suburban settlements. In the past 20 years, 45 million people in their peak years of employment had chosen this direction, precisely at a time when they should have been saving money. In this so-called idyllic environment, the family is transformed from a one to a three or four-car household. During the period 1870-1917, the US with about 30% of its current population, constructed dozens of interurban rail facilities, subways in its largest cities, streetcars in nearly all cities with more than 10,000 people, and integrated the nation with a massive rail system. Therefore, to make mass transit profitable, population densities must increase. Since more people reside in suburban regions and not in central cities, mass transportation is not expected to become economically viable until national policy reverses trend. Sixty-eight percent commute to work by car, and given the pace of suburbanization, reductions in the horizontal movement of people by auto will not occur until energy costs escalate to levels that eventually force people to move back to high-density venues. The average daily commute by automobile in America is 45 minutes, 3.7 hours weekly, or 185 hours yearly. If one includes driving during a two-week vacation, 10 holidays, and personal travel during the year, we have an additional 800-plus hours of driving. Therefore, the advantages of urban living are obvious: proximity to work and services, diversity, and high population density to enhance competition.

The utopic notion that suburban living leads to increased longevity, supreme happiness, reduced crime, etc., is nothing but propaganda. The biggest cost of suburban living is energy, and when one factors the cost of the home, suburban living is expensive in real dollars. When maintenance and other purchases of unnecessary items are taken into account, costs escalate. America over the course of the past 55-plus years has quietly but steadily reduced the size of its central cities and expanded suburban development. This growth brought smaller families but ever-larger houses, cars, swimming pools, lawns, air conditioning and heating systems–all built and purchased on the theory that low energy costs and continuously rising disposable incomes would remain favorable to the continuance of this lifestyle. The problem with suburbia is that it relies on horizontal movement for everything. Once having made the move, the new suburbanites have come to realize they are now captives of their own fantasies with no way to reduce the rising fixed costs of their existence. The national investment to suburbia is so massive; an immediate reversal is nearly impossible which means that the nation will have to muddle through the excesses of the post-WWII period with considerable pain. Suburbistan is wasteful because it destroys central cities and "open land," and piles up enormous subsidies to promulgate a "Shangri La" called "urban sprawl." It lives and breathes cheap oil; it cannot function nor survive without it. As the cost of transportation rises ($10,000 per car annually) at a time when personal incomes are declining in an atmosphere of rising debt, the wisdom of living and expanding suburbs further seems imponderable. The process of gentrification of central cities, already in process, will accelerate as people begin to retrace historic footsteps back to high-density living; the bulk of the current domestic migration is overwhelmingly to central city locations and not to rural and suburban locations as in the past. The global situation is different: In 2013, 59% of global population resided in urban areas, more than any time in world history, thus entering a new paradigm. Out of a total population of 7.5 billion people, 4 billion reside in cities, a figure that is expected to grow to 6 billion by 2030. Interestingly, 14 of the world's largest 20 fastest growing cities are in Asia, 4 in Africa, and 2 in Latin America. The four tallest buildings are in Asia. Since 1985, the world has added 3 million people a week to an urban environment, and by 2025, more than 70% will be classified as urban.

When contemplating buying a home, think of it as having two specific components–an investment and shelter element. The former is sheer speculation above inflation, and the shelter portion is quite expensive as it expresses social status. Never consider your home as an investment as it produces no income, and for the vast majority of homeowners, no appreciation in real terms. Real net home prices rise less than inflation and maintenance, and total returns are less than the long-term Treasury, even when factoring tax benefits. It is a myth, therefore, to think that a home is a capital good as it is nothing more than a consumable item in constant need of repair, and it is not a retirement investment as many baby boomers have discovered. Its value has a lot to do with location, time of purchase, and lifestyle. A home produces considerable psychic value, and is therefore important, but it is never a retirement asset, but a liability. The price of the median home rose from $88,000 in 1990 to $233,000 in 2006; it now sits at $155,000.

For most people, home equity is dead money as the outflow of money for upkeep, taxes, etc., outweigh the eventual sale value of the home. Many, in the right location and ideal economic conditions, do realize spectacular gains, but "real" gains are rare when compared to alternative investments. Peace of mind is good, pride is good, but over time, one must keep the finger on the pulse of the entopic and not the utopic world. Housing and energy are large expenses. While figures vary when mortgage, utilities, maintenance, and transportation are included in the cost of suburban living, the figure exceeds 65% of gross wages. In addition, if one adds the cost of food, healthcare, etc., there is nothing left for saving. Therefore, the next real estate wreck will occur in the suburbs. As energy, costs escalate, and inflation rises, and as personal debt becomes so overbearing, the demise of American suburbs will come to a screeching halt and eventually become the future slums of America. In fact, the collapse of the American suburb has begun. Since 2000, suburban poverty has risen from 10 to 26 million, and for the first time, more people are living in poverty in suburbs than in central cities.

# CHAPTER 4

# MARKET BEHAVIOR AND INVESTING PRINCIPLES

*The best way to predict the future is to invent it.* - Alan Kay

*Those who have knowledge don't predict; those who predict don't have knowledge.* - Lao Tzu

*Bull markets are born on pessimism, grow on skepticism, mature on optimism, and die on euphoria.* - Sir John Templeton

*"To the moon, Alice."*- Ralph Kramden

*"I invest in anything that Bernanke can't destroy."* - David Stockman

# Cyclical and Secular Markets

Secular markets are characterized by stages of trough, upward motion, peak, downward motion, and trough. The time generally exceeds 30-plus years and is characterized by "bull" and "bear" components. Each secular phase contains both cyclical segments of "bull" and "bear" elements distinguished by periods of less than five years. The leading economic indicator approach is to identify these repeating events and take action about asset allocation. The 20th century has had three secular bull markets: 1921-1929, 1949-1966, and 1982-2000. Secular bear markets occurred in 1929-1948, 1966-81, and the latest began in 2000. Therefore, because of their infrequency and variability, investors have difficulty observing secular cycles as people historically did not live long enough to observe more than one as an adult. There are no straight lines in economic matters. Most investors had never experienced anything worse than a four-year recession, and, therefore, had no clue about the dangers, dimensions, and consequences of secular bear markets. Cato the Elder said that people are more concerned with "the pebble in the shoe," than broad macro-associated problems. In addition, data is unreliable, and a number of indicators are no longer relevant as they once were. Country comparisons, furthermore, are rarely applicable as the character of national economies is not subject to strict comparisons.

Secular markets are of significance to investors because bonds outperform equities in deflationary times, underperform equities during times of inflation and bull markets, and are average during range-bound markets. Growth investors outperform during bull markets, are flat or just below during range-bound markets, and underperform during inflationary periods. In the middle position are value investors who are above average performers during bull and range-bound markets, but do not suffer as much as growth investors during inflationary and deflationary episodes. Business fluctuations, like true love, are never smooth or predictable; disequilibrium, not stability, is the rule; and just as extinction is followed by succession and neap tides follow spring tides, so are the ways of alternating secular bull and bear markets. In both instances, a catharsis prepares markets for new directions. Secular bull markets are never homogeneous–from beginning to end;

there is considerable sector rotation as most secular markets are associated with favored sectors. It happened with railroads in the second half of the 19th century, radio and motion pictures prior to the Great Depression, the "nifty-fifty" of the 1960s, gaming and commodities in the 1970s, equities and bonds in the 1980s and 1990s, Japanese equities in the 1980s, EMs and technology stocks in the 1990s, real estate during 1990-2007, bonds since 1982, and commodities since 2001. All securities run in multiyear cycles of above and below average streaks. Just as glamour eventually fades, so do all tales of perpetual financial bliss.

Market declines of less than 10% are commonly called "dips," a decline between 10% and 20% is a "correction," and a decline greater than 20%-plus is described as a "bear market." The ultimate decline is a secular bear market where the fall is greater than 40% and lasts a long time. In all of the above, there are innumerable "rotational" corrections in which specific sectors, sub-sectors, and styles go through their periodic bouts of cyclical gyrations. No matter what the general market does, there are always economic sectors that are moving up or down. It is during these endless periods of rotational corrections where the exceptional professional trader makes serious money, and where amateurs lose. The interesting character of economic and business history has been an intricate and convoluted environment where market cycles of every character and magnitude cavort against an intricate background of economic, cultural, and political events. How investors interpret cyclical elements is complicated and shrouded in controversy. Analysis differs widely by historical period fueled by emotional responses to events with each explanation confusing issues further. What is eminently important is the markets line of march that illustrates its most important ingredients–GDP growth, interest rates, and inflation–all of which are never static but evolving into minor, intermediate, and long-term cycles.

## Secular Market Features

1. The introduction of new technologies with revolutionary structural effects in terms of cost reduction, employment, and the elimination of and/or destruction of old technologies are the prime forces that generate growth in one area and decline in others, thus establishing new business cycles. 2. Monetary inflation promotes a propensity to produce cheap credit considered the mother of all bubbles. 3. The dangerous emotions of fear and greed play a role in the business cycle, the former dominates the trough and the latter the peak. In the words of Agesilaus: "It is circumstance and proper timing that give an action its character and make it either good or bad." 4. Since 1965, there have been 5% declines 48 times, 12% declines 18 times, 15% declines 11 times, 20% declines 9 times, and 25%-plus declines 7 times. Each year, there is a 70% chance of gain. Despite the 1987 crash, the 1994 Tequila crisis, the first Gulf War of 1990, the 1997 Asian financial crisis, the Russian default of 1998, the Y2K scare of 1999, the crash of 2000, 9/11, etc., markets recover and move on. 5. Within secular bull and bear markets, there are cyclical counter trends. While it is quite possible for the individual investor to

identify the secular trend and ride it to its conclusion, taking advantage of cyclical countertrends is more difficult, and often, dangerous. One thing is certain; the limits of both secular and cyclical trends from peak to trough are characterized by extreme sentiment. The signs of market tops and bottoms, therefore, offer clear psychological reactions that are unmistakable. At market peaks, the euphoria is so pervasive; there is no stopping the momentum until it is too late and the same for the bottom when investors become discouraged. These features characterize all bull tops and bear bottoms. Reality stares the investor in the face, but his perception of the future is the inertia of the past that ultimately spells ruin. 6. How to spot a secular bear market top and bottom? The Dow Jones dividend yield bottomed in 1999 at 1.5%, the lowest level in its history, and a figure that coincided with the market top of the most robust secular bull market in history. New secular bull markets will develop when the dividend yield exceeds 5%. The other sure sign of a secular market reversal is the PE ratio. Fourteen is average with market tops synonymous with ratios above 20. The ratio exceeded 33 in 1929, and in 1999, it reached 48. 7. No one knows when new bubbles erupt and when they burst. However, one thing is certain: Just as trees do not grow to the sky, neither do markets. Look at secular markets from Winston Churchill's point of view: "We have reached the end of the beginning at the top of a bubble, and are about to enter the beginning of the end of the cycle when the bear market takes hold." Mean reversion always occurs due to technical over and under fundamental valuations. 9. Why should the ordinary investor respond to secular trends? Because DB plans do, as the Federal Reserve reports for the years 1950, 1975 and 2002. In 1950 75% of all assets were allocated to bonds, 16% equities, 5% other, 4% cash; in 1975, 46% equities, 30% bonds, 15% other, 9% cash; and in 2002, 55% equities, 20% bonds, other 18%, 7% cash. 10. Markets do not move in straight lines. They always retreat on the way up and vice versa, and bull and bear depth and length gyrations cannot be accurately and consistently predicted. 11. Bull and bear markets are mainly creatures of Fed policies, as in the events of 1973-1974, and post-2000.

In addition to secular and cyclical, there are other types of economic fluctuations. History indicates that many are unexpected while others, random, continuous and while there are many classifications as to types, several are constantly in the news. 1. Seasonal investing behavior is important for those societies that are essentially primary, but in recent decades, this applies to trading strategies like buying in early winter and selling in late spring/early summer. Diamonds are mainly sold during the period of Thanksgiving and New Year's, and to a lesser extent, in May-June. November-December holiday season is generally the strongest retail and consumer discretionary period of the year, and financial, industrial and technology companies end the year on a strong note. The Santa Claus and Chia pet rallies come on the last five trading days of the years and the first two days of January. 2. Miscellaneous random fluctuations, or accidental occurrences are events devoid of rhythm, but statistically significant in that they do occur within all of the above cycles. Examples include war, terrorist attacks, political assassinations, etc. "Made-up" patterns like the "Friday Effect," referring to the tendency for markets to fall on Friday, rise on Monday, fall between 10:30 A.M. and rise at 1:50 P.M., etc. These "made-up" cycles are attached to presidential cycles (Interesting to note that bear markets have taken place in the first two years 89% of the time and second-terms are characterized by lower secondary output, negative inflation-adjusted house prices, reduced income, higher federal debt, and lower GDP.), football teams, the "January Effect," and other non-symbiotic relationships. Rarely, however, do they trace exactly and, hence, the frustration. There are people who have spent lifetimes in search of the perfect cycle in order to profit, and while they plot symmetrical and asymmetrical combinations, the determination of exact length leaves much to the imagination. Confusing the picture is the endless variety of weather (cicada cycle), celestial occurrences like sunspots, bee populations, bio rhythms, pig iron production, sneaker consumption, counting trucks under a highway overpass, pumpkin cycles, hair color cycles for women, width of tie cycles for men, length of woman's skirts, wine auctions, lipstick sales, and "year of the pig." You name the variable; it has been studied in one way or another in forecasting market behavior. There are also short to long-term academic cycles: Kitchen's short-wave cycle of 3-5 years duration, Clement Jugular's 7-11 year cycle, Kuznets's medium wave cycle of 15-25 year duration, and Kondratiev's long wave cycle of 45-60 year duration. However, life is not simple: there are calendar cycles that end in "4," "0," or any other number. The science is not exact, and deadly when attempting to forecast the future primarily because the correlation between cause and effect is rarely definitive.

## Secular Bull Markets

## Figure 5

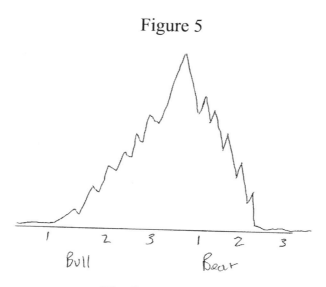

The Secular Market

Stage 1. This stage is coincident with an extremely high degree of pessimism expressed by frustration as the economy remains in a negative psychological mindset. Equities trade below intrinsic value. People are defensive, have no interest in the market as stocks trade in a narrow range, and characterized by a flat trend line, often experiencing three bottoms before the secular upturn. With time, excess money and credit creation, sustained price increases, all symbiotic in nature, take hold and prices rise. This is a critical phase where "smart" money takes a long-term position and "sits tight" during the initial stage of "accumulation." These "early adopters" enter quietly and their innocuous and unassuming character remains unnoticed. This group adds to their positions on dips, confident of the fact that the secular bear is over. Once the market makes new highs and higher lows, new buyers are attracted. When the market PE is below 10 and the dividend yield above 5%, is to buy "ideal."

Stage 2. This is the stage where buyers overwhelm sellers. There will be several cyclical bear markets and much noise about reversals, but the true believers add to their positions during the "dips." There is a long period of further accumulation of shares as more participants are brought in with more publicity in "a wall of worry" type environment. As the economy improves, capital investment accelerates, unemployment ameliorates, and other economic metrics begin to assert themselves. Media coverage fuels the urge for investors to enter in an atmosphere of higher highs, higher lows, and increased volume.

Stage 3. This stage is characterized by sustained price appreciation and massive public participation, thus boosting prices higher with media attention increasing in intensity as the incipient manic condition sets the stage for "no price is too high." Wall Street gurus scream for investors to buy the dips with higher prices creating an urgency to "be in the market," and, thus, the bull attracts ever-growing pools of money. As acceleration quickens, people begin to feel richer, and the invariable, former, risk-averse investors undertake more speculative positions, open margin accounts, and succumb to the "momentum" syndrome. An explosion of investment newsletters takes place with radio and television gurus spreading half-truths and outright falsehoods, and when newsletter sentiment rises above 70%, markets decline and, hence, offer excellent, contrarian indicators.

This stage is noted by a flagpole-type of price appreciation pattern. It will expand far longer than most people expect and usually with a double top. While bullish sentiment dominates and small buyers enter, the "smart money" is exiting, marking the point where the early arrivals begin "distributing" their shares. In the words of Oliver Wendell Holmes: "When I want to understand what is happening today or try to decide what will happen tomorrow, I look back." When you look back at historical norms and determine what the averages were, present-day unbalanced metrics will revert to mean. This is true of PE ratios, interest rates, inflation rates, soybean prices, oil prices, gold to silver ratios, etc. This stage is not only characterized by massive consumer participation and the introduction of

IPOs, but there is a feeling of rapture pervading the market. Buyers undergo a mindless process of buying with no regard to fundamentals, and near the top, investors bid up prices because they believe that bids will be higher tomorrow, next week, next month, and forever. This is the stage when PE ratios skyrocket (they double from start to finish), and speculation in unproven companies intensifies. Therefore, when PE ratios exceed 40, and bulls run in the narrow streets of Pamplona with microscopic earnings and prices rise beyond the stratosphere, it is time to take money off the table. At the top, markets are all risk with little reward. "This time it's different," is the motto for those who think that the top will never succumb. It is the phrase uttered to justify crowd behavior; a frenzy that is not perceived in real time. Sooner, rather than later, economic gravity will exert itself and the market will fall. A good indicator is margin debt: when it reflects a hockey stick, the decline in prices cannot be far behind as in 1929 when it equaled 30% of equity value. When margin debt rose quickly in the late 1990s, Greenspan's Fed did not raise margin requirements, a negligent act that precipitated the bubble burst in March of 2000, a fall that was to wipe out more than $6 trillion from the aggregate equity market. At market peaks, the scent of *Chabochard* is mixed with a doubtful future; anxiety replaces assurance; fear replaces optimism; PE ratios plummet and dividend yields rise.

## Bull Market Strategies

1. In Stage 1 and 2, buy the Total Market and/or other broad indexes, high-yield bonds, LEAPS, transportation, small-caps and technology. In Stages 2-3, buy basic materials, energy, forest products, precious metals, capital goods and service industries. 2. In a secular bull market, the first 50% or so of upward price movements will encompass 90% of the bull's time requiring extended periods of backing and filling, but the remaining 50%-plus gains are realized in less than 10% of the time. 3. Plan and become a critical observer because a secular bull is a relative state. Not everything was good during the stock market boom of the 1920s as hundreds of banks failed each year, farm values declined, and income discrepancies widened. For a good portion of the rural population, and in the Deep South and its western fringes, incomes declined. The wealth of the US was concentrated in a narrow belt between Boston and Washington, D.C., and along the southern fringes of the Great Lakes.

## The Secular Bear Market

Stage 1. This is the stage where sellers overwhelm buyers with an initial 20%-plus decline that many believe is just a "correction" in a bullish trend and no one is concerned. As the decline continues, investors gradually grow fearful and selling pressure intensifies with lower lows followed by additional lows. In short, secular bear markets begin with fear and progressively give rise to denial, panic, despondency, depression and capitulation. 2. You know you are in a bear when securities trade under their 50, 100, and 200-day moving average; more insiders sell than buy; dividend yields rise, and PE ratios fall. 3. Since fear is a much stronger emotion than greed, bear markets descend steeply, and offer exceptional short selling opportunities. The secular bear begins when heavy volume is not confirmed by price escalation, and Newton's third law takes hold. As the selling frenzy explodes, the panic begins in earnest with a dramatic descent. *Ersatz* wealth easily evaporates.

Stage 2. This stage is noted by furious volatility between steep declines and spectacular counter-rallies. If one fails to sell near the high, the loses may be greater than 60%, and it will take decades to approach prices seen during the bubble stage. The QQQQ Index, the stellar performer of the 1990s, has yet to recover, and probably will not see its 2000 high for some time. Investors enticed by spectacular short-term price increases, think that they will miss a major "run," and assume new positions only to see potential gains turn to loses. The stock market rallied 15 times after 1929 before reaching the bottom and losing 85% of its value in the process. In 2009, the market rose 50% and considered the largest countercyclical market rally since the 1930s; in March of 2009, the Dow had its 10 best days since 1938, a good indication of the explosive power of countercyclical rallies. The Great Depression had seven -20%-plus declines in the DOW, and reached a low of 44 before recovering. During the 1966-1981 secular bear market, Wall Street made five failed attempts to rally past 1,000. When it made a low of 607 in 1974, it marked the worst 40% decline in the Dow since the Great Depression. This period was marked by a constitutional crisis, an unpopular war, oil shock, rising interest and inflation rates, and social conflict. Japan illustrates what might happen to the US. The Nikkei over the past 23 years rallied 8 times by more than 30%, and yet, the Nikkei remains 29,000 points lower than its all-time high of 40,000. When adjusted for inflation it is one of the world's greatest financial disasters in history. The US is not far behind, because since 2000 it experienced a lost decade, with another underway.

Stage 3. In this stage, anxiety, fear, and capitulation are defined by considerable pain, anguish, and suffering. Expressions like "never again" surface, indicating that the investor, who lost much, renounces Wall Street. Eventually the frenzy to sell will result in *Gotterdammerung*–a tragic and final end to the existing calamity when massive daily declines for days at a time and with ever increasing volume devastates net wealth. A similar expression, *torschlusspanik*, refers to the ultimate fear among investors where everyone rushes for the door at the same time. With capitulation, the "misery index" climbs to new levels fueling anger, social, and political discord. The bottom of a bear market arrives when PE ratios below 10 occur as in 1919, 1939, 1949, 1975, 1979, and 1982. Overvalued conditions when the PE was over 20 occurred in 1921, 1929, 1934, 1946, 1960, 1990 and 2000. In its final phase the selling pressure reaches a climax of frenetic trading that produces one of four outcomes: the classic "V" shape indicating a huge sell off on high volume and a quick rebound to the upside, a "W" pattern that frustrates many investors, a broader "U," an "L-shaped" market, and often with a double bottom.

## The End of the Current Secular Bear

A number of negative mechanical and immutable forces influences today's secular bear market. How much confidence does an economy have when burdened with historically high multiple deficits, a 2% savings rate, historic debts, and expensive and damaging wars? Furthermore, capital investment is nearly comatose, and there is a general malaise that pervades the once fruited plain. More than 17% of the population relies on food stamps, 11 million are on "disability" (includes stress, aches and pains, etc.), and 50% of the population is too poor to pay federal taxes. Wage growth is the lowest in memory, and without rising wages, the housing recovery is mute. Therefore, the secular bear market is encased in uncertainty and fear and fueled by active federal intervention in free markets. Therefore, the US is currently in a secular bear market manifested, some say, by depression, others by recession, and still others by stagflation. It is the largest economic contraction since the 1930s, and while spikes in several economic indicators will occur from time to time, the trend is to muddle through the previous economic excesses before the ultimate bottom is reached.

Therefore, a large number of shoes need to fall, not all at the same time, but eventually, all will have to be re-soled, dyed and polished. Here is an abbreviated list: 1. Government spending is increasing 7% annually with deficits and debts increasing at higher rates. 2. The erosion of the $US relative to gold and other currencies is continuing. 3. The tendency for dual citizenships and the migration of wealth overseas is intensifying. 4. The looming pension/retirement crisis is worsening because few will be able to retire even at poverty levels, thus straining public assistance programs. 5. Commercial real estate has more room to drop. 6. Measured by historic metrics, equities are overpriced by more than 20%. 7. As long as interest rates are less than the rate of inflation, debt expansion will continue, as $20 trillion of bad debts have to be eliminated. The deleveraging of the private and public sectors will be a painful long-term process. It would require the emergence of an "El Cid," or a "Lycurgus," a name synonymous with "austerity," to offer guidance and structure. Extreme by today's standards, "austerity" is highly controversial, but timely in the sense that a reduction in entitlements, size of government and spending are necessary to reduce debts. Nevertheless, the US will survive the current financial crisis, and will emerge stronger than before. As the secular bear market unwinds, the American market will offer extraordinary opportunities in technology, biotechnology, real estate, financials, and the durable goods sectors. The US faced many challenges in the past, survived all, and those who had short the US, failed.

Given the fact that the government has only three ways to raise money–by printing it, by taxing it, and by borrowing it, the options are limited, as all three strategies have reached their limits. The government has already printed too much, and should the supply of dollars escalate further, it would spell disaster. The government may increase the marginal tax on the top 20%, but in today's world, they would merely move their money offshore and begin asset liquidation at home. The remaining 80% have no additional money to be taxed. The last option has also been played out, as creditors are no longer enthusiastic of lending money at negative real returns. Military adventures, contrived international incidents, and political spins have come to resemble the boy calling "wolf" once too often. The time has come for America to face reality and admit that expenditures will have to be reduced, military adventures curtailed, and corruption reduced. One thing is certain: the US is unable to grow out of its present morass; secondary output is as good or better outside the US, innovation and discovery is increasing faster overseas and productivity is no longer exclusively an American monopoly.

## Bear Market Strategies

Since the government is committed to a parallel policy of monetary expansion and low interest rates, what is the investor to do? 1. If you are buying a home, do so with a 30-year fixed mortgage as you will never again see lower interest rates. 2. Do not buy long bonds. Buy productive assets: commodities, utilities, healthcare, and EM equities. 3. Prepare for Murphy's Law. Anything that can go wrong will go wrong. Never take anything for granted. 4. Stay calm, do not panic and review all assets frequently. 5. Remain debt-free. 6. When the capitulation phase approaches, begin DCA in those assets that will benefit from the early stages of impending growth. 7. Build cash reserves, so that you will have the means to buy when the market bottom arrives. 8. Sell high PE and beta stocks at the beginning of the decline. During a market crash, stocks with the highest valuations will decline the sharpest and remain low the longest. 9. In the words of Jim Rogers: "Bottoms in the investment world don't end with four-year lows; they end with 10 or 15-year lows."

### Mark Twain on Seasonal Trading

"October. This is one of the peculiarly dangerous months to speculate in stocks. The others are July, January, September, April, November, May, March, June, December, August, and February." Short-term market behavior can be extremely volatile and, hence, dangerous. "Stock picking" is a notion that the investor knows more than the market, but it is impossible to track markets so meticulously so that they can trade to perfection. Few are able to handle losing short-term positions without remorse and disappointment.

## The Evolution of Commodity Companies

Stage 1. During secular bear declines, investment diminishes and mines are neglected or abandoned, situations that can last for decades. Under these conditions, prices can remain extremely low for such a long time that nearly all investors are unable to entertain thoughts that prices would ever rise again. However, they do. Once commodities embark on a secular uptrend, it may take three steps forward and two steps backward until momentum improves. What propels bullish commodity cycles are monetary policies when central banks begin to print monopoly money. Stage 2. This stage is characterized by pricing power as the economy progresses. Individual investors remain un-phased, but the smart money enters as vigorous capital investment re-enforces its upward channel. Stage 3. This is the stage of maximum euphoria, a hockey stick formation in price escalation. Magazine articles now feature the commodity on the cover. Producers experience windfall profits as margins widen in a spectacular manner. The profits per barrel, ounce and ton rise, thus warranting extremely high multiples. Once the bubble bursts, the descent is sharp precipitating a rush of bankruptcies. A number of observations:

1. The historic process of supply/demand imbalances produces business cycles, something that Harry Schultz calls the "pig effect." When pig prices rise, farmers breed more to meet demand and raise profits. The price rises energize all pig farmers to do the same, and in less than two years supply exceeds demand and prices plummet until the cycle begins anew. This type of economic behavior is universal in scope affecting all commodities. The only difference is the lead-time necessary to increase supply. With poultry, the time interval is 1 year; cattle 3 years; ship construction 5 to 7 years; coffee 5-plus years; cacao, 6-8 years; a quality wine vineyard 11 years; high quality olive trees bear fruit after their 5th year and improve for centuries; and quality cork oak begins after the 25th year.

2. Low prices never offer an inducement for capital investment to encourage exploration, production, transportation, processing and fabrication. For nearly 20 years, the energy industry had been stymied with pipe, drilling rig, and skilled labor shortages. Since it takes time, money, and huge human resource investments necessary to bring new commodities on line, the entire process can only occur if the industry is assured higher sustainable prices. When NG prices rose sharply in 2007, new supplies through new technologies brought additional supplies to market, thus depressing prices, closing operations and promulgating bankruptcies and mergers. Furthermore, there has always been a negative correlation between equities and commodities. Commodities rose between 1906 and 1920 when equities were flat, and equities rose during 1921-1929 as commodities fell. During 1933-1950, commodities rose at the expense of equities. In the 1970s, equities remained flat and commodities rose. During the period 1982-2000, equities rose and commodities fell. This has been the pattern for nearly 200 years, with equities and commodities alternating leadership in cycles of about 18 years.

3. Withdrawing metal and other mineral matter from the earth's bowels is expensive in terms of capital expenditures for exploration, site development, and

infrastructure and plant development. One must also supplement the list of endless problems and obstacles associated with political and geopolitical interventions such as bureaucratic red tape, regulations, *baksheesh* and legal issues.

4. The last time the US had a commodity secular bull market (1970s), gold increased from $34 to $800oz, oil rose from $1.50b to $80b, and nearly all other commodities increased in excess of 1,500% in less than 10 years. It was a time when investors lost faith in cash and bought real assets. The process reversed in 1982 when interest rates declined and the equity and bond markets went on to an 18-year secular bull market. During this period, mines closed, farmers went out of business, oil-drilling rigs were mothballed, and capital investment shriveled to insignificance. Eventually, demand outstripped supplies and prices began to rise. This is where the commodity markets are today–in the middle secular bull stage. Commodities companies suffer from the following risks: country, currency, operational, market, and commodity.

## Historic Bubbles and Panics/Crashes

Market bubbles, crashes, etc., are sudden increases and declines in market value noted by greed and fear gripping the investment community. They are more numerous than most people realize, and noted for market turmoil. What propels most bubbles is a rapid rise in the money supply leading to easy credit, outrageous and euphoric predictions, and a good dose of corruption and fraud. A panic is most commonly described as overpowering terror that affects many people at once, but on Wall Street, it generally refers to a sudden rush to sell at any price. Within a short period, selling begets more selling, with new lows made in abnormally short intervals. Panics and crashes have a tendency to disfigure facts and bewilder the thinking processes of investors. When the price of anything increases at more than twice GDP, you have asset bubbles. A short listing among 900 bubbles, panics and crashes since 1634 include the most notable, mainly US, for illustrative purposes.

Tulip Bubble of 1634-1637: The rage to own tulips in Holland captivated the imagination and actions of an entire population. During the height of the mania, the asking price for tulips was hundreds of times their weight in gold. In a similar vein, Americans sold their homes to buy lottery tickets in order to increase the odds of winning, and a casino mogul from Macao bought at auction in Florence, Italy, a 3.3-pound truffle for $330,000.

South Sea Bubble of 1720: A scheme, hatched by Robert Harley produced the ill-fated "South Sea Trading Company" which implicated Sir Isaac Newton, the king of England, and Parliament. This was one of the most notorious scandals in English history that attempted to create a trading monopoly in order to retire the national debt, the latter brought about by the costly and protracted war of the Spanish Succession.

The Mississippi Company Bubble of 1720: This misadventure involved a Scottish opportunist, John Law, who sold non-existent resources in Louisiana through the Mississippi Company to investors, many of whom were the French monarchy and the national treasury. Given a monopoly to take advantage of the imagined "riches" of French possessions in North America, the fraudulent scheme never generated profits. What it produced were incredible quantities of money and credit, excessive speculation in which nearly half the nation owned shares, and, as usual, mania set in, followed by the inevitable crash.

Depression of 1861: Civil War and Confederate debt sent the nation in an economic tailspin with a short-lived depression in the North, and a three-generation depression in the South. A combination of defaulted southern loans and business failures in the north led to the issuance of worthless currency commonly referred to as "greenbacks."

Panic of "Black Friday," September 24, 1869. Monetary inflation in the aftermath of the Civil War to finance war debts and corner the gold market produced a severe market crash leading to bank "runs," and many financial and political scandals.

Panic of 1873: This panic, a product of railroad, land and business speculation, scandals, inflation, bank failures and removal of silver as a medium of exchange resulted in the closing of the NYSE for 10 days.

Panic of 1893: Proposed tariff legislation, the gold standard vs. inflationary fiat money creation, Florida land speculation, and easy money and credit, combined to produce a rash of business and bank failures and high unemployment.

Panic of 1907: Consolidated Copper, a company that controlled more than 50% of domestic copper production, and wished to corner the remaining supply, borrowed huge amounts of money, defaulted, and the market declined 48%.

Panic of 1919-1921: After WWI, commodities plummeted; heavy European debts, excessive money creation, inflation, currency devaluations and eventual defaults weakened the American financial system and capital markets.

The Crash of 1929 and the Great Depression: Black Thursday, October 1929, marks the start of the largest secular bear market (that lasted 20 years) and known as the Great Depression. The Dow fell from 385 to 40 within three years, industrial production fell by more than 50%, commodity prices declined by 40%, and foreign trade declined by more than 34%. A combination of easy business credit, the largest explosion in consumer installment debt, new federal programs requiring new taxes, the introduction of trade barriers, business frauds on Wall Street, and low margin requirements, all combined to produce a depression.

Panic of 1973-1974: Arriving during the conclusion of the Vietnam War and the Watergate scandal, the crash, the largest since 1929, drove the Dow from 1,067 in 1973 to a low of 570 one year later. Caused in part by the Middle East Oil Crisis, this secular bear market, lasted to 1982.

Panic of 1987: More than 35% of stock market value was depleted within a 48-hour period. Although short-lived, the panic revealed major systemic financial flaws.

Crash of 2000: The 1982-2000 secular bull market was a function of several unique factors that converged to produce spectacular returns in equities and bonds: positive demographic forces, favorable monetary policies, the phenomenal growth of technology and globalization, and deregulation. The problem is that all of the above were trumped by phenomenal increases in the federal debt, household debt, state, and local government debt, a widening trade deficit, a declining dollar, stagnant to declining real wages, and near zero saving rates. The year 2000 began with the highest valuations since 1929. The S&P fell by 38% and NASDAQ by 57%. The Fed promises free money forever.

Crash of 2008: By lowering the Fed rate below 1% and keeping it there for a prolonged period, Alan Greenspan promulgated a horrendous credit crisis and triggered housing speculation that precipitated a crash of major financial institutions. He was responsible for a decline of nearly $10 trillion in the value of all assets and the demise of Bear Stearns, Lehman and AIG. In the past, consumers reduced spending, paid down debt, and increased their savings rate. The "zero decade" of 2000-2009 was something unlike any other. Equity markets achieved a negative return; negative job creation became the new normal; gold quadrupled in price; two cyclical bear and two cyclical bull markets within a secular bear market came and went; the effects of 9/11 ushered a new era of waste and corruption; record-low interest rates and personal savings combined to misappropriate investment capital; and Hurricane Katrina, household insolvency, financial bailouts, stimulus packages involving enormous amounts of money, record deficits of all types and magnitude, five destructive wars, financial and political scandals *du jour*, and the acrid whiffs of corruption from the canyons of Wall Street and Washington have stained the cultural and political fabric of America. The crashes of 2000 and 2008, collectively wiped out three decades of equity wealth creation in the US, and $27 trillion from the global equity market. The median net worth of the American household declined by 46% from 2007-2010. In the meantime:

1. Nothing has changed; history has produced an endless array of bubbles, crashes and panics. They occur at irregular intervals. The names may be different, the venues may vary, the sums may stagger the imagination, but they repeat themselves whenever cheap money fuels speculative fever. World history offers a plate of repeated manias and busts that ranged from camels, black pepper, vanilla

beans, cane sugar, tobacco, gold, swampland, mountain real estate, cloves, green tea, stamps, stocks, bonds, baseball cards, rare books, railroads, and everything else that the conscious mind is able to proffer. Financial crises occur because disposable incomes are unable to support debt servicing. 2. Fed policies have not worked for many decades, and there has been a total lack of financial reform to prevent financial crises. 3. In the past 100 years, the element of contagion has increased. 3. The tendency for investors not observing signs of decline are quite common with inflection points always identified after the fact. 4. Before the Industrial Revolution, many bubbles were attributed to weather related events as they affected agriculture. With the advent of the Industrial Revolution in the 1700s, the business cycle changed, thus captivating the minds and political hearts of economists, factory workers, and heads of state. For the first time in history, bubbles have been introduced in a tertiary environment increasing their duration.

## Behavioral Investing

Behavioral finance is a school of thought, which seeks to identify the forces that explain why investors buy and sell when they do, particularly in erratic fashion at the extremes. The notion is based on the simple premise that human emotions, not reason, drive markets. The concept has evolved into a highly refined subject spawning seminars and many books. Central to this notion are greed and fear, both of which are affected by the herd mentality propelling individuals to mimic the actions of many and behave as a mass. With instant communication, positions are switched in *milliseconds* inducing the individual to participate in the prevailing "momentum." In time of panic, people lose their nerve, forget what they were taught, disregard discipline and patience, and generally behave contrary to how they should. In the final analysis, common sense, prudence, patience, and discipline continue to be the basis for successful investing as all four are significant in controlling impulses, emotions, and desires. Never forget that people are emotional beings with imperfect memories.

What makes people follow each other? While the definitive results are subject to dispute among psychologists, one thing is certain–investors do not wish to stick out from the group. By "belonging," they seek recognition and not disapproval, acceptance rather than rejection, comfort and not anxiety. Most important, the fright of standing alone is too much for most to bear. The herd instinct is prevalent in man, not just lemmings with investors seeking to emulate the momentum of "the market." Just before the great crash in 1929, the prevailing wisdom "on the street" was that the market would continue rising and the herd instinct prevailed. One of the few dissenters, Charles Merrill, strongly urged his clients to sell the year before the crash and no one listened. Moreover, months before the crash, Merrill implored President Coolidge to address the issue of excessive speculation, but to no avail. When the "instinct" grips Wall Street and Main Street, it is totally irrational and devoid of all reason and conscious effort to buck the trend. When a large number of investors move in the same direction, they can exert a massive shift in objectives, thus moving the pendulum to extremes. People never think of themselves as lemmings, but they certainly behave like them, and as the crowd discards caution and rational behavior, false prophets guide human actions to the precipice and beyond. Hemingway said, "Anyone would behave badly if given the opportunity." Therefore, never follow the crowd, as it is habitually wrong. Should you wish to avoid the negative effects of following the herd, the remedy is simple: be disciplined, tune out the noise, become a contrarian, and remember the words of Mark Twain: "Whenever you find yourself on the side of the majority, it's time to pause and reflect." To be avoided are "groupthink" environments in which members suppress all contrarian opinions. In the words of Dale Carnegie: "When dealing with people, remember you are not dealing with creatures of logic, but creatures of emotion." Remember that for every emotion there is a counter move, and for every buyer a seller.

### Apollo and Dionysius

Emulate and admire Apollo and not Dionysius. The former was the ancient god of moderation and the latter, the god of wine and revelry. One is responsible, the other irresponsible; one is practical and sensible, the other impractical and foolish. One lives a life of moderation and the other a life of excess. Unlike Dionysius who looks at the "little picture," Apollo looks at the "big picture." It is a strategy of being aware of long-term trends, being patient, picking your moments, and investing wisely and not foolishly. The little picture is analogous to a tiny worm crawling in a random manner on an intricate oriental rug, moving from one color and pattern to others in an endless manner, unable to observe the "whole picture." Moreover, such is the view of Dionysius who thinks he "sees" inflection points where none exists. The little snippets of daily market behavior never seem to combine into a perception and appreciation of broad market behavior. He does "this" on Monday, "that" on Wednesday, and "whatever" penetrates the deeper recesses of his clueless mind on Friday. In the end, he has missed the trend, bought late, sold late, and has lost money. Apollo does not behave in this manner. He understands and appreciates market behavior, is not prone to irrational actions by the daily missives of media "gurus," and questions everything.

Addictive behavior is driven by brain activity where rational thought processes are superseded by impulsive behavior. Even when aware of the adverse effects, addicts are unable to stop when they wish as the body and mind both wish additional stimuli to satisfy. It is also not exclusively related to a substance, but to any disrupting process, that produces the illusion of insatiable pleasure. Whether it is alcohol, shopping, heroin, or the crap table makes no difference. The element that drives behavior is dopamine, a chemical that induces elation while lowering cynicism and uncertainty. The production of dopamine by the brain is neither constant nor fully understood, but what is familiar to the scientific community is that the brain requires unexpected stimulation as in the expectation of outrageous rewards from a "hidden gem" yet undiscovered by Wall Street. Most investors simply cannot defy the adrenaline flows that seem to overpower wisdom and purpose. Anything mundane and repetitive dries up the supply of dopamine; hence, the need for investors "to do something." After a successful trade, the release of dopamine increases risk taking. That is why most people after selling a position immediately turn around and make other purchases often to their detriment because they did not step back, relax and reflect. Dopamine is the enemy of patience and discipline.

Greed and fear move in a never-ending pattern like the predictable movements of a pendulum–from one extreme to another. On one end, greed generates inertia, as perceived danger appears to diminish, while fear exaggerates perceived hazards on the other end. In matters of investment, people are no better as they act contrary to their economic interests. Most often, the eyes see, but the mind fails to believe. Of the two, fear is a visceral emotion than greed and trumps the latter by a significant margin because fear of capital losses amplifies risk. Excessive sanguinity disguises risk and leads to the accumulation of high-risk investments. When excessive pessimism replaces optimism, the reverse occurs. Investors become overly cautious and postpone important decisions that have long-term consequences. Not only does fear play a large part during a selling frenzy, but also it is the most difficult emotion to restrain, as investors are unable to calculate market probabilities. Fear either acts to paralyze or enables the investor to enter uncharted areas. A primary investing objective, therefore, is to control fear and greed. A greedy investor is destined for misadventure as he will enter early and remain late, and a fearful investor will arrive late and leave early. If individuals can ignore the fear that grips them during periods when stocks fall precipitously and accumulate instead, they can make a lot of money. However, there is a problem: the Janus personality is present in every investor. Patience vs. impatience, discipline vs. anarchy, and fear vs. greed all act as countervailing forces, and rare is the investor with the ability to apply good sense. Most investors simply cannot defy the adrenaline flows that seem to overpower wisdom and a sense of purpose. The Janus-type emotions of fear and greed, alternate more frequently than the individual realizes, and as the pendulum swings to and fro, so do powerful passions. Fear is irrational, utterly random, and capricious; it is an all-enveloping emotion that governs investment decisions. When there is blood in the streets, fear grips the investor and he does not enter as his fears are reinforced when all are selling. Fear propels immediate reaction as it represents a survival mechanism. Following the herd, the investor switches from one "hot" stock to another, from one timely fund to another, and from one sector to another, with no strategy save that of realizing significant short-term gains. Therefore, it is necessary to marinate your emotions in order to prevent and minimize mistakes.

In addition to greed and fear, one must also add hope, optimism and overconfidence as dangerous emotions because they often compound the mistakes that arise from irrational passions. It is human nature to hope and be optimistic because it makes people feel good. The opposite extreme, pessimism and negativity lead to anger, apprehension, a repetition of mistakes, and depression. Investors are on the wrong side of a position when they hope that several market actions are certain to take place. It is hope that prevents an investor from selling rather than watching the stock touch new lows week after week, and this is not an emotion that Mr. Market recognizes. Investors are similar to troops in battle. No matter how hopeless the position, they are committed to the eventual outcome. Investors want maximum gains no matter what the probabilities, and the stray bullet consumes those that resist market forces and common sense when its least expected. Overconfidence also heightens risk-taking, and when it is negatively correlated with experience, poor performance is magnified. In addition, when excessive trading, lack of experience, and overconfidence combine with rapid, on-line compulsions, net returns decline. Extreme optimism, therefore, is not always a virtue. France thought that "Christmas in Moscow" was an attainable goal, The Pentagon thought that the Iraqi war would cost less than $50 billion, and many investors dreamed of Dow 34,000 in 2000. "Overconfidence" states John Nofsinger, "causes people to overestimate their knowledge, underestimate risks, and exaggerate their ability to control events." In addition, he states that, "People have the tendency to believe that the accuracy of their forecasts increases with more information. This is the illusion of knowledge–that more information increases your knowledge about something and improves your decisions. However, this is not always the case, as increased levels of information do not necessarily lead to greater knowledge. There are three reasons for this. Information can mislead. Many people may not have the training, experience, or skills to interpret the information. People also tend to interpret new information as confirmation of their prior beliefs." Overconfidence, therefore, must be controlled because it promotes excessive trading, and when negatively correlated with experience, underperformance is magnified. At all costs, discipline must be exercised.

Four words summarize the psychological impairment of the investor: greed, fear, denial, and desperation. We all know what these words mean, but they have a counter side to them as well–self-esteem, moderation, acceptance, and grit. All of these emotions are in constant interaction most often leading to rising anxieties, distraction and ultimately bad decision-making. Chance plays a far more important role than most people think. When it results in something positive, it is hardly ever considered "luck." There is the chance, however, that you will actually come to think that you are naturally lucky, and that this luck will continue forever. Napoleon Bonaparte used to say, "Give me lucky generals." Some were, but, like most investors, not all were "consistently" lucky. "Feelings," "instincts," "intuitions," should also not enter the equation as they distort decision-making processes. Once you develop a bias for such "instincts" and "feelings" there is an overwhelming compulsion to view choices in a more favorable light. Also noteworthy is the "Stockholm Syndrome" a psychological expression to denote that the human mind can be held hostage regardless of financial harm. The name is derived from a robbery in Stockholm, Sweden, whereby the criminals took hostages. These things happen every day somewhere in the world. But in this case, the victims became emotionally attached to their captors and even defended them upon their release. The Stockholm Syndrome is of concern because investors make excuses for their dishonest brokers, financial planners, and for their own blunders. When investors become hostage to specific unworkable strategies, they remain true to the destructive course by making unwarranted excuses. Therefore, disavow market timing, overweighing, chasing performance and miscalculating risk.

### Time to Invest?

For a few investors, extreme pessimism is the perfect time to invest new money because that is when the market bottom generally has been met. This is hard to appraise at any given time, but history suggests that when consumer sentiment reaches and remains below 40%, it suggests a buying opportunity, and that when consumer confidence rises above 70%, it is time to sell. When prices are up, investors are optimists, and when down they are pessimists. The psychology of the problem is as endless as time. Investors dislike stocks and sectors when they are in the doldrums, and flock like lemmings to buy when prices are going through the stratosphere. Investors buy late and sell late. Successful investors do not lose their nerve, apply common sense, are disciplined, and patient. If the prudent investor evades emotional terror on either side of the trading desk, he is in an enviable position to take advantage of the stupidities of others. Psychologically, when times are good, people think that they will continue along their present projectory forever. Remember that markets are composed of crowds with unlimited opinions and slick charlatans. Markets often make no sense, becoming irrational and trending to extremes until violent corrections occur. History is sated with examples of market euphoria and depression, as in hoola hoops, narrow ties, Cabbage Patch dolls, dot.com stocks, or time-shares in the South Bronx. Remember: the worst loans are made in the best of times.

Flawed people lie. In the words of Bernard Baruch: "Nobody buys at the low and sells at the high–except liars." Significant is the fact that many investors, and primarily day traders and those obsessed with timing markets, suffer from cognitive dissonance, or the manifestation of concentrated and extreme anxiety when they attempt to accommodate two or more conflicting thoughts in their head at the same time. In avoiding disharmony, the notion is filled with emotional frailties that combine to frame false market impressions that lead to serious mistakes. Whether good or bad, habits are powerful and difficult to change. They can, however, be altered through focused determination. Once negative habits are broken and discipline and patience dominate behavior, financial success is nearly assured as fewer mistakes are made and, more importantly, fewer repeated.

Whether acute, chronic, or periodic, the average investor must learn to manage stress levels. If not, the disruptive forces of fear, greed, peer pressure, and propagandist elements will precipitate deleterious actions. Acute stress preoccupies the life of many investors 24 hours a day. Quite common with day traders, the acute nature of the malady progresses rapidly during the course of the day until the element of fatigue and psychosomatic disorders overwhelm. Obviously, mistakes compound, and these individuals, who began with overconfidence and enthusiasm, find themselves on welfare due to fear-based decisions. Worry manifested in obsessions, physical ailments like high blood pressure, etc., lead to mental illnesses that are more serious. One such individual, who dropped out of college at age19 in 1956, amassed a $6 million fortune as a day trader two years later. Harry soon became an alcoholic, and self-destructed at age 25. Being skilled at what you do, being smart, and managing your financial affairs, is simply not enough to become successful. Something was missing in Hurry's emotional and mental state and it was that he could not contain his arrogance and self-centered personality. The illusion of unique insight and intuitive manifestations has destroyed more than one investor, and it is best to know yourself and keep delusional ideas in check. Emotions tend to cloud good judgment: you do not know yourself as well as you think, and because of that, "Hail Mary" plays should not be encouraged. And in the words of Marilyn vos Savant: "Being defeated is often a temporary condition. Giving up is what makes it permanent." In this connection, I am persuaded that an investor cannot profit without good financial discipline, for without financial discipline one is destined to get caught up in the emotions of the markets, buying into greed that forms market tops and selling into fear that forms market bottoms. Without good financial discipline, one will ultimately wind up following the rapid waters of the crowd, sloshing with the currents of emotion headed inevitably toward the waterfalls of financial failure.

When one stops to consider that there are thousands of people making economic predictions, it is statistically possible for one or two to be correct at any given time. However, ask to see the color of their money on the next bet, and they will no longer be available. Even the shaman of Wall Street and the oracle at Delphi are, and were, unable to do it. However, the language is always cleverly peppered with "if," "perhaps," "should," "could," or "might." In the end, prognosticators lie in order to sell. In an attempt to prove that England was the birthplace of Homo sapiens, Piltdown man came into being, one of the greatest hoaxes ever perpetrated. The supposedly missing link found and engulfed the highest echelons of British science that sought to prove that the village of Piltdown became the most famous venue on the planet as it attempted to prove that human origins were on the hallowed ground of Britain. Even the legendary Sir Conan Doyle was implicated. Charles Dawson a swindler made the "discovery" and soon drew into the web of deception the Natural British Museum and many scientists. For nearly half a century, many who knew that Piltdown Man was a hoax allowed the deception to continue. Piltdown holds many lessons once a concept becomes firmly encased in the mass psyche of a population. People become frightened by exposure and, hence, bad decisions are made until the bogus theory is exposed. Sadly, most investors see only what they want to believe. Thinking and believing are the two most dangerous perceptions that an investor can have when pondering a decision. Terrible things occur when reality is ignored.

## Investing Principles

Investing is defined by wikipedia.com as, "...the accumulation of some kind of asset in hopes of getting a further return from it. Examples include building a railroad, or a factory, clearing land, or putting oneself through college. In finance, investment means buying monetary paper assets, real estate, bonds, or postage stamps. These investments may then provide income and increase in value." Despite the simplicity, few individuals manage to bring themselves to invest, preferring, instead, to spend. While it is easy to say that the lack of discipline is the singular cause, there is more to the story. The condition is a manifestation of the times in which self-indulgence is the main driver, something that pervades every facet of society. In the end, investing is a matter of common sense, discipline and patience. The sooner investors understand the investing landscape, the better investor they would be. Therefore, learn the basics of successful investing, and acquire the essentials of economic history. Investing is a conscious effort to enhance wealth by measured paces and by taking appropriate risks. Prudent, value investing works over time because the equity markets outperform both cash, bonds, and mirrors the growth of the national economy. The sapient investor is rarely impatient and reckless.

"Speculation" is defined as "to enter into a transaction or venture the profits of which are conjectural or subject to chance." By its very definition, the odds are stacked against you finding the lone needle in the haystack, the jackpot in a casino, and the winning Powerball number. Periodically, one does indeed get lucky, but over the course of a lifetime, you as an individual, will not be. Speculation is a utopic notion pregnant with illusory and delusional components, and it behooves the prudent investor to concentrate on the entopic world of cold, hard facts. Do not be fashionable! All novelties fade with time, and often, quite suddenly. Every generation succumbs to "hot" issues that vary from gaming, dotcoms, tulips, "pet rocks," etc. In the words of Jesse Livermore: "Another lesson I learned early is that there is nothing new on Wall Street. There cannot be because speculation is as old as the hills. Whatever happens in the stock market today has happened before and will happen again. I've never forgotten that." Therefore, before you begin investing, develop a serious attitude towards saving and accumulating wealth as a long-term objective. Consider your net assets as part of a corporation and appoint yourself CEO. For the rest of your life, your objective is to make the net assets of the corporation grow. In addition, place blinders on either side of your head to force you to cultivate a positive attitude on life and your financial health, because the combination of nurturing a positive attitude, life objectives, and skills is what will separate you from your peers. To achieve goals a well-structured existence with like-minded individuals is essential.

## Investors Come in All Sizes and Flavors

1. Speculators and aggressive investors suffer from dangerous feelings of infallibility and truly believe that a pot of gold exists on the other side of their last trade. They invest on steroids, lose control of their emotions, and are programmed to follow the herd. Their mantra is to buy on the belief that some other "fool" will pay a higher price. They fail because in the words of Lord Keynes: "The market can remain irrational a lot longer than you can remain solvent." Speculators seek to outperform by attempting to select investments that will go one better than the market, and their overconfidence is further heightened by passion and a profound belief that huge capital gains are a certainty. For the vast majority, it involves frequent trading, leverage, higher expenses, and more mistakes. Aggressive investors, much larger in number than speculators, are only slightly better in terms of longevity and success. The laws of probability bankrupts them–it just take a bit longer. They exhibit absolute disdain for low PE ratios, stating that there is nothing wrong in buying high and selling higher. While this sounds good, history precludes a long-term success record. Any "value" stock is to be avoided for the simple reason that if it were good, it would command a much higher PE. The only significant item that matters to them is growth and not fundamentals. They forget that dice have no memory.

2. Program, market timers, day traders, and companies who enable the habit by offering "signature" trading, "private client" trading, trading seminars, software packages, etc., offer stories of successful trading adventures on television replete with yachts in the background. They are engineered to speculate on that which is "hot," with margin, and distinguished by classic daredevil elements. Their number has skyrocketed with the advent of on-line trading, but due to the high tuition, few survive. The above would like to be Ted Williams who got base hits 40% of the time, the all-time record. How many speculators have a 40% success record with their individual investments? These investors can never beat the market over a long period through indiscriminate market timing, day trading, or any other "get rich scheme." Because the preoccupation for a "kill" is so pervasive, few investors accurately calculate taxes, expenses, inflation, etc., over a long period. Yet, despite the never-ending history of failure, more than 85% of all investors continue failed strategies in their quest for the "needle in the haystack." According to Benjamin Graham, "The investor's chief problem-and even his worst enemy-is likely to be himself." This cohort simply gets intertwined in their underwear. Nevertheless, to be a good trader you need unlimited amounts of luck and a wealthy mother-in-law who loves you.

3. The "clueless" investor is the one who "sees," but does not observe, has no inkling about what his life objectives are, and lacks a saving plan. Much like a jumping bean, he never stands still, never looks at the broad picture, never reflects, always impulsive and easily influenced by fly by night suggestions, thus producing underperformance. This investor usually sprints into the wrong asset at the wrong time.

4. Contrarians seek to invest in those assets that are discarded and ignored, wishing to find value in a universe that nobody craves. Lord Keynes described the contrarian spirit and investor as one in which, "It is in the essence of his behavior that he should be eccentric, unconventional, and rash in the eyes of average opinion." To be a contrarian, one must disallow prevailing judgments in secular markets and seek quality, out-of-favor assets. Therefore, due to the emotional nature of all markets, utopic and entopic perceptions are often confused and/or misinterpreted leading to price anomalies, and, in order to profit, contrarians must have nerves of steel, defy temptation, and be oblivious to the noise that ricochets in the canyons of Wall Street. According to Charles Ellis, "The only way to beat the market is to exploit other investor's mistakes." Remember the words of Robert Frost: "I took the road less travelled and that made all the difference."

5. Value investors are a bit older, wiser, and more cautious with money. They buy quality index funds, trade less frequently, are more successful due to a more balanced approach to investing, and are often referred to as "fundamentalists" as they are immersed in the methodical approach to investing. They have a much higher level of municipal bonds, and use all manner of tax mitigation approaches to their investments. In terms of size, these successful investors are in the minority, but control 80% of financial assets. They are the perfectionists who have a comprehensive plan, and adhere to a household budget.

6. "Income" investors are obsessed with current yield: there are those that require income to live as in the case of retirees, and those individuals who are determined to preserve their capital through interest, dividends and modest capital gains.

## Elements of Successful Investing

1. Become a value and passive investor by emphasizing index funds. 2. Increase the level of knowledge necessary to invest properly and wisely. 3. Live a prudent and sensible lifestyle in which frugality receives a central role, and eliminate all those items that are unnecessary in your life. 4. Buy quality and hold for the duration of a secular bull market. 5. According to David Dreman, avoid short-term trading because it does not work: "…there are no billionaires who made their money with short-term trades." 6. Reinvest and divide assets into taxable and tax-sheltered accounts and allocate assets accordingly. 7. Asset allocations should conform to secular markets. 8. Avoid "hot" stocks and mutual funds. 9. Buy during a market crash. 10. One way of alleviating stress and bad decisions is to be debt free. 11. Tax-defer as much money as possible. 12. Further those elements that are subject to your control such as asset allocation, expenses, and risk. 13. Being master of your emotions promotes and enhances wealth formation. 14. Buy when share price is below book value, dividend rate is between 5% and 7%, PE below 10, price to sales under 1.0, ROE greater than 15%, and when companies are buying back stock and increasing dividends.

## Buying Securities

Consider the following: darts; hot tips, educated tips, brokers buy lists, and doing your own research. The dart approach is strictly random, and while it is possible to get "lucky," long-term, this is a dangerous strategy. Hot tips pose the biggest danger to your financial health, as most concern small, little known companies on the precipice of bankruptcy. "Educated tips," the product of TV and radio personalities, magazines, etc., are also dangerous since the information is both tainted and dated. Broker's buy listings are always yesterday's news and, hence, useless and dangerous. Doing your own research, in the words of Lynch/Rothchild, is the "highest form of stock-picking," but this process requires considerable effort. If you do your due diligence, you do not have to rely on the constant "noise" about this stock vs. that one. However, in the course of the year the average investor lacks the time and ability to fully research more than ten specific companies, then sit back, and look for a good entry point. If Jesse Livermore had been unable to crack the secret code of the stock market, what makes the lowly retail investor think that he can? The ability to select a winning stock repeatedly eludes everyone. Therefore, what to do? If one considers money to be serious business, listen to the sage words of John Bogle: "The effective means of building wealth is simply to emulate the annual returns provided by the financial markets, and reap the benefits of long-term compounding. This goal, as it turns out, can best be achieved by minimizing the costs of investing-sales commissions, advisory fees, taxes, and the like-and seeking to earn the highest possible portion of the annual return earned in each sector of the financial markets in which you invest, *recognizing, and accepting, that that portion will be less than 100%*. To achieve this goal, the ideal investment program includes four elements: 1. *Simplicity: Matching*, not *beating* the markets; asset allocation that is *strategic*, not *tactical*. 2. *Focus*: Maximizing the *productive economics* (earnings and dividends, interest yields) of investing; minimizing the *counterproductive emotions* of investing (changing price-earnings ratios). 3. *Efficiency*: Economical operations; minimization of the frictional costs of fees and commissions and taxes. 4. *Stewardship*: Placing the interest of the client first; unyielding emphasis on human beings and eternal values-integrity, honesty, candor." The best time to buy is at peak bearishness (after a steep sell-off, a condition that sets up an investment opportunity), and the best time to sell is at peak bullishness. The ability to pick the absolute bottom and top is an impossibility.

When and what to buy: 1. Since most investors do not engage in meaningful research, decision making is best left to index funds. 2. Buy when the market is exhausted, and in the words of John Templeton: "The greatest bargains can only be found at the point of maximum pessimism." It is always too late to buy when the sector move becomes visible to most investors, or in the words of Warren Buffett: "If you wait for the robins, spring will be over." Historically, more than 80% of all individual stocks follow the sector trend. 3. The cheapest markets are those with low PEs and high dividends, and when the two combine, buy as much as you can afford. 4. The direction of interest rates defines "acceptable" investments. 5. When an opportunity arises. 6. When corporate fundamentals turn positive. 7. When you wish to increase quality. 8. Buy the best of the best as value companies dominate their sector, and exhibit high sustainable free cash flow, high return on equity, and high sustainable margins.

## Selling Securities

Selling securities is more intricate than buying. In the words of Chinese sages: "Easy to buy, not so easy to sell." The average holding period for a stock today is 22 minutes, a direct result of high-frequency and day trading practices, with the former responsible for more than 70%-plus of all trades. The problem is further compounded by excessive trading in tax-sheltered accounts, and the abandonment of the "buy and hold" philosophy of investing. 1. Every security requires an exit strategy. Part of disciplined investing is to exert a will to sell, and remember the sagacious words of J.P. Morgan: "I made all my money by getting out too early." And here is an example of the not so smart: The Bank of England, with all its enormous resources, sold billions of dollars of gold near the very bottom in 2003. 2. Sell when the security is out of sync with its asset allocation percentage; when the PE rises more than 50% above its historical average, when it makes a "double top"; when competition is eroding market share; when company internals like price to sales, book value, etc., begin to deteriorate; when the reasons you originally purchased are no longer valid; and when company turmoil due to scandal, criminal activity dominate headlines. 3. Never sell because of hunches, horoscope prognostications, etc. 4. Parabolic rallies are always selling opportunities, particularly when its price has increased five times its dividend yield in six months. Market tops are always recognized as periods of excessive euphoria, excessive bullishness, with nary a bearish comment from the media. When the waiter offers stock tips, you know that the top is in place. 5. The time to sell a security is when you have found a much better asset to replace it.

## What Influences the Purchase or Selling of Securities

1. Suggestions from a friend (a major percentage) 2. The investor engaged in exhaustive research (negligible). 3. Broker advice (at one time, a major source, but with on-line trading less so) 4. Advice from a registered advisor (limited to the top 10% of investors) 5. Selection of mutual funds within investment plans is a function of limited listings 6. Television and radio financial programs (increasing in frequency) 7. Print media (increasing in influence) 8. Financial newsletters (subscriptions vary with current market performance) 9. Rating services (affecting less than 10%) 10. Advice from anonymous sources from internet company chat boards (increasing in number and a dangerous trend) 11. The *illuminati* often become the inflection point as they define and dominate investor sentiment. Once a bubble begins, it requires nutrition and momentum, something that these individuals wish to preserve and expand. 12. In a letter to shareholders in 2005, Warren Buffett stated,

"Investors should remember that excitement and expenses are their enemies. And if they insist on trying to time their participation in equities, they should try to be fearful when others are greedy and greedy only when others are fearful."

## Buy and Hold Philosophy

There are three basic ways to invest: the short, intermediate, and long, all of which lead to the following outcomes: outperform the market, match market performance, underperform the market, or lose principal. Investors outperforming the market on a consistent manner are rare; matching market performance can be accomplished by purchasing index funds; and underperformance can be avoided by not becoming a stock picker. Short-term investing, either daily, weekly, or monthly is doomed to failure as it implies that the investor has unique insight into market internals. The intermediate approach seeks to profit from unpredictable cyclical patterns. Since interest rates, inflation, the general economy, commodities, etc., all follow long-term cyclical patterns, it is possible to buy at or near the low and then hold for the completion of the cycle. Consider historical advantages of holding "the market." There is a 30% chance that the S&P 500 will decline within 12 months after purchase, but if held for 10 years the downdraft is reduced to 10%, and to 0% if held for 20 or more years. The notion of buying forever, therefore, is because market volatility is reduced dramatically the longer an investor holds. Given the fact that only rare individuals are able to select the "needle in the haystack," the alternative is to hold index funds, as they will shield the investor from the ravages of poor stock selection. The strategy is to hold, not trade, and to select those with the lowest possible expenses and DCA. Over the long run, index funds will return the index minus expenses. You will never outperform the index, but you will also never experience catastrophic losses. Negative returns will occur for more than one year, but the fund will recover when its underlining benchmark recovers, and all have recovered throughout history. The issue is patience and discipline. In addition, no individual will have access to information about the Total Market that is not available to everyone else. The concept of "buy and hold" differs among investors. For some it means to buy and hold "forever." If it refers to a broad index, one can make a case, but it cannot and should never refer to individual stocks, as the uncertainties in "forever" are fraught with excessive risk.

The imbroglio continues: 1. By buying broad index funds, and holding, the investor will perform at market levels. Note that the Total Market cannot revert to zero, and that throughout history, its highs have always been surpassed. If one "holds," providence will reward. According to Penelope Wang, "Buy-and-hold is the worst form of investing except for all those other forms that have been tried." "Buy and hold" does not mean buy and never sell. One can and many do, the problem is timing: when to get out and when to get back in. It should also be noted that history also relegates political and economic events as "irrelevant" over the course of time. For example, the 1970s were more than turbulent as a president and vice-president resigned their offices, more than 57,000 American lives were lost in Vietnam, a major bear market ravaged markets, a hostage crisis, a nuclear plant accident, gas rationing, political riots, etc., but eventually, markets recovered. Today, America is mired in several wars, as well as political, social, and economic uncertainty, a secular bear market, etc., all of which, will eventually become minor footnotes. 2. Another reason to buy and hold is that most stocks make the bulk of their returns in short-term bursts that are difficult to predict. The investor finds it difficult to be sitting on cash waiting for an entry point. First, he does not know the actual bottom or its duration, and when there is a sudden 4% rise in a given day, he may hesitate to buy on the theory that the market will retrace. But suppose it doesn't for weeks at a time, then rises 2%, declines 1% over the course of the next few months, rises 2% over a period of five months, declines 2% the next month, and then rises 10% in a matter of days. By the time the investor sees a chart of a steady rise over a period of a year he might have lost the opportunity to buy at the low or near low, and he is then forced to buy much higher. While it is tempting for the investor to wait for the absolute low, reality rarely produces this perfect scenario. Short-term emotions simply cloud, obscure, and confuse the picture. 3. In the past 100 years, the Total Market experienced several declines of more than 40%, yet it recovered and subsequently attained new highs. And while recoveries take time, they do not take into account individual circumstances, of which age is the most prominent. If in March 2000, for example, you at the age of 70 were 100% invested in the Total Market, and held, would life be better 14 years later? Should you disagree, go like Diogenes, and produce individuals that have successfully applied the pleasures of market timing for more than 20 years. A buy and hold strategy never works for the stock picker, but fares much better for the index investor. 4. Over the long run, wealth is accumulated by holding and not trading. While the investor suffers paper loses during cyclical downturns, the history of the market has always had an upward bias (The Dow has increased from 206 in 1945 to over 15,000 in 2013.). "Holding forever," therefore, will only work if you are younger than 60, DCA, and have a strong disposition to tolerate large declines. In addition, indexing is a buy and hold investment strategy which is much less expensive than active portfolio management. "Buying and holding" index funds is rewarding because it is the sauce that visually defines the finished product as it dismisses day trading and market timing by holding forever.

### The Needle in the Haystack

Thoughts of finding the needle in the haystack are the ultimate investment alchemy. The needle is here, there, everywhere, and yet nowhere. The "Pareto Principle" or "20/80 rule" states that of all the daily trades occurring at any given time, fewer than 20% are successful. This 20% has a certain patina of personal achievement that must be clearly understood should one wish to imitate success. These individuals are loaded with enthusiasm, have high energy levels, live on the edge in terms of making difficult decisions, are receptive to new ideas, and are able to deliver on their mission of making money. "Picking" the winning stock is what John Bogle says is equivalent to "finding the needle in the haystack." It is not only difficult to do occasionally, but nearly impossible on a consistent basis, and for the ordinary "retail" investor, impossible. Yet the allure of finding that undiscovered elusive needle that would generate spectacular market returns forces investors to make untold unforced errors. No method ever devised by man, deity, sage, or well-dressed huckster from the canyons of lower New York, can help you either. It literally is impossible to select the one Dow, S&P 500, or one stock from the Total Market, that will, over the course of 25, 50, 75, or 100 years, be the stellar out-performer. Therefore, do not attempt, and do not listen to those who profess otherwise. There is much that the ordinary investor can do to increase the odds against failure: select no-load index funds; never buy "concept" stocks; and if history teaches anything, it is that no single valuation method works perfectly and consistently. Emulate the "old-school of investing by choosing quality dividend-payers and index funds.

## Why Investors Fail to Match the Market

1. The implementation of a long-range investment strategy is essential, and yet, the vast majority of investors have none, or if they did, they abandoned it for the pleasures of *la dolce vita*. Investors cannot resist the "free cheese" in the mousetrap when affected by propaganda. 2. A lack of discipline and patience 3. Not paying attention to expenses Every adjustment in your portfolio requires an expense, and over time, the drip, drip, drip effect of transaction costs erodes your capital stock. 4. The belief in the power of "new paradigms" 5. Allowing the emotional inner to dominate investment decisions, as in "instincts," "hunches," etc. 6. The "I have discovered the perfect system to making money" strategy (as in reliance on mechanical and intuitive stock picking systems) is very likely to produce a "winner" every so often, similar to the proverbial blind pig that finds an acorn. However, there is no investment alchemy that can consistently produce winners to beat the market. Chances are that if the investor loses grip of the true reason for that occasional triumph, he will lose those winnings on subsequent "chances." 7. Taking things for granted. When anything appears possible, not everything is probable, and it is the latter that should guide investor behavior. 8. Many "swing" for the fences, avoiding "singles," and in

the process strike out frequently. 9. Not paying attention to simple math: when a stock declines by 50%, it must then rise 100% for the investor to break even. Whenever an investor invests money and loses, he repeats the bet, and loses again. The more he loses, the greater the propensity for the most fatal of all flaws—"I am due to win now." 10. Besides increasing transaction costs, portfolio churning is an insidious activity that spells trouble. The most obvious and serious issue deals with the fact that the investor must be accurate twice—once when he sells and once when he buys back. 11. Buying concept stocks that lack earnings, are on the margin of solvency, and dearly priced. 12. Excessive day trading 13. Chasing past returns: It seems that investors love to shop when they see a sign in store window advertising a 60% discount, but when it comes to investing, people are reluctant to invest when prices are low or depressed. 14. During the course of a secular bull market when stock prices appear to be an endless road to nirvana, investors develop bad habits. 15. The individual remains on the periphery in any attempt to capitalize on price anomalies; he may get lucky periodically, but in the main, the casino will always have the edge because they have analysts, computer models and inside information.

## A Number of Insights

1. Fashion is endemic on Wall Street. If you wait long enough, some concept will float your way to entice you, and most often, it is old wine in a new bottle. 2. The most expensive real estate is that between your ears. Nurture it, develop it, and constantly feed it with good, sensible information. 3. At market tops and bottoms, the most dangerous words are: "This time it's different." 4. There is no "sure thing" in investing. 5. Often, what is comfortable is seldom profitable. 6. Passive investing should be the preferred avenue for the investor. 7. The winner is the investor who remains in the game the longest. 8. It always pays to be an agnostic in investing: listen carefully, do not believe everything you hear, take your time making up your mind, and question everything. 9. Because markets are not efficient, they always provide opportunities. 10. Will Rogers: "It's easy to make money, just figure out where people are going and then buy the land before they get there." 11. Not paying attention to your investments is much like your kitchen knife drawer. If you do not use a particular knife often, it falls to the bottom of the pile, and you do not see it. 12. There are no "free" lunches. In a German restaurant, when you ask for the bill, you ask for *die rechnung*, or "the reckoning." 13. Indexes capture a much larger portion of market efficiency than individual stocks. 14. Buying last year's top performers is a failed strategy. 15. The Fed can levitate the market by providing unlimited access to credit at no cost. 16. All markets return to the mean, excesses are never permanent, flat markets are not corrections, investors buy more at the top than bottom, and when the majority agree, something else will happen. 17. All the historic axioms on wise and prudent investing are discarded on expectations of ever-rising stock prices. 18. The most successful investors are those who are not forced to sell during crashes. 19. Those assets that had risen the most during the previous secular bull are the ones to drop

the most during the succeeding secular bear market. 20. Opportunities are found in all markets. During the years 1930-1937, more than 10,000 new millionaires were created. 21. There is no investment strategy that is always successful. 22. Equities and real estate always go up in the long-term.

## What It Takes to be a Successful Investor

1. Cultivate a proper state of mind. In order to save and invest one must sacrifice, and sacrifice for a long time. Just as a child prodigy must sacrifice "play time" with friends and spend ten hours at the piano, so must an investor sacrifice spending activities in order to feed the hungry investing machine. If you are one to not listen, dislike reading and taking prudent advice, stick to horseracing and casino gambling. But if you are the antithesis of hedonistic behavior, and are able to control your emotions by emphasizing moderation, common sense, and are able to restrict passions, then long-term investing will prove rewarding. Remain committed to your objective to build wealth and never waiver. 2. Get educated. Knowledge is the wellspring of successful investing. 3. Buy companies that are circumscribed by good fundamentals and wide "moats." 4. He who loses the least wins. Apply Warren Buffet's golden rules: "Rule No. 1: Never lose money. Rule No. 2: Never forget Rule No 1." 5. A major reliable indicator of future performance is the expense ratio. 6. Provide a margin of safety in order to prevent mutilation of principal. 7. Maintain efficient tax strategies. 8. Pay attention to the "time value of money." 9. Be frugal. Over the course of a 40-year working career, if you reduce all those items that are unnecessary in your life, like excess consumption of soft drinks, coffee, alcohol, reducing driving by 5,000 miles each year, taking care of your clothing, and by not wasting food will generate savings of about $1.4 million over the course of a lifetime. 10. Enhance portfolio returns by selling covered calls and buying long-term options (LEAPS) in a secular bull market. 11. Long outperforms short horizons. 12. Expected rates of return should be reasonable. 13. Control your temperament. 14. Broad investment opportunities are created when there are major demographic shifts, economic shifts between primary, secondary, and tertiary sectors, technological innovations, discoveries, and global shifts in productivity. 15. One cannot outsmart the market. 16. In the words of Steven Jon Kaplan: "The good news is that there are thousands of ways to make money in the financial markets. The bad news is that there are millions of ways to lose money." 17. Detach yourself from minute by minute obsessions about market movements and take time to smell the roses. 18. Resist irrational overconfidence. If not, you will overtrade, overpay, and under perform. 19. Take advantage of opportunities. In an atmosphere characterized by turbulence, remember the words of Mao Zedong: "There is great disorder under heaven…the situation is excellent." 20. Discipline and patience are indispensable. 21. Create appropriate goals and stick to them. 22. Create a balanced portfolio and stick to it. 23. Since no one is able to accurately predict market behavior and the individual stocks that will outperform, buy index funds. 24. A frugal existence and saving are the first steps toward investing.

## Nineteen Investing Commandments

1. I shall not follow the herd. 2. I shall not believe official data. 3. I shall not squander time. 4. I shall not panic. 5. I shall not speculate. 6. I shall not borrow from my retirement accounts. 7. I shall never time the market. 8. I shall never forget the erosive force of inflation. 9. I shall not overpay. 10. I shall never confuse luck with talent. 11. I shall not ignore fundamentals. 12. I shall never ignore probabilities for disaster. 13. I shall never lose sight of the advantages of thinking and acting in a contrarian manner. 14. I shall fall in love with my children, spouse, flowers and pets, but never with financial instruments. 15. I shall never lose money. 16. I shall never ignore risk. 17. I shall never buy the notion that markets react to the same news twice. 18. I shall never believe that markets are efficient. 19. I shall never forget that total return is a much better investment goal than dividend yield.

# The Best and Least Expensive Buying Strategy

When investors "sieve" all available alternatives, do what the smart money does, buy the Total Market or the S&P 500 Indexes, thus purchasing the "haystack." Why attempt all manner of investment strategies when the market freely offers "market performance"? Both indexes have proffered 10.5% over time while returns of the average investor have been less than 4%. The reasons for the dramatic discrepancy are simple to explain but hard for investors to understand. The ordinary investor pays too much, buys, sells at the wrong time, and lacks the ability to select worthy individual securities. Instead, place your bet on these two indexes that guarantee market returns and whose value doubles every seven years with no commissions, minimal fees, and few headaches. DCA each month for 40 years without deviation, and you will outperform 90% of all fund managers. The following is also noteworthy: About 20% of stocks are responsible for the bulk of market gains, a similar percentage lose at least 74% of their value, 66% of all stocks underperform the Total Market, and more than 50% of all individual stocks prove to be unprofitable over 10-plus year intervals.

### Investment Myths

1. You can beat the market by timing the market. 2. Investors are rational. 3. The stock market is a landscape where only the wealthy and privileged can profit. 4. Serious money can be made by following the crowd. 5. Markets are efficient. 6. Trends are linear. 7. "Blindly stay the course" is a good axiom to follow. 8. Diversification eliminates risk. 9. Investing is easy; anyone can do it. 10. Investing is a science. 11. Economics is a science. 12. According to the Fed, the business cycle is "abolished." 13. The American economy is a perpetual growth model. 14. Individuals are unbiased in their examination of present and future market behavior.

## What We Know About Investing

1. Equities outperform bonds and cash, but not all the time. Equities often remain flat for extended periods, and under those conditions, bonds and cash outperform and are necessary for stability. 2. A portfolio of equities and bonds will reduce risk. 3. Index funds and domestic and international income-producing securities should dominate your core positions. 4. Depending on market conditions, significant sector exposures are necessary to extend diversification and enhance performance. 5. In the battle between growth and value, it is wise to veer toward value. 6. In addition to losing capital, one can also lose opportunity. 8. The "odds" lie with Wall Street and never with the retail investor. 9. More than 90% of all economic predictions miss their target. 10. The hallowed halls of academia and the concrete pavements of Wall Street are littered with false prophets. 11. Small-cap growth and value should overweight portfolio composition. 12. For those under the age of 60, foreign exposure should not be less than 20%. 13. Sentiments alter over time as each generation produces its own *zeitgeist*, and the prudent investor must be aware of these manifestations. 14. While it is impossible to predict market movements, the identification of events after they occur is not difficult. 15. Successful investors invest with a "focus." 16. The number of up and down days by at least 2% has increased from fewer than 20 days prior to 2007 to more than 50 during the period 2008-2011. 17. While individual equity prices can vacillate to zero over years, returns for the Total Market over time have been remarkably consistent at 10.5%. 18. There is no such thing as "buy at any price." 19. Don't trust your broker and financial advisor. 20. Not all market sectors move in unison, thus offering opportunities. 21. Take advantage of the 3%-6% Dow tenet: Historically, the Dow theorists proclaimed an overvalued market when dividends stood under 2%, and undervalued when greater than 6%. 22. Markets are much like wine. Two glasses of red wine may look similar, even smell similar, but may taste very different. To discern accurately, it takes experience, time, and a degree of expertise to observe accurately and consistently. 21. No one should invest for emotional reasons. 22. No stock/market sector is immune to financial gravity. 23. It is rewarding to buy the most neglected portion of the market. 24. Becoming a *frugalisto* augments wealth. 25. When panics begin, it is difficult to think rationally. 26. Valuation and sentiment matter.

## Black Swan Effects

There is always risk in matters investing. Somewhere, somehow, today, or tomorrow, some unknown event will, in one way or another, interfere with statistical averages and great expectations. Be prepared for the unexpected! One of the most notorious surprises was, "All safe deposit boxes in banks or financial institutions have been sealed and may only be opened in the presence of an agent of the IRS." Black Swan events occur more frequently than one thinks. They are atavistic events that come and go with irregular frequency, and are therefore the reason why one should always be defensive in the world of investing. Furthermore, there are times, when investors think that they have observed an immutable pattern, but the rules often change just when they anticipate the pattern to repeat. Furthermore, there are always exceptions on Wall Street: every textbook states that during an economic downturn consumer spending declines and saving increases, something that has not occurred during the current secular bear. Who would have bet on a baseball team with but 83 victories in the regular season to win the World Series? "Stuff happens," and happens more frequently now than before. Investors should always keep the significance of the Titanic in mind when investing. Icebergs are ubiquitous and nothing should be taken for granted. In fact, investors should always be looking for black swans. Just as the Titanic proved to have been sinkable, "riskless" investments can disappoint.

## Twenty-Four Investing Principles

1. Among long-term investing in the nation's largest central cities, real estate has been the greatest wealth-building machine ever in the US. 2. The second best investment is small-cap stocks, which have outperformed the general market for 100-plus years. 3. The third best investment is the Total Market/S&P 500 indexes. 4. Investors are unable to outsmart the market. 5. Over the long-term, equities are no riskier than bonds. 6. Total real return is a function of dividend yield, plus capital gains, plus compounding, plus dividend increases, minus expenses, minus inflation, minus taxes. The successful investor must be cognizant of the mandatory *bella figura*, the only true measure of performance. 7. Wealth is transferred from the impatient to the patient. 8. Invest for a specific economy by paying attention to interest and inflation rates. When interest rates peak and begin to fall, buy bonds and stocks; when inflationary pressures, begin switch to commodities. 9. Index funds are primary investment vehicles because they are inexpensive, and tax-friendly. 10. Regression to the mean is inevitable as all markets adjust all previous excesses. 11. The best time to invest is now! Postponing even $1 is costly over the course of a lifetime. 12. When the market is flat to falling, the market favors and rewards value stocks. When the market is rising, it favors growth stocks. 13. As long as the Fed prints fiat, equity markets will rise. 14. Equities offer high risks and high returns. Cash offers low risk and low returns. Long-term Treasury bonds fall somewhere between these two extremes. 15. Other than buying at absolute secular lows, there are no perfect "buy and sell" signals that guarantee winning trades. It is best to DCA. 16. Stocks are only to be considered investments relative to their fundamentals, and never to their historic price levels; what is important are "current" fundamentals and future expectations. In this connection, the "20 yard fake-out" refers to that; fact that what looks very attractive at 20 yards turns out to look worse at a shorter distance. And so it is with investments. Do your due diligences, stay educated, and do not believe everything you hear and read, and question everything. 17. In certain wine producing regions, like Bordeaux, vintage years are important. These vintage years also vary in the Mosel River, Napa, and Eastern Long Island, and all other wine growing regions. Even king Tut mentioned unequal wine quality in Egypt. Vintage years are also important in the investment

industry, as "streaks" and "runs" of above-average years alternate with bad years for all national economies, and all sectors and sub-sectors. 18. There are no categorical imperatives in finance. 19. Always invest with a plan. 20. Stock market tops and bottoms are difficult to time and trade. 21. Equity markets are a zero-sum game. 22. Low market-to-book and low price-to-earnings portfolios outperform the market by significant percentages. 23. Market predictions are wrong nearly 100% of the time. 24. Never invest for *du moment*.

# CHAPTER 5

# THE RECIPES

*All things in moderation.* - Aristotle

*Reasonable people assemble ingredients and cook before they get hungry.* - Armenian adage

*Make your money first, then think about spending it.*
- J. Paul Getty

It is prudent for the executive financial chef to develop and determine his financial destiny. In the investing arena, not all chefs are similar as they vary in age, experience, gender, and family history. Most of all, there is the key feature of desire, the most indefinable but crucial element in the equation. The chef must want to be in the kitchen. He must be focused and committed to long-term financial goals. Therefore, one of the most practical ways of planning for future comfort is to look at the most important elements that confront an individual after graduation from high school, or receiving a doctorate from a university. The life cycle consists of the following critical events that have key financial implications: graduation from public school and/or college, first job, marriage, first child, last child, last child to leave home, divorce and/or remarriage, change in employment, retirement, and death of a spouse. In addition, investors ought to pay attention to the "spending cycle," an important demographic determinant. Awareness of these events means that one can plan, with a minimum of expense and inconvenience, investments on the road to critical mass and beyond. However, market return expectations can often become cloudy and confused, as investors begin to diverge in their opinions of a "reasonable" return. If the investor does not consider a 10% return "reasonable," he is asking for trouble. A 10% total return, with dividends and interest reinvested and compounded over the course of an entire working career is an excellent return, and it should be the benchmark when making soup, as a consistent 10% return is neither watery, thick, salty, nor flavorless.

## Portfolio and Asset Allocation

A portfolio represents the aggregate investable assets found in the kitchen, and asset allocation refers to individual components that are placed in the various cupboards expressed in percentages. The four asset classes are: cash, bonds, real estate, and equities, and each one may be sliced as thinly as one wishes. In the case of equities, by size, style, geography or sector; in the case of bonds, by duration, corporate, sovereign, or municipal. In addition, all four-asset classes have a time and place dimension in the sense that all exhibit different periods where their intrinsic value remains stable, declines, or increases. For example, in 2009, an all-stock portfolio returned 35%, and the Total Bond Index 8%. For the period 1998-2008, however, equities were -.29% and bonds 6%. These extremes are reduced if one holds a portfolio consisting of 50% equities, and 50% bonds. Therefore, the creation of an asset allocation rests on seven factors: 1. The nature of the prevailing secular market. 2. The identification of non-correlating assets. 3. The selection of core positions, or a cluster of assets that are value oriented, indexed, and always long-term in nature. Because of safety and familiarity, domestic securities dominate the core segment of the portfolio and, taken together, the market returns of this segment should always exceed the rate of inflation. 4. The placement of assets in taxable and non-taxable accounts. 5. Time. A portfolio, like fine wine, requires time to fully mature. 6. The asset allocation contains eight basic elements: value, innovative companies, growth, commodities, foreign, small-cap, real estate, and income. Consider an asset allocation a "yoke." If investors wish to make straight furrows, the integrity of the yoke is vital.

## What Confronts the National Economy and Portfolio Strategies

Nothing is more fundamental to the health of a portfolio than the nutritional elements of its asset allocation, often referred to as the "93% solution." In 1986 and again in 1991, Gary Brinson and associates found that 93.6% of portfolio returns to be the product of asset allocation, with individual security selection, market timing, and other factors contributing the remainder. The 93.6% of total returns are much like a fine bottle of Bordeaux. To most people a bottle of Bordeaux is red in color and comes with two names: Cabernet Sauvignon or Merlot. Life, however, is not so simple. Red Bordeaux is a mixture of Cabernet Sauvignon, Merlot, Cabernet Franc, Malbec, and Petit Verdot. The wine maker cultivates these grape varieties to reduce the risk of having a reduced crop of one variety vs. another and to balance and maximize staying power, aroma, body and flavor. The strategy for the investor is similar: The need to assemble large-cap growth and value, small-cap growth and value, bonds, REITs, foreign large-cap growth and value, foreign small-cap growth and value, foreign bonds, etc. Asset allocation is the single most important element that produces high, mediocre, or low total returns.

According to the law of averages, all excesses revert to their means, and monetary debt, real estate bubbles, etc., will, and must "correct." 1. The current policy of debasing the dollar is disastrous and unsustainable and history dictates that the days of $US hegemony must decline. Fiscal and monetary policies have produced a credit bubble of epic proportions. 2. The nature of the economy with its stagnant wages, housing foreclosures, credit problems and deficits, are unsustainable. The post-2009 recovery appears to be a fraud as presented by governmental statistics. The CPI and inflation are much higher and GDP much lower. America's basic industries have been dismembered and replaced by low-wage tertiary employment; college graduates are selling shoes and hamburgers; real personal income is declining; and personal net worth is falling. 3. Rising aggregate debts are unsustainable. 4. America's generational standard of living has declined for the first time since Jamestown. 5. The current account deficit is increasing, and it is debatable that America's principal trading partners will continue to fund the deficit. 6. Long-term interest and inflation rate increases are inevitable. 7. Federal, state, and local budgets are in crisis. Deficits are getting bigger with states relying more and more on tobacco, lotteries, and casino gambling revenues to pay bills. 8. The official Washington policy to "kick the can" down the road with higher taxation, higher government spending, and larger government will continue. 9. Foreign military adventures are devouring human and financial resources. The centripetal forces creating and maintaining imperial power are strained. 10. It is a myth to entertain thoughts of the business cycle ending, "New Economy" dominating, and QE programs triggering economic growth. Fifty-five percent of all workers have (ex-house), less than $25,000 in investments and savings, and no pension. 11. The Prudent investor must recognize that the economic character of the US has been altered: Treasuries have lost their triple-A rating, half of the population is described as "poor", unemployment and underemployment are high, the lack of economic opportunity stands at historic lows, looming fiscal crises are ever-present, and declining real wages and income disparities act as centripetal social and political forces. In addition, corporatocracy will accelerate and Washington lobbying shall remain a growth industry. The barbell economic recovery favors the rich. The poor are rising in number and the middle class is dwindling in number. Globalization will continue to depress wages and one must scale back lifestyle and become mean and lean. 12. The Fed will continue to "ease" unless forced to do something else.

There are many paths to wealth creation and preservation of capital: capital appreciation to match the performance of the Total Market; aggressive capital appreciation by the assumption of additional risk to outperform the Total Market; capital preservation in which long-term returns are less than 5%; or a "balanced" strategy that produces 7%-8% returns. The key elements to investment success are, buy and hold, asset diversification, controlling emotions, paying attention to taxes, remaining knowledgeable, and reducing expenses. Therefore, whatever your proclivities during the current secular bear market: 1. Start a business. 2. Allocate 50%-plus of all money to real assets. 3. Keep at least 50% of your total portfolio in income-generating securities. 4. Invest at least 20% in small-cap funds, more than 70% in index funds and at least 25% in international securities. 5. Do everything to stay ahead of inflation and be skeptical of schemes promising above average market performance. 6. A "one asset allocation fits all" portfolio does not exist. The basics of asset allocation consist of two major concerns. The first is the focus on a time horizon as there is a big difference between a young 22-year-old investor and a 75-year-old. The second consideration concerns your personal circumstances of employment, family conditions, assets available, etc. In both instances, an asset allocation must be flexible, and conform to current secular features. In addition, if an investor is unable to tolerate losses greater than 5%, then the equity portion of the asset allocation ought to be restricted to less than 15%. Should the individual be able to tolerate 50% declines during severe secular bear markets, then an equity percentage could exceed 80%. 7. Avoid complex themes as they distract and rarely produce the desired effects. 8. Strategic asset allocation involves balancing asset classes of different correlations in order to minimize risk and maximize total returns. Tactical Asset Allocation is a strategy that seeks to anticipate asset and sector direction movements, and thus the necessity of shifting the percentage of cash, bonds, stocks, etc., as secular market conditions warrant. 9. Until the conclusion of the current secular bear, be realistic and bear in mind that real total returns for the Total Market might be less than 4% annually. 10. In the present low interest rate environment, one successful investment is real estate (especially commercial property), and secure a long-term fixed mortgage. The contrarian trade of the decade, however, lies with commodities, particularly with miners and real estate. 11. Think and invest long-term; the S&P 500 has had positive returns over 20-year periods, 97% over 10-year periods, and 72% in 1-year periods. 12. Internationalize as much as possible. 13. Be aware that until circa 2020, the highest annual returns will probably be in EMs and commodities.

## The Recipes

Since nothing is written in stone except the need for discipline and patience, consider the following not only with a grain of salt, but also with a jaundiced eye toward customizing "recipes" appropriate to individual needs. The Vanguard Group, the largest fund family is a company that offers something for all investors: more than 100 investment choices among equity, balanced, bond, etc., and without prejudice, it is used as the default investment group for illustrative purposes. The Admiral shares, with lower expenses and better performance require larger entry amounts. Dimensional Fund Advisors, Fidelity, Meridian, and Dodge & Cox offer additional alternatives. Listed below are ideas of the basic default portfolios to be placed in appropriate tax-sheltered and taxable accounts. Before presenting the recipes consider historical portfolio returns: CDs have returned between 2%-5%; a 100% bond portfolio between 5%-7%; 60%/40%, 8.8%; 80%/20%, 9.5%; and a100% equity position returned 10.5%. It is important to note that these are nominal returns; when inflation is factored, the 100% equity portfolio is reduced to about 6.5%. Just as there are differences between a *bistro, brasserie, taverna,* and *rotisserie* establishments, the investment choices available to American investors are just as varied. Not all brie is alike. There is brie that may look like the authentic product, but when made with skimmed milk, it is not worth the effort of consuming it. However, when one discovers the wonders of a dozen authentic variations made with triple-cream, and consumed with walnuts/toasted hazelnuts and a fine aged wine, then satisfaction rises to a new level. All recipes can be adjusted to suit individual circumstances and specific age cohorts, and all have ETF equivalents.

Whatever your choices among the many sample recipes, pay careful attention to seven key elements: 1. Total return expectations should be reasonable. 2. Contain your expenses. Choose no-load funds over loaded versions and select those with the lowest annual expenses. When choosing a broker, choose one with low costs and trade on line as expenses over time have a serious impact on total returns. 3. Control portfolio risk. Since all assets contain some measure of risk, the prudent investor should evaluate those potential dangers before investing. 4. Monitor portfolio performance in relation to benchmarks, and adjust accordingly. 5. Never confuse any market theory or investing strategy as science. They are not, have never been, nor will they ever be the final word, and this holds true for any computer model that may be available for sale to the unwary or greedy. The equity risk premium is never constant and shifting sentiment and exogenous factors enter the picture to complicate matters further. 6. Reinvest all interest, dividends and distributions. 7. Diversify to manage risk.

**Core (#1-#8) "Lazy" Holdings To Be Bought and Held as Long as DCA Occurs.** Core positions should have low PE ratios, pay good and rising dividends, and not be subject to whimsical trades

Recipe 1. **US Total Stock Market Index** (VTSMX): This is the definitive "plain vanilla" one stop investment containing growth, value and large, medium and small-cap stocks. It is inexpensive, offers 10% annual returns (a rate that will double your money in less than 7 years with no commissions, minimal fees, and few headaches) and because it contains a little of everything, it is the ultimate *smorgasbord*. DCA each month for 60 years without deviation, and you will outperform 80% of all fund managers. How simple, and yet, few people will attempt this strategy because it is considered too boring. In general, the longer the "market" is held the greater the probability that it will be profitable. Despite its KISS character, it lacks international exposure, and stability from fixed income instruments. Ideally, it should be purchased in the depths of a secular bear market and held. Its PE ratio is widely followed to gauge market direction. For all under 70, taxable or tax-sheltered.

Recipe 2. **US S&P 500 Index** (VFINX): This is a large-cap index (and rich as a quiche) that outperforms more than two-thirds of all managed funds. Throughout its history, the fund has achieved total returns of 10%. In the past 35 years, it has risen 28 and declined 7 years with the best 1-year total +33% and the worst -37%. While it tracks the 500 largest US corporations, the 300 largest in the index can comprise about 90% of its value. History shows that while the S&P 500 and the Total Market have several disparate elements, their performance over the long run is negligible. The DALBAR research group reports that over time, the S&P 500 has returned 12.2% while those of the average investor have been but 2.6%. Therefore, buy the S&P 500 index (or the Total Market), DCA, and keep it forever. If one had invested $10,000 in the S&P 500 in 1929, it would have grown beyond $8.6 million at the time of this writing. What prevents this simple approach are discipline, patience, and common sense. For all under 70, taxable or tax-sheltered. Substitutions or additions are allowed as in large-cap Index (VLACX), large-cap value Index (VIVAX), large-cap growth Index (VIGRX), etc.

Recipe 3. **US/International REIT:** 50% each, REIT Index (VGSIX), Global ex-US Real Estate Index (VGXRX). For those under 60, tax-sheltered.

Recipe 4. **US/International Tax-Managed:** For those with a high net-worth wishing to diversify and minimize taxes. Balanced (VTMFX), Growth and Income (VTGLX), Capital Appreciation (VTCLX), Small-Cap (VTMSX), International (VTMGX). For any age, taxable.

Recipe 5. **US/International Aggressive Small-Cap:** Equal weight, International Explorer (VINEX), Small-Cap Growth Index (VISGX), Small-Cap Value Index (VISVX), Small-Cap Index (NAESX), FTSE All-World ex-US Small-Cap Index (VFSVX), Explorer (VEXPX), Explorer Value (VEVFX). For those under 60, taxable or tax-sheltered.

Recipe 6. **US/International Value:** Equal weight, Value Index (VIVAX), International Value (VTRIX), Mid-Cap Value Index (VMVIX), Small-Cap Value Index (VISVX). For those under 65, tax-sheltered.

Recipe 7. **US/International Balanced:** 50% Balanced (VBINX), equal weight FTSE All-World ex-US Small-Cap Index (VFSVX), Global ex-US Real Estate Index (VGXRX), Small-Cap Growth Index (VISGX), REIT Index (VGSIX), High Yield (VWEHX). For all age groups, tax-sheltered.

Recipe 8. **US/International Bond:** Equal weight, GNMA (VFIIX), Inflation-Protected (VIPSX), Long-term Investment Grade (VWESX), High-yield (VWEHX), Convertible (VCVSX), Total Bond Market Index (VBMFX), Total International Bond Index (VTIBX). For all age groups, tax-sheltered.

Recipe 9. **US/International *Basso Profundo* for the Present Secular Bear Market:** There is fresh apricot, a dried apricot, and then there is apricot *glace*–the ultimate–designed to please the palate and outperform the current secular bear market. It consists of US and foreign dividend stocks, foreign real estate, small-cap growth and value for both domestic and equivalent foreign equities: 25% each of Precious Metals (VGPMX), Energy (VGENX); 10% each Materials Index (VMIAX), Emerging Markets (VEIEX); 5% each FTSE All-World ex-US Small-Cap Index (VFSVX), Global ex-US Real Estate Index (VGXRX), REIT (VGSIX), Utilities (VPU), Small-Cap Growth Index (VISGX), Explorer Value (VEVFX). For those under 60, taxable and tax-sheltered, DCA.

Recipe 10. **US/International Buy and Hold "Decadent" Equity for the Current Secular Bear Market:** A value-oriented, dividend yielding, 5 *puttonyi* portfolio offering income, appreciation, and diversification. It is composed of companies having a history of raising dividends, offering steady income and outperforming inflation. Many are members of the Dividend Aristocrats group, have strong cash flows, sustainable earnings, and low debt levels. It is imperative that investors diversify across and within all asset classes. Investing in *dividend* paying stocks that produce both income and capital gains is a sound strategy representing a powerful investment tactic to the retail investor. For all under 70, tax-sheltered, may be considered a Core holding, DCA. Choose from the various sectors for a custom-made "forever" fund.

**16% Commodities:** Agrium (AGU), Anglico-Eagle (AEM), Alcoa (AA); Anglogold Ashanti (AU), Archer-Daniels-Midland (ADM), Barrick (ABX), BHP Billiton (BHP), Bunge (BG), Cameco (CCJ), Cliffs Natural Resources (CLF), Freeport McMoran (FCX), Goldcorp (GG), Gold Fields (GFI), Impala Platinum (IMPUY), International Paper (IP), Kimberly-Clark (KMB), Newmont (NEM), Mosaic (MOS), Plum Creek Timber (PCL), Potash (POT), Rayonier (RYN), Rio Tinto (RIO), Royal Gold (RGLD), Silver Wheaton (SLW), Southern Copper (SCCO), Terra Nitrogen (TNH), Vale (VALE), Weyerhaeuser (WY), Yamana (AUY).

**16% Energy:** British Petroleum (BP), Buckeye Partners (BPL), Cenovus (CVE), Chevron (CVX), Conoco (COP), Encana (ECA), Energen (EGN), Energy Transfer Partners (ETP), ENI, Enterprise Products (EPD), ExxonMobil (XOM), Helmerich & Payne (HP), Kinder Morgan Energy (KMP), Magellan (MMP), Marathon Petroleum (MPC), MarkWest (MWE), National Oilwell Varco (NOV), Oneok Partners (OKS), Questar STR, Royal Dutch Shell (RDS B), Sasol (SSL), Schlumberger (SLB), Sempra Energy Partners (SRE), Sunoco Logistics (SXL), Targa Resources (TRGP), Total (TOT), UGI Corp (UGI), Williams Partners (WPZ).

**15% Healthcare:** Abbott Labs (ABT), Amgen (AMGN), Astrazeneca (AZN), Baxter (BAX), Becton, Celgene (CELG), Dickinson (BDX), Bristol Myers (BMY), Cardinal (CAH), Covidien (COV), CR Bard (BCR), Eli Lilly, (LLY), Express Scripts (ESRX), GlaxoSmithKline (GSK), Johnson & Johnson (JNJ), Medtronic (MDT), Merck (MRK), Novartis (NVS), Novo Nordisk (NVO), Patterson (PDCO), PDL Biopharma (PDLI), Pfizer (PFE), Roche Holdings (RHHVF), Sanofi (SNY), Steris (STE), Stryker (SYK), Ventas (VTR).

**11% Utilities:** AGL Resources (GAS), Alliant Energy (LNT), American Water (AWK), Aqua America (WTR), Brookfield (BIP), Black Hills (BKH), CPFL Energia (CPL), Consolidated Edison (ED), Dominion (D), Duke (DUK), Empresa Nacional (EOC), EQT (EQT), FirstEnergy (FE), First Trust (FXU), Exelon (EXC), MDU Resources (MDU), National Fuel Gas (NFG), National Grid (NGG), New Jersey Resources (NJR), NiSource (NI), NRG Energy (NRG), OGE Energy (OGE), Oneok (OKE), Pacific Gas (PCG), Pennsylvania Power (PPL), Piedmont Gas (PNY), Sempra (SE), Southern (SO), South Jersey (SJI), Vanguard Utilities (VPU), Vectren (VVC), Trans Canada (TRP), Westar (WR), Williams (WMB), Wisconsin Energy (WEC), York Water (YORW).

**11% Industrials:** 3M (MMM), Air Products (APD), Alcoa (AA), Berkshire Hathaway (BRK-B), Deere (DE); Bemis (BMS), BMW (BAMXY), Canadian National Railway (CNI), Carlisle (CSL), Church & Dwight (CHD), Comcast (CMCSA), Compass Minerals (CMP), Crane (CR), Dover (DOV), Dow Chemical

(DOW), Dupont (DD), Eaton (ETN), Ecolab (ECL), Emerson Electric (EMR), Expeditors (EXPD), Fastenal (FAST), Fedex (FDX), Ford (F), General Dynamics (GD), Gentex (GNTX), Illinois Tool Works (ITW), International Flavors & Fragrances (IFF), Ford Motor (F), General Electric (GE), Johnson Controls (JCI), Honeywell (HON), Kennametal (KMT), Leggett & Platt (LEG), Lockheed Martin (LMT), LyondellBasel (LYB), Navios Maritime (NM), Norfolk Southern (NSC), Northrup Grumman (NOC), Nucor (NUE), PPG Industries (PPG), Pall Corporation (PLL), Pentair (PNR), Praxair (PX), Raytheon (RTN), Roper (ROP), RPM International (RPM), Sealed Air (ECL), Seaspan (SSW), Sherman-Williams (SHW), Siemens (SI), Stanley (SWK), Syngenta (SYT), Toyota (TM), Union Pacific (UNP), United Parcel Service (UPS), United Technologies (UTX), Waste Management (WM).

**11% Financials:** ABM Industries (ABM), Ace (ACE), Aetna (AET), AFLAC (AFL), Allstate (ALL), American Express (AXP), Annaly Capital (NLY), Arthur Gallagher (AJG), Arrow Financial (AROW), Astoria Financial (AF), Assured Guaranty (AGO), Axis Capital (AXS), Banco Bilbao (BBVA), Bank of America (BAC), Bank of Hawaii (BOH), Bank of NY Mellon (BK), Bank of Nova Scotia (BNS); Bank of Montreal (BMO), Bank of the Ozarks (OZRK), BlackRock (BLK), BRE Properties (BRE), Canadian Imperial Bank (CM), Chubb (CB), Cincinnati Financial (CINF), Citizens Financial (CZFS), Citigroup (C), Commerce Bancshares (CBSH), HCP (HCP), Eaton Vance, (EV), Equity Residential (EQR), Erie (ERIE), Fisery (FISV), Franklin Resources (BEN), General Growth Properties (GGP), Hartford Financial (HIG), HCC Insurance (HCC), HSBC Holdings (HBC), ING Groep (ING), JP Morgan (JPM), Mastercard (MA), Lincoln National (LNC), Marsh & McLennon (MMC), McGraw-Hill (MHFI), MetLife (MET), MFA Financial (MFA), M&T Bank (MTB), New York Comm. (NYCB), Old Republic (ORI), Omnicom (OMC), Oritani Financial (ORIT), Ozark (OZRK), Peoples United (PBCT), PNC Financial (PNC), Realty Income (O), Redwood (RWT), Royal Bank of Canada (RY), Sun Life Financial (SLF), Travelers (TRV), T. Rowe Price Group (TROW), US Bancorp (USB), Vornado (VNO), Waddell & Reed (WDR), Washington Real Estate (WRE), Wells Fargo (WFC).

**8% Information/Telecom/Technology:** Accenture (ACN), Apple (AAPL), Applied Materials (AMAT), AT&T (T), Automatic Data Processing (ADP), Baidu (BIDU), BCE, Inc. (BCE), Brady (BRC), Broadcom (BRCM), CA Inc. (CA), Century Link (CTL), China Mobile (CHL), Cisco (CISCO), Cognizant Technology (CTSH), Eaton (ETN), EMC Corp. (EMC), FranceT (FTE), Harris (HRS), IBM (IBM), Intel (INTC), KLA-Tencor (KLAC), L-3 Communications (LLL), Microchip Tech. (MCHP), Microsoft (MSFT), Molex (MOLX), Oracle (ORCL), Portugal Telecom (PT), Qualcomm (QCOM), Teradata (TDC), Texas Instruments (TXN), Verizon (VZ), Vodafone (VOD).

**8% Consumer Staples:** Archer Daniel Midland (ADM), Clorox (CLX), Colgate Palmolive (CL), Conagra (CAG), Cosco Wholesale (COST), Danaher

(DHR), General Mills (GIS), Heinz HNZ, Hershey (HSY), JM Smucker (SJM), Kraft (KFT), Kellogg (K), McDonalds (MCD), McCormick (MKC), Mead Johnson (MJN), Nestle (NSRGF), Newell Rubbermaid (NWL), Procter and Gamble (PG), Sysco (SYY), Target (TGT), Unilever (UL), Walgreen (WAG), Wal-Mart (WMT).

**4% Consumer Discretionary:** Altria (MO), Anheuser-Busch (BUD), British American Tobacco (BTI), Brown-Forman (BFB), Anheuser-Busch (BUD), Coca-Cola (KO), Constellation Brands (STZ), Diagio (DEO), Dunkin Donuts (DNKN). Fortune Brands (FO), Home Depot (HD), McDonalds (MCD), Nordstom (JWN), Panasonic (PC), Pepsico (PEP), Philip Morris (PM), Reynolds American (RAI), Samsung (SSNLF), Target (TGT), Universal Corp (UVV), Yum Brands (YUM). For any age group with sufficient funds.

**US/International Equity For The Next Secular Bull Market:** Once the current secular bear market ends, a change in allocation is warranted, and the percentages offered in Recipe 10 must be adjusted: reduce commodities and utilities to 5% each, industrials to 8%, energy to 9%, financials and information and technology 18% each, consumer staples 13%, consumer discretionary 9%, and healthcare 16%.

Recipe 11. **US "Couch Potato" Index:** Equal weight, S&P 500 (VFINX), Large-cap Value (VIVAX), Extended Market (VEXMX), Mid-cap Value (VMVIX), Small-cap Growth (VISGX), Small-cap Value (VISVX), Small-cap (NAESX), REIT (VGSIX). For all under 70, taxable and tax-sheltered, DCA.

Recipe 12. **International "Spicy" Portfolio:** Equal Weight, FTSE All-World ex-US Small-Cap Index (VFSVX), Global ex-US Real Estate Index (VGXRX), Explorer (VINEX), International Growth (VWIGX), Emerging Markets Index (VEIEX), FTSE All-World ex-US Index (VFWIX), Total International Stock Index (VGTSX). For those under 60, tax-sheltered, DCA.

Recipe 13. **US/International Aggressive *"Parfait"* for Those With Means and a High Risk Tolerance for the Next Secular Bull Market:** 10% each Explorer Value (VEVFX), Explorer (VEXPX), International Explorer (VINEX), All-World ex-US Small-Cap Index (VFSVX); equal weight, Total International Index (VTWSX), Small-Cap Index (NAESX), Small-Cap Growth Index (VISGX), Large Value (VIVAX), Emerging Markets Index (VEIEX), Global ex-US Real Estate Index (VGXRX), REIT Index (VGSIX), Energy (VGENX), Healthcare (VGHCX), Capital Opportunity (VHCOX), PRIMECAP (VPMCX), recipe #10. Taxable or tax-sheltered, DCA.

**Balanced portfolios:** The principle behind a balanced portfolio is that the two primary assets–bonds and equities–move in opposite directions. When equities decline and bonds rise, owning both will lower portfolio volatility and market risk.

For example, a 70/30 portfolio, for the past 70 years, captured 92% of equity returns with only 70% of the risk, and a 60/40 mix captured 87% of stock returns with but 60% of the risk. A 20% equity exposure will not induce more than a 5% market loss in normal market corrections. A 100% equity exposure can, in secular bear markets, produce losses exceeding 50%, and these declines may continue for a prolonged period of time. The "classic" balanced portfolio consists of equal percentages of equities and bonds, producing more than 8% in total returns over time. A balanced portfolio is described as pedantic, dull, and arcane as it is unable to outperform a 100% equity portfolio. The Vanguard Group reports that a 70% equity, 25% bond and 5% cash portfolio only experienced 24 down years from 1930 to 2010. Many dislike balanced portfolios liking them to a combined laxative and sleeping pill, but for those who wish to sleep well, there is nothing wrong with a long-term return of 8%-plus that doubles its value every 8 years when dividends and interest are reinvested. The fact that a good, balanced fund can offer, over time, more than a 8% total return with practically no effort, time and worry, it is a wonder that so few make use of them. Among the wealthiest Americans, the balanced approach is preferred, the only variation being a 10%-25% deviation between equities and bonds to capture advantages from prevailing secular trends. Fixed-income securities should not play a critical role in the life of those under 30, unless there are special circumstances. For those in their 30s and 40s, the fixed-income percentage can vary between 20% to 30. After the age of 50, the income portion of the portfolio should dominate and vary between 50% and 80%. In the final analysis, a balanced portfolio can only be described as a "Maginot Line," or one that is defensive, risk-averse, and conservative in nature. All balanced portfolios may be bought and held from current market levels in tax-sheltered accounts. DCA religiously.

Recipe 14. **US 50/50 Xanthum Gum Portfolio:** Equal weight, Total Bond Index (VBINX) and Total Market (VTSMX). It is a "couch potato" portfolio that can also serve as a core holding.

Recipe 15. **US/International "Minestrone" Buy and Hold:** For aggressive investors seeking diversification this portfolio offers something for all under 65. Equal weight: GNMA (VFIIX), Long-Term Investment Grade (VWESX), and T. Rowe Price Emerging Market Bond (PREMX), S&P 500 Index (VFINX), REIT Index (VGSIX), Small-Cap Growth (VSGAX), Small-Cap Index (NAESX), Small-Cap Value Index (VISVX), Strategic Small-Cap (VSTCX), Explorer (VEXPX), Explorer Value (VEVFX), Energy (VGENX), Equity Income (VEIPX), Precious Metals (VGPMX), Recipe #10, Large Value (VIVAX), International Growth (VWIGX), Emerging Markets (VEIEX), FTSE All-World ex-US Small-Cap (VFSVX), Global ex-US Real Estate (VGXRX), Developed Markets (VDMIX), Convertible (VCVSX).

Recipe 16. **US/International "Lazy" *Du Moment* Solution for the Current Bear Market**: Equal weight Inflation-Protected (VIPSX), Total Market (VTSMX),

GNMA (VFIIX), High-Yield (VWEHX), Precious metals (VGPMX), Star (VGSTX), REIT Index (VGSIX), Global ex-US Real Estate Index (VGXRX), Energy (VGENX).

Recipe 17. **US/International "Coffee House":** This inexpensive and amazingly productive portfolio consists of 40% Total Bond Index (VBMFX), and 10% each of REIT (VGSIX), Total International (VGTSX), Small-Cap Value (VISVX), Small-Cap (NAESX), Large Value (VIVAX), and S&P 500 (VFINX). It is a portfolio that one can buy at any age and hold. It seeks diversification, captures the returns of each asset class, and performs above average in bull and bear markets. For those under 65. Insurance companies employ the nation's finest mathematicians who constantly deal with probabilities in order to effectively manage risk. They rarely make mistakes outperforming professional portfolio managers 80% of the time. Their portfolio management technique is simple–60% equities and 40% bonds, both components, well diversified. It provides reasonable yield, appropriate stability, exposure to many sectors, and yields 9% over time. The allocation assumes a low risk component, but given the fact that secular bears and bull markets alternate; the percentages can be tweaked to enhance total returns. For example, at the time of this writing, the bond portion can be reduced to 20%, and the international percentage increased. When the secular bear begins to dissipate, one should tweak the allocation again.

**"One-Stop Recipes": Fund of Funds and Target Retirement Funds:** Many large mutual fund companies offer one-stop shopping based on age in which cash, bonds, and equities are represented in "buy-and-forget" packages, such as Target Retirement, and Life Cycle Funds, both of which seek to take the guess work out of retirement investing. Target funds select the fund closest to retirement and the fund family takes care of the asset allocation and rebalancing. It is essential to select the low cost fund and compare the asset allocation of the three main asset classes. Target funds are not similar and vary enormously in terms of annual expenses, asset mix, and quality of positions.

Recipe 18. **Target Retirement Funds:** 2015 (VTXVX), 2020 (VTWNX), 2025 (VTTVX), 2030 (VTHRX), 2035 (VTTHX), 2040 (VFORX), 2045 (VTIVX), 2050 (VFIFX), 2055 (VFFVX), 2060 (VTTSX), Target Retirement Income (VTINX), for those already in retirement. Choose the one appropriate to your age and DCA. All may be considered Core holdings.

**In Search of Income:** "Fixed income" refers to an asset class in which fixed payments are made over varying periods from CDs, Treasuries, Agency bonds, investment grade, high-yield bonds, etc. There are many reasons why investors should have fixed income or income generating securities in their portfolio. One is that they provide income for living expenses if one is retired, and for those who are still working, they provide ballast by balancing market volatility. Another is to help reduce overall risk and accumulate cash to be used to take advantage of buying opportunities. The use of municipal bonds offers tax relief for those in the 28%-plus tax bracket. Global bonds and related instruments may offer above-average returns. Income-bearing securities are assumed to be the ultimate buy and hold investments as their primary function is to provide income and safety of principal. Because of governmental intrusions in free markets, and Fed purchases of debt, Treasuries are overpriced, represent the next bubble burst along with college loans, and reverse mortgages. In all instances, more yield means more risk. In the words of Casey Research, one must "navigate the politicized economy" carefully.

Many investors are lured to fixed income investments because of safety, steady income, comparatively low risk and portfolio diversity. The paucity of real total returns over the past 15 years, coupled with low interest rates has driven many investors to speculative income-bearing instruments and adventurous equities in search of higher yields. Declining interest rates since 1982 infer serious impending dangers as rates are poised to rise substantially. No one knows exactly when, but be aware that increases in the short-term will seriously impair portfolio values.

Recipe 19. **US Conservative Income Portfolio For The Current Secular Bear Market:** 30% each, GNMA (VFIIX), TIPS (VIPSX); equal weight, Short-Term Treasury Fund (VFISX), Short-Term Investment Grade (VFSTX), High-yield Corporate (VWEHX), Utilities (VPU), recipe 10, Managed Payout (VPGDX). Any age, DCA.

Recipe 20. **Income for the Current Secular Bear Market:** A couple aged 65-plus with $150,000 in savings, a home valued at $150,000, a $15,000 pension, and $20,000 from S.S.. This couple should continue working, the home sold with all cash invested: 40% laddered 6-month CDs, 20% each in Short-Term Corporate (VFSTX), Target Retirement Income (VTINX), and GNMA (VFIIX).

Recipe 21. **US Income and Growth, For The Current Secular Bear Market:** A couple with $500,000 in savings, a home worth $200,000, and a $40,000 pension. Continue working to age 70-plus and save every penny. The home should be sold with proceeds invested. The portfolio, for the duration of the current secular bear, offering moderate risk with some capital gains: 25% each of GNMA (VFIIX), Inflation-Protected (VIPSX); equal weight Short-Term Corporate Investment-Grade (VFSTX), Value (VIVAX), Equity Income (VEIPX), International Value (VTRIX), Recipe 10. DCA.

Recipe 22. **US/International Tax-sheltered Income For The Current Secular Bear Market:** For high net-wealth individuals with no need to withdraw money, 70%-plus in state-specific municipal, 30% Tax-managed Intl. (VTMGX). Taxable, DCA.

Recipe 23. **US/International Aggressive Income and Growth:** For high net-wealth individuals with no need to withdraw money: equal weight, High-yield

Corporate (VWEHX), Corporate Investment-Grade (VWESX), REIT Index (VGSIX), International Value (VTRIX); Emerging markets Select (VMMSX), Healthcare (VGHCX), Energy (VGENX), Explorer Value (VEVFX), PRIMECAP (VPMCX), Recipe 10, Managed Payout (VPGDX). DCA.

# Investment Strategies For The Nursery And "Puppy" Years

The things that one can elect to do with money are limited. Wanton spending is instant gratification that never enriches. You can lend to a bank, state, or government when you buy a CD or a bond, and while good in terms of safety, rarely will these instruments outperform inflation. Saving and investing are long-term disciplined endeavors that forego current for future consumption. Giving money away foolishly is never a good habit. Gifting children is always a good habit. With diligence and discipline, there is no reason why people cannot retire a millionaire several times over. Guidelines include:

1. The most important, two-decade period in the life of an investor is the period from birth to high school graduation. These early years are critical because learning the value and importance of money is the foundation of what follows until death. It guides the personal and professional evolution of one's life, all relationships, and employment. For working teenagers, beware the tendency for hedonistic behavior and debt. The road to financial ruin is littered with easy credit, something that must be resisted at an early age. Therefore, it is imperative for the investor, at the earliest age to accumulate assets that produce passive and portfolio income and to reinvest all dividends and interest forever.

2. For the rest of your life the following factors will influence your investment future to retirement: age at which the first dollar is invested, propensity to save, restraining spending proclivities, asset allocation, and aggregate dollars invested. At the earliest moment, contribute maximum levels to ROTH and 401(k) accounts, and monitor credit. Remember the old Chinese proverb: "The best time to plant a tree is 20 years ago. The second best time is today. Do not procrastinate.

3. A newborn has three secular bull and bear markets ahead of him, and given the fact that equities with time, outperform both cash and bonds, parents should be as aggressive as possible with all monies in their child's name. This is no time for extreme timidity. Invest for growth and diversify among the major growth

components such as technology, real estate, healthcare, pharmaceuticals, biotechnology, small-cap, and foreign equities. In addition, at least 50% should be invested in value stocks among large, mid, and small-caps. No bonds, no CDs, no "ultra-safe" investments need apply. When a grandchild is born gift at maximum levels each year. Forget market volatility, add additional monies as they become available, and above all, remember that your grandchild does not have to sell until retirement. In this regard, a gift of $5,000 at age one in the S&P 500 Index would translate to $4-plus million by age 70. As a parent, the best gift that you can offer your children is to sacrifice vacations, expensive presents, etc. and begin gifting as much money as possible. Instead of having your children begin their life with nothing, have them start with something. All progress requires sacrifice: it may be little or a lot, but sacrifice is an indispensable ingredient in successful investing. Sacrificing for children may sound like a novel idea, but it is sound policy. In addition, provide work for your children as soon as possible and invest the income.

4. Obviously, baby steps are necessary as large contributions will not be automatic at birth, but over time the small amounts from birthday presents, odd jobs, and gifts, etc., begin to accumulate into serious sums. The fact that parents are in a position to begin investing early in their child's future, time can be put to advantage. In addition, parents should emphasize frugality, discipline, patience, and the avoidance of forces that detract from wealth creation. Children should be taught the benefits of saving and investing, and the toleration of mistakes with their allowance a given. Eventually, if your sage advice perseveres, they will learn from any missteps. It should be remembered that retiring, as a multi-millionaire is not a difficult assignment. All you need is patience and discipline (this is the hardest), time (the easiest–more than 70-plus years of investing), money (you have the rest of your life to make it), and a strategy to increase, not lose wealth. Children should be encouraged to not "follow the crowd," but to question, to think about the future, and to consider the impossible. Your children may not always be enamored by these virtues at the time but, as they get older, you are guaranteed to be viewed as a much wiser and smarter parent. While few in their late teens ever think that they have six decades to invest, this notion is of critical importance to those with a sense of purpose and expectations. Therefore, it behooves a person to take time seriously, as every passing year diminishes the opportunity for wealth accumulation. The objective is to start saving and investing as early as possible and curb the proclivity to spend.

The investing business attempts to beat time because the decision of when to buy, sell, or hold is time-based. Assuming that you have bought quality, time is the most valuable asset in your arsenal. At birth, the individual has maximum time; at 20 years of age, the individual will have a minimum of 50 working years, and with the passing of each year, time, like sand in an hourglass, is lost and will never be retrieved; at 70, there is little time left, as you have lived most of your years; at 80, you need glasses to see the sand in the upper part of the hourglass; and at 90, you need a magnifying glass to find any sand particles. The advantages of an early start are immense and irretrievable. Let us assume that an 18-year-old opens an IRA, contributes $60 a month until retirement at age 65, and receives a 10% annual compounded return. His total contribution of $33,840 would grow to more than $500,000. If the same individual opened an IRA at age 45 and contributed $200 a month, for a total contribution of $48.000, he would have less than $152,000 at age 65. Given the fact that the average investor has five decades to invest as an adult, there are advantages in beginning as soon as possible. Therefore, the first investment phase, from birth to age 40, is the accumulation stage. Plato said more than 2,000 years ago that, "The beginning is the most important part of the work." For those under 18 years of age, yesterday was the time to begin saving and investing, and because of an extended time horizon, the youth of America are presented with an exceptional opportunity to tolerate and assume risk.

5. The first important event that can happen in the life of a young person is the adoption of the work ethic, as the experience will teach an important lesson about the nature of the real world. The second best thing that can happen is to have a losing trade and to hopefully learn from the mistake. The third best thing is to learn to save in order to appreciate the value of money. The worst thing that could befall the young investor is a spectacular first trade, something that might lead him to think that he has extraordinary talent rather than dumb luck, as chance plays a far more important role in investing than most people think.

6. Youthful investing offers a number of behavioral contrasts that are not easily reconciled: One recognizes the need for maximum saving and investing in order to capture the rewards of compounding over time, but finds it difficult to restrain spending urges in order to "have a good time" in the present. In addition, limited income suppresses the urgency for saving and investing, as the small sums available do not appear to be important. However, if you save, you will spend less and have more to invest.

7. Children must be taught not to waste. In an absolute manner, everyone does, but one ought to strive to reduce the degrading habit to a minimum. The less you waste the greater the saving potential and the more you have to invest. The sooner one learns this lesson, the faster one reaches critical mass. Children must be taught to view their portfolio in a holistic manner with them as the CEO. Every investment decision, whether good or bad, has consequences because "it's all about money, and the rest is conversation."

8. Make every attempt to emulate the more successful as it is a rewarding strategy.

9. Four, important variables confront women: a longer life expectancy then men; lower pay; fewer years in the workforce; and since there are more single mothers than single fathers, all of the foregoing affect investment decisions. Women need to invest more effectively—and most do.

10. Part of this cohort is referred to as "millennial" that refer to a large group (88 million) that face severe challenges. They will inherent the bulk of parental debts in a stagflating economy for an extended period. Their future is clouded with uncertainties, and in order to survive retirement, they must become extremely productive and vigilant and learn to reduce or eliminate the most notorious parental money blunders. If not, they will be remembered as a lost generation. In this connection, remember the wise words of Will Rogers on how people learn: "The ones that learn by reading. The few who learn by observation. The rest that have to pee on the electric fence and find out for themselves."

11. Invest in yourself, forever because you would require in excess of $25 million at retirement age. This journey will be an uphill climb.

## Recipes

Due to the small initial amount of money involved, begin with the simplest core recipe and gradually morph into the complicated. As the child gets older and assets accumulate, carefully separate monies into taxable and tax-sheltered accounts. DCA religiously.

#1 or #2; #3; #5, #6; for conservative investors #7, #10, #11, or other balanced funds. All may be purchased now and held. Should substantial funds become available, double all holdings, and add the following: #9 or #13.

# For Those in Their 20s

Understand that you will be "able" to earn more throughout your working years than the person without a college or university degree. That is all! It does not mean that you will save more, invest more profitably, retire more comfortably, nor that you will be a better citizen, a better parent, or a better spouse. Graduate in four years or less. More than 60% of all undergraduates do not, and, in the process, waste time, money and effort. Bad friends and bad habits go together; hence, the importance to choose and socialize with older, more successful associates. Habits are acutely powerful (whether good or bad) and difficult to change (particularly the latter), but they can be changed through discipline and focused determination. Once negative habits are broken and discipline and patience dominate behavior, financial success is nearly assured as fewer mistakes are made. In a knowledge-based economy, education usually means higher earning power as higher degrees earn more. While few doubt that this relationship between education and money earned exists in real life, there are several, essential aspects of this mix that should be noted. The first is that historic differences have been bridged. At least 40% of all college graduates do not make more money than skilled workers without a college degree; 50% move back home after graduation because they cannot afford to live alone; and fewer than 60% find suitable employment in their major. Today's colleges are much different from those in the past. Nearly anyone who is breathing and with cash in hand is accepted and able to graduate with a "B+" average. Standards have fallen, and most graduates find it hard to compete with their cohorts from other nations. Chances are if you are a "C" student, you will graduate at age 24, and upon graduation, will find employment in fields that are not considered "professional." Therefore, why invest money, time, and effort for six years and graduate indebted when you can begin working, saving, and investing at age 18? At the time of this writing, I have seen advertisements for Ph.D. starting salaries at the rank of assistant professor for $65,000. Does anyone think that this is "good money" after investing one-third of a lifetime in the classroom? A college education is a good thing, but not for everyone, and certainly not for society as a whole as it costs $400,000-plus to produce one undergraduate degree. This is not written to disparage those who do not go to a college, but to mention the fact that not everyone is college material.

Make a list of your educational and professional priorities, stick to them, and resist the temptation to deviate. Your career must be your first priority, as it will produce income. The amount of money that you will make is a function of the knowledge and skills procured and your attitude toward your profession. Consider your person as the number one investment, as it will determine how you accumulate wealth. Further your career at all costs by improving your skills in order to augment your income as much as possible. If it means additional education, get it by sacrificing other activities to meet your career objectives. Treat work with respect and never neglect it. Whatever your education and age, take several Dale Carnegie courses on self-improvement, effective speaking, etc. Read the business section of newspapers, investment books and magazines. Take accounting courses, and as many investment classes as possible. Apply the "law of relativity," to every aspect of your life. (When the population saves 1% of gross income, you save 20%.) Sacrifice short-term burning desires and contemporary life styles for something better in the future. Clearly distinguish between saving, investing, speculating, and gambling, and remember that gambling is not investing, speculating is not investing, and that investing requires time, patience, discipline, and knowledge. Remember that a person only has a 52-year window to amass wealth, raise a family, and buy a home. For the rest of your life focus on how much you keep rather on how much you earn. Learn to speak Mandarin and graduate "debt free." A few essentials include:

1. Place yourself in the following picture: You have graduated college and are currently employed in a position with a future, and have moved into your new apartment. Besides furnishing your bedroom and living room, you must also invest in a kitchen. The organization of refrigerator and cabinets is essential. First, purchase high quality knives that would last a lifetime. If you use sugar, flour, or other dry goods in sizeable amounts, buy in bulk. Buy with coupons, and fruits, vegetables, and meat products when on sale. Cook for two to three days at a time, and never waste food. These are major expenditures and a full weekly accounting is important. If you exert discipline in the kitchen, you will also exercise similar behavior with your investments. In fact, your success in kitchen management is identical with the management of your investments: reduce costs, purchase on a timely basis, do not waste, and never overindulge. Prepare a "to do" list, and update it annually for the rest of your life. This includes a ledger of all your assets and liabilities, savings, wages and all other income, employment goals, familial obligations, etc. In addition, monitor all expenses and seek ways to reduce them. Remember that money does not come with instructions, and providence does not control our lives. Take charge, read, attain as much knowledge as possible, and question the financial media. Furthermore, create sensible investment goals, a proper asset allocation, and exert discipline.

2. Saving a minimum of 20% is your main priority. In addition, save some more. A lifelong saving strategy is the first step in a series leading to prosperity, the latter quite elusive without a saving ethic. Save all free money, that comes your way in the way of an inheritance, bonus, pay raise, etc. No matter how small the amount, save and invest. When you consciously do not consume the extra coffee or soda, place the money in a jar, and should this be done daily, by the end of the month, you have enough to invest, no matter how small the amount. The crucial aspect of this behavior is that it be done, and done yesterday. Wealth creation does not occur in the abstract but begins instantly when the individual saves that first dollar and continues to do so on a regular basis forever. Should you expect to receive an inheritance, preserve it and do not spend it, and should you consume the legacy foolishly, you, essentially, have insulted the person(s) who gave it to you. If the young investor remembers anything in life, it should be the words of Charles Darwin: "It is not the strongest of the species that survives, or the most intelligent, but the one most responsive to change." Therefore, remain focused, learn to adapt, and bear in mind that no one has a monopoly on expertise, knowledge, insight, and erudition. Remember: the spending curve is rising. If it is possible to live at home, one is able to save more than 70% of disposable income. If it is possible to relocate and eliminate the car, one can raise the saving level further.

3. Contribute maximum levels to retirement accounts. Save 20% and begin the process with the first paycheck, and without interruption. How you structure your financial life at this early age will determine where and how you live the rest of your life. Establish a clear life-long discipline that you will not spend more money than you earn, to be frugal, and not borrow. The importance of saving as much as possible and as soon as possible is enormous. Never borrow from retirement accounts, as this money must never be put at risk and always resist lifestyle inflation at all costs. It is hard for this cohort to make sound retirement investments. It is, however, the most critical age cohort for future financial comfort as money has a long time span to grow.

4. For those with a family, keep in mind that there is a 14% chance that you will die and a 28% chance to be disabled before 65. Buy term insurance! There are other long-term issues to be faced: possible multiple marriages, multiple families, multiple careers, and multiple retirement plans. Try to keep your life simple and trouble free.

5. For those without a college education, the challenges for saving and, hence, retirement are not as bleak as they appear, as there are many with incomes above $200,000 and no money in the bank. Frugality, common sense, and prudent behaviors will provide for your retirement. The critical issues are to save as much as possible, exercise extreme discipline, and never place money in jeopardy. A poor investment and wasted time is to graduate college with a useless degree, $37,000 in loans and no job prospects. The future of the US is in human capital and not the production of useless capital. Choose your career path wisely, supplement

your skills and be prepared to migrate where employment opportunities present themselves.

6. Live as close as possible to work and services in order to minimize transportation costs. If you live in exurbia, your biggest cost will not be housing or food, but transportation. The sooner you purchase a two or three family home, the better, as you will essentially live rent-free for the rest of your life. Resist the temptation to move often, as any move no matter the distance, generates expenses and headaches. Consider the purchase of a home cautiously because few homes appreciate in value when adjusted for inflation.

7. At this age, many "forks in the road" tempt one, and the likelihood of a bad fork chosen is quite high. Be prepared, therefore, to endure many hardships in order to acquire insight. As in the classic, *The Alchemist*, where Santiago pursues worldly treasures, you, the young investor, face a similar journey. The alchemist, promising riches, does not exist, never has, and never will. It is up to you to acquire the essential wisdom to achieve wealth creation. How you handle adversity in youth will define your future.

8. Become responsible. It is most important at this age to take stock of what surrounds you and make appropriate decisions for you and your family. Note that half of all American workers do not participate in a retirement account and fewer than 20% contribute the maximum allowable. If you do not save and invest for retirement, would you prefer to be like the 50% of all Americans 65 years and older whose main income is S.S.? Do you wish to struggle under the yoke of perpetual debt? There are only six parallel avenues available to provide for a comfortable future–frugality, saving, judicious investing, patience, and discipline. Mastering control of your daily habits will guarantee financial success in future decades. The abridged list that will add more than $1 million for the next 50 years include: the use of mass transit, the local library, a shopping list, the avoidance of impulsive purchases, paying off the credit card balance each month, increasing deductibles, reducing "fixed" costs, never buying a depreciating asset with borrowed money, and gambling. Stay out of trouble as we live in a highly litigious society.

9. Divide your dollars into three pots. The first pot contains your fixed-cost monies necessary for your monthly living expenses. Do not live in a place you cannot afford, drive a car you cannot afford, and surround yourself with household electrical gismos you cannot afford. The second contains discretionary items that are usually not important to daily existence and should be reduced. This is the pot that is most appealing to people in their 20s, and should be resisted as these expenditures reduce the size of the next pot. The third is your wealth-creating pot containing monies that are to be invested for the future. This is the most important pot, and the one that must be nurtured.

10. Be aware of the various types of income—earned, passive, and portfolio. The first is that which emanates from work activity, and is fixed to hours, days, weeks, or months of engaged work. Passive income is that which is the product of a period of work with a stream of money continuing after the initial work activity has ceased. Portfolio income is the income received from dividends, rent, interest, etc. The key to becoming wealthy is the conversion of earned income to passive and portfolio income, and taking advantage of compounding as these assets continue to produce a capital stream. Remember that the government taxes earned income at a higher rate than passive and portfolio income, and since a complete working career is before you, concentrate on developing passive and portfolio income.

11. At this age just starting out in life and giving birth to a career, you have several options when it comes to money: a. Spend all of it and enjoy life. b. You are so smart that you will concentrate on stock picking to make easy money. c. You become an expert at market timing. d. You take the ultra-safe road and invest in CDs and Treasuries. e. You follow the asset allocation guidelines of the 401(k) at work. All of the above options are inappropriate. The first thing that you should do is to get smart by acquiring investment knowledge. The second important item you should consider is taking the subject of saving and investment seriously, and the third thing is to stop entertaining thoughts that you will find the "needle in the haystack." Remember: Your primary focus should lie with your career and not "playing the market," nor "timing the market," or chasing "hot tips"; pay close attention to your asset allocation, but be prepared to over and underweight sectors in conformity with secular markets; participate in all retirement plans and maximize your contributions; for the rest of your life, your objective is to make "net assets grow."

12. Create the widest possible information field, or the most diverse "range" of close associations. Just as a successful investor does not overly concentrate on a particular asset class, but diversifies, the successful "alpha" diversifies friendships. Therefore, associate with people who are older and more successful than you are, as they have accumulated more wealth and experience. All associations must be committed to making straight furrows.

13. The best investment a young investor can make is to pay off existing debt, and not assume any additional debt. At this age, the use of credit is irresistible because credit "gets you things" sooner, but at a price, and that is the payment of interest. Part of this behavior lies in the fact that youth are myopic. They rarely project into the future and go through life unaware of the benefits of saving and long-term investing. The American youth have been conditioned to think of "now" and never "later"; conditioned to spend and not save; to squander and not be thrifty.

14. The following imperatives will do much to enhance wealth: do not marry a spendthrift, do not deviate from a strict saving habit, and purchasing assets on credit that depreciate with time.

15. Recognize the fact that should you wish to dictate your destiny, you must control the balance sheet. If you fail to manage your finances, you cannot control your destiny.

## Investment Strategies

1. "The time has come to talk of many things," said the walrus in "Alice and Wonderland," and when you are in your 20s, it would behoove you to begin taking saving and investing seriously because more than 90% of all in this age cohort have negative net worth. What to do with your first dollar? Save it; then invest it; and then reinvest all interest and dividends. What not to do: spend it on jewelry, tobacco, beer, and tattoos. Also, be prepared to endure many hardships in order to acquire insight. 2. For those earning $30,000 annually, the first thing to do is to get a second job, and place the income in a ROTH. 3. Over the course of the next 7-plus years, the current secular bear market will be characterized by stagflation. Therefore, due to the presence of treacherous water, it is best to overweigh commodities, EMs, TIPS, REITs, and securities whose total returns are greater than inflation. 4. This cohort will reverse the parental profligate behavior of past decades; employment will not be secure, wages will not be rising rapidly, work benefits will be curtailed, and unless prudent and wise saving and investing takes place retirement will not be secure. Do not depend on government and never entertain thoughts that it will protect you and your assets. The future is uncertain, and one must, at the most elementary level, self-insure and prepare to fund a personal retirement. Speaking before Congress in 2005, Alan Greenspan, in one of his rare candid moments said: "I fear that we may have already committed more physical resources to the baby-boom generation in its retirement years than our economy has the capacity to deliver." The "American Dream" is in jeopardy; for 60% of the population, it has literally disappeared. Therefore, what are the available avenues for wealth accumulation? You may prevail in an extremely lucky manner in a lottery, but that is unlikely; inherit wealth, but that applies to less than 20% of the population; marry wealth, also highly unlikely; or you may triumph in a legal dispute, also highly unlikely. However, anyone can accumulate wealth by being disciplined and frugal. Curtailing the small, seemingly incidental and unnecessary expenditures, and investing the proceeds as soon as possible will always prevail as an unfailing policy. In fact, through the grace of compound interest, the strategy is mechanical and immutable. 5. With equities too expensive, slow GDP growth, and aging boomers struggling, equity markets are poised to deliver below average historic returns. Therefore, select companies and sectors that benefit from slow growth: utilities, exporters, countries with a healthy economy, and companies with a good balance sheet paying steady dividends. 6. From now on, emphasize real estate, small-cap and value stocks. 7. You must be

prepared to save much more than your parents did in order to retire in 2060. How much more? At age 72, you would require in excess of $20 million to retire comfortably. Unfortunately, the 20-30 year age cohort currently earns less than $30,000 annually with 76% not saving for retirement. 401(k) accounts contain less than $3,000. However, saving 8% of a $30,000 income (and increasing it annually) will produce a nest egg greater than $1.4 million over 40 years. This cohort has suffered much since 2007. 8. Buy "forever stamps." They are liquid, guaranteed to appreciate, outperform inflation, and there are no capital gain taxes.

## Recipes

Select and hold recipes #1 or #2, #3, #5, #6, #7, #9, #10, #17, or balanced funds. For the college graduate receiving a large "gift" consider #13.

# For Those In Their 30s

It is estimated that 36% of the population, aged 30-39, faces a future of mounting debts. Yet it appears that lassitude reigns in this age cohort as individuals show little concern about retirement. Those in their 20s are too busy spending and have the notion that white hair and wrinkles will never be experienced. Those between 30 and 39 are too busy working and spending, thinking that life will be good to them in perpetuity. This cohort is in deep trouble as it will be forced to pay the mountains of debt of their parents, and since many acquired profligate habits, they will be under enormous pressure to curtail expenditures. They will inherit little, will have to save more and work harder longer. One bright spot is that when they reach their 40s the current secular bear market will be over so the equity portion of their investments will have the potential of generating higher returns. Nevertheless, this cohort, if it wishes to retire in comfort, must boost the savings rate dramatically, because, while not in the most productive working period it will critically test discipline and patience. 1. There are many distractions that will drain cash flow: mortgage, family, peer pressure, and the illness of "I must keep up with the Joneses." The spending curve is rising rapidly. 2. Concentrate on the production of passive and portfolio income. Monitor investments in tax-sheltered accounts carefully, and for those who are more risk-averse, reduce growth by 5%-10% and increase fixed-income and dividend-paying securities to 50%. Reduce debt, save as much as possible, and fund retirement accounts to maximum levels. 3. As the aggregate value of your investments increase, maintain your investment educational level, and start thinking of the legacy that you will be leaving your children, because what you do in the rest of this decade will determine your future financial productivity. 4. Never use home equity to invest in equity markets. 5. Should you lose your employment; the next job will pay 20% less. 6. For this cohort, current net worth is $14,250; earnings $43,000; credit card balances $8,335; home equity $2,000; and the 401(k) is worth $14,000. Sixty-five percent have experienced a decline in net wealth of 30% since 2000. Interestingly, more than 50% of the nation's unemployed is under 40. If the 18-40 age cohort does not heed the advice in previous pages, it will eventually become a "lost" generation.

Since 2008, more part-time positions have been created than full-time with the 60-plus age cohort taking market share from younger workers.

## Recipes

Select, purchase and hold recipes #1 or #2, #3, #5, #6, #7, #8, #9, #10, #13, and #17. Gradually increase income and balanced funds.

# For Those In Their 40s

The vast majority of all working Americans in their 40s are not adequately prepared for retirement. Few realize what the probabilities to age 75 and beyond are and how much retirement will eventually cost. Given the current state of company pension policies, the prudent investor should not rely on company plans. For those in public service the picture is much brighter, but plans are being altered as we speak, so there is an element of risk there as well. Be prepared for higher taxes and reduced S.S. and pension benefits, and that includes healthcare. Beginning at age 40 and continuing into the 50s, the spending curve peaks. Since a good deal of this spending amounts to profligate behavior driven by children and conspicuous consumption, the rate of spending must be reigned and the saving rate increased. This is also an age cohort that is vulnerable to divorce, something that triggers foolish expenditures by both parties. One would also encounter conflicting obligations, and the easy road of indebtedness not be taken. The 40-50 age cohort "yearns" for things, most of which are unnecessary, expensive, and dangerous to financial health. The pressure to assume more debt rises to new levels, and like the previous age cohort, it will test your demeanor to remain resolute in your convictions and to stay financially sound. If you have not seriously begun saving and investing for retirement, consider the fact that most retire on less than $140,000, net worth.

Age 40 is critical because if the individual does not alter past habits, the future will be bleak, as this will be the last opportunity to make up for past hedonistic behavior. Therefore, tear up credit cards, become more frugal, save more than 20% of gross income, drive your car longer, and raise your deductibles. If you have not saved, nor invested toward your retirement, you must immediately play "catch-up" with 50% of your portfolio composed of income producing securities. Another goal is to capture market returns of the remaining secular markets remaining in your lifetime. Furthermore, due to the inherent inefficiencies of a suburban society, life style changes are crucial, of which high-density living will intensify. Those living in rural areas greater than 50 miles from a central city will become more self-sufficient, less spendthrift, and less mobile. Real estate values will decline in these areas, and increase in central cities as the post-WWII suburban migration reverses. By age 45, one should have saved six times annual salary. Few individuals reach that goal, and should that be the case, double the saving level. All bonuses, tax refunds, inheritance distributions, and other "found money" should be invested. Should you lose employment in this age cohort, the next job would pay 22% less. This cohort has a net worth of $60,000, earns $48,000, 76% own a home valued at $140,000 with 20% equity, 50% maintain a credit card balance of $9,900, and 48% have a 401(k) worth $41,000. About 40% have negative net wealth. This cohort has experienced net wealth decline of 35% since 2000, and would require $5 million to retire.

## Recipes

Select, purchase and hold recipes #1, #2, #3, #4, #5, and #6, #7, #8, #9, #10 and #18. Should you feel uncomfortable, reduce #9 and #10, #17, and add a combination of balanced and income funds. From now on income bearing instruments should exceed 50% of the portfolio.

# For Those In Their 50s

This age cohort, born after WW II and extending to 1964, commonly called the "baby boomer" generation, represents 40% of the American workforce and has started to retire. It involves 80 million people who have enjoyed the longest longevity, the lowest birthrate, and have become the most notorious spenders in the nation's history. Spoiled enormously throughout their lifetime, they will be a burden for decades because they are the most indebted. They also became the most obese, drug-afflicted, and wasteful generation—features that have progressively gotten worse as they aged. Blighted with wanton consumption, they will be unable to adopt a frugal lifestyle in retirement because this "consuming" generation continues to deny that a financial disaster looms beyond the horizon. Blithely, baby boomers are caught in a secular bear market–a market that will inflict serious psychological and physical damage to themselves and their investments. The "me now" generation, after the death of their parents, are left without a protector and, for the first time in their history, are left without a financial rudder. More than 50% are unprepared for this treacherous journey past the age of 65. Producing just 1.2 children, they will be faced with expensive houses, high stock valuations, and huge quantities of personal debt and overpriced Treasuries. More than 10,000 baby boomers are retiring every day; more than 50% have an outstanding mortgage of more than $85,000; more than 70% say they cannot reduce their spending habits; and 80% are facing lower living standards. In 2006, the first baby-boomer began retiring and, along with that event, a steady stream of selling of accumulated assets has begun, begging the question: Who will purchase these assets in future years? This torrent of selling will accelerate and, by 2017, a huge avalanche of additional mandatory selling will begin to take place, thus depressing markets.

Unfortunately, their problems are not about to disappear, but compound. 1. More than 60% maintain unacceptable debt levels. 2. Not only do they have a mortgage that is entirely too large, but 10% also finance a mortgage on a second home. 3. Falling home and stock prices have reduced their wealth by more than $7 trillion in the past 13 years, and more than 70% will die in debt. 4. Twenty-five percent have raided their retirement accounts on grounds of "hardship" (some withdrawing 60%-plus of their contributions). 5. Most have lost their DB pension plans and invested poorly in their DC plans. 6. Incomes, when adjusted for inflation, have been reduced by more than 30% since 1999, and the prudent have reduced spending. 7. Physically mobile and imbued with a spendthrift attitude throughout their lifetime, they now find themselves on the edge of poverty in a secular bear market, the worst possible pre-retirement and retirement scenario. In order to get back on track, they must embrace austerity and save more than 50% of their disposable income. Emergency measures must be established. 8. The vast majority will not exit the workforce until they are at least 72; while it is the most indulged and the most educated, it is a cohort that saved the least and will suffer the most in retirement, as more than 75% cannot afford to grow old. A similar percentage has insufficient retirement funds. For a comfortable retirement, boomers need a much larger nest egg than their parents; unfortunately, this is an elusive goal, as DB plans are history, life expectancy has increased, falling interest rates have circumscribed income creation, healthcare costs and inflation have risen, stagnant/declining wages, bad investment decisions, and a flat stock market for 14 years with two 45%-plus market declines has decimated wealth. One thing is certain: they will dabble less on Wall Street and spend less on Main Street. They have less than $44,000 in savings. After borrowing from 401(k) accounts, the net wealth has been reduced to $331,000, 40% less than in 2000. At retirement they would require $3 million.

# Preparing For Retirement

1. Be cognizant of the following major life-altering events: At 62 you become eligible for S.S., Medicare at 65, and at 70½, you must begin taking minimum required distributions. Lurking in the shadows is the ability to maintain an acceptable living standard. Furthermore, retirement is not what it is cracked up to be. Americans are consumed with the utopic notion that once out of work, they can play golf and tennis each day, eat out every evening, go cruising, etc. Nothing can be further from the truth. As the "rusty" years approach, higher interest rates and inflation, and a lower standard of living will greet you. Therefore, do not believe the propaganda of "early retirement" being "peachy." Working people live longer, are much happier than those who retire early, and do not fall into an abyss of bad habits. In addition, the timing of retirement is particularly crucial for those without a pension, as financial strategies will vary whether one is retiring at the beginning of a secular bear or a secular bull market. Since nearly all assets decline during a secular bear market, let us assume that a couple of humble means were planning to retire in 2000 when the current secular bear market began. If they were on the cusp of solvency and needed income, they had few pleasant alternatives to stop the erosion of their net wealth.

2. Pre-retirees have now reached the autumnal period of their life–maximum earnings, an empty nest, with investing capabilities circumscribed. Major, but gradual, shifts are about to occur in terms of lifestyles, health, employment, and mindset. Most important, these events are arriving to the point where time is no longer an ally. Choices made in the midst of the current secular bear market will have either positive or devastating effects as the number of people in the 60-plus age cohort, with little or no retirement savings, continues to increase. Therefore, this cohort falls into two groups: those that have prepared for retirement, and those who did not. The former is about 20% of the cohort, and appears to be well endowed until it meets its maker. Individuals who are addicted to spending and debt characterize the second group. The youngest will require between $3.5-$4.5 million to retire comfortably, and this is a very disconcerting issue since few have the means. Since 46% of Americans have less than $10,000 saved for retirement,

baby boomers have a 80%-plus retirement gap, meaning that they will reach retirement age with less than 80% of necessary assets to maintain their traditional lifestyle, and in the words of Ben Bernanke: "Baby boomers will strain the American economy." And let us not forget the words of George Forman: "The question isn't at what age I want to retire, it's at what income." Two ways of augmenting retirement income is to increase savings and max "catch-up" contributions. In addition, eliminate all debt (get liquid) and consider all taxes in retirement.

3. Plan for inflation. Every bond interest payment will progressively purchase less and less. The principal is paid in nominal, not real dollars, and the bondholder suffers from devalued principal at maturity. Furthermore, expunge all "I want to get rich quickly" schemes in order to make up for lost time. While it is advantageous to benefit by overweighing certain market sectors, your primary objective is to "preserve capital" with acceptable levels of growth to stay ahead of inflation. In addition, reduce your overhead. If downsizing does not occur consciously, inflation and economic exigencies will do it for those who procrastinate. Two practical ways of reducing overhead is to change to a smaller home or apartment and alter your lifestyle. By living in an apartment in a central city, it is easy to reduce "fixed costs" by eliminating all cars, be closer to services and be able to take advantage of social and recreational opportunities that are available at little or no cost. Often, an aging couple, and eventually a sole survivor, is overwhelmed by the maintenance of a house.

4. Should you require an income of $100,000, the necessary assets needed would be a minimum of $3,000,000, at a 3% annual return. This does not take inflation into consideration, which means that should you live to the age of 90, you may require a nest egg of $6 million. Also to be considered is long-term healthcare. Simple nursing home care amounts to more than $300 a day, or $110,000 annually. About half of all Americans over the age of 75 spend some time in a nursing home, and 85% aged 80-plus reside in a healthcare facility. It should also be noted that in 1936, there were 43 contributing workers for each S.S. beneficiary, and today there are fewer than five.

5. Consider the retirement venue for your remaining life. Living costs in the US are not equal, as many cities and states are more "dollar friendly" than others. Property, gasoline, sales, pension, S.S., capital gains taxes, etc. vary by venue. Taxes vary from a low of $2,400 in Cheyenne, Wyoming, to $18,627 in Bridgeport, Connecticut. Seven states do not tax earned income as well as dividends and interest. Tax consequences matter and increase in importance with age and the size of net worth. Some states will honor the sanctity of public pension distributions from other states and many will not exempt private pensions from state taxes. The number of permutations are many and financially significant.

6. Plan on living longer; that is the good news. The bad news is that you have to save more to live 10-plus years longer. The 65-plus cohort increased from 3 million in 1900, to 7 million during the 1930s, 17 million in 1960, and 27 million in 1980, and it is expected to more than double by 2030. More than 1.5 million are 90-plus. At age 65, a person is expected to live another 18 years; at age 70, another 14 years; at age 75, another 12 years; at age 80, another 9.3 years; at age 85, another 7 years; at age 90, another 5 years; and at age 95, another 3 years. It is prudent to expect to spend one-third of existence in retirement, and the need to outlive retirement assets requires effort and considerable discipline.

7. Plan on working longer. The civilian labor force participation rate for those 60-plus years has risen from 20% in 2000 to 31% in 2013. Forty-two percent say that they will work until they die.

8. Economic insecurity grows with age. Four-fifths of all adults scuffle with poverty, unemployment, and dependency on public assistance programs. More than 58% above the age of 60 are officially classified as "poor," and more than 80% cannot find work.

## Recipes

Select, purchase and hold recipes #1 or #2, #3, #4, #5, #6, #7, #8, #9, #10, #11, #12, #13, #17, or #18. For the more conservative add balanced funds, and for those with limited funds emphasize the safest income funds.

# For Those In Retirement

## Retirement Myths

1. That your expenses will be reduced at retirement by 30%. Chances are that your life style will not be curtailed to any appreciable degree, and due to tax creep, inflation, and S.S. swindles, chances are that you will need more money, not less. Assuming that retirees will live for another 20 years, the remaining life will essentially be without children and work, and, therefore, a new social order will be born that will exert a colossal influence in the market place in terms of consumer expenditures and political voting behavior. 2. "My income stream is strong enough to outperform inflation." Reality suggests otherwise. Fifty percent of all Americans have less than $10,000 in savings. 3. Government will see me through the roughest moments of retirement. S.S. and modest savings will prove to be insufficient. Be prepared for a 30% cut in S.S. benefits and draconian means testing. 4. Your pension, from either a governmental agency or a corporation, is as solid as Fort Knox. Severe modifications and future disbursements may be reduced, and not keep up with inflation. 5. "I know what I'm doing." "I can outlive my assets even if I withdraw10% annually." Reality suggests otherwise. 6. That equities do not belong in a retirement portfolio. You need growth, and, that means equities. 7. That $1 million is a sufficient nest egg to see me through my remaining 20-35 years. Hardly! One million dollars is no longer the symbol of wealth as the amount returns only $10,000 at 1% at the local bank. 8. Early retirement is good. The longer you work the greater the propensity to defer taxes, increase future S.S. distributions, save more, improve your physical and mental health, etc. 9. That Treasuries are a vital element in wealth creation. They are a vital element in wealth preservation. Interest rates are rising for the duration of current retirees' life span.

## Retirement Problems

1. Avoid one of the dictionary definitions of retirement–"withdrawing into seclusion," and make every effort to stay alert and active, both physically and mentally. Boredom is particularly worrisome as it can affect your mental state and promote bad financial decisions, as senescence degrades investment skills.

Disinterest in economic, political, and social affairs, and a need for solitary living compounds the many problems listed. 2. While able to control key elements of a portfolio's performance, the retiree has no control over the erosive effects of inflation. This is particularly deadly for those without an inflation adjusted pension, and sufficient funds. During the interval 1965-1974, inflation averaged 5.2% while stocks gained but 1.2%, and the period 1975-1982 was far worse. In fact, the erosion in purchasing power during the last secular bear market for the unfortunate retiree rose by more than 50%, and while inflation is nothing new, it is accelerating no matter what Washington says. At 4% inflation, $100,000 erodes to $82,193 after 5 years; $67,556 after 10 years; $55,526 after 15 years; and $45,639 after 20 years. Currently inflation is more than 5%. 3. Personal appearance and lack of grooming is an indication of indifference, or worse. 4. Preservation of capital is paramount, as only one out every 10 retirees outlives their money. 5. Be prepared for market downturns. During the market meltdown in 2000, many investors lost anywhere from 40% to 90% of their portfolio value. During the 2008 meltdown, many investors lost 35% to 60%. 6. Senior citizens have been decimated in recent decades through increased taxes and fees and artificially low interest rates. The standard of living of nearly all retirees has declined, and the outlook is even worse under the current stagflating environment. 7. Because of increased longevity, retirement has become more expensive, and the ability of retirees stretching their retirement dollars is limited. 8. Among DMs, the US ranks near the bottom in the provision of secure retirement accounts for its aging citizens. The safety net has been lowered and fully 80%-plus of the population eventually becomes, for all practical purposes, a ward of the state. The average retiree has a net wealth of less than $40,000. Under these conditions, most retirees do not budget and they need to in order to track every cent. 9. Taking S.S. early. About 60% do so, and it is a huge mistake. 10. Assuming a reverse mortgage. There are nearly 1 million fraudulent loans outstanding. 11. Never underestimate the cumulative costs of inflation, taxes, fixed expenses, hobbies, and relatives. 12. Should you lose employment at 65, the next job would pay 51% less. 13. Not having sufficient funds. Low saving levels frame a dire picture perfectly, in which reliance on S.S., Medicaid, and Medicare dominate. Three in five retired persons live below the poverty line, and their number is increasing. 14. Not moving to venues with lower living expenses. 15. Retiring with no plan for steady income.

## Sources of Income

Income investors are of two types: those that have large sums of money to protect, and those with more humble assets who wish to avoid the vicissitudes of daily living challenges. The first group may have a significant portion of their net wealth in more lucrative growth investments, to live either on income-generating securities, or to compound interest. The second group who wish to preserve capital fall in a category called "no-growth seekers." They merely seek to live on monthly returns from an income portfolio. Depending on circumstances, the bulk of monies will be from bonds and cash. If the retirement account along with S.S. and other assets is sufficiently large to outlive the individual, a variable portion should be invested in equities to provide growth. For the average retirement couple that lives on less than $35,000 a year, the options are limited. For both groups, the dilemma in retirement investing rests on the inflation risk offered by cash, Treasuries, municipals and corporate bonds, and counterbalanced by capital risk offered by foreign, small-cap and all other equities. In addition, prudent retirees should be cautious of "income for life model" retirement strategies as they are pregnant with hazards. Nevertheless, retirees ought to pay attention to the "rule of 100," or the percentage of bonds relative to equities and other assets. The amount is determined by subtracting your age from 100 with the resulting sum devoted to equities and the remainder to bonds and cash. The rule is not ingrained in granite, but it varies with individual circumstances.

The dominant sources of income include Treasuries, CDs, municipal bonds, high-yield bonds, investment-grade bonds, dividend-paying equities, agency bonds, S.S., pensions, personal savings, and exotic assets. At the time of this writing, retiring on CDs and Treasuries is not a viable option due to low yields and the inability to withdraw 4% is impossible in a low-yield environment. The importance of S.S. for retirees in terms of income is both revealing and disturbing. Of those on the bottom 70% of the income scale, 94% rely on S.S., and 3% each on pensions and savings. Pension income comes in four varieties: Adjusted for inflation; not adjusted for inflation; adequate in maintaining a comfortable lifestyle; inadequate in the maintenance of a historic lifestyle. Like S.S. disbursements, inflation adjusted pensions never keep up with inflation, thus requiring additional protection. Income from savings and investments should be the largest segment of a retirees total income package, but, unfortunately, it is becoming smaller and smaller as fewer and fewer individuals properly saved and prudently invested. Retirement sources for the top 10% is primarily from savings and accumulated wealth (65%); 25% from pensions; and less than 5% from S.S. For the middle class, 31% of all income is derived from pensions; 29% from savings and accumulated wealth; and 40% from S.S.. While the top 20% do not need S.S. in retirement, it is astonishing how the remaining 80% of the population is so dependent; a percentage that can only increase as stagflation increases its grip on the economy. For example, more than 60 million people rely on S.S. checks that average less than $1,150 per month, a stark reminder of the plight of those aged 65 and older. In retirement, many investors want income to arrive as reliably as a Zurich streetcar. Unfortunately, S.S. and pension COLAs never keep up with inflation so that there is purchasing power erosion of at least 3% annually. Treasuries and CDs are currently earning a negative return, pension distributions are being reduced, and passive income affects only a minority. Seventy-two percent of dividend income is reported by people older than 60. Despite low interest rates, bonds continue to play a principal role in income retirement portfolios. Save as much of your pension income as possible.

## Investment Strategies

Upon retirement, many people metamorphose mentally and physically into a series of significant stages. The first is the "Jacuzzi" stage in which the individual or couple, after decades of denial, now wishes to act as children and spend money on unnecessary travel, a new residence, golf courses, restaurants, casinos, etc. This continues until money runs out, the death of a spouse, the onslaught of ill health, or common sense. All too often, retirees fail to keep a schedule, taking unnecessary naps, watching an excessive amount of television, etc. The second stage, or "reflective years," is the period after the initial glamour of retirement wears off, and punctuated with boredom, isolation from close relationships, and lack of intellectual stimulation. Travel, clothes, etc., become less important, medical concerns more immediate, discretionary expenses decline, and people become more philosophical as they prepare to meet their maker. They respond to community activities on occasion, wish to see old friends after an absence of decades, and downsize most aspects of daily living. During this phase, travel is closer to home and even closer to an easy chair, sleep becomes more important and the appetite for exotic travel, winter skiing, and other activities diminishes dramatically. In fact, after a certain point in retirement, the loss of desire intensifies, and others will do garden work. The third stage is one of "supervision," a phase that can take place at any age due to illness or physical impairment, expressed by dependency; a stage not too dissimilar to infancy. This last stage of retirement consists of a host of hard to imagine scenarios of physical and mental infirmity, all of which lead to a final destination. This, therefore, is retirement with all aspects identified as "unknown" in terms of time and quality. At the university where I worked and in my department, history was not kind to my colleagues. One retired at 62 and died within a month without collecting a single retirement check; the second died within two years, the third lived for five years, and the fourth died within seven years. On the other hand, a retired colleague was golfing every day at age 85. Therefore, remain mentally alert, work part-time, maintain a positive attitude, exercise, maintain close relationships, volunteer, and budget your time effectively.

Note the following: 1. A simple asset allocation is one that offers safe income. Therefore, CDs, Treasuries, TIPS and Ginnie Maes are the vehicles that guarantee capital preservation. Under no conditions should retirees with limited funds attempt to chase yields during secular bear markets. 2. Should a serious secular bear market commence as you approach retirement, market risk plays a serious role as it takes a long time to recover from 40%-plus declines. You do not want to retire just as inflation and economic uncertainty begins. Therefore, the timing of retirement relative to secular market trends is critical: those who retire at secular bear market bottoms will outperform those who retire at market tops. Remember the words of Benjamin Franklin: "By failing to prepare, you are preparing to fail." Capital gains will be limited or non-existent in a falling or flat stock market. Taxes will be rising, the investor will be squeezed for real income, and fixed income will not outpace inflation. Once you retire, you will enter the final period of your life as an unemployed person; hence, you will be required to have a well-planned "exit strategy." A "no plan" philosophy leads to a failed future. 3. Withdraw as little money as possible from your portfolio. A 10% withdrawal ($1 million portfolio) at age 65 will deplete your funds by age 75; an 8% withdrawal will see you through age 77; 5% will enable you to live conformably to age 94; and a 4% withdrawal will see you to age 107. 4. There is no correct strategy for creating a successful retirement roadmap. The number of variables determining "the plan" begins with family discussions. 5. With increasing senescence, short-term, income-generating securities should dominate. 6. The ultra-conservative investment strategy for those with a small or no pension and limited savings is the unwavering preservation of capital. For those fortunate to have a large pension, savings, and are in good health, consider "the pension" your bond allocation and focus on value, dividend-paying equities. For most people, keeping assets working to pay bills trumps all else. 8. Preservation of capital remains a primary consideration. 9. Low-cost index funds are the primary choices for market exposure. 10. A short retirement prescription is to spend less, save more if possible, downsize fixed expenses by 50%, and concentrate on wellness. Retirees are presently living in a stagflation environment, and best to remain defensive. They have progressed from "golden," to "tarnished," to "rusty."

## Recipes

Select from #4, #6, #7, #8, #10, Target Retirement Income (VTINX), #14, #16, #17, and #19-#23, most suitable to circumstances. For those with significant wealth accumulation, it is never too late for #9 and #13, especially if they rest in a trust.

# CHAPTER 6

# SOURCES OF INFORMATION FOR KNOWLEDGE, WISDOM, AND ERUDITION

*"Knowledge is power."*- Francis Bacon

*"Only the educated are free."*- Epictetus

*"All men by nature desire knowledge."*- Aristotle

*"Educate yourself."*- Gautama

*"As a general rule, the most successful man in life is the man who has the best information."*
-Anonymous

Augmenting your mind with useful information is constructive, and if taken to maximum limits, it will enable you to improvise and not panic at every minor or major market swing. Remember: Wall Street is not in the business of educating the retail investor; they enjoy keeping you in murky waters and having the pleasure, for a fee, to manage your money, mostly at marginal levels. The only way that the investor is able to protect assets from the corrupt and fraudulent financial world of distortions, misrepresentations and half-truths, is to become and remain informed. There is no substitute for information. Knowledge is the key to your financial success. Knowledge is power, and the mind is much like a parachute as it works much better when its open. Read, inquire, and become informed. Knowledge is the biggest key to investment success; it protects you from the sharks encircling lower Manhattan, and empowers the investor to remove the wheat from the chaff. It is the best capital you can acquire. Always read and listen with a critical eye and ear. In the words of Barbara W. Tuchman: "Books are the carriers of civilization. Without books, history is silent, literature dumb, science crippled, thought and speculation at a standstill." The list presented below is incomplete, but it serves as a guide and a good, first effort.

# Books And Magazines

Addison, Wiggin. The Demise Of The Dollar…And Why It's Great For Your Investments.

Alexander, Colin. Timing The Stock Market; When To Buy, Sell, And Sell Short.

Armstrong, Frank. The Informed Investor; A Hype-Free Guide To Constructing A Sound Financial Portfolio.

Bernstein, William. The Intelligent Asset Allocator; How Build Your Portfolio to Maximize Returns and Minimize Risk. The Investor's Manifesto.

Block, Ralph L. Investing In REITs.

Bogle, John C. Common Sense on Mutual Funds.

John Bogle on Investing: The First 50 Years.

Bonner, Bill, and Addison Wiggin. Financial Reckoning. Empire of Debt; The Rise of an Epic Financial Crisis.

Boroson, Warren. Keys to Investing in Mutual Funds.

Brandes, Charles H. Value Investing Today.

Brinson, Gary P., et al. "Determinants of Portfolio Performance," *Financial Analysts Journal*, July/August, 1986.

Brown, Stephen J., William N. Goetzmann, and Stephen A. Ross, "Survival," *The Journal of Finance* 50, No. 3 (1995).

Callahan, Gene. Economics For Real People; An Introduction to the Austrian School.

Carret, Philip L. The Art of Speculation.

Carter, Anne P. "The Economics of Technological Change." *Scientific American*, April 1966, Vol. 214, No. 4, Pp. 25-31.

Chancellor, Edward. Devil Take the Hindmost; A History of Financial Speculation.

Coghlan, Richard. Strategic Cycle Investing.

Coxe, Donald. The New Reality Of Wall Street; An Investor's Survival Guide To Triple Waterfalls And Other Stock Market Perils.

Davis, Ned. The Triumph of Contrarian Investing; Crowds, Mania, and Beating the Market by Going Against the Grain.

Dent, Harry. The Next Great Bubble Boom.

Dines, James. The Invisible Crash.

Dines, James. Mass Psychology.

Dreman, David. Psychology and the Stock Market.

Dreman, David. Contrarian Investment Strategies: The Next Generation.

Easterling, Ed. Unexpected Returns; Understanding Secular Stock Market Cycles.

Ellis, Charles. Winning the Loser's Game.

Evans, E. Richard. Earn More (Sleep Better); The Index Fund Solution.

Fabozzi, Frank J. Bond Markets; Analysis And Strategies.

Farrell, Paul B. The Lazy Person's Guide to Investing.

Ferri, Richard A. Serious Money; Straight Talk About Investing For Retirement. All About Index Funds. Protecting Your Wealth in Good Times and Bad.

Fleckenstein, William A., Frederick Sheehan. The Age of Ignorance at the Federal Reserve.

Florida, Richard. The Flight of the Creative Class; The New Global Competition for Talent.

Fox, Justin. The Myth of the Rational Market; A History of Risk, Reward, and Delusion on Wall Street.

Gasparino, Charles. Blood on the Street; The Sensational Inside Story of How Wall Street Analysts Duped a Generation of Investors.

Gibson, Roger. Asset Allocation: Balancing Financial Risk.

Gordon, Robert N., Jan M. Rosen. Wall Street Secrets for Tax-Efficient Investing.

Goetzmann, W.N., and Nadav Peles. "Cognitive Dissonance and Mutual Fund Investors," *Journal of Financial Research*, Summer 1997.

Graham, Benjamin. The Intelligent Investor.

Graham, Benjamin, David L. Dodd. Security Analysis.

Greenwald, Bruce C.N., Judd Kahn, Paul D. Sonkin, Michael Van Biema. Value Investing; From Graham to Buffett and Beyond.

Griffin, G. Edward. The Creature From Jekyll Island; A Second Look at the Federal Reserve.

Haugen, Robert. The Inefficient Stock Market. The New Finance; The Case Against Efficient Markets.

Hebner, Mark T. Index Funds; The 12-Step Program For Active Investors.

Ibbotson Associates. Stocks, Bonds, Bills and Inflation Annual Yearbook.

Ibbotson, Roger, and Gary Brinson. Global Investing; The Professional's Guide to the World Capital Markets.

Katsenelson, Vitaly N. Active Value Investing; Making Money in Range-Bound Markets.

Kindleberger, Charles P. and Robert Aliber. Manias, Panics, and Crashes; A History of Financial Crises.

King, John L. Human Behavior and Wall Street. How To Profit From The Next Great Depression.

Knowles, Harvey C., and Damon H. Petty. The Dividend Investor; A Safe, Sure Way To Beat The Market.

Knox, Paul, and John Agnew. The Geography of the World Economy.

LeBoeuf, Michael. The Millionaire in You.

Leuthold, Steven C. The Myths of Inflation and Investing.

Lindgren, Henry C. Great Expectations; The Psychology of Money.

Lips, Ferdinand. Gold Wars; The Battle Against Sound Money as Seen From a Swiss Perspective.

Longman, Phillip. The Return of Thrift; How The Collapse of The Middle Class Welfare State Will Reawaken Values in America.

Lynch, Peter. Beating the Street.

Lynch, Peter, John Rothchild. Learn to Earn: A Beginners Guide to the Basics of Investing and Business.

Mackay, Charles. Extraordinary Popular Delusions and the Madness of Crowds.

Malkiel, Burton. A Random Walk Down Wall Street.

McClelland, David D. The Achieving Society.

Morris, Charles R. The Trillion Dollar Meltdown; Easy Money, High Rollers, and the Great Credit Crash.

Napier, Russell. Anatomy of the Bear; Lessons From Wall Street's Four Great Bottoms.

Nelson, Charles R. The Investor's Guide To Economic Indicators.

O'Higgins, Michael B., and John McCarty. Beating The Dow With Bonds.

O'Neil, William J. How To Make Money in Stocks; A Winning System in Good Times or Bad.

O'Shaughnessy, James P. What Works On Wall Street; A Guide To The Best-Performing Investment Strategies Of All Time.

O'Shaughnessy, Jones P. How To Retire Rich; Time-Tested Strategies To Beat The Market And Retire In Style.

O'Shea, Peter, and Jonathan Worrall. Beating the S&P With Dividends; How to Build a Superior Portfolio of Dividend Yielding Stocks.

Perritt, Gerald W., and Alan Lavine. Diversify; The Investor's Guide To Asset Allocation Strategies.

Phillips, Kevin. The Politics of Rich and Poor; Wealth and the American Electorate in the Reagan Aftermath.

Rogers, Jim. Hot Commodities; How Anyone Can Invest Profitably in the World's Best Market.

Rostow, W.W. The Stages of Economic Growth; A Non-Communist Manifesto.

Rothchild, John. The Bear Book.

Schiff, Peter D. Crash Proof; How to Profit From the Coming Economic Collapse.

Schultheis, Bill. The Coffeehouse Investor.

Schultz, Harry D. Panics and Crashes; How You Can Make Money Out Of Them.

Schumpeter, Joseph. Business Cycles.

Siegel, Jeremy J. Stocks For The Long Run.

Simon, W. Scott. Index Mutual Funds; Profiting From An Investment Revolution.

Spare, Anthony E., and Paul Ciotti. Relative Dividend Yield; Common Stock Investing For Income and Appreciation.

Stanley, Thomas J. The Millionaire Mind.

Stanley, Thomas J., William D. Danko. The Millionaire Next Door: The Surprising Secrets of America's Wealthy.

Stathis. America's Financial Apocalypse; How To Profit From The Next Great Depression.

Stovall, Sam. Standard & Poor's Guide to Sector Investing.

Swedroe, Larry. What Wall Street Doesn't Want You To Know; How You Can Build Real Wealth Investing in Index Funds."

Swensen David F. A Fundamental Approach To Personal Investment.

Taleb, Nassim N. The Black Swan; The Impact of the Highly Improbable.

Tigue, Joseph. The Standard & Poor's Guide to Long-Term Investing. The Standard & Poor's Guide To Building Wealth With Dividend Stocks.

Tigue, Joseph, and Joseph Lisanti. The Dividend Rich Investor; Building Wealth With High-Quality, Dividend-Paying Stocks.

Tuccille, Jerome. Mind Over Money; Why Most People Lose Money In The Stock Market And How You Can Become A Winner.

Tvede, Lars. Business Cycles; History, Theory and Investment Reality.

Vick, Timothy P. Wall Street On Sale; How To Beat The Market As A Value Investor.

Warwick, Ben. Searching for Alpha: The Quest for Exceptional Investment Performance.

Weiss, Geraldine and Gregory Weiss. The Dividend Connection; How Dividends Create Value in the Stock Market.

# Web Resources

www.aii.com The site of the American Association of Individual Investors; general to specific information on stocks, mutual funds and bonds, and investment strategies, etc.

www.afr.org An alternative site to the evening news.

www. api.org The site of the American Petroleum Institute.

www.allthingsfrugal.com An indispensable site on the subject.

www.ameinfo.com A good site for Middle East news, Arab stock markets, data, commentary, etc.

www.atimes.com A superb site for Asian news and commentary.

www.bankrate.com A good source for CD rates and investment information.

www.bea.gov Site for the Bureau of Economic Analysis.

www.betterinvesting.org The site of the National Association of Investors Corporation.

www.bio.org The site of the Biotechnology Industry Organization.

www.bls.gov Website for the Bureau of Labor Statistics.

www.cepr.org The site of the Centre for Economic Policy Research.

www.coffeehouseinvestor.com A common sense investment site.

www.crestmontresearch.com Excellent economic commentary.

www.dailyreckoning.com A great site for economic and political commentary.

www.djindexes.com All about Dow Jones.

www.dividendgrowthinvestor.com An educational site with interesting commentary.

www.dowtheory.com Site for *Dow Theory Forecasts*.

www.dumblaws.com  About things dumb, not necessarily frivolous.

www.economagic.com  The complete site for economic statistics.

www.eia.doe.gov  The site of the Energy Information Administration.

www.emgmkts.com  A site for EM investing.

www.financeasia.com  Asian news and commentary.

www.financialsense.com  A must for financial/economic commentary.

www.fpanet.org  The official site of the Financial Planning Association.

www.freemoneyfinance.com Useful information on wealth building.

www.fundadvice.com  An indispensable site for all manner of portfolio options.

www.iie.com  The site for the Peterson Institute for International Economics.

 inflationdata.com  A superb site of interest to every investor.

www.investorguide.com  A site offering comprehensive investing information.

www.kitco.com  A precious metals site with commentary.

www.lcurve.org  An interesting site dealing with unequal income distribution.

www. marketwatch.com  A comprehensive site for economic and investment information.

www.mfea.com  Site of the Mutual Investors Center.

www.mineweb.com   An international site for the precious metals and energy sectors.

www.mises.org. The site of the Ludwig von Mises Institute.

www.morningstar.com  The leading site for news and commentary for mutual funds.

www.municipalbonds.com  Indispensible for bond selection by state, education, etc.

www.mutualfunds.about.com  A good site on all matters including ETFs.

www.napfa.org  The site for the National Association of Personal Financial Advisors.

www.NAREIT.com  A comprehensive site for REITs.

www.nber.org The site of the National Bureau of Economic Research.

www.plansponsor.com  A site for retirement news.

www.prudentbear.com  A great site for commentary and market history.

www.retirementliving.com  Practical advice and information about the rusty years.

www.safehaven.com  Excellent commentary on all aspects financial.

www.smgww.org A site for stock market games and simulations for kids.

www.treasurydirect.gov For treasuries, saving bonds, auctions, and more.

www.vanguard.com The mother of all mutual fund sites.

www.yahoo.com A large, supermarket investment site offering much.

www.zealllc.com Superb commentary and market analysis.

# Index

CPSIA information can be obtained at www.ICGtesting.com
Printed in the USA
BVOC01*2216180315

392323BV00006BA/11/P